CIRCULATE 9|99

'Winning Isn't Everything . . .'

BY THE SAME AUTHOR

DAVE BOWLER

'Winning Isn't Everything...'

A Biography of Sir Alf Ramsey

VICTOR GOLLANCZ

LONDON

07553921

First published in Great Britain 1998
by Victor Gollancz
An imprint of the Cassell Group
Wellington House, 125 Strand, London WC2R 0BB

© Dave Bowler 1998

The right of Dave Bowler to be identified as author of
this work has been asserted by him in accordance with
the Copyright, Designs and Patents Act, 1988.

A catalogue record for this book is
available from the British Library.

ISBN 0 575 06601 6

Typeset by Rowland Phototypesetting Ltd,
Bury St Edmunds, Suffolk
Printed in Great Britain by
St Edmundsbury Press Ltd, Bury St Edmunds, Suffolk

98 99   10 9 8 7 6 5 4 3 2 1

To Mom and Dad
I owe it all to you.

And for Denise
At first I was scared . . .

Always,

David

Contents

Acknowledgements

Piecing this book together has been a long, but rewarding task. I'd like to thank a number of people who helped make it possible:

Foremost among them is Sir Alf Ramsey who will, I hope, recognize himself in these pages and won't look upon my efforts too harshly. Many friends and colleagues have been gracious enough to speak to me, and I am especially grateful to them: Gordon Boreham, Joe Mallett, Ted Bates, Ian Black, Sir Tom Finney, Sir Walter Winterbottom, George Robb, Ron Reynolds, Ray Crawford, Jimmy Leadbetter, Ray Wilson, Jimmy Armfield, George Cohen, Geoff Hurst, Peter Thompson, Francis Lee, Peter Osgood, Roy McFarland, Colin Bell, Mick Channon, Rodney Marsh, John Oakley, Ken Jones, Kevin Dillon and Tony Want. I'm also grateful, as usual, to John 'globetrotter' Roberts for many helpful suggestions – may I recommend his excellent book on the Busby Babes, *The Team That Wouldn't Die*. Letters from George Curtis and Tommy Harmer were also gratefully received. I've been informed and inspired by the books listed in the bibliography – my thanks to their authors. Thanks too to David Witchard and everyone at *Matchday* in the USA, the world's foremost bi-monthly football magazine. Final thanks to Frank Zappa, Beth Orton, Miles Davis, Peter Gabriel and Genesis for providing the soundtrack.

Once again, Ian Preece at Gollancz has been an excellent editor who has contributed immeasurably to the finished text. And he didn't laugh too much when Forest beat Albion – I'm not sure which is the more important. Thanks too to all in the production, sales and press offices for their efforts. At the agency, thanks are due to Tanja Howarth and Mark Hayward for putting up with everything without complaint. Greetings to Carrie, possibly the most namechecked person in acknowledgement history. Denise helped me start, finish and do all the bits in the middle. Thank you is inadequate, but I can't say more. Not in a family book anyway. And finally, thanks again to Mom and Dad, who encouraged me in everything.

Introduction

'Winning Isn't Everything . . .'

It's the big question. What do we want from the England football team? More accurately, as Posh Spice (a latter-day Nobby Stiles to David Beckham's Martin Peters) might have it, what do we really, really want? It's a question that's hung in the air since 1966, and still there's no definitive answer. From time to time, journalists, fans, players and managers flirt with the laudable idea that the purpose of the national side is to play modern, elegant, even beautiful football: players combining slickly, nary a pass going astray, knocking the ball around foreign fields with panache, blending the grace of Cruyff, the wit of Best, the intellect of Blanchflower, the assurance of Beckenbauer, the glamour of Platini, the star quality of Pelé. Stir in a dash of Law, a hint of Puskas, a pinch of Krol, a soupçon of Ardiles and a dollop of di Stéfano and, the theory goes, you have the ideal left-back. Of course, England have long employed Stuart Pearce in that role. That's the English conundrum. Pearce is a devoted Englishman, committed, strong in the tackle, powerful, inspirational, passionate in everything he does on the field. But even Pearce would concede that he falls a shade short of the graceful footballing ideal. And when it comes to it, England will always look for a Pearce rather than a Junior, not just at national level but at every level, down to your local school, searching for soldiers not artists. We then find ourselves in a vicious circle – we don't look for a full-back like Brazil's Junior or Carlos Alberto, so we don't produce one. And if we don't produce one we have to be pragmatic and play a good, solid, English pro. But we pretend we don't like it. And that's all it is, pretence. Because our view of the game suggests that when it comes to the crunch, Pearce is the kind of man you want in your side, the Tommy you'd want beside you in the trenches, as the awful, inappropriate analogy goes. Indeed, warlike metaphors are the root of most of our footballing evils. Press and fans encourage our players to spill blood for the cause, to approach a game with the Germans as if they're going over the top at the Somme, urging them not to wilt in the heat of battle. If you put that kind of pressure on footballers and managers, it's no wonder they are often struck dumb, look for the easy option, lump the ball out of harm's way. But what do you put in place of fear?

If we're being honest, we have to admit that as a nation we talk a great game, but we don't actually care. We just want to win – how else could we hypnotize ourselves into believing that the Euro '96 team was the primal force that the newspapers told us it was? How could we drool at the performance England gave in Italy to qualify for France '98 if anything except the result mattered? Hoddle's men played out a superbly professional, thoroughly well drilled game plan that gave them the 0–0 result they required, but only the most rabid, blinkered patriot could ever say that it was a great advertisement for the beautiful game. And had the tables been turned, had Italy come to Wembley in the final game and blotted England out, they'd have been castigated for being cynical, assaulted for betraying the principles of football. It's true that Terry Venables was a modernizer, Glenn Hoddle is too, but New England aren't that far removed from Old England: hard working, hard to beat, efficient, but Shearer and, fitfully, Gascoigne apart, short of brilliance. The truth is this: despite having our best collection of talent since the boys of '66, England still lack truly world class, technically adept footballers. There have been considerable improvements in recent years with the emergence of David Beckham, Sol Campbell and Paul Scholes, but ask yourself how many Englishmen would get a game in Serie A for Milan or Juventus – and how many of those would really star there?

We are not alone in our apparently schizophrenic approach to the fortunes of the national team. So many people see the Brazilians of 1970 as football's ideal. England could not compete then on an individual basis and nor can we now. Nor, perhaps, can the Brazilians themselves. Like the Hungarians of the early 1950s, or the great Real Madrid side that once owned the European Cup, sides of joyous sophistication emerge but rarely. Furthermore, our domestic set-up, our temperament, perhaps even our climate, militates against us ever producing a team that can match those heights. Peter Thompson, one of the wingers famously jettisoned from Alf Ramsey's teams, recalls a tour to Brazil in 1964: 'We went out on the Copacabana and there were thousands of these little kids, penniless, flicking these makeshift footballs up in the air, doing all these tricks and then they realized we were there. They came over to Bobby Moore and Bobby Charlton, saying, "You do this trick?", but we were all saying, "No, no!" We couldn't do them!' If the great Moore and Charlton, fixtures in football's hall of fame, couldn't match these Brazilian youngsters, who can? Again, we are not alone in this. The Germans are very similar to us in many respects, but they have had a great advantage over the last twenty or thirty years. They've been ruthlessly honest with themselves. Certainly they've offered better coaching and have therefore had many highly accomplished technical players, some much better than that – Beckenbauer, Netzer, Muller, Rummenigge, Matthäus, Klinsmann – but they've never indulged themselves, never dreamt that they could take on a great Latin side and play them off the pitch by footballing genius alone. The German mentality has long been that a plan be devised, the players comprehensively briefed in it, given freedom to adapt when necessary, but instilled with the overwhelming belief that the system will provide. How often is a German side apparently in trouble, only to come through with an equalizer or a winner in the dying moments, simply because they retained faith in their system? Whose is the better record in the thirteen World and European Championships since 1970? The Germans have won two World Cups and been Finalists twice, have been European Champions three times and runners-up twice – nine times out of thirteen they've reached a Cup Final and have never failed to qualify for a finals series. England have missed out altogether on five occasions and have pieced together two semi-finals, where we have been dismissed, albeit on penalties, by the Germans. Yet in that period, we have had quality players such as Lineker, Shilton, Clemence, Keegan, Robson, Hoddle, Wilkins, Platt, Gascoigne, Ince, Shearer, all of whom have moved between clubs, even across the globe, for phenomenal amounts of money, though in fairness to Ramsey's successors, it should be said that none have had the benefit of such a spinal column as Banks, Moore and Bobby Charlton. So why the shortfall in performance? Inadequate preparation and inconsistent team selection and policy are at the root.

There has been no greater admirer of the German philosophy than Sir Alf Ramsey. He might never concede that they represented a superior force, but he was always impressed with their method-ology, their values, their determination and their ability to concen-trate when it mattered most, to focus on the greater goals. Essentially, he valued their ability to play for results and their refusal to be deflected from their aim. Little wonder he was so impressed by them. It was a lesson that he had taught the world with England in 1966. The most single-minded of England's managers (although Hoddle may yet match him), he knew that whatever happened, when the dust settled on a competition, the only thing that mattered to the great majority was the name engraved on the trophy. He heard the dissident voices that would have had him play wingers, the flair players, Greaves instead of Hunt, but he ignored them, steeled with the knowledge that his was the correct vision. 'I am employed to win football matches. That's all,' was his motto. He was neither hypocritical nor, his critics would say, imaginative enough to broaden his horizons beyond that single task. He saw that as his grail, his simple truth, and everything he did as manager of England was dedicated to achieving success. Since his departure, some of his successors have set off with that in mind, but have been blown off course by unforeseen events and injuries, have been coerced into playing a different game, selecting players they wouldn't have otherwise chosen at the behest of the press and public. Others have had their own principles compromised by public ridicule and found it impossible to return. England's managers aren't always the problem – sometimes it's us, the supporters, aided and abetted by the media. Sir Alf stuck by his values through thick and thin, sometimes perhaps to his and the team's detriment, more often to their great advantage, giving him one unanswerable riposte to criticism: the summer's day in 1966 in balmy north London, when he captured the World Cup. And when have England ever looked like doing that again?

Ironically, it was that very victory that set us off on the trail of 'good football', football that would stir the soul, pleasing our aesthetic instincts as well as bringing in the results. No England manager has had the nerve to persevere with such a philosophy for long, but it's a debate that regularly rears its head, fed by its very insolubility. It cropped up within weeks of Bobby Moore lifting the World Cup. It was nice to be World Champions, of course it was, but perhaps Alf was too hung up on industry, preferring workhorses to thoroughbreds. And all this running around that Alan Ball and Nobby Stiles had to do was perfectly laudable, but couldn't we find a player that would look more polished, who would stroke passes around Wembley to even greater effect? Alf himself always seemed so aloof, so self-contained. Couldn't he show a bit more emotion, be a bit more approachable, put on a show for the cameras? In the glow of victory, there was very soon a feeling abroad that we could have achieved the same ends by more pleasing means, a typically English reaction of self-flagellation rather than self-satisfaction – had Italy won in 1966 by wholly pragmatic means, we'd have complained that it wasn't pretty then stood back and, however grudgingly, admired their professionalism. It also ignored the real truth, that England were a highly accomplished side who could pass the ball around as well as any other – disbelievers need only look at the video of the 1966 World Cup Final to have their prejudices disproved. After the intervening thirty years of hurt that have gone down in popular song, we're a bit less choosy, hence the hysteria accorded to Hoddle's negativity in Rome. But if Glenn dreams of carrying off the World Cup in Paris, he might be wise to revisit the ancient proverb and reorder his priorities. If Hoddle does win the World Cup, following a brief honeymoon, the rest of his England tenure will be a personal nightmare – what can he do for an encore?

Given a knighthood five months after his great triumph at Wembley, Sir Alf's England days were almost inevitably doomed to end in anticlimax. Yet none of the later disappointments of Leon, Katowice or Wembley can mask the fact that here was a very formidable footballing man. He assembled a collection of thirty-two England caps, having come to the game late after the war. Winning a Championship medal with the great push-and-run side at Tottenham, he went into management four years later to mastermind one of the greatest coups in the English game. In seven years he took lowly Ipswich Town, then a backwater team struggling in the Third Division (South), to the League Championship at their first attempt in 1961–62 with a team put together for less than £30,000. Even allowing for inflation, that wouldn't buy a season's worth of boots for Stan Collymore. From Portman Road, Ramsey then went to Lancaster Gate and on into history.

The 1960s were a seismic decade in England. We'd never had it so good, but then neither had Profumo. When he and the 14th Earl of Home made way for the 14th Mr Wilson, Britain was going to grasp the white heat of technology and reinvent itself as a new power for the computer age. The Beatles ruled the world and Carnaby Street swung, but our currency collapsed, possible involvement in Vietnam terrified us and then, at the end of the decade, John Lennon informed us that the dream was over. In spite of all that went on, for many the 1960s are still most fondly remembered, or most easily called to mind, by reference to Wembley Stadium, 30 July 1966, and unforgettable pictures of Geoff Hurst exploding a left-foot shot past the West German goalkeeper, of Nobby Stiles jigging a jig and baring his fangs, beaming at the world's cameras, of Bobby Charlton in tears, of Bobby Moore wiping his hands on the way to receiving the Jules Rimet trophy from the Queen. If a week was a long time in politics, 120 minutes was an eternity in football, throwing up scenes of powerful drama and emotion, scenes that have not been repeated here since. In the eye of the storm was a short, stocky, middle-aged figure in a blue England tracksuit, utterly placid, apparently just waiting for the inevitable victory – a victory he had promised an expectant nation three years earlier – to be delivered. When it was, he did not exult, did not indulge in ludicrous nor extravagant celebration, did not place the Jules Rimet trophy on his head, did no lap of honour, didn't even say, 'I told you so,' but seemed quietly satisfied with a job well done, and made his way calmly back to the dressing room, his dignity intact, even as 100,000 people chanted his name.

That was the essence of Alf Ramsey. Nobody loved the game of football nor abhorred its showbiz periphery more than he, for football was too important to become a game show, reduced to mere entertainment. Nobody was more immersed in its tactics, its possibilities, its practices. Like most of his generation he was robbed of a full education by the politicians of the day, but he was an intelligent man, a voracious reader, an enthusiastic self-educator, keen to improve himself and his station in life. Where football was concerned, the man was an academic with an honours degree in his subject. His detractors would point to his dissection of the game as though it were a laboratory animal, arguing that it robbed football of its poetry, that rather than the art form they craved, he had reduced it to a science. It's an assessment that he would not disagree with, one which he might well take as a compliment. For he saw football as a tactical exercise, a mental as much as a physical sport, a series of confrontations in which you sought to nullify the strengths of the opposition first and foremost and then, that crucial task achieved, impose your own attributes on them – you can't win a game of noughts and crosses if your opponent keeps making a line of three. It was a strategy that his England carried out with aplomb: destroyers like Stiles and Jack Charlton, busy men like Alan Ball, George Cohen, Roger Hunt and Ray Wilson, combining to pave the way for Bobby Charlton, Bobby Moore, Geoff Hurst and Martin Peters to express their considerable gifts. If it sometimes lessened the spectacle, particularly at home, then that was a necessary evil.

Ramsey's soul was infused by the pragmatic rather than suffused with beauty – on an England trip to Moscow, acting on behalf of the entire party, he passed up the chance of a visit to a command performance of *Sleeping Beauty* by the Bolshoi Ballet in favour of a screening of an Alf Garnett film at the British Embassy Club. English was always best.

One might have thought that with all England's talent available to him, Ramsey would possibly have become more flamboyant on the field, giving rein to quality footballers the like of which he could never have signed for Ipswich. But Ramsey was no career manager, looking for personal success. He was a fervent, rampant patriot, one for whom there could be no greater honour than playing for England. When he took on the job as England manager – and he was not the first choice to replace Walter Winterbottom – he spoke of a sense of obligation, a duty to accept the task when his country needed him. His guiding principle was that England should not be humbled nor embarrassed at any cost. He knew the consequences of humiliating defeat – he had been in the side that had lost to the United States in the 1950 World Cup and was still questioned about it. He had played his final international in the side devastated by Hungary at Wembley in 1953 and was still furious at the outcome, claiming that since so many Hungarian goals had come from outside the box, they should never have been scored and that their victory was freakish. The pain of those singular defeats still burned within him, not because of his part in them but because they had reduced England's standing in the world. That was the greatest crime of all. His appointment as manager signalled the start of a single-minded crusade to restore England to footballing greatness, whatever the cost.

Football management is an enormous paradox. The more successful you are, the greater the demands placed upon you. As the cliché goes, the only certainty in management is that it will end in the sack. If you produce purely functional sides, then results are all: if you fail to produce them, you are left with nothing. At club level, the likes of George Graham, Howard Wilkinson, Gerry Francis and Don Howe have all found this out the hard way – they gain grudging respect but not much affection. If you insist on putting industry before quality, you need a Germanic winning streak to keep you in employment. Sir Alf Ramsey discovered who his friends were in 1974 when England were not party to the World Cup Finals for the first time since we'd deigned to enter the competition back in 1950.

Truth was, by then he didn't have many. Rightly or wrongly, fans had grown bored with his insistence on picking Peter Storey, Norman Hunter, Allan Clarke and Martin Chivers, while Stan Bowles, Rodney Marsh, Peter Osgood and Frank Worthington withered on the sidelines. An increasingly important media had long grown irritated and frustrated by Ramsey's perceived lack of interest in them, his refusal to co-operate by feeding them stories and quotes, as Brian Clough, Bill Shankly and Malcolm Allison did so brilliantly. And with his brusque attitude to the FA, he had stored up enough enemies there to last several lifetimes. Once Ramsey's method began to falter, he could not live off a fund of goodwill, was not given time to turn things around.

It has been suggested that Ramsey lost his job as much because his later sides were uninspired as because they missed out on going to Munich in 1974, but how true is this? David Pleat tried to add style to the hard graft that had made Sheffield Wednesday difficult to beat in the Premiership. He produced a side that produced some very nice football but without results. A third of the way through 1997–98, he was gone. Ossie Ardiles tried to stay true to Tottenham's traditions, won acclaim for the famous five forwards he employed, but barely lasted five minutes as results went wrong. Danny Blanchflower failed at Chelsea when trying to get his young side to play with a smile, Newcastle's board and merchant bankers were patently relieved to see the back of Keegan when it became clear that his principles stood between them and the Premiership title. (Incidentally, it's revealing that neither Ardiles, Blanchflower nor Keegan needed football management to earn a crust. The freedom to play attacking football may well be inextricably linked to a manager's financial independence, a luxury that Ramsey did not enjoy.) Everywhere you look, there are clubs making the tacit admission that Ramsey was right – results are all, and as long as you get them, by any means necessary, you'll be all right. If Martin Peters was ten years ahead of his time, as Ramsey averred, then he himself was thirty years ahead of his. For the arch-believer in results before all else, he had made a rod for his own back. Once they went against him, by his own creed he had to go.

Much of the accepted wisdom surrounding Sir Alf Ramsey is a myth. His sides were not the dour battlers of legend, he did not sacrifice intelligent football for moronic long-ball, he was not the aloof, cold-hearted general that many longed to execute. Look at the players he used, for heaven's sake: Bobby Moore, Ray Wilson,

Bobby Charlton, Alan Ball, Geoff Hurst, Martin Peters, Jimmy Greaves, Roy McFarland, Terry Cooper, Colin Bell. Don't they atone for Nobby Stiles, Peter Storey and Norman Hunter? Doesn't almost every successful side need the balance these players provide, anyway? Didn't the glamorous Italians of 1982, with Rossi, Antognoni, Conti and Tardelli, have Gentile marauding at the back, hatchet in one hand, maimed forward in the other? And it wasn't Ramsey who gave Nobby Stiles – supposedly, and unfairly, the symbol of all the terrible damage Ramsey wrought on the game – his chance. That was genial Matt Busby, who used him in his glittering Manchester United team, Stiles' contribution to which is often overlooked. Many thoughtless preconceptions cloud the true picture. Undoubtedly England did become more defensive, more physical, towards the end of Ramsey's reign, but that was where the strengths lay. Even then, England could still pass the ball around the midfield with some assurance, following their manager's mantra that possession was all, it should never be given away, that openings would emerge if the team remained patient. His, admittedly belated, employment of the gifted Tony Currie in midfield gives the lie to accusations that Ramsey was averse to 'flair players' *per se*. If he felt they would fulfil a function, give the side an option he felt it needed and do their job reliably, they got their chance – have we produced many players with more flair than Bobby Charlton, a fixture in his team? Indeed, Ramsey's sides relied on flair, for it was that quality which gave them an edge. The system won him the majority of play, while individuality often provided the finishing touch. While the artisans worked, the fulcrum of the side was given licence. Peter Osgood avers that, 'Bobby Charlton was Alf's jewel, he loved having him in the side.'

The charge that Ramsey was unconcerned about people, rude and aloof is another superficial reading of his character, at best. Like the proverbial swan, Ramsey was serenity personified on the surface, but was paddling away furiously beneath. Mick Channon, another kept on the sidelines for perhaps a little too long, knows that Ramsey was a ferocious spirit: 'Alf wouldn't have this rubbish about friendly internationals – there was no such thing. Everybody wanted to beat England and he was passionate about winning, it was all about national pride, you had to win. I knew he was a very proud man, and you could just tell he loved beating the foreigners! He didn't swear much, but when he did it was usually an aggressive adjective to show that he really wanted to stuff it up 'em! He did it with a bit of class, a bit of dignity, he never let it show with clenched fists and this jumping up and down that some managers do, but after a game you could tell he was so pleased to have won.'

Ramsey was no one-dimensional archetype, but a compelling mixture of attitudes and characteristics, a man shaped by the turbulent times that he lived through. That he was our most successful national manager is beyond dispute. How he achieved that status is a little more complex.

1 Homes Fit for Heroes

Every story has a source from which it springs. Some come from the sophisticated boulevards of Paris; others rise skyward from the hustle and bustle of the New York streets. More are born in a blazing sunrise or a romantic sunset in the tropical isles. And then there are those that come from the prosaic surroundings of Dagenham. It was this Essex town that bore and bred Alfred Ernest Ramsey, and its environs also played host to the formative years of Bobby Moore, Jimmy Greaves and Martin Peters, all of whom played starring roles in Ramsey's crowning achievement forty-six years after his birth. Perhaps there's something in the water.

Now synonymous with Ford Motors, Dagenham has undergone dramatic change this century, notably in the inter-war years, when Alf Ramsey was growing up. Prior to the Great War, Dagenham was described as 'surrounded by cornfields and market gardens. The soil is exceedingly fertile and being flat is easily worked. The village is quaint and old world, many of its houses being boarded with gable roofs.' If it had a native trade, it was agricultural, its proximity to London giving local farmers a ready market. Alf's father Albert took advantage of the local geography, running a smallholding near their bungalow cottage in Halbutt Street. He was obviously a man who knew the value of hard work, for in addition to this he toiled for the District Council, Alf's school friend Gordon Boreham recalling that he drove the local dustcart every Saturday. Albert and his wife Florence needed to work hard, for they had four boys to look after, Alf, Albert, Len and Cyril.

Although Dagenham was still a rural paradise, signs of change were to be seen even as Alf, born on 22 January 1920, was taking his first steps. After the carnage of the Great War, British soldiers were coming home after the Armistice. In many cases, they returned to poverty and woefully inadequate housing. Mindful of the Bolshevik uprising that had wiped out Russia's ruling classes in 1917, British politicians were quick to realize that men who had given their all at the Somme, Ypres and Passchendaele would not put up with that for long. They had lost comrades, given their own health in many cases, given their youth and their innocence in every case. Life was harsh, they appreciated its realities. They had not gone through four years of hell to come back to live like animals in squalor, especially while the wealthy, who in most instances had sacrificed comparatively little, still had their mansions. To combat the rising anger, the Prime Minister, David Lloyd George, proclaimed that we would build 'a country fit for heroes to live in'. With that as the nation's peacetime goal, he was able to mollify the masses and head off any thoughts of a 'peasants' revolt'.

In London, conditions in the East End were abysmal. Recounting their experiences in Age Exchange's book *Just Like The Country*, those who lived there offer tales of children sleeping in iron cots until they were fifteen; bug-infested homes; rampant TB, bronchitis, rickets; homes without even an outside lavatory, but a communal wash house; of no running water. The tenement slums weren't fit for dogs let alone heroes. The difficulty was in finding replacement housing. Ultimately, the slums would be razed to the ground, but first the people had to be rehoused. Built-up and overcrowded, it was simply impractical to build new houses in the East End itself. The solution lay on their back doorstep. Dagenham in Essex had plenty of land to spare. Just ten miles from Charing Cross, it allowed people to stay close to their roots, giving them the chance to visit family and friends who might be left behind. One of several sites, Dagenham was chosen as the home of a new housing development that would provide working people with the conditions they deserved. The Becontree estate would be built on 2770 acres of prime farmland; 25,769 houses and flats were to be constructed, increasing the population from 9000 in 1919 to 120,000 a decade later. Becontree was later described as Britain's first new town, the largest development in Europe. Future fashion designer Hardy Amies was one of the first outsiders to move into the area – his father worked for the London County Council and assisted in purchasing the land. There was great co-operation from the locals, who felt it was their patriotic obligation to help build this land fit for heroes. Amies recalls, 'The farmers were very happy with the money they got, and most of them were happy about selling. I remember them saying to my father that they were grateful for what he had done, and that he had done his duty.' That sense of pride and of national duty was ingrained in Alf, just as it was in all schoolchildren at a time when the map of the world was still largely red, indicating the sprawl of the British Empire.

Although there were few complaints about the building work, it was obvious that life would change for ever. Amies wrote that, 'When we first moved there I had to bicycle four miles to Chadwell Heath station to get to school. I would pass about four houses.' The Ramseys thrived in this rural isolation. Alf recalled in his book, *Talking Football*, that, 'We were happy in the country, the town and cinemas offering no attractions for us.' This idyllic existence was further improved by a meadow at the back of their home. The boys spent all their time out there, and Alf admitted that it was here, playing mainly with a tennis ball, that he mastered the rudiments of football. Sent off to school at the age of five, he and his brothers Albert and Len had quite a walk along the country lanes. Going to and from Beacontree Heath School, they clocked up about four miles every day, an ideal way of keeping fit. To entertain them on their way along the deserted country lane that led to the school, the three always took a small ball. Although their classmates were welcome to join in, Alf noted later that it was usually just the Ramsey boys who took part, an early sign of shyness perhaps, a reflection that it could be hard for outsiders to penetrate their tightly knit, fiercely loyal family circle. To be fair, there weren't too many pupils who could walk to school with them – the school had just 200 pupils, ranging from infants through to those of leaving age, then fourteen. Even so, Gordon Boreham recalls that, like most boys who are good at football, 'Alf had plenty of friends.' If you shared an interest, Alf was willing to talk.

Alf was a seriously minded individual even when an infant. Reflecting on those long walks on the way to and from school, he noted that the country lanes had ditches on either side which, after heavy rainfall, could be two- or three-feet deep in water. If the ball found its way into the ditch, the brother who put it there was charged with fishing it out again. It fell to Alf to retrieve a rare stray pass on one such occasion and he found himself out of his depth. He spent a week in bed with a stinking cold, drawing the following moral some twenty years later: 'It impressed upon me the need for accurate passing, and I am certain that those daily kick-abouts with my brothers played a much more important part than I then appreciated in helping me secure accuracy in the pass and any ball control I now possess.' It had its virtues even as a child, for at the tender age of 7, Alf was picked for the school junior side, lining up at inside-left, with brother Len to guide him at inside-right. This elevation meant that he needed his first proper pair of football boots, purchased for 4s 11d (25p) – his mother having provided the 4s, the self-reliant Alf having saved up the eleven pence himself. 'If those boots had been made of gold and studded with diamonds I could not have felt prouder,' he wrote, emphasizing his devotion to his parents. The boots represented a sizeable purchase, and Alf was suitably grateful.

Within a year, life would change irrevocably as the trickle of incomers from London grew into a torrent. Inevitably, such major changes had an impact on the atmosphere in Dagenham. From a country hamlet, it was now very much a part of London, part of the capital city. Further changes came when Ford started to build their factory in 1929, an industrial plant the size of ten football fields finally opening in 1932. These changes weren't entirely to Alf's tastes – he remained a country boy, and was lucky that his was one of the areas of town least touched by the new developments. Gordon Boreham was born in the town in 1924 and recalls that, 'At our end of town things didn't change much until just before the war. It stayed farmland. We got on with the people from the "new estate", as we called it, and quite a few went to our school. The people all mixed very well together, it was a happy community. There was plenty of work, you could walk into a job straightaway. There was Ford's, and they had lots of little factories working for them.'

Alf was pleased that work was in plentiful supply, for he never felt that football offered a future. His headmaster recognized something in him though, and by 1929 he was the school captain, having moved back to centre-half, a key position in the days of the WM formation – two full-backs on the right and left, three half-backs ranged across the pitch, and five forwards. In junior football, talented players can dictate a game. Playing at centre-half, though nominally marking the opposing centre-forward, Alf could also act as playmaker – with most of the game laid out in front of him he was in an ideal position to feed his forwards. Alf surmised that he had been elevated to the captaincy because he'd been in the junior side for so long, but he was their best player, the long hours spent kicking a ball to school making him an excellent passer. If he had a deficiency, it was a lack of pace, something disguised by his positioning at the back. To mask this failing, Alf became a reader of the game, encouraged by the centre-half role. With so much happening in front of him, his intuitive football intelligence took control to such an extent that he could snuff out trouble before it started, make telling interceptions before the ball could reach an opponent.

His ability was recognized locally when he played his first representative game for Dagenham Schools, against West Ham Schools in the Corinthian Shield, leading in turn to a place in the Essex County Schools side, then on to a trial game for London Schools. It was here that he received his first setback. A slight figure, at five feet tall and 87lbs, he confessed he resembled a jockey more than a centre-half. Giving ten inches and 53lbs to the opposing centre-forward was a deficit that no amount of clever play could claw back. When his opponent scored three, Alf accepted that his hopes of progressing to London Schoolboy honours were gone. He was extremely sensitive to criticism and disappointments. This débâcle hurt him deeply, and he dismissed any hopes of a future in the game. It hardly helped his state of mind when he was sent off for arguing with the referee at the age of 13 – he promptly wrote to the Dagenham Schools FA to apologize for this uncharacteristic petulance. Nevertheless, it underlined his passion for the game and the way his quick temper could get the better of him. That had to be controlled in future. For the time being, it would not impinge on his football. Leaving school in 1934, he had to give it up for a couple of years.

Like most of his contemporaries, he applied for a job at Ford, understandably so given that an unskilled man might earn £3 10s for a forty-hour week when qualified tradesmen working elsewhere would be lucky to bring in £2 for longer hours. The competition was fierce and Alf failed to get in. (One employee, Ted Knightly, noted, 'My father helped me to get a permanent job there, which I wouldn't have got without that connection,' providing an example of the old-boy-network Alf despised – he was in favour of meritocracy.) Hopes dashed, and following a family conference, Alf declared that he wanted to become a grocer, a successful one at that, which was a revealing ambition in many ways. It further confirms his loyalty to his parents, for the grocery trade was one step removed from the smallholding his father worked. It suggested that he did not wish to stray from his roots, that he recognized that with the booming population in the town there would always be a demand for food. Most interesting, perhaps, is the fact that it's a vivid illustration of his pragmatic mind. How many youngsters dream of becoming a grocer? Aren't their dreams of adventure, of exploring the world, of playing professional football? But young Alf was a realist, knew the value of money, wanted to grow up with a solid, reliable trade behind him, valued security rather than excitement. Becoming a *successful* grocer is important too, making it clear that although his chosen vocation might be mundane, he was personally ambitious. Perhaps the proximity to the capital encouraged such ambition. Always portrayed as the centre of national wealth, the city where fortunes could be made, those who lived in rural Dagenham were close to its glittering promise, but far enough away to be living in a different world. While the Ramseys didn't like the pace of city life, they were drawn to its vision of success. Alf wanted to achieve on his own terms, to have the best of both worlds.

Pursuing his hopes, he was apprenticed to the local Co-op store. Starting at the bottom, Alf became an errand boy, cycling around the district delivering to all and sundry, for twelve shillings (60p) per week, of which ten shillings went to his mother. It's hard to picture him as a prototype Granville from *Open All Hours*, bike piled high with boxes, teetering around the new Becontree estate, but it was a job that he enjoyed. There was plenty of work, for although the Five Elms shopping parade had about twenty shops, many of Dagenham's new residents had to have their groceries delivered because their houses were so far away and public transport was still poor as the new town took shape. It kept Alf out in the open air; the constant cycling kept him in shape, converting him into 'a hefty lad'. The drawback was that his half-day off was on Thursdays, and he had to work all day on Saturday. With no football on a Thursday afternoon and no 'official' fixtures allowed on a Sunday by Football Association decree, there was no opportunity for him to get a game. Other interests claimed a little of his time too, for at fourteen and now a working man, he made his first visit to the local cinema. It's surprising he hadn't been before, for Dagenham wasn't short of picture palaces – there was the Grange (known locally as the 'Bug House'), while the Saturday morning flicks were shown in the Central Hall ('the tuppeny rush'), featuring the latest serials for the kids, *Flash Gordon*, *The Invisible Man* or the new Tom Mix.

Alf also spent a little time at Dagenham Stadium, fostering his abiding interest in greyhound racing. But compared with today, there were few recreations on offer, an article in *The Times* in May 1934 noting that, 'At Becontree, where there are 65,000 children and young persons, there is only one boys' club and girls' club with accommodation for 100, and a few units attached to religious bodies.' There wasn't much transport either. Although the District Line had been extended to Dagenham in 1929, Alf's disinterest in London meant that was of little use. Gordon Boreham recalls, 'My parents would take the family into London and it was a day out – nowadays you can get in in thirty minutes! There weren't many buses then. If you wanted to go to Romford, a couple of miles away, you had to walk, because buses were few and far between.' Along with his brother Albert, Alf managed one pilgrimage to Upton Park to watch West Ham take on Arsenal, but that was his only exposure to League football. As Gordon Boreham points out: 'Dagenham had its own team, but West Ham were our idols around here.'

The teenage Ramsey was a fairly typical Essex lad, a little quiet perhaps, but a hard worker. With the Depression taking work away from great swathes of the country, he knew how fortunate he was to be in regular employment. He was grateful for the opportunity and wouldn't squander it. It was an attitude he carried through life – grab your opportunities when they come, make the most of them, behave in a conscientious and professional manner. With such an outlook, there's little doubt that he would have been successful, whatever trade he'd turned to. If he had no great social pretensions, no aims beyond doing a good job and providing for himself, he did hope to 'better himself' in some way. This was indicative of a wave of social change. Previously a boy was often brought up to do the same job his father had done for thirty or forty years. But by the mid-thirties, the changing attitudes to work were in part the result of some quite sophisticated social engineering that attended the Becontree development. The people coming into the area looked on Dagenham as 'the real countryside life' and were keen to make the most of it. With rents that were comparatively high, they knew they needed to work hard to keep a roof over their heads. By taking people out of the slums and putting them into houses, Dr Robert Home, a distinguished architect, notes that 'the London County Council, through a paternalistic management style, sought to inculcate in its tenants new social values, training them into the lifestyle of an aspiring lower middle class.' If the development could be faulted, it was in breaking up the spirit of community simply because the place was so big, another report suggested: 'The sprawl of the estate as a whole, and the failure to provide a lively civic centre or local corner shops and pubs, have discouraged the development of social mixing.' The Ramseys were no great socializers but looked instead at the benefits of the new estate. Now part of a town that had changed beyond all recognition, Alf entered into the spirit of change, looking to build a better future. In time he would graduate to the position of counter hand at the Oxlow Lane Co-op, and could look forward to a future in store management. Had he continued with his chosen profession, in time he would surely have married, settled down and looked to take out a mortgage, all within the confines of Dagenham, in doing so becoming father to the mythical 'Basildon Man', who shaped successive elections in the 1980s and 1990s.

In spite of the advances he was making at work, Alf was beginning to miss his football, complaining later that he pined for 'the thrill of kicking a ball'. Eventually, salvation came from an unlikely source. The manager of a sweet shop near the Co-op, Edward Grimme, decided that there were too many young lads in the same position as Alf, all working in the retail trade, with only Thursday afternoons, early closing day, as their half-day. And there were so few leisure facilities available to them, they spent their spare afternoons kicking their heels. In an effort to give them something better to do, Grimme formed Five Elms United, named after the district where his shop lay. Even then, the reticent Ramsey did not come forward, and it was only when the team were a man short that someone remembered that he'd played with distinction at school. He was invited to join, and played his part in what became a social as much as a football club. The lure of the game was such that he did not protest when asked to pay sixpence a week in subscription fees (since he religiously saved a shilling a week, that only left him with sixpence to spend elsewhere). Keen to reacquaint himself with the game after such an absence, money was no object. Five Elms United was a young side, made up of errand boys and apprentices, and most fixtures were played against older and bigger men, but Alf considered that these matches provided him with 'among the most valuable lessons of my football life'. Playing in the back garden of the Merry Fiddlers pub, he settled into his customary centre-half role and immediately felt the benefit of the height and weight he had put on since school. All those miles on his bike had given him powerful legs, and though he still wasn't quick he had reserves of stamina, was stronger in the tackle, and could not be brushed off the ball without a struggle.

Enjoying his football to the full, the more so since he had been deprived of it for so long, the exposure to a better class of play sharpened his skills. By 1937–38, after a year or so with Five Elms,

Alf came to the notice of scouts from Portsmouth. Although he was now a very competent footballer, it would be wrong to say that he was an obvious professional in the making, something borne out by his own shock at Portsmouth's advances. Informed of their interest by the Five Elms secretary, he went home to give the news to the family. His reaction was typical: ' "Young Alf" a footballer! The idea was too fantastic to be taken seriously – and take it from me, I was among the greatest doubters of the "Portsmouth want Ramsey" rumours.' The stringent strain of realism that coursed through his veins meant he could not countenance the possibility of a career in football, certainly not with a top side. That sort of thing didn't happen to ordinary people, despite the fact that the country supported 88 clubs and well over 1000 professionals. It was a typical working-class attitude, born out of years of struggle to make ends meet. The ideal for a young working-class boy was to get a solid trade, not waste his time day-dreaming; a state of mind typical of 'know-my-place', class-ridden England. It was a small-minded attitude that he turned against later, as he made determined strides to improve his education and prospects, but for all the gradually changing attitudes and widening horizons in Becontree, it was still the prevailing mood. To their credit, Alf's family rose above such feelings and made no attempt to dissuade him from looking into Portsmouth's interest, nor from making his own decisions. But in the back of his mind was the nagging fear that he wasn't up to the task, that he was no footballer, that he'd be found out and returned to the scrapheap, perhaps with no job to go back to – this wasn't long after the Depression, after all. He remained insecure, a legacy of his encounter with West Ham Schools a few years earlier.

Portsmouth's interest indicated he'd improved, for they were willing to offer him amateur terms, a stepping stone on the way towards professionalism. Scout Ned Liddell approached him and two colleagues, painting a glorious picture of life as a pro, calming many fears. Even so, he refused to sign forms on the spot, but insisted on taking them home for his parents to look through. Liddell's persuasive tongue, allied to the fact that the terms offered meant he could continue working at the Co-op, convinced Alf to sign on the dotted line, feeling he was risking nothing. But after all that soul searching, Portsmouth failed to write back. All those dreams that he had allowed himself of an exciting career in the game he loved were shattered. This was by no means uncommon, for these were the days when footballers were mere serfs, owned lock, stock and barrel by the clubs. To act courteously, never mind with human decency, was a thought that did not occur to the vast majority of directors, the men who ruled the roost. If the footballers didn't like it, they could bugger off back down the mines or wherever they came from. There was always somebody else willing to take their place.

This was a pivotal experience in Alf Ramsey's life. Certainly it reinforced his belief in having a trade to fall back on. But there were positive effects. It gave him confidence in his ability as a centre-half. If one football club had expressed an interest in him, others might too. He was still 18, not too old to get into the game. Even so, Portsmouth's cavalier treatment of him, their abuse of a young man's ambitions, was a terrible blow to a sensitive youth. To crush someone's dreams without the courtesy of an explanatory letter was appalling. His family had taught him the value of loyalty; this episode taught him the value of justice, the need to treat people with the proper respect. When the time came, when Alf found himself judge and jury of a player's future, he thought back to Portsmouth and treated players as he would have wanted to have been treated himself.

Having Portsmouth attempt to wreck his career was one thing. Next, Hitler got in on the act.

2 Your Country Needs You

Any thoughts Alf might have had of furthering his career in football were brutally ended when Hitler invaded Poland (Poland always put a spanner in the works for Alf). On the outbreak of war in September 1939, meaningful football was brought to a close for the foreseeable future. Continuing to work in the Oxlow Lane Co-op, he recognized it was just a matter of time before he'd be off to serve King and country. That call came in June 1940. He was dispatched to an Infantry Training Unit in Truro, the other side of the world for one whose greatest adventure thus far had been taking the train to Brighton. Alf conceded that his had been a sheltered upbringing and that his enforced stint in the Army 'was one of the greatest things which ever happened to me . . . I was pitchforked into the company of many older and more experienced men. I learnt, in a few weeks, more about life in general than I had picked up in years at home.' Prior to his basic training, Alf had been a homebody, spending next to no time outside the family home. His school was small, and although his work had brought him into contact with many people, these were the briefest of encounters, pleasantries exchanged over the shop counter. In short, he had little experience in relating to people and knew little about how to make friends and influence people. Now he had to learn pretty quickly.

The new experiences came thick and fast, making a lasting impression. He had his first stay in an hotel, twelve to a room, but wrote to the folks back home about this unaccustomed 'luxury'. Awe-struck by a 'swagger hotel', it gave him a first taste of what life would be like for those higher up the social ladder. Never motivated by money for its own sake, certainly not a greedy man, Alf's exposure to the comforts of a good hotel was an eye-opener in another way too, for it confirmed in him the belief that men with a job to do should be treated to the very best facilities. If they were to give their all, they should be treated as important people, not dismissed as second-class citizens. He might have reflected that the Portsmouth directors who had ignored him would be used to staying in such majestic surroundings when their team played away from home, while their players travelled third-class and stayed in far cheaper accommodation.

Within a few months, he was moved to St Austell and helped form a battalion side. To his surprise, Alf was appointed captain, and played centre-half. His participation was restricted by regular postings around the south before he finally arrived at Barton Stacey in Hampshire, where he was able to resume playing and take on the mantle of captaincy once more. Filling out still further following basic training, Alf was a strapping figure, which did a great deal for his game. He enjoyed another priceless advantage too. He would see out the war on home soil, rising to the rank of Company Quarter-Master sergeant in an anti-aircraft unit, further evidence of innate qualities of leadership. Commanding officer, Colonel Fletcher, was a football nut, having represented the Army himself. His men were encouraged to spend as much time as possible on the field once their duties were discharged. For several years, Alf was able to play as much football as ever he'd managed as a child. It was the next best thing to being a professional.

There was a gulf between the standard of football in the Army and that played by real football clubs. Alf found that out in August 1943, when the battalion were summoned to the Dell to play Southampton in a pre-season friendly. Sergeant Ramsey captained a team that included Arsenal's Cyril Hodges, and the *Southern Daily Echo* recorded that although 'the soldiers are a very useful battalion team, they had not the experience to withstand the more forceful play of the Saints.' They escaped with a 10–3 thrashing, Southampton scoring five in each half. Ramsey admitted that he had much to learn, marvelling at the speed of movement – not the last time that his lack of pace would be exposed – and, crucially, of thought displayed by Southampton who, while a decent side, were not yet in the First Division and were missing several players of their own. Nevertheless, the Army had proved good opposition and were invited back to the Dell the following week to play Southampton's reserve side. Pride was restored with a 4–1 win, evidence that some of the lessons of the previous week had been assimilated. As captain, Alf had played an important role in shoring up morale and in bolting together a more effective defence for this second game, and there were many at Southampton who were impressed with his performance.

During wartime, it was always difficult for any club to put out a regular side. Many decent amateur footballers were given the odd game, making up the numbers almost as they would in a park game on a Sunday. It should not have come as any great shock when Southampton asked Alf to play for their first team, but again events are revealing. Ordered to report to Colonel Fletcher's office, his C.O. asked him if he'd harboured any dreams of playing football for a living. 'I've never considered I was anywhere near that class,' came the reply. Modesty can be a virtue, but it can be taken too far. Alf must have known he'd given a good account of himself in difficult circumstances, that the defeat couldn't be laid solely at his door. His self-critical outlook, his determination to meet the highest standards whatever the task, had clouded his judgement, the smallest error making him fret, leaving him unable to see the wider picture. His sensitivity to criticism, to sporting humiliation, also meant his apparently fragile self-confidence was open to lasting damage.

He was fortunate that Colonel Fletcher had more faith in him. Arrangements were made for Alf to meet the Southampton players, prior to travelling to Luton Town. Leaving the office, Alf admitted to doing 'a little tap-dance with delight'. This unexpected call-up also fired his imagination. For the first time since signing amateur papers for Portsmouth, he began to wonder if he might be able to make his way in the game in the post-war world. Those thoughts must have been at the root of one of the more celebrated deceptions in football. Precisely when Alf began to put it about that he was born in 1922 rather than 1920 is uncertain, but the reason is obvious. To be a couple of years younger would help get a contract once hostilities had ceased. By October 1943, the course of the war was turning. Victory for the allies was by no means certain, but the prospects were far brighter than they had been in the dark days of 1940 and 1941. Whatever the outcome – and a patriot like Ramsey would never have considered the possibility of defeat – it was obvious that the war could drag on for another two or three years. Life would not return to normal until 1945, '46, even '47, by which stage Alf would be 26 or 27, a considerable age for a debutant footballer, especially one who had not attracted the interest of a club prior to the war. As Tom Finney, later an England colleague, puts it, 'Having not played before the war, that two-year difference might have swayed the issue as to whether he got signed on or not.' It was a pretty harmless white lie for, after all, if he failed to make the grade as a footballer, it wouldn't matter. And if he was good enough, why should age stand between him and a life in the game he loved? In effect, he was simply asking to be judged on merit, not on preconceptions.

Having taken a swig from the fountain of youth, Alf needed to maintain the subterfuge right through his playing career and on into management. Consequently, in his own book *Talking Football*, published in 1952, he played fast and loose with dates, suggesting that he had only just turned 22 on his debut. In fact, when he turned up at Kenilworth Road for his first senior game, he was nudging 24, and a bag of nerves. Masking them with the inscrutable countenance that was to become his trademark, he took the field, desperate to make the most of his big chance. Southampton performed confidently and were 2–1 ahead with ten minutes to go. With victory in the bag, Alf brought down Luton's Ted Duggan (eight years later he showed a trace of dissent, saying that the referee 'considered' it was a foul, making it clear that he did not) and conceded a penalty. Duggan converted the kick, but Alf was rescued by Southampton's Don Roper, who scored a last-minute winner. In spite of playing a part in a useful away win, Alf was concerned that he had been the weak link, though the *Southern Daily Echo* recorded that 'the defence as a whole functioned satisfactorily, without having to meet much opposition'. Three weeks later, Alf played in a side that was hammered 7–0 by QPR, the local press reporting that, 'Ramsey at centre-half rarely countered the combined skill of the opposing inside-forwards.' His play was inevitably naïve, understandable in one so inexperienced in the game. He'd only been to one League game, and so had had little chance to see how professionals combined together. He took the defeat badly, personally, and wrote of his relief when he was posted to Newcastle shortly after the game, glad to escape the scene of his embarrassment. Lacking in self-belief, Alf made no approach to any of the north-eastern clubs while stationed there, surprising since, under the relaxed registration rules of the time, he could very easily have turned out for any team he chose.

Perhaps this absence from the game gave him time to reflect on what he had achieved. His progress had been faltering, but perhaps he was too hard on himself and his perceived inadequacies. Meticulous in all he did, Alf was struggling to come to terms with the fact that passes were going astray, that he was hurried into errors. But these were wrinkles that would be ironed out by persistence, by playing more games, by working at his craft. That he had some talent was confirmed when, on being posted back to Southampton in the summer of 1944, he was invited to the Dell for another trial. Clearly the club had faith in him, so perhaps he should show more in himself.

Such resolution was hard to learn. Immediately following that trial, Southampton's manager, J.R. Sarjantson, offered him the chance to sign professional forms. Initially, Alf refused, arguing that he knew nothing about the game at that level, adding that he might not enjoy playing for Southampton, suggesting that for all his modesty, he thought that he might make the grade but that Southampton might not be the club for him. With the war entering its final phase, maybe he did not want to be tied to a club that would play its football in the Second Division on the resumption. It was only after Sarjantson agreed that he would be free to leave at the end of the 1944–45 season if he chose, that Alf put pen to paper, earning £2 a match but forgoing the £10 signing-on fee. Then, he wrote, he was plagued with self-doubt once more, asking, 'Am I really good enough?' An injury picked up in pre-season for his battalion against Southampton gave him six weeks to brood. The odd game that he'd played here and there for Southampton was now irrelevant. He was coming to the crunch. He had a season to prove that he could play football to good professional standard. He was on the verge of the big time, and although footballers were not fantastically well paid they earned a decent living. The rewards were there but so were the risks. If he took up the challenge and failed, what then? If he turned his back on the job that was waiting for him at the Co-op in Dagenham, passing up the trade he'd worked towards before the war, might he live to regret it? The next few months would be crucial.

Following his injury, he didn't return to the side until Christmas, when Bill Dodgin was injured. Alf played in the visit to White Hart Lane, where Southampton met Arsenal, Highbury being out of commission. His immediate opponent was Ted Drake, who had five England caps and six international goals to his credit and who had famously scored all seven in Arsenal's 7–1 win over Aston Villa in 1935. Previously, Alf might have been cowed into submission by his reputation but this time he stuck to his task well in a 4–2 win, the *Southern Daily Echo* reporting, 'Ramsey, stocky and perhaps an inch or two shorter than Drake, did much that pleased, although the Arsenal leader scored two goals.' Where Alf had worried about errors in the past, this time he chose to dwell on the positive. Growing in confidence, he was willing to move to inside-left when the need arose. His first appearance there was at Luton, scoring four in a 12–3 win, but a poor performance the following week against Watford persuaded him, and Sarjantson, that his future lay at the back. When the season closed, Alf had eleven appearances in League and Cup and, though considerably happier with his own displays, was forced to admit that little had been proved. Nevertheless, Southampton wished to retain his services and Alf agreed to play on in 1945–46.

It was another frustrating year. Looking to make the centre-half position his own, to prepare himself for the inevitable resumption of League football the following year, Alf found himself little more than a makeweight. So expendable was he at the back that when Southampton had an injury crisis Alf found himself at centre-forward. He made a good fist of it, scoring seven in the first eight games, including a hat-trick at Newport, but it was obvious that he was simply filling in, and he began to lose heart, sure he wouldn't become a Southampton regular. A posting to Palestine in December 1945 did little to soothe his fears, though it boosted his morale to captain the Services XI and skipper players such as Arthur Rowley. Again the contrast between Ramsey's own assessment of himself and that of others is striking. Wherever he went, Southampton apart, he was captain of the side. Clearly he showed qualities of leadership, was an accomplished footballer and carried out his duties with assurance. Back at Southampton, he was nervous, uncertain and unable to break into a team consistently weakened by military absences.

He was demobbed in June 1946 and found a letter from Southampton waiting for him at home in Dagenham. Bill Dodgin had taken over as team manager, with Sarjantson becoming secretary. Having coached the side in 1945–46, Dodgin wanted to retain Alf, reasoning that while some of Southampton's pre-war players could still play, a transfusion of new blood was required. With Alf still just 24 according to the records, he looked a good prospect. Since Dodgin would not be playing himself, he needed cover for his centre-half, Eric Webber, and invited Alf to contact the club to discuss terms. There was no tap-dance of delight this time around, and the Ramseys had another conference at which Alf expressed typical caution: 'What folk forget to mention, when they're talking about the successes, are the failures . . . football isn't so easy as some would have you think. Anyway, I'm yet to be convinced that I am good enough to earn my living at the game.' With his job at the Co-op waiting for him, he had all but decided to return to the

Oxlow Lane store. Out of loyalty to Southampton, he felt he should talk things through with Dodgin and hear what Southampton had to offer – £4 in the summer, £6 in the season, £7 in the first team. It was not enough to prise him away from Dagenham, and Alf told Dodgin the offer would not do, resolving to play his football for Five Elms. If it was a bluff it was a brave move, for had he walked out on Southampton there's little chance he would have found another club. It's more likely that Alf was simply being his pragmatic self. At 26 he knew he had perhaps five or six good seasons left in him – even if he did well, by the age of 31 he might be dropping down the divisions, earning less and less money. He knew too that the first season would be a tremendously difficult one as teams came back to full strength, providing a level of competition far fiercer than any he'd known. If he'd been unable to establish himself in the war years, what chance did he have now? Even if things went well, he'd still be a year closer to retirement with little to show for it, and of course if things went badly and he wasn't retained, what career prospects would he have?

A couple of days later, he received another letter from Southampton, inviting him to the Dell for further discussions. The Saints had upped their offer to £6 in the winter, £7 in the season, £8 in the first team. These were substantial increases, enough to tip the balance and persuade him to take the gamble that was to change his life.

3 Saint Alfred

If Alf had known that within a matter of weeks of returning to the Dell he'd be playing centre-forward for Southampton's reserves, even the increased terms probably wouldn't have prised him away from Dagenham. He might not have known much about professional football, but he knew he was no centre-forward. This switch, brought about by injuries, was an unwelcome move for someone who had just started to settle into the pattern of playing for his living. Pre-season training had returned to something like its pre-war state, players able to dedicate themselves to their game rather than snatching practice as and when they could. If his time in the Army had brought him to a high level of physical fitness, these workouts made him fit to play football. A perfectionist, it was always going to take the move to professionalism to turn him into a player. Slow, particularly on the turn, with little inside knowledge of the game, he needed to be toughened up, made fitter and faster and given time to work more methodically on his skills. Only then would his talent come through. Bill Dodgin had taken a gamble on him, viewing him as a rough diamond that needed to be polished. To have Dodgin's support was a great fillip.

In his wartime games for Southampton, the meticulous Ramsey was always looking to play the killer pass, make the perfect tackle, measure the long through ball to the inch. These were laudable aims, but in striving for such high standards a player needs only to be a fraction off the mark for his efforts to end in failure. Since he was still little more than a glorified amateur at the time, Alf hadn't the time to master those skills, ambition getting the better of him. He needed the chance to work on every facet of his game before he could become the accomplished footballer he wanted to be. With every training session he nudged closer to his ideal and his confidence began to grow. The finishing touch came when Dodgin recognized that Alf had been playing out of position. In late September, he suggested that he play in the right full-back position.

It was an intelligent move, one which played to his burgeoning strengths. It allowed him to see the play coming towards him, placed him in a position where his lack of pace was less of a hindrance, and gave him the opportunity to read the game. By now he was a more assured passer, and from the rear he had the chance to spot forwards and feed them. Inside-forward Ted Bates recalls: 'He was very solid, very right-sided, football-minded, with an excellent right foot.' Full-back was a slot for a dependable type who could be relied upon to do the right thing at the right time, one who would look for safety first. This was Alf's game in some respects, but Dodgin realized that as a student of the game, he might expand the horizons of the position. Rather than having the stereotypical clogger at the back, here was a cultured footballer who would look to be a main-spring of attack whenever he could. In short, he might give the team a new option.

Settling down to work with assistant trainer Sydney Cann, himself a former full-back with Manchester City and Charlton, Alf looked to master the basics. Using the replica football pitch painted on the floor of the dressing room, he and Cann explored all the possibilities that he would have to master on the field of play. He was especially grateful to Cann and recorded, 'The way to get any footballer's respect is to treat him as a "student" anxious to learn thoroughly his chosen profession.' Cann offered wise counsel, not only on the way to play but on having the patience to master his new craft before looking for a first-team berth. This was good advice, for the first-team right-back, Bill Ellerington, was making that position his own. Fortunately for Alf, with a month's experience at full-back under his belt, Ellerington picked up a minor injury and Alf was called into the first team to play at home to Plymouth on 26 October 1946. Three months short of his 27th birthday, Alf was about to get his big chance. 'My heart went pit-a-pat, my legs felt a trifle unsteady – and I felt like cheering,' he recalled.

Plymouth were not the strongest side and with the match taking place at home, things looked set fair. Needless to say, nerves set in again and Alf was lucky to be lining up alongside club captain Bill Rochford at left-back. Rochford was an excellent captain, looking to help out the less experienced members of the side. Inside-forward Joe Mallett recalls Rochford as, 'A very intelligent full-back, he had a great football brain. He used to save Alf from a lot of trouble with his knowledge.' Prior to the game against Plymouth, Rochford took Alf to one side and told him that it was the captain's job to do any worrying that needed doing, and that Alf should concentrate on his own game. He continued, 'It's another of my jobs to put you right, so always look to me for guidance if you don't feel too happy.' Rochford schooled him through his debut, a 5–1 win. A less favourable performance at Filbert Street the following Saturday saw Southampton lose 2–0, whereupon Bill Ellerington resumed his position in the side. Alf took his demotion well and professed that, 'Frankly, I was rather relieved! . . . it quickly dawned on me how little about football I knew. Everybody on the field moved – and above all else, thought – considerably quicker than I did.'

To be relieved that he'd been dropped was a worrying admission. There would be far better teams than Plymouth and Leicester to combat if he wanted to succeed. This persistent lack of confidence was potentially damaging, and not entirely rooted in reality. In his first two games he hadn't disgraced himself. That quiet, retiring attitude, understandable in a country lad who'd grown up in a tiny town, had to change. Alf was now faced with crowds of 20,000 watching his every move. Physically fit, he needed to add mental strength to his repertoire. The next few months saw a substantial change as, by an effort of will, he began to alter his outlook, learned to control his doubts so that they would not impinge on his career. Relieved to be dropped in November 1946, soon things were very different. Joe Mallett joined in February 1947 and says, 'I'd be surprised if Alf ever lacked confidence!' Clearly, within three months, he'd become a very different man to the one who had darted back to the reserves.

There are many who suggest that although Alf had a gift for the game and a natural football intelligence, he became a fine player largely by an effort of will and application. He was a slave to practice, returning to work on certain skills in the afternoon, working on facets of his game back home in Dagenham in the close season. He set himself a task, to become a thoroughly competent and utterly reliable player. With the basics mastered, his tactical grasp of the game, his vision, would then take charge, propelling him into a higher league. Such an approach requires enormous reserves of character, of concentration, of determination, a compelling desire to maximize your gifts. The playing career of Kevin Keegan is not dissimilar – twice European Footballer of the Year, that puts him in a select band of repeat winners that includes Beckenbauer, Cruyff, Platini and Van Basten. Keegan did not share their incredible natural talent, but made himself an indispensable part of any team by his intelligent application of his lesser gifts. For Alf, this was not the only battle. If his protestations of nerves and of self-doubt are taken at face value, then he needed to resolve them before he could really make his mark. If he exerted an effort of will on improving his physical game, it required equal mental strength to emerge victorious from his own mind games. His motivation was simple – he just *had* to succeed. How could he face going home in failure? He was growing in confidence as it became clear that the full-back position was his niche. With each game, it became increasingly apparent that he could actually play the game to a high standard, thereby mitigating his earlier worries. As it was gradually revealed that football was his *métier*, that he instinctively understood its pace, its rhythms, that too increased his self-belief. But equally, he had to make a stand, had to resolve to overcome the fears that beset him. Simply, he had to convince himself that he was a first-class footballer, that he had every right to stand on the same pitch as the likes of Matthews, Wright or Finney. The results were remarkable. On Boxing Day 1946, Alf got another chance in the first team following a further injury to Ellerington. By all accounts Alf had a good game, but the crowning glory came late on. With Southampton trailing by a goal in front of a good holiday crowd of 21,556, they were awarded a penalty in the last minute. Bill Rochford gave Alf the ball and he cracked home the equalizer, a feat of quiet assurance almost unthinkable two months earlier. Playing again two days later in a 5–1 win over Newport County, Alf confessed, 'I felt myself getting more into the game.' The *Southern Daily Echo* noted, 'Ramsey had another good game at right-back and if there was a less accomplished back than Ellerington established in the position, Ramsey's claims to the place would be strong.' Now at home in the first team, Alf's confidence began to rocket. Any problems in the future would be of over-confidence or an occasional refusal to accept his own mistakes.

Although his game was coming on, he was still second choice. Ellerington was a year younger than Alf (even after the amended birth date) and is described in the *Complete Record Of Southampton F.C.* as 'arguably the most cultured and elegant right-back ever to be on the Saints' books'. Ted Bates confirms that, 'Alf had a continual competition with Bill. There wasn't anything to choose between them.' When Ellerington regained fitness, he was straight back into the side, interrupting Alf's run of three matches. Had he retained his health, Alf would never have broken into the team, so it was Ellerington's further misfortune early in the new year that gave him his break. Alf travelled with the team to Whitley Bay, where the side were to have some 'special training' prior to a fourth-round Cup-tie at Newcastle. While they were there, in the midst of that harshest of winters, Ellerington was hospitalized with pneumonia. Alf would deputize and could expect a decent run in the side. The local press had no qualms about the change, describing Alf as 'a level-headed player [who] is not likely to be upset when he walks on to the field with sixty, or more, thousand northern fans cheering for the Newcastle side'. They were correct in that assessment, for nerves were now a thing of the past, masked by that passive face. Of course there was the odd flutter before the game, but he was in control, recording, 'Something inside me seemed to say: "Don't worry, Alf, you can only do your best. The fellows you're playing against are, after all, only human."' This was a huge shift in attitude, the more so since his opponents included the likes of Len Shackleton, Roy Bentley and Charlie Wayman. Neither they nor the St James' Park crowd intimidated him, and he played a full part in taking Southampton to a one-goal lead at the break. In the second half the tide turned and a Wayman hat-trick decided the game. Alf was turned inside out by Tommy Pearson on the wing, but Alf felt that it hadn't been his inadequacies that had caused the trouble, but the fact that Pearson put on 'a display of ball control I've never seen equalled, [making] me dizzy'.

In the post-mortem that followed, Alf was not crushed, but sat down with Rochford and Dodgin and went over the game blow by blow, analysing his faults. He was fortunate to be able to call on their combined experience, Ted Bates describing the club captain as 'an excellent player, we all respected him. Alf always admired Bill and the information he gave him about the game.' Taking responsibility for Alf, since it had been his decision to move him to full-back, Bill Dodgin was just as happy to point out to Alf where he was going wrong and, as important, what he was doing right, encouraging him at every opportunity. Ellerington would be out for some time, and Alf had to grow into the position quickly. Their efforts soon bore fruit, for when the side returned to Newcastle three weeks later, Southampton won 3–1 and Alf had a commanding game.

Within weeks, it was as though Alf had been Southampton's full-back for years. If not the dominant presence he would become, he was utterly dependable. Having reached an acceptable standard of performance, the relentless self-improver wanted to move on. He accepted that his play was safe rather than spectacular. If the ball came into his area, it was dispatched to the other end of the field pretty sharply. Whether it found another Southampton player was as much a matter of luck as judgement. To improve his distribution, Alf accepted he had more work to do. As Joe Mallett recalls, 'Normally, we used to train for about ninety minutes. We got plenty of the ball in training, though not as much as they do today. We weren't starved of the ball, as they were at other clubs, although the fact that a few of us stayed on after training may tell you we still didn't get enough! But we had a problem with the pitch, it was poor and they tried to keep it for the game on Saturday. Alf was one of the few, like myself, who used to stay behind, just to do a little bit more practice, passing the ball around.' Alf's keen football brain made it clear that he should work on the passing game, for possession was crucial, and the higher you went in the game the more important it became. Bill Rochford was an excellent exponent of the art of constructive defence, as was another player that Alf encountered. Manchester City, that season's Division Two Champions, were the visitors, and at full-back was veteran Sam Barkas, then almost 38 and in his final season. An England international before the war, winning five caps, he was still a considerable player. Alf was certainly taken with him, crediting Barkas with a change in his entire approach to the game: 'The brilliance of Barkas' positional play, his habit of making the other fellow play how *he* wanted him to play, all caught my eye. What impressed me most of all was Sam Barkas' astute use of the ball. Every time he cleared his lines, he found an unmarked colleague . . . [he was] the first defender I had ever seen play this kind of game. He passed the ball with the same confidence and accuracy I expected from so great an inside-forward as Alex James . . . I had found a man upon whom I was determined to try to mould my style.'

Assiduous practice was called for, but this was no hardship for Alf, scarcely the most sociable of men. In bed at 10, taking ten hours of sleep, not smoking, rarely drinking, he kept himself to himself. His only vices were an occasional visit to the dog track near the Dell for a little flutter on the greyhounds and a penchant for the music hall where, he wrote, he got his 'biggest kick out of the comedians [and could] literally roll in the aisles with laughter'. Hard though this may be to imagine now, Joe Mallett confirms it to be the case: 'If the material was right, he was a proper Cockney, was Alf!' At work, goalkeeper Ian Black notes, 'He was very much his own man. He wasn't disagreeable in any way, he was easy enough to get along with, but he didn't mix a lot with the rest of the players – apart from training and matchdays, we didn't see a lot of him.' Ted Bates agrees, adding, 'He was very reserved, wouldn't go out of his way to talk to anybody, but if you wanted his advice, he'd give it. When we played, early on, I roomed with him, and he was always the same: very quiet, getting on with the job.' Now bursting with confidence, he certainly knew his own mind. At Southampton, he shared digs with a fellow Londoner, Alf Freeman. In their early months together, the two would talk long into the night, but according to Joe Mallett, their friendship soured: 'They were close but they had a disagreement, and though they lived together Alf would never speak to Freeman. If you got on the wrong side of Alf, that was it, you were out! You couldn't talk him round, he would be very adamant. If he didn't like somebody or something, he didn't like them. There were no half measures! I don't think he had anyone who was really close to him in the game. He was a very difficult man to get to know. He was a man you could get so far with, so close to, and then there was a gap, he'd draw this curtain and you had to stop. I don't think he liked intrusion into his private life. Alf wouldn't tolerate anything like that, he'd be abusive to people rather than put up with it. He wasn't frightened to say exactly what he thought! That's why people couldn't get close to him.'

Once Alf thought something was a good idea, he clung to it like a limpet. Perfecting the Barkas style was his *raison d'être* for some months, though he was shrewd enough to notice faults in his game as they developed. Against Birmingham, on an icy pitch, he was given the runaround by their Welsh international George Edwards, who was too quick for him, forcing him to turn and leaving him for dead. Shortly afterwards, Alf spent hours 'wearing spiked shoes, [practising] turning and getting off the mark from either a walking or running position'. Although there was no immediate improvement in him, he persisted and gradually began to pick up pace. Underlining his thoroughness, he continued to practise this aspect of the game throughout his career. Even so, Joe Mallett points out, 'He was always a bit slow, one-paced, any quick opponent could take advantage of that.' Unable to eliminate the fault, Alf looked at the problem from another angle. Rather than taking wingers on, he concluded, he should put them in a position where they couldn't threaten. Mallett notes, 'Alf was thoughtful, played with his head. He was very single-minded, keen, liked things done thoroughly; he was meticulous in many things. In defence, he read the game well, had very good anticipation, would cut out danger before it had started.' To add to his armoury, 'He passed the ball well, which was unusual for full-backs then, they were really there to play the ball long, but he liked to pass it to feet.'

At the end of 1946–47, Alf was established. With Bill Ellerington still unwell – he wasn't to come back to fitness until October – he had little competition, but no one could have displaced him. He had twenty-four appearances to his credit, nineteen in a row. His colleagues accepted him as a valuable member of the side, and the local press sang his praises. There was no need to worry about returning to the Co-op. He did go back to his parents in the close season, unable to afford to stay in digs throughout the lowly paid summer. Every day, he would take a ball on to the local playing field and, for an hour or two, attempt to place a pass to the inch. On his return to Southampton for pre-season training, the improvement in his game was clear. Nevertheless, he knew football was a team game and that he would need help from his colleagues if he were to be able to make the most of his new asset. He felt that Southampton's play needed to change to suit his style – he'd put all the work in, so they should adapt accordingly. It was obvious to anyone that a shorter pass would have a greater chance of reaching its target than a long ball, so he asked right-winger Eric Day to come deep to collect a short ball from him rather than chase a longer pass knocked into space. By combining in this way, Southampton rarely lost possession once Alf had the ball under control, moving smoothly from defence to attack.

With a year's football under its belt, the whole side was coming together, ready to make a challenge for promotion after a mundane first season. Alf was to play a central part, an increasingly valuable asset. At the back, he was committed to snuffing out goalscoring opportunities, the *Daily Echo* recording that against West Bromwich Albion, 'Ramsey, twice, was positioned perfectly to save his goal. In the second half he dived to the base of the post to head the ball away – a great effort,' adding that he was 'strong, incisive, resourceful'. Weeks later, against Doncaster, he proved his worth in the attacking half, by scoring with a twenty-yard free-kick. Ted Bates found his free-kicks to be a fruitful source of goals too: 'I played up front and was pretty good in the air. Any free-kicks on the right, Alf used to stick them on the far post and I used to get on the end of them. On the ball, he was very accurate.'

A poor start to the season, though, seemed to have put Southampton out of the reckoning, but the signing of Charlie Wayman from Newcastle helped kick-start their challenge. Scoring seventeen goals in twenty-seven matches, Wayman helped keep Southampton in with a chance of promotion until a poor spell over Easter and beyond meant that they could only finish third. Nevertheless, it had been an encouraging season, with a Cup run taking them to the sixth round. Sunderland were beaten at the Dell in the third, Blackburn overcome in the fourth round, 3–2, Rochford showing his value with his 'thinking-ahead play' as the local press described it. With Swindon swept aside, only Tottenham stood between the Saints and a semi-final. The week before the Cup-tie, Southampton had held them 0–0 in London, and with the Cup match at the Dell, there was much optimism. Spurs, then several places below Southampton in the League, squeezed through by the only goal, but Southampton did themselves justice. The *Daily Echo* was particularly taken by Alf's performance, pointing out that he was now a pivotal member of the side: 'Alf Ramsey was one of the big successes of the match and Welsh international left winger Ernie Jones made little impression there. Ramsey is playing so well that he is consistently building up a reputation which should bring some soccer honour to him. He certainly impressed highly in this game and is steadily and intelligently profiting under the experienced guidance of his partner and captain Bill Rochford.'

Timing is vital in any career, certainly in Alf's. England did not have an embarrassment of riches at right-back following the war; the man in possession was Arsenal's Laurie Scott. By the end of 1947–48 he was 31 and the selectors were casting around for replacements. With his sterling performances at club level, Alf was among the names discussed. The England team manager, Walter Winterbottom, had 'seen him at Southampton, and I knew Ted Bates well. He spoke very highly of Alf, and I thought a lot of his opinion. He came quickly through. We called him one of the gentlemen of soccer, he never looked like committing a foul when he was playing. He was the interceptor of play, using his intelligence, going for a tackle, pretending to make it and then getting the ball thereafter by throwing an opponent off balance, making him attempt a pass that Alf wanted him to make. He loved to intercept passes.' With that in mind, Alf was selected to accompany the England party that would play a full international against Italy in Turin and then a 'B' game against Switzerland in Bellinzona. His call-up was described by the *Daily Echo* as 'well-earned recognition of a grand full-back and grand sportsman'. His selection came at the worst possible time, coinciding with a summer tour of Brazil which Southampton had already arranged. He could not, nor would he ever dream of turning England down, but the visit to Brazil would be of great value. It was agreed that once Alf returned home from Switzerland, he would fly out and join his team-mates for the latter part of the tour.

Elevation to the fringes of the England team was the ideal end to a season where Alf had latterly been an ever-present for his club. Not only had he overcome competition from every other English right-back, but he had persuaded the selectors that his lack of experience – just seventy first-team games, and those with a Second Division club – was no handicap. As Tom Finney points out: 'In today's football, as soon as you have a promising youngster in the lower divisions, he'll be snapped up by one of the big boys. Then, players couldn't move so easily [even the great Finney had to spend two years marooned in Division Two with Preston], so there was talent in the lower divisions, and although it was unusual for a Second Division player to get picked for England for the first time, it wasn't unheard of. Even so, he was pretty well unknown to us prior to that tour to Italy.' That was underlined as Alf sat in the lounge of the Great Western Hotel, Paddington, where the FA party convened. Virtually all his team-mates filed past without recognizing him, not surprising in the days before television made the most humble face familiar. He knew his colleagues well enough, for there assembled was one of England's finest ever squads. Tom Finney believes, 'That was the best England side that I played with,' and the line-up confirms his opinion: Swift, Scott, Howe, Wright, Franklin, Cockburn, Matthews, Mortensen, Lawton, Mannion, Finney. To be on a par with men of that quality only confirmed Alf in his belief that he was now a top-class player.

Not surprised to miss the full international, Alf still took his place with the squad to listen to Walter Winterbottom's pre-match talk. Alf recorded that he 'pointed out to us the importance of everything being correct and the fact that our soccer prestige was at stake ... his outlook on Italian methods and temperament left a lasting impression upon me ... [he] did not waste time trying to sell ideas to footballers who have already proved themselves [but rather, he acted] as chairman of the meeting at which ideas were pooled, with Walter himself explaining how he thought our opponents would play.' Such professionalism made a nice contrast to the slightly shambolic hotel arrangements, with the England team beset by local newsmen. Even then, the gentlemen of the press were not making a good impression on Ramsey.

The game in Turin was astounding. Walter Winterbottom remembers, 'It was billed as the "Match of the Century" in the press simply because Italy had been playing remarkable football. At the time we played them they had, unfortunately, lost some players when Turin were involved in a plane crash, taking four internationals out of the side. I watched Italy play France in Paris and they played such remarkable football and won so easily – in the second half, they were putting on a show, passing the ball, deliberately keeping it on the ground. The centre-half controlled a kick out from the opposing goalkeeper in the centre-circle with his head, going forward with three other bounces off his head, then shooting and scoring! At the end, they carried the manager, Pozzo, off the field, which was quite amazing treatment of a manager at the time. We arrived untested in European football, after they'd had two wonderful post-war seasons in Europe. We went to a cinema on the eve of the game and saw a newsreel about the previous England–Italy games, and at the end of the film the President was asked his opinion on the game. He said, "Being very modest, we shall win 4–0"!'

Italy had two goals disallowed for offside and put England under terrific pressure before, as Walter Winterbottom explains, 'Mortensen scored an amazing goal from outside the penalty area, near the goal-line, into the net at the near post. A few moments later, he centred and Lawton cracked it in from the edge of the box. We came off at half-time 2–0 up. Our players were suffering from the heat and humidity, but I pointed out that the Italians were worse than we were, squirting water from soda siphons over themselves to cool down!' Tom Finney admits, 'Had I been Italian I should have felt very disappointed to come off losing after playing so well, but it was often apparent against Continental sides in those days that they seemed to lose heart once you got in the lead. We ran out very comfortable winners, 4–0.'

There can be few better introductions to international football than to watch one of England's greatest ever wins. It was a lesson Alf absorbed, writing, 'I could not have been in a better position to feel the atmosphere of the match had I taken part in it, and the FA policy of taking with them on such trips young players who might develop into international players is one I commend.' As one of the five to sit out the Italian game, Alf was given his chance to play in Switzerland. In a 5–1 victory, Alf 'pleased all the critics' according to the Southampton press and underlined the fact that he would soon be pushing Scott for a place in the full side. The contrast between this assurance and the diffident full-back of eighteen months earlier was marked. He had finished constructing the bubble of confidence which he would inhabit for the rest of his career.

His worth was further illustrated when he reached Brazil. He noted that they had lost their first four games. His arrival, he seemed to suggest, would help stem the tide. Flying out of Heathrow via Lisbon, Dakar and Natal, he finally arrived in Rio only to find no one to meet him, something which must have angered him, the more so since he hadn't a word of Portuguese nor any Brazilian currency. After two hours, he was met by a representative of Botafogo FC, Southampton's hosts. The two had to communicate by sign language, but it was a relief to meet anyone who could help. The two went to the Palace Hotel, prior to flying on to São Paolo. There, Alf had a meal and was interrupted by a local journalist who 'nearly spoilt my dinner by trying continuously to draw me into conversation about England's victory over Italy . . . I naturally would not commit myself as a newcomer to the FA scene, and it was with some relief that [the Botafogo official] finally broke up the party.' On his flight to São Paolo, 'the air hostess was kind enough to bring me some local newspapers to read . . . and I nearly jumped out of my seat with surprise. Looking out of the front page of one paper was my photograph, while the name "Alf Ramsey" was in the headline . . . maybe, I thought, Brazilian words took up more space than they do at home.' Following hard on the heels of the disruption caused by the Italian press, he was certainly cultivating a distaste for some reporters. Under FA regulations, he was unable to comment on the England performance, a situation which persisted for many years. As a creature of habit, that enforced silence was hard for him to break in later years.

Once reunited with the rest of the team, Alf began to look forward to playing against the Brazilians. The first fixture was against the Corinthians. It also led to another encounter with the Brazilian press who, 'rushed up to us and demanded – yes, demanded! – our views'. Forty-five years on, you can still feel the outrage in his words. The very idea that a professional should be subjected to such demands before a game! Whether it affected his concentration or not is hard to say, but early on he missed a penalty and then conceded one at the other end – another poor decision, he reflected later – to put the home side a goal ahead. Southampton fought back to lead 2–1, but when one of the Brazilians was sent off for fighting, the crowd went berserk, the local militia having to calm the situation. When the dust settled and the game restarted, the Corinthians had replaced the man sent off with a substitute, but even that wasn't enough to pull the game back. With Southampton the winners, the crowd demonstrated outside the dressing room for more than an hour. At the after-match banquet, Alf found himself sitting next to one of the opposing players who refused to speak to him. It made 'this banquet among the most embarrassing I've ever attended. I tried to speak to him and in return received only a fixed glare.' Summing up the events with a diplomacy that was to elude him in 1966, he wrote 'I must emphasise that although the match . . . had its unfortunate moments, there was nothing on the field, apart from the one incident to really upset us.' For all that, the tension that he experienced on and off the pitch made a lasting mark on him. His view of football was that it should be hard but fair, that you should never deliberately foul an opponent and should take defeat in sporting fashion. The evidence of this tour was that the South American attitude was radically different. Although he appreciated the ball control of the Brazilians, and even recorded that 'their method of always trying to use the ball coincided with my own ideas of how the game should be played', he also began to mistrust Latin behaviour.

The team flew on to Rio, Ian Black recalling, 'It was marvellous – the conditions weren't ideal from our point of view, it was very hard to play in such hot conditions, but the hospitality was incredible, they couldn't do enough for us. Botafogo sponsored the tour, laid everything on and we had an ideal hotel on the Copacabana.' Alf chose to comment on the devotion to practice of his team, noting that they were early to bed every evening. He captained them in a 3–1 win against Flamengo, Rochford returning for the final fixture against Vasco Da Gama, a 2–1 defeat. It was a sad note on which to end, but the tour had been important in formulating a new outlook and bonding the players, and Alf wrote, 'I learnt a good deal which in later seasons . . . I was to try out with singular success.' That self-effacing modesty that characterized his early days in the game had long gone.

The England tour had turned things upside down. An eager new member of the side at the start of the season, by the end he was, in many ways, Southampton's senior player. Joe Mallett saw a change, recalling, 'I think after the England tour in 1948, he'd made up his mind that he wanted to leave Southampton. When players from smaller clubs went away with their country, you'd often find other clubs putting out feelers, lots of people used to get tapped, though I wouldn't know if that happened with Alf. Playing in the England set-up, he'd probably look at the other players and think he was as good as them, and he could be playing somewhere else.' If he did have eyes for another club, it didn't show, as Southampton built on the work done in Brazil. Winning four of their first five, they set the pace at the top and remained there or thereabouts for most of the season, and Alf's name came under discussion when England teams were formulated. For a time, he looked a certain starter in the game against Denmark in September, but the selectors sprang a surprise when they chose him to represent the Football League against the Irish League instead. In the game at Anfield he lined up with players such as Milburn, Ditchburn, Shackleton and Matthews, so this wasn't far short of a full England outfit. The Irishmen were dispatched 5–1, their only goal coming five minutes from the end. With everything apparently under control, Alf slipped on the edge of the box, giving space to the Irish winger Kelly who pushed the ball through for the centre-forward Jones to score. It was an error that Alf declined to mention in *Talking Football*, evidence that he would not allow his confidence to be grazed by the occasional aberration. Instead, he preferred to discuss the interplay between himself and Matthews. He noted that 'to my surprise, he played football as I believed it should be played between full-back and winger', referring to Matthews' preference for a ball played into his feet. It's a quote that has haunted him down the years, his detractors pointing to it as evidence of extreme arrogance – how dare such an inexperienced footballer suggest that the great Matthews was only right because he played the game according to Ramsey's rules. Hadn't Matthews been terrorizing defences when Alf was still on the meat counter at the Co-op? It was a tactless comment, but not malicious. It could be taken to mean that Alf was surprised to find his thinking was in tune with that of Matthews, and that therefore he himself must be doing something right, or that he was surprised to find the great individualist was also a team man. And if it was an example of his own super-confidence, there wasn't much wrong in that. Every great player has to have an ego, for how else would they do what they do? Would Matthews have taken on a string of defenders if he wasn't arrogant enough to think he'd slice through them? Although Alf wasn't a great player, merely a very, very good one, he at least *thought* like a great player. That effort of will was bearing dividends.

For all that he tried to ignore his error at Anfield, it affected him. Throughout October he had a run of awful form, and his cherished hopes of playing for England seemed to be ebbing away. Aware that time was running out – more aware than those who thought he was still 26 – he knew how important it was that he force his way into the England ranks. Ironically, his elevation to the England side and his visit to Brazil in the summer was having a detrimental effect on his game. Confidence had spilled over into a belief in his invulnerability, the new ideas he'd absorbed overshadowing the importance of the basic defensive job he was paid to do. Where he had been steady at the back, he was now trying to express his attacking instincts, over-playing at times, his backers at the *Southern Daily Echo* noting in the course of a 1–1 draw at West Ham that 'he did at times try to do more than was necessary'. Eventually form returned and, with Laurie Scott suffering a serious knee injury, Alf was called to the full England side for a game against Switzerland which took place at Highbury on 2 December 1948.

The game was actually put back twenty-four hours because of thick fog, but when the teams did take the field, it was easy for England, winning 6–0. It was an ideal debut for Alf – the defence were rarely threatened, he had a chance to settle into new surroundings and make his mark. He did so as early as the second minute, when he headed clear from under the bar. The *Daily Mail* thought, 'Ramsey looked suave and cool as a city businessman,' *The Times* adding: 'Ramsey kicked beautifully and was perfectly at home.' It was no accident either that most observers felt Matthews enjoyed one of his best ever games, for he and Alf struck up a good partnership, just as they had with the Football League XI. England captain Billy Wright was impressed too: 'In his quietly efficient manner, Alf Ramsey made the knowledgeable critics . . . raise their eyebrows. His special brand of "constructive defence", which entailed holding on to the ball until good use could be made of it, appealed to everyone . . . I must admit I found it a little disconcerting at first to have a full-back behind me who was cool as an ice-cream soda . . . I soon learned that nothing could disturb this footballer with the perfect balance and poise, no situation, however desperate, which could force him into abandoning his immaculate style . . . he strokes the ball along the grass with radar-like accuracy.' Alf was initially less effusive about playing with Wright, as he forced him to adapt his own game. He wrote that, 'I found his attacking tendencies rather worrisome, for he was prone to carry the ball forward and, if things went wrong, was caught out of position, which made things rather awkward for right-back Ramsey!' Once he became used to Wright's style, however, Ramsey became a big fan of the England captain.

These were important observations, offering suggestions as to how he would like to see the game played. Wright played right-half, directly in front of Alf. As he went forward so much, it curbed Alf's own attacking instincts, for he was obliged to cover Wright in case a move broke down. At a time when he was enjoying linking with Matthews, constant defending had become a chore. Nevertheless, Wright's ability on the ball reinforced the lessons learnt in Brazil, that a team could build moves by precise passing from the back. When Wright moved to centre-half to cover for the loss of Neil Franklin, he continued to be a constructive footballer. In later years, Bobby Moore was to be employed in a similar role, though following Alf's experience with Wright, Moore was always given a minder such as Jack Charlton, placed there because Alf knew he wouldn't trust Moore not to lose the ball. If he did, Charlton was on hand to mop up. In a sense, this antipathy towards a player bringing the ball forward bled into a mistrust for all but the finest wingers, a Matthews or a Finney. In general, Alf felt that the ball could be moved out about quicker and safer by passing rather than dribbling it.

The Swiss game seemed to have established Alf in the England side for some time to come and he returned to Southampton more assured than ever. Yet his problems had only just begun. Just as he'd wanted to get forward with England, he wanted to do the same with Southampton. In more evenly matched games than England had had against Switzerland, this could prove to be a liability. Joe Mallett remembers, 'Alf had his own ideas and that might have been his downfall at Southampton: he wouldn't conform to the team aspect. Because of his lack of pace he could have problems. Any player that went away from him, gathered the ball and ran at him quickly, could get the better of him, even though he was a good tackler. Players who used to run behind him could exploit his slowness on the turn. To combat that, we played offside, and Bill Rochford was an expert at that. He rescued Alf time and again. Alf really took advantage of this, took liberties with it. If you're the right-back, if the ball's on your side of the field, you continue to play, because you're unable to play offside – you don't know what's happening on the other side, you've got your eye on the man you're marking. Players would run past Alf, but Bill would be watching from the left, move up and catch them offside. At the same time, Alf should have been playing to the whistle, but he didn't, he took it for granted that Bill would sort it out. My lasting impressions of Alf's trouble at Southampton came at Sheffield Wednesday in a Cup-tie. We got beat 2–1 simply because of the offside problem and Alf not playing to the whistle. That was the beginning of the end.'

The following Saturday, Southampton went to Plymouth for a friendly. Slipping as he went into a tackle, Alf seriously injured his left knee – the pain was such that his first thought was that he might be finished with the game. That proved to be a premature diagnosis, but it was bad enough to keep him out for several weeks. In a neat reversal of roles, Bill Ellerington stepped into the breach and made the right-back position his own with accomplished performances. He even took Alf's place in the England team that played in Norway and France in the summer of 1949. Southampton embarked on a run which was to see them win eight and draw the other two of the next ten games, leaving them well clear at the top of the Second Division by Easter. With Alf still hobbling around the Dell at the beginning of March, Bill Dodgin came to him to say that even when fit, he would find it very difficult to displace Ellerington in the team. Alf was outraged: 'As at the time I could not even trot round the track, I took a very dim view of his remark and felt very upset ... in my view the Southampton manager could have shown a little more understanding of my personal feelings at a time when I was still on the injured list. To some this may appear just a trivial incident, but with time on my hands it became an obsession with me.' Alf's reaction, which included the idea of giving up the game altogether, was extreme, another example of his sensitivity. Equally, it was insensitive timing on Dodgin's part, although perhaps he was trying to gee him up, to get him fitter, faster, worrying that, as an England player, he might feel he could take his time working back to full fitness. If that was the case, then he had misread Alf's character, for he was desperate to get back into the team as quickly as he could. Joe Mallett's summary of the situation is probably nearest to the mark: 'We were lucky that we had Bill to replace Alf – he was a better player in some respects, though not all. He was younger, open to ideas, and that appealed to Bill Dodgin. Alf, on the other hand, was a bit set in his. Alf took umbrage when he couldn't get his place back, didn't want to be an international playing in the reserves, so that was that.' Dodgin must have known that the final decision over Ramsey or Ellerington had been coming for some time, and that one of them was bound to leave. Ellerington was younger and more suggestible; Alf had his own ideas about how he wanted to play and, as an international, was likely to bring in more transfer money. This dispute seemed a sensible, if awkward, way of forcing the situation.

To Alf, this was rank bad man-management, and he lost some of his respect for Dodgin. He felt that, above all else, a manager should have the welfare of his players uppermost in his mind at all times, and that Dodgin had fallen short. The inevitable consequence was a transfer request. With the transfer deadline looming on 16 March 1949, Alf put in his request on the 7th, and although the board asked him to reconsider, it was approved within a couple of days, an obvious pointer that Dodgin was happy enough to see him go. By the 10th, and with Alf still not back in the reserves as yet, several enquiries had been made. Sheffield Wednesday, Tottenham, Liverpool – who wanted to swap him for Joe Fagan – Bolton, Luton, Norwich and Burnley all had offers placed on the table, but by deadline day, the field had narrowed to just Sheffield Wednesday, then in the Second Division and way behind Southampton in the table. Although terms had been agreed between the clubs, Alf refused on the grounds that he did not wish to move so far north. Tottenham had maintained their interest but had understood that he was off to Hillsborough and pulled out of the race. When they were informed Alf was still available, they concluded it was too late to renew talks before the deadline. Alf was stuck at the Dell for the rest of the season. With a transfer fee in the region of £20,000, Spurs were only too pleased to let him play in the reserves at Southampton's expense before splashing out on a player who might not recapture his fitness. He proved he had done so at the beginning of May when he played for the reserves in the Football Combination Cup Final against Bournemouth. Although they lost 5–3, the *Daily Echo*'s correspondent wrote, 'I must make special reference to Alf Ramsey who played a grand game. He could not have played better had he been wearing an England shirt.'

Had Southampton won promotion, perhaps Alf might have withdrawn his request, the prospect of First Division football keeping him there, although as a stubborn man of principle, it's hard to see him working with Dodgin again. As it was, the Saints crumbled and took just four of the last fourteen points to miss out on promotion by one point, Fulham and West Bromwich Albion going up instead. Now, there was no reason to stay.

4 Push and Run

Having dismissed the advances of Sheffield Wednesday on deadline day, it became obvious that Alf would move to Tottenham Hotspur. They put in a sizeable bid for his services and were genuinely keen to take him to London. Alf cherished dreams of turning out at White Hart Lane and was merely biding his time. Briefly, however, the deal seemed to be in real jeopardy. It had been Joe Hulme, Spurs' manager, who had first expressed an interest in Alf. Suffering from a bout of ill health, he sent his assistant, Jimmy Anderson, down to Southampton in March to try to wrap up the Ramsey transfer but, to Hulme's great disappointment, Anderson had been unable to do so. Hulme had assembled a very useful side, just short of fulfilling its potential, and he saw Alf as the final ingredient he required to turn Spurs into promotion certainties. Returning to work later that March, the Tottenham directors suggested that if he was not fit to resume his duties, he could resign. Hulme declined their offer. A month later, acting with the generosity of spirit for which football directors are renowned, they sacked him. Alf was left wondering if his replacement would still see him as the ideal, footballing right-back the club so badly needed.

He need not have worried. On 4 May 1949, Arthur Rowe was appointed. Rowe was a football man through and through, anxious to see teams play the right way and in the right spirit. Before the war he'd made his name with Spurs as a centre-half, the new position pioneered by Herbert Chapman's Arsenal, the 'third back'. Traditionally the centre-half had been a half-back position, but Chapman pulled his number 5 into the back line and used him as a 'stopper', taking advantage of a change in the offside law: where it had previously decreed that three opposing players were required to keep a forward onside, in the late 1920s it was amended to two in an attempt to make the game more exciting. There was an avalanche of goals as a result, but Chapman was quickest to adapt. He added the third defender and immediately stemmed the flow. Meanwhile, opponents still had just two backs, giving Arsenal the opportunity to rack up the goals. They dominated English football for a time but, inevitably, other clubs followed suit, and before long the middle of defence was ruled by great dinosaurs, slogging their way through a season. There were exceptions to the rule, of course, and Arthur Rowe was one such. Just as Ramsey was to develop the full-back position, Rowe had seen that centre-half offered greater potential. Rather than whacking the ball fifty yards out of defence, only for it to come straight back again in a giant game of ping-pong, Rowe liked to maintain possession, looked to guide accurate passes out to his own men. His playing career at an end, he accepted a coaching post in Hungary, but was there just six months before the war called a halt to that, and he had to scuttle home. However brief his stay, it was valuable exposure to the methods that would ultimately create a national team of unsurpassed genius. Back home, Rowe managed the Army XI for much of the war before becoming manager of Chelmsford City, winning the Southern League in his first year, moulding a lively and entertaining outfit. This was merely an apprenticeship, the non-League game could not hold on to such talent for long. His arrival at Tottenham was inevitable.

An old-boy, Rowe kept an eye on the team's progress from his Essex exile. In his initial discussions with Jimmy Anderson, the perennial assistant, he agreed that a new right-back was required and accepted that Alf fitted the bill. Ramsey was no unknown any longer, his performance against Switzerland winning him a powerful reputation as a constructive player with good vision, the sort that Rowe had been. Yet why should Ramsey want to go to Tottenham? They'd finished fifth in Division Two, two places and five points adrift of Southampton. As Ted Bates avers, Southampton 'had probably as good a side then as we've ever had', so Spurs didn't provide an obvious step up. For all that Southampton were on the fringes of the footballing world, isolated on the south coast in spite of Bill Dodgin's relentless promotion of the club, Tottenham were not the legend they've since become. In May 1949, their only major honours were two Cup wins, the last of which had been in 1921. Even so, there was an allure to their name: they had good support, far better than Southampton could ever hope for; and they were a London club, which held twin advantages for Alf – it put him nearer the football press, which could only bolster his hopes of international recognition, and it also meant he could move back to the family home in Dagenham. Indeed, he stipulated that he should be allowed to live there before he signed for the club. This was an important consideration for him financially, and it also helped him manage his energies properly, illustrating the serious attention he gave to every detail of his career. By living with his parents, he could rely on them to help relieve him of chores he could well do without, leaving him free to concentrate on his game. In return, as a young man on a decent income, he could make a valuable contribution to the family budget, something that mattered a great deal to him, though he pointed out, 'There's no fortune in football, just a comfortable living for those who want to get paid for doing something they enjoy above all else.'

Domestic arrangements were not the only reason he made such a choice, of course. Liverpool aside, there were no First Division clubs in the running for his signature once he'd gone on the list. For an England player, this was amazing, but perhaps it worked to his benefit in that it clarified matters: it was Tottenham or Southampton. Since staying at the Dell was out of the question, he was bound for White Hart Lane. (Ironically, selling Alf was Dodgin's last positive act at the Dell. Within weeks, he'd moved to Fulham.) The paucity of choice forced Alf's hand, but he was excited by the potential on offer in north London. As Joe Mallett explains, 'I think he fitted in to Tottenham's style of play better than he did ours. They were probably a better team to play in, and his own game was guided by those around him who were more his style.' Southampton were a traditional English outfit, and for all that Alf liked to talk of his relationship with Eric Day on the wing, he was still required to play longer passes more often than not. Equally, he was shackled with more defensive duties than he wanted. At Tottenham, he could see that things were happening, that the game would be played more to his liking. In *And the Spurs Go Marching On* . . . Arthur Rowe expanded on the game he wanted Alf to play: 'I put it to Alf Ramsey that while I knew he was brought up on using long, measured passes, these tended to leave him out of the action once he had played them. But had he ever thought how much more accuracy was guaranteed, how much more progress could be made if he pumped fifteen- or twenty-yard passes to a withdrawn [outside-right, Sonny] Walters. The opposing left-back would hesitate to follow Walters back into the Spurs half, which was definitely no man's land to the full-back then, thus giving Walters the vital gift of space. And Sonny could now also make an inside pass if Alf followed up and made himself available. We had one more option: with Ramsey's precision, once advanced, he could drive the ball down to the right for Les

Bennett, coming to the near post, to turn the ball inside with his head.'

This was the root of 'push and run', a style that was to reap great rewards and become synonymous with Tottenham for many years. Rowe was expanding an idea that Alf himself had been coming towards in his own play. Running with the ball was inherently risky. Trying to hit a raking sixty-yard pass was risky. Pushing a ball to a colleague ten yards away and making yourself available to take a return pass was simple and straightforward for any pro worth his salt, and much safer. With Rowe offering Alf an important role in that kind of team, Spurs was the right move. As Walter Winterbottom points out: 'His great skill was his use of the ball. He could spot openings very quickly and play a long ball extremely accurately, but he was better known for the short ball which Tottenham were famous for. It was a passing game at Tottenham, using intelligence.' For a record fee for a full-back, officially pegged at £21,000 – left-winger Ernie Jones moved in the opposite direction as makeweight – Alf was on the move.

With Rowe dispensing maxims like 'make it simple, make it quick' and, most influential of all, 'the team makes the stars, not the stars the team', Tottenham got off to a storming start to the 1949–50 season. There was strength in every position: Ted Ditchburn was a completely reliable goalkeeper; Charlie Withers, a pacy left-back who had just displaced Vic Buckingham; Harry Clarke, a powerful centre-half. In the engine room Ronnie Burgess was perpetual motion at left-half, Bill Nicholson a willing partner on the other flank. Up front, there were the diverse talents of wingers Sonny Walters, fast, direct and an accurate passer, and the more unortho-dox, wandering Les Medley. Eddie Baily, a creative livewire, and the elegant Les Bennett were formidable inside-forwards and fed the dependable Len Duquemin in the middle. The only surprise was that such a good team had been consigned to the Second Division for so long. They destroyed the competition, winning nine of the first ten games and losing just twice before the turn of the year. In November, they humiliated their close rivals Sheffield United 7–0 at home. *The Times* was moved to report that, 'Spurs, as one prefers to think of them, on this form are in a class of their own in the Second Division. One would go even farther. They would make the leading sides in the Championship sit up and think.' Alf's contri-bution was singled out for praise, the reporter stating that, 'Ramsey was feeding his forwards beautifully.'

Promotion never looked in doubt, even allowing for a slump in form in the new year, an inevitable slackening off once much of the hard work had been done. In fact, much of that work had been done before a ball was kicked in anger. In pre-season, Rowe's approach and enthusiasm for the game energized the players. His vision came together on the training field in double-quick time, everyone warming to their task. Alf wrote that the club was awash with football talk: 'All over the field during training, at lunch, even on the way home, the Tottenham players never ceased to discuss ways and means of improving the standard of their play.' There was the unspoken suggestion that Alf himself was the hub, yet he was actually a more peripheral figure. Ron Reynolds, the young reserve goalkeeper, remembers that Alf 'was a loner, a quiet man, not someone you could easily talk with. I don't think anyone at Spurs really got to know him, not even Syd McClellan. Both came from Dagenham, and they'd travel in daily. Syd would say that on some days Alf would chat away, but on others you wouldn't hear a thing from him. He used to say Alf was hard to pin down. Of all the players I had dealings with, he's one I could never figure out. Even later on, when I got in the team, and in fact in training, I normally stripped next to Alf, and he rarely had much to say. Then, once training was finished, he was gone.' George Robb, who joined the club initially as an amateur in December 1951, confirms the point: 'You couldn't say, "Right, who's Alf's mate in the dressing room?" He didn't deliberately set himself and not want to join in – if you went up to him, he'd love it, he'd talk about the game, but where on the coach there might be a bit of noise going on, Alf wouldn't be behind it. But nor would he resent it. He was a little less rowdy, a quiet, introspective chap.' This was the remaining manifestation of the shy nature that had created those doubts about his own ability. Alf was not an unpleasant, not even an unsociable man. He simply didn't have the social skills necessary to succeed in that way, was not a master of small talk, wasn't a comedian like Eddie Baily, nor naturally loquacious like Danny Blanchflower. If he had nothing to say, his lips were sealed.

That season was a vital one in which the methods that would stand Spurs in good stead in future were tried and tested. Perhaps they were fortunate to still be in the Second Division, so that they could formulate their play in slightly less demanding company, though very shortly it was apparent that they were a class apart. With promotion all but sewn up by the turn of the year, they turned their attentions to the FA Cup, seeing it as an opportunity to test their progress against better opposition. They saw off First Division Stoke at the Victoria Ground by a single goal, though the margin of victory should have been far greater. Sunderland were next in line, this time at White Hart Lane. Sunderland finished that season in third place in Division One, missing out on the title by one point, but on that January afternoon they were no match for Tottenham, and were thrashed 5–1. Spurs went out at the next hurdle, losing 1–0 in a tense game at Goodison Park, but their point had been proved. The First Division need hold no fears for them.

A game at Queens Park Rangers on 1 April offered the chance for them to book an early passage to the top flight. Previewing the game, the *Daily Mail*'s reporter noted, 'Tottenham manager Arthur Rowe and right-back Alf Ramsey have for the past two months been carefully guarding two bottles of champagne sent them by admirers for the team celebration when Spurs gains promotion to Division 1. Yesterday Mr Rowe said to Ramsey: "Shall we take our bottles to Shepherd's Bush tomorrow?" The England back answered: "No, the lads want to celebrate at Tottenham."' Rowe treated Alf as an equal, almost looking upon him as a captain, even while Ronnie Burgess was doing such a fine job in that role. It confirms Bill Nicholson's feeling that Alf was Rowe's favourite player of the time. This was not surprising since Rowe noted that, 'Alf would come back after practice to perfect his kicking. He would spend hours seeking accuracy and perfection.' This was the dedication he'd encountered in Hungary before the war, a determination and willingness to learn and improve that he loved to see in his players. The two were close professionally and Rowe was a great influence on Alf's career in management, as Ron Reynolds explains: 'I think Arthur was lucky in that he perfected this style and was fortunate to already have players who fitted that style. His back-room staff were good, Cecil Poynton as trainer, for example. On top of that, Vic Buckingham, who was just finishing at the club, was well in with one of the top coaches for the Football Association. Vic and Freddie Cox from Arsenal held the very first course for a preliminary coaching certificate outside the usual FA centres, and that was held at Tottenham. Vic believed strongly in that side of things. That permeated down and everyone talked football all the time. The funny thing was that Alf was on the fringe. You never really heard from Alf in the discussions. In fact, as a colleague, you very rarely got any assistance or advice verbally from Alf, but he was always listening to Arthur and picking things up from him.' So many of Rowe's maxims, so many of his ideas on creating space, of moulding a team, found their way into his own methodology. As Alf spelt it out: 'In football there is no such thing as a defender or attacker. Every member of the team should be working together to *score* goals!' This was a lesson right from the Tottenham training ground, one that Alf took into management, where he also made the reverse true, that every member of the side should be working together to *prevent* goals. And although Rowe always used wingers at Spurs, it was his view on running off the ball rather than running with it that put Alf on the path towards his rejection of specialist wingers.

That Tottenham side was one of almost industrial efficiency, although that's not to say they were mechanical or stereotyped. They were a fine *team*, shorn of great eye-catching individuals. No man won games alone, each had a job to do, moving the ball with speed and accuracy, always having options available. It was a game that demanded physical fitness and tremendous footballing intelligence. Eddie Baily confirmed, 'We were always playing for each other, it was genuine team spirit . . . you played with a pride in yourself and the team.' As Rowe said time and again, 'The team makes the stars, not the stars the team.' That was as true for Alf as it was for others – he was recalled to England colours in November 1949 and never looked back. It's testament to Tottenham's effectiveness that few other members of the side amassed more than a handful of caps. Unable to play the virtuoso game that would captivate the press and the spectators, their talents were generally overlooked – Alf aside, only Ronnie Burgess got into double figures in international appearances, playing thirty-two times for Wales. Yet if individuals did not receive the requisite acclaim, the team did. That was the object of the exercise. Promotion was clinched by the handsome margin of nine points, Sheffield Wednesday accompanying Spurs into the First Division on goal average from Sheffield United – Wednesday even had Tottenham to thank for that, for it was their 7–0 beating of United that had tipped the balance.

For Alf, it had been a triumphant season. He had established himself in the Spurs team without any question, his side had won their divisional championship with almost contemptuous ease, and he had established himself in the England side with a visit to Brazil to take part in the fourth World Cup to crown his year.

5 You Cannot Conquer America

Of all seasons, 1949–50 promised to be the most exciting in a long time. England had, finally, deigned to enter FIFA's World Cup, scheduled for the end of the season in Brazil. Having turned up their noses at the prospect of competing for the greatest prize in world football, having lacked the vision to grasp the importance of the tournament, the penny had at last dropped in Football Association HQ. Alf did not want to miss out on this once in a lifetime opportunity.

Proving yourself an England player was harder in the early 1950s than today. Since players weren't seen much on television or even on newsreel, to establish a national reputation, you had to perform well every week on every ground – the people in Newcastle might see Alf just once a year, and if he had a stinker at St James' Park, they'd have little interest in what he did elsewhere, but mark him down as useless. Equally, for all that the game is quicker and more pressurized, young guns like Paul Scholes and Robbie Fowler have only to please Glenn Hoddle with their performances in order to get England caps. It wasn't always so straightforward. Walter Winterbottom was England's first manager, although this was only a small part of his duties given that he was Director of Coaching. As he explains, 'There was a sideline, being manager of the England teams! I worked with a selection committee, I didn't pick the teams alone, as they do today. We had eight selectors and a chairman, and the committee went through the side position by position! We had nominations for goalkeeper, and when he'd been selected we went on to right-back. The committee would meet the Wednesday before the international the following week. They would pick a side and then a reserve side, position for position. If on the Saturday a player got injured, the reserve would slot in, quite irrespective of whether or not he was suitable! There was no thought of building a team, just choosing players. As a manager, you're always looking for new talent. The whole business of restructuring a side took a long time because of the committee, many of whom were well established and thought a lot of themselves, enjoyed the glory, but had no experience at all of playing in Europe or further afield. Their thoughts were on picking people who had been loyal to their clubs, who they thought deserved an honour, an international cap, rather than picking a team for a particular purpose. For example, the Bolton chairman was a typical Lancastrian with a hard-headed view that football was centred up north, not down south, and that we should select players accordingly. Then you'd get the opposing view elsewhere on the committee. They'd travelled little and seen too little of international football to judge it.'

The selection committee made life difficult. It was virtually imposs-ible to maintain any consistency, making it harder to stick with a playing policy. Yet it was not that unusual at the time. At many clubs, it was the directors who selected the side, the manager coming in, tugging his forelock and meekly offering his suggestions. If you looked at the England team in which Alf made his debut, the side that beat Switzerland 6–0, you would think it had done a good job. The next game showed five personnel changes and one positional. Injuries played a part, but changing half the side was scarcely the recipe for success. (England lost 3–1 to Scotland at Wembley.) The players felt undermined and Tom Finney admits: 'When Walter first came, as far as we knew, he picked the side, but you read things that said otherwise. It became common knowledge that he would go in with a selected side and would talk it through with the commit-tee, who would have some say in the final team.' Ray Wilson, who came into the England reckoning in the latter days of Winter-bottom's reign, recalls 'In 1954, long before I got in the side, I remember Len Shackleton having a marvellous game at Wembley when we beat West Germany 3–1, the year they'd won the World Cup. Shack went into print saying what a great result it was, but also said, "I bet we only have half the team playing in the next international", and that was so.' Seven changes were made, Shackle-ton one of them – he never played for his country again. Every player was on trial, there was no security, no hope of a run of five or six games to find a new level. Only a few players were guaranteed a place, certain of beating the inadequacies of the selection system – Tom Finney, Stanley Matthews, Billy Wright and, by early 1950, Alf Ramsey.

Following his knee injury, Alf had missed seven internationals. Several players had been tried in his position – Manchester United's left-back John Aston, Blackpool's Edward Shimwell, Alf's nemesis at Southampton, Bill Ellerington, and Derby's Bert Mozley – but none had looked as secure as Alf in his only appearance to date. Even the committee could see that. Having proven his fitness for Spurs, he was selected for the fourth international of the year, the visit of reigning world champions Italy, Mozley having succumbed to an injury of his own. Alf's prospects weren't harmed by the fact that the game took place at White Hart Lane, the FA committee always having an eye on the extra gate money they might generate from including a home favourite in the team. Glad to be back, he was under no illusions as to the strength of the opposition, having seen them outplay England for half an hour or so in Turin eighteen months earlier. In addition, Walter Winterbottom made sure that his charges were well prepared, the *Daily Mail* explaining that, 'One of the reasons why he is such a success at his job is that he has a card index, complete with diagrams, life history and assessment of playing skills of most of the world's star players.'

Whatever information he was able to impart did little good in the opening exchanges, for the Italians were irresistible, let down only by their inability to finish. *The Times* pointed out that Alf was given a torrid time as 'Carapellese too often for comfort found an inside path past Ramsey', the *Daily Mail* adding that 'England were lucky not to have been beaten 3–0 ... Ramsey and Aston were guilty of lapses early on, but came back well enough to earn honourable mention.' Alf confessed that he had learned a great deal from the game, particularly that, 'It is sometimes more important to watch the man rather than the ball.' Having absorbed the lesson, by the second half, Alf was secure, causing Billy Wright to conclude, 'Alf turned in a grand display to make the right-back position his own.' This was confirmed by the result, a 2–0 win, goals from Jack Rowley and a fluke from Wright himself overcoming the Italians. The game was a personal triumph for goalkeeper Bert Williams, whose performance was described as 'magical' by the *Daily Mail*. All observers agreed that he had been the difference between an England victory and catastrophic defeat. All, that is, except Alf. His view was pragmatic to the point of asceticism: 'I did not agree with those who afterwards remarked that we were very lucky to have Williams. After all, the idea of having a goalkeeper is to try to stop the other fellows from scoring.' This was Ramsey the complete professional coming through. Every player in the side had a job to do, that was what they were paid for, so they should get on with it. If they did their job properly, anything they achieved, however extraordinary, was only to be expected. If they had the ability in them, they should show it every time they went out on the field. Failure to do so was worthy of mention for that showed they were doing something wrong, but success was an inevitable by-product of applying the principles. It wasn't an attitude that necessarily endeared him to too many, though he was still highly regarded, Tom Finney recording, 'He was very serious-minded compared with the majority of players. He was a bit of a loner, but if you had a discussion on anything, he talked a lot of sense.' Comments such as Alf's merely add to the impression that he was a detached, aloof character, ruthless in his decision making. Yet this was the paradox from which he drew strength. His perceived aloofness might be better described as shyness, but his introspection helped him turn himself into a calculating logician. A deep thinker, his voluntary solitude gave him time to think things through and come to great insights, though he often came to them via his turbulent emotions, his obsessive perfectionism and passion for winning. If an accomplished footballer did not do his job as he should, it would drive Alf to distraction. He learned to channel such anger, using it to his advantage, recognizing that if a player drew his wrath, he needed to be put back on the straight and narrow. It led to a fondness for the reliable rather than the capricious. Similarly, his enthusiasm could lead him to become besotted with footballers who always did the right thing at the right time, men like Sam Barkas, Billy Wright or Manchester United's captain Johnny Carey. Alf's combination of relentless logic and total commitment to a cause was a potent mix.

He was now a fixture in the England side, despite lacking in pace and aggression. His Spurs colleague George Robb points out, 'His timing was immaculate. You wouldn't find him going in with a rash tackle. He'd prefer to go an extra yard or two and make it a good firm tackle as opposed to diving in, which was unusual – if you were a full-back then, you went in and got the ball however you could and got the winger out of it as well!' Having turned himself into a first-class player, he always had a soft spot for similar players, men like Roger Hunt and Alan Ball, who never sold themselves short, the hallmark of his own play.

In common with his international colleagues, Alf had to wait five months to get another cap after the Italian job, for England had no game until April 1950 – this in a World Cup year! With such long breaks in between games, it was little wonder that the players struggled to find a pattern. International football of the 1950s looks very disjointed from a modern perspective. Today's calendar is cluttered with European or World Cup qualifiers, a result of the exponential improvements in international travel. Back then, England existed almost exclusively on a diet of friendlies, albeit friendlies with a more competitive edge than most of those played today. It was thus harder to maintain the level of preparation and concentration required at the highest level, never mind prepare England for the World Cup. That was all the more difficult since even the qualifying group was merely an extension of the Home Internationals, England battling it out for one of two places in the finals with Scotland, Wales and Northern Ireland. Playing against teams that played the same basic style hardly equipped England to take on the South Americans or teams from Continental Europe.

Alf's third cap came in the final World Cup qualifier at Hampden Park. Having beaten Wales 4–1 and Northern Ireland 9–2, England were certain of taking one of the two qualification places. Scotland had been equally successful, defeating the Welsh 2–0 and Northern Ireland 8–2 and so they were also sure of coming at least second – a draw would ensure a tied Championship in the pre-goal-difference days. However, to add spice to the encounter with England, the Scottish FA had come to the ludicrously truculent conclusion that their side would only travel to Brazil to compete if they won the qualification series. The *Daily Mail* summed up the situation confronting the Scots: 'Scottish officials have in effect said: "Win or draw and you get an eight weeks' holiday trip to South America plus the possibility of six international games at £20 a time in the World Cup play-offs. If you lose there is nothing."' Under such heavy pressure, the Scots were unable to raise their game. Roy Bentley scored to seal an England win. Many of the Englishmen offered consolation to their opponents, Billy Wright insisting that the players should petition their FA and force them to change their mind. Alf was rather more sanguine about the affair, for as Tom Finney points out, 'For some reason, he was very bitter towards the Scots. Whenever we played them he really wanted to win.' That determination had brought out the best in his game, the *Mail*'s after-match summary pointing out that, 'Among the certainties for Brazil on Saturday's form are Alf Ramsey . . . [he] begins to look like Wadsworth and Hapgood rolled into one.'

The season ended in early May, with England's first World Cup game set for 25 June in Rio. A brief tour into Europe was arranged in mid-May to give the players some much-needed experience of playing together. In Lisbon, Portugal were defeated 5–3, Tom Finney scoring four goals. In criticizing the team, despite winning so well away from home, the press' false picture of England's standing in the world was revealed. One report suggested that 'England's chances in the World Cup were dented today at the National Stadium in an inconclusive display ... the defence which took everything Scotland could throw at Hampden Park in April looked like shifting sands against the quick-moving, tip-tapping Portuguese forwards.' If the analysis was correct – England were not invincible – the tone of the reports nonetheless suggested that a team like England should simply squash these European insects. The great technical and tactical strides that were being made on the mainland were ignored by the media, ultimately to England's cost. Not only that, the press and public failed to make allowances for a savage blow that had been inflicted on the side. Ever since the war, Stoke's Neil Franklin had been England's centre-half. A top-class player, he was disenchanted by the paltry maximum wage, and on the eve of the World Cup he walked out on Stoke and joined Santa Fe, a Colombian club who offered far greater rewards. To move was against FIFA regulations, since Stoke held his registration. Franklin made himself ineligible for England selection and a replacement was needed. But players like Neil Franklin don't grow on trees. As Tom Finney remembers: 'It was a terrible blow because I always considered Neil was the best centre-half I ever played with. For him to up and leave was terrible. We played Scotland and by the next weekend he was off! It took us a fair time to replace him – that was why Billy Wright came across to centre-half later on. Neil going just made things harder. We'd probably just gone past a peak from that 1948 side, losing players like Carter, Lawton, Hardwick and Scott. Younger players were coming in. They were good players, like Alf, but they were in their early internationals, which is difficult.' Alf understood how hard it would be to replace Franklin, having played alongside him, but such was his anger at this 'betrayal' of the national team, he could not bring himself to mention Franklin's defection in his account of the 1950 World Cup, despite its great impact on results. Franklin was simply blanked out – the Ministry of Truth couldn't have done a better job of rewriting history.

Defensive frailty was shown again in the final tour game, when Belgium were beaten 4–1 having taken a shock lead. The *Mail* described the game as 'inspiring, glittering, thrilling ... [but] the defence must learn the secret of playing against Continental-style forwards without losing their positions or their heads ... Ramsey [though] was the best of the defence.' Alf himself felt that they showed promise, arguing that 'on many occasions it "clicked" so well that I thought with plenty of match practice it could be developed into a really first-rate combination'. That was a statement heavy with irony. Having played in Brussels on 18 May, the players returned home and disbanded, only reconvening in London a month later for a four-day get-together prior to flying out to Brazil. In the restrained language of the time, Alf expressed his disapproval: 'The thought of hanging about at the end of a season waiting for "Cup time" to come around was in my view rather a waste of time. I would have preferred to have gone to Brazil, get accustomed to the conditions, and, of course, have a series of trial matches under the conditions we should have to face – and of course overcome.' There would be no such mistakes under Alf's own regime. His comments are endorsed by Tom Finney: 'We had a month after the end of the season without meeting. That was the way football was run in those days – nowadays a team would be in South America for two or three weeks to get acclimatized, whereas we went three days before our first game!' Walter Winterbottom was forced to toil as England's manager in less than ideal circumstances: 'Normally, the only time we got them together was in the week before the game against Scotland, which was always played on a Saturday. That gave us the time to play against West Ham or Tottenham, asking them to play in a particular style, so that we might at least get a feeling of the way the French played or the Italians played. If we were playing in Scotland, we might play Bolton or Manchester United. They used to get stuck in, they wanted to beat England, and this was good for us. A lot of clubs objected to this because it was something new!'

Although such difficulties in getting hold of players in the season might be understandable, surely in the close season, things would be easier? Far from it, according to Winterbottom: 'We didn't pull off World Cup football because I think very often we were physically exhausted when we came to play these matches. They came right at the end of the season, and it was a psychological as much as a physical problem. In those days, the clubs would tell their players to take a complete rest through the summer because they were exhausted and needed to come back ready for the new season. It was impregnated in the players, and so they were coming to me psychologically tired, whereas now players accept that if they are fit and prepare properly, they can play almost all the year round. Instead, they were jaded and it was hard to pick them up for a tournament that was about to begin. Equally, they didn't have the experience of foreign tactics and were caught out on a number of occasions. The clubs came first, no doubt about that. You had to go on bended knee to get your players. We had a get-together before we went out to Brazil, playing amateur sides because all our club sides had finished for the season. We couldn't use proper grounds because they were being reseeded, so we had to play on pitches at amateur clubs too, though we did get one session at Wembley! The handicaps are extraordinary if you look back at them today. The clubs wanted their players to rest in the close season, and the press were all with this. You simply couldn't give them hard training at that stage – we tried to, but a lot of the players soon began to complain they were tired: "Don't take too much out of us, Walter!"'

Although Finney's assessment that England had gone past a peak is a fair one, they still had a useful squad for the 1950 series: Williams and Ditchburn as goalkeepers; Ramsey, John Aston, Scott and Bill Eckersley at full-back; Wright, Laurie Hughes, Jimmy Dickinson, Nicholson, Jimmy Taylor, Henry Cockburn as half-backs; Milburn, Mortensen, Bentley, Mannion, Finney, Matthews, Baily, Jimmy Mullen and Willie Watson selected as forwards. They looked formidable and should have gone a long way in the competition. Preparation, such as it was in England, was good, Tom Finney explaining that, 'Walter was a tactician and a very good coach – he was very well respected on the Continent. He was a coaching manager.' Even this caused its problems: many players of the time, brought up in the simpler pre-war world, were, like Stanley Matthews, almost allergic to coaching, and argued that players good enough to play for England should be left to get on with the job. There is a grain of truth in that, but equally, in combating unusual opposition styles, even great players need to have some framework to work within. Walter Winterbottom is a great believer that, 'Real coaching is about bringing about team understanding so that they can work with one another . . . if Stanley Matthews said, "Look, Walter, I don't want any through balls for me to run on to, I want it to feet," we'd all try to contribute by doing that, and Alf, of course, was very good at that. On the whole, you couldn't dominate players the way in which you might if you were a club manager. We would try to discuss the opposition wherever possible and discuss what we wanted to do in the game, but it just wasn't possible to go into any depth. Alf didn't like to talk at our meetings. He thought a lot, and we might speak privately, but he was very reserved and didn't like to speak up at meetings.' Billy Wright, though, remembered him doing so on occasion: 'He has the priceless ability of being able to put over new ideas in a splendid fashion, encourages his colleagues to reveal their own theories, and in every way he is a remarkable character whose contribution to the game has definitely helped to improve the standard of defensive play . . . he has brought something new to the full-back art.' Alf could be relied on to come up with good ideas on a one-to-one basis, but he still shrank from being the centre of attention. He was also reluctant to put forward ideas in a situation where he was not in command, where he did not have the opportunity to make sure things were done to his liking. He would not take the blame for an idea gone wrong if he could not be charged with full responsibility for putting it into practice.

However hard they prepared in England, it could scarcely approximate the conditions they would meet in Brazil, playing in heat and humidity, at unfamiliar altitude, and with a three-hour time difference. The party flew out of London on 19 June, bound for Rio via Paris, Lisbon, Dakar and Recife, a daunting thirty-one-hour flight. They reached their destination on the 21st, jet-lagged and exhausted. Tom Finney recalls vividly the shock of arriving in Brazil: 'We went from a mild English summer to something in the eighties or nineties. It was a huge difference to what we'd been used to at home.' For all that, the tournament was already a foregone conclusion according to the newspapers. Brazil would be a tough nut to crack on their own soil, but them apart, England would have things very much their own way. Finney remembers, 'Looking from our point of view, we were rated pretty highly in Europe, but what people never understood was that we never knew much about the South American teams. We hadn't really seen them because there was no TV, and all we knew was what we'd read about them in magazines – Arsenal had played out there the year before and they came back full of what they'd seen, the great skills they had. We were fortunate enough to see the opening game of that tournament, Brazil v Mexico, which Brazil won 4–0. We arrived about a day before that and we were really in awe of what we saw – I just hadn't seen anything like the skills they produced. We knew then we were in for a hard time against the South American sides.' Walter Winterbottom was equally uneasy with England's status as hot favourites:

'The press were very blinkered. Nobody had seen Brazil play – even I hadn't, which was terribly wrong. We saw them in the first game and I feared them then – they had three forwards who were so fast, the speed of their inter-passing was tremendous. I admired their style of football, they pushed it to the feet of an attacker who came away from the defence, he pushed it back and someone else ran through on the blind side of the defender. It was very difficult to counter this, because we didn't experience it in club football.' Of England's party, only Arsenal's Laurie Scott and Alf himself had met Brazilian opposition. While the other members of the party were in awe of their virtuosity, Alf took it in his stride. After all, Southampton had done well in Brazil two years earlier and England were a far better proposition than Southampton. Apply the English virtues and victory would follow.

Fortune had smiled on England, for at least they wouldn't meet the stiffest opposition until the second phase of the competition. In perhaps the most chaotic World Cup of them all, four sides would qualify from four qualifying groups. In the second stage, these four would then play each other in a round-robin, the team topping the group emerging as World Champions – for the first, and only time, the competition would not culminate in a World Cup Final! England's pool saw them grouped with Chile, Spain and the USA; nothing to frighten our players, the theory went. Although the opposition seemed weak, England were unfortunate to be in a group of four. Just as Scotland had refused to compete after qualifying, so too did Argentina and Czechoslovakia, yet all three were included in the draw. The upshot was that FIFA was left with two groups of four, one of three and one of two! Had fortune looked on them more kindly, England could have found themselves in Uruguay's position, having to play one game to progress.

In an attempt to get used to conditions, England made use of Botafogo's facilities, but Alf soon made note that all was not well: 'During practice matches I found it very hard to breathe. Secondly, at the conclusion of even an easy kick-about, I felt infinitely more tired than after a hectic League match at home.' Tom Finney recalls, 'The altitude made things very difficult. They had these oxygen masks to help us breathe, and this was just foreign to us!' Even England's base did not help them. Walter Winterbottom cannot hide the despair that he felt on arrival, even now, almost fifty years after the event: 'The accommodation was hopeless – we were stuck on Copacabana beach. Arsenal had put us up to it, they stayed there the year before, but of course they were on an end-of-season tour, so to be on the beach was uproarious to them! The kitchens were dreadful, the smell used to go up into the bedrooms, the food was swimming in oil [most players suffered 'Rio stomach' at some stage], there were other guests there and, of course, the players were always wanting to go and enjoy the beach! We decided that it was off limits after 10 a.m. because we were told the sun on the sand gave off rays that caused lethargy and sapped the energy. The players were discontented with the situation – many hadn't even experienced travel abroad. It's a miserable experience when you find that players are worried about the atmosphere they'll be playing in, scared to death of the supporters when, if you'd been here before, you would have realized it was simply crowds having fun! We were very unfortunate in so many ways. We asked to have some lightweight boots made for training, but when they came they were almost heavy gardening boots! They were made of Wellington material!'

With such problems to overcome, it's to Winterbottom's credit that he got a team on the field at all; such was his run of luck, he almost lost Stan Mortensen one evening. The local officials had been busy beautifying their city for the arrival of the world's greatest footballers. Trees were removed, broad parades put in their place. Unfortunately, one worker tore up a tree and forgot to fill in the hole. In the darkness, Mortensen disappeared into it. Fortunately, no harm was done and he took his place in the side that faced Chile at the Maracanã in pouring rain. The rain helped the Englishmen battle against the conditions, and a goal in each half, one from Mortensen, the other from Mannion, saw them through. Yet it was anything but comfortable, Billy Wright admitting that, 'We all knew in our hearts that the team had not "clicked" as we had hoped . . . owing to the humidity, breathing became quite an effort . . . the conditions underfoot, too, were entirely different to those we were accustomed to in Britain. Our boots sank ankle deep in the thick grass . . . for the first time in my life I felt tired long before the end of the game.' That weariness was England's biggest worry. If nothing else, England teams were supremely strong and fit – Wright made a point of noting that Winterbottom 'insisted on physical fitness'. It was their power of endurance that had rescued games against superior sides in recent years. If their effectiveness was to be so reduced, they had problems. Even so, the *Daily Mail* appeared happy: 'England came through the first test fairly satisfactorily considering the strange conditions and the hostility of the crowd . . .

all things considered England should take the game against US in their stride as a preparation for the stiff test against Spain.' At least they had points on the board and could only get better as they became more accustomed to life in Brazil. Not only that, but their second game, against the USA, would be played at lower altitude, just 1000 feet above sea level, offering an altogether more comfortable atmosphere.

Tom Finney recalls the attitude in the England camp: 'America were no-hopers. They were a mixed-nationality side, players that were there to make the numbers up.' Even so, England did not underestimate the task. The full, unchanged, side was selected, the only note of controversy centring around the continued absence of Matthews on the right-wing, though since he had not played for England since April 1949, this was no surprise. With Finney on the right and Jimmy Mullen picking up on the left-wing, Matthews was not the loss that might be imagined. For Finney, it provided another chance to combine with Alf: 'Alf liked to have his winger drop deep, which was my sort of game too, picking it up deep to get away from the full-back – if he came with you that was just what you wanted, because he was pulled out of position. I enjoyed playing with Alf, he always played the right pass.'

Following the Chile game, England flew out to Belo Horizonte. Alf described the journey and the sights that met them in *Talking Football*: 'When we shot through an opening in a mountain range we found Belo Horizonte stretched out below us ... nearly 300 miles in the wilderness [we found] a beautifully planned city with "baby skyscrapers" ... the pilot swooped low to give us a close-up of the newly constructed stadium which is the pride and joy of the citizens.' The city was home to many English expatriate, working for the local mining company, hence England's visit to this outpost at FIFA's insistence. It was a move they could have done without, at the very time they were coming to grips with Rio. For the duration of their stay, they were based at a training camp in Morro Velho, fifteen miles from the stadium. The journey to and from the camp did little to settle nerves, as Alf explained: 'Never will the England footballers who made the journey to the camp forget the nightmare experience of being driven around 167 hairpin bends on a road which seemed to cling to the side of the mountain ... [the driver] was possibly the only fellow aboard the coach who did not give an anxious thought to the possibility that the coach might hurtle hundreds of feet into the valley below. Every time a car passed us a nasty red dust would come hurtling into our coach and we were all holding handkerchiefs to our faces.'

Following that ordeal, it seemed things couldn't get any worse. But they did. The Belo Horizonte stadium was incomplete – the dressing rooms were so primitive that England got changed in the Minas Athletic Club, five minutes' coach ride away. The field was surrounded by a twelve-foot-high wall, like 'playing in a prison' according to Bert Williams. Above the wall was an extremely hostile crowd, the English representation notwithstanding. England had suffered this in the first game against Chile, but in the tight little stadium at Belo it seemed all the more venomous. The Brazilians had marked England down as the biggest threat and were doing all they could to undermine them. But even their support could not save an American side there for the slaughter – even the Americans thought so, having held a party the night before the game, several players not getting to bed until the early hours.

England started confidently enough, but after half an hour still hadn't scored. The Americans, who had acquitted themselves well in their 3–1 defeat against Spain in their first game, were clearly outclassed but were riding their luck, Wright writing of three saves the American goalkeeper made with his face. With five minutes to go to half-time and the scores level, America broke free. Walter Winterbottom recalls with horror, 'We were murdering them but they had a shot from well outside the box. It struck an attacker on the head as it was going through, and Bert Williams had to change direction. He was on his hands and knees trying to stop it rolling over the line! Totally against the run of the play.' A goal down, England became more and more frenzied in their attacks, Winterbottom pointing out: 'Our players get worse when they have to fight like that, they put too much into it, expend too much effort, but even so, we scored a genuine goal which was disallowed. But these things happen. Maurice Smith, who wrote for the *People*, was doing some statistics and reckoned we hit the woodwork eleven times! Once they scored it was a case of handle the ball, handle the players, the crowd were loving it, and it was just one of those days when we were poleaxed! I've often wondered why that game was never filmed; if we could have had any film of it, we could have shown people what sort of game it was, but we've had to suffer ever since. I've been round the world on tours with FIFA and so on, even to New Zealand and Australia, and everywhere I went, they wanted me on TV, and the first question was always, "What happened when you played against America?"!' Tom Finney remembers England's most famous reverse with similar clarity: 'There was no question of the players taking it easy, it was just one of those games where the longer it went on, the more desperate we became. They had a couple of attacks, scored from one of them, and then pulled everybody back behind the ball and made it very difficult for us. The pitch was very, very poor – there's no way it would be used for a World Cup game in this day and age – and that levels things up, like it does in the FA Cup. We had more than enough chances to have won comfortably. We knew we were in for a lashing from the press because to lose to the US made us the laughing stocks of the game, really, and it was dismal. Rightly, the press were incensed. When it was over, as a player, it was one of those times where it doesn't seem to dawn on you that you've lost to a side like that. How could you possibly lose to a side as poor as that? All we wanted to do was get home and forget about it! But we had another game to play.' As expected, the press were remorseless in their criticism. The *Daily Worker* complained of 'probably the worst display ever by an England side' while the *Daily Mail* called it 'the biggest soccer upset of all time . . . England played ridiculously badly . . . the US gradually got on top and on the left-wing, the Souzas, Eddie and John, played a victory march against Wright and Ramsey . . . they were beaten because of bad shooting, over-anxiety in the second half and failure to settle down on the small pitch . . . [the stadium was] unsuitable for a match of World Cup importance.'

Despite the setback, flying back to Rio, England knew that victory over Spain would mean a tie at the head of the table and a play-off. But the American game had left scars that could not heal in three days, Winterbottom pointing out: 'That game really took the morale out of the side, a tragedy, really.' Changes were made by Arthur Drewry, the only England selector to accompany the side to Brazil. Bentley, a deep lying centre-forward, was dropped to make way for the more robust talents of Milburn. Eckersley replaced Aston at left-back, Mullen was ousted by Matthews, Finney switching back to the left-wing, and Baily came in for Mannion. Stung into action, England turned on a display lauded by the Brazilian critics as the best of the tournament. Tom Finney recalls, 'Jackie Milburn scored the first goal of the game and was given offside, but his header had gone past the keeper and the full-back who was stood on the line! We played really well against Spain, but again missed chances. The refereeing wasn't much help.' With a good goal struck off the record by the Italian official, England began to feel the world was against them, the more so when the Spaniards took the lead against the run of play. Walter Winterbottom remembers: 'Alf played a short pass that was intercepted and the cross was headed in by the centre-forward, and after that they were doing anything to stop the play, dirty tactics all the time.' Alf's memory of the goal was a little different: 'I fancy I might have been watching the left-winger rather than the ball when it was swung over from the right. If I had not made this slip there is a chance I might have prevented Zarra, their crack leader, running on to it. But then, one lapse such as this, costly though it proved to be, would have meant very little had the Spaniards played football in keeping with the rules of the game.' It was richly ironic that England's 1950 challenge was stymied by refereeing according to the Latin interpretation of the rules – precisely the opposite phenomenon would help Alf to glory sixteen years later.

Although the refereeing was poor – Brazilian radio said England played against twelve men in the Spanish match – England weren't up to the task. Winterbottom had done all that could be expected, as had the players, the American defeat notwithstanding. The English authorities had turned up expecting to win and the FA's unjustifiable arrogance cost them dear. Imagine enduring a thirty-one-hour flight into the southern hemisphere, to altitude, days before kicking-off in the World Cup! The Englishmen were being asked to play with their legs tied together. Little wonder they stumbled. It was also time to face up to fundamental deficiencies within the English game, many of which lay with the forwards, perceived as our greatest strength. Wright wrote, 'The England forwards were brilliant in their approach work. Time and again they tore wide gaps in the defence which tried to halt their progress, but once the penalty area was reached! I can assure you that schoolboys would have been spanked by their masters for missing the same simple chances . . . the primary lesson being that too many English forwards in their mania for football perfection overlook the fact that it is goals that count most of all.'

Matthews, forced to watch the Belo Horizonte humiliation from the stands, put it down as 'One of those days. We could have played for twenty-four hours and not scored.' We've all seen the odd game like that, but when did that happen to truly *great* sides, especially twice in a row? When did it happen to the Hungarians, to Real Madrid, to Brazil, to Liverpool in their prime? This 'better luck next time' attitude was one Alf could not stand. He accepted that, 'We had a year's bad luck ... [but] I repeat we cannot hope to win matches if we don't take our chances ... we can never shut our eyes to the fact that the England forwards had chances which they would have snapped up in the most confident manner in an ordinary League match.' It's interesting that he should savage the forwards, fairly enough, yet spare himself and the defence when it was goals conceded that cost England, his error that helped lose the Spanish match. Again, this was evidence of the defence mechanism that protected him so thoroughly, and it was never more necessary than now. So angry was he at England's abject failure, it was to change his outlook on the game. Defeat on that scale became unacceptable to him. For all his slightly pompous comments on the sporting nature of Englishmen, our refusal to descend to the Latin level, Alf made sure that all of his sides would have players well enough acquainted with the euphemistic 'professionalism' necessary to protect a lead and make life uncomfortable for opponents. If Winterbottom's team embraced the Corinthian ideal, Alf's teams would accept the new realities of world football and fight dirty as and when necessary. Winterbottom himself says, 'We had a cultured full-back with Alf's arrival, but there were times when you wished he would tackle more! I think because of that, in his own mind throughout his career, he favoured getting players with steel in his team – Nobby Stiles was a typical example of that.' The pain of that American defeat in particular was almost physical. He could not bear to be tainted with England's most devastating humiliation. If Walter Winterbottom and Tom Finney were continually quizzed on that game against the USA, you can guarantee that the same happened to Ramsey. The memory of the Brazilian fans taking out their hankies to wave goodbye to England during the last minutes of the game left its own vivid scar: 'It did not altogether please us,' he recorded. A super-patriot and one who took defeat badly, almost personally, from then on he became a driven man, obsessive about doing anything he could to restore English fortunes. The misery of 1950 was a stain that had to be expunged.

Although Alf refused to dwell on England's defensive failings in Brazil, his critique of the forwards was no buck-passing exercise. It was an honest appraisal of shortcomings, an analysis which Tom Finney accepts: 'I think to a degree the way we played, the 2–3–5 system, meant that we were behind the times. There were always lots of goals in English football because, defensively, there was nowhere near as much thought going into that as into attacking. We stood still as others passed us. Some of the foreigners had really gone into the game, trying out different formations, thinking there must be better systems to try. This competition was the first glimpse we got of the South Americans, who were really well organized in attack *and* in defence. As a professional it was obvious to me that we had a hell of a lot to learn from these so-called youngsters of the game. They were very, very skilful throughout their sides.'

English football refused to learn anything from the 1950 World Cup. The harshest lesson of all was still some three years away, a lesson that we had to take seriously. Even that should not have been the surprise it was though, for one English team was already playing the Hungarian way. Back to Tottenham.

6   Champions of England

So England's footballers did not return home to the fondly imagined heroes' welcome with the Jules Rimet trophy tucked safely away in Walter Winterbottom's luggage. Instead, they came back to a mixture of apathy and derision, emotions which added to the exhaustion they all felt following their ridiculous itinerary. Billy Wright said it all when, on arrival, he told the waiting press that he wanted a 'jolly good rest'. Their final game in Brazil had been on 2 July. The new season resumed on 19 August, less than seven weeks later. Small wonder some had little appetite for the work ahead.

Alf was an exception, for he had something to which to look forward – his first season in First Division football. Looking ahead to 1950–51, he did so with confidence. He wasn't alone in that, for most experts felt Tottenham would hold their own in the rarefied atmosphere. Little changed in terms of personnel or style, Arthur Willis coming in for Charlie Withers, Peter Murphy and Les Bennett fighting for the inside-right position. The better playing surfaces they would encounter in Division One lent themselves to push and run, and as few First Division sides had been exposed to it, there would be a shock value inherent in it. More important, it was a damn good system, intelligent, entertaining and hard to counter. Tottenham historian Ralph Finn became euphoric in describing it: 'Away went old traditional styles based on stereotyped play. Away went long-held beliefs in defensively based and negatively biased football. Away went predictable patterns and tired techniques. Formula-ridden football had no part in the team's brilliant new play. Rapid interplay, fast interchanging of position, short sweet passing of meticulous accuracy, insistence on possession . . . all these, allied to quick thinking on the field of play, gave birth to a new style of football.'

English football was caught in a time warp. The World Cup had shown that. But Spurs were in the vanguard of a new style of play, scientific, precise, forensic. It didn't need the traditional strength and power that monopolized English football (as Rowe pointed out 'there was no thuggery in our game'), but players had to be very, very fit to carry it off, as so much depended on off-the-ball running. As such, tactical work in the season was kept to a minimum, training was for simply maintaining the peak condition players had achieved in July and August, where the emphasis was on building stamina. The routine was simple. On Mondays, the players would do a couple of laps of the training field and a little ball work. On Tuesday, they'd do eight laps, some gym work and then some specialist work on a new move, perhaps ending with a light practice game. Wednesdays would see some five-a-sides, Thursday further lapping and sprinting followed by a massage. On Friday there'd be a couple of laps, eight sprints and then a talk about the following day – 'player discussions', as Alf termed them, rather than tactical talks. Everyone was encouraged to contribute, George Robb remembering, 'The likes of Alf loved to talk about the game. In team talks Alf certainly played an important part – he was full of deep thinking about the game but very quietly spoken. He was appreciated by the rest of us as being a cut above, tactically, calm, unruffled. You'd go in the dressing room for training and you'd have Eddie Baily, a tremendous clown, making a terrific row and Alf would just sit there, taking it all in, occasionally coming in with a shrewd observation, a cooling statement; he was ice-cool, just as his game was. Alf was looked upon as classy, constructive, so he set a new pattern.' That Alf was so much more forthcoming with suggestions than at Southampton or England level was down to the personal relationship he forged with Arthur Rowe. Rowe was hugely popular at White Hart Lane because he treated players properly, treated them as equals, understood their problems. George Robb had long been an amateur and might have been lost to the game had it not been for Rowe: 'Arthur was an excellent fellow and a man of his word. He persuaded me to turn professional and everything he promised came through without a problem. I was allowed to carry on teaching full-time and so on. I liked him very much. He was a thoughtful, quiet man – he and Alf were on the same lines. He was very basic, down to earth, didn't want to try anything special. As long as we were knitting together well, into a team pattern, that was what he wanted. He was on good terms with all the players. Arthur created a new idea of what a manager should be.' Ron Reynolds, reserve goalkeeper, agrees, adding, 'I had every admiration for Arthur, he had a great feeling for the players and he always kept you informed if a club was after you and so on. You knew where you stood with him. Portsmouth came in for me while I was still in the reserves and Arthur told me that he'd had an enquiry, but because I was his only cover for Ted Ditchburn, and Portsmouth had nobody they could let him have, he wasn't going to let me go. That was fine, that's what you want to know as a player. He got your complete respect.' Of course, if a manager delivers success, it will sway opinion – all players want to win medals, and if a manager can help them towards that goal, then great. And Rowe had the golden touch.

The Cup-ties of the previous season against Stoke, Sunderland and Everton had given the players self-belief, but that could easily have been dented on the opening day of the season. Blackpool, just four points shy of being Champions the previous year, visited White Hart Lane and promptly won 4–1. For all Blackpool's success, there was still room for optimism, the *Daily Worker* talking of 'a hard baptism for Spurs on returning to League I. But the football qualities are there.' The *Daily Mail* was equally positive, pointing out that the difference between the two sides was a small one: 'For a fatal twenty minutes midway through the first half, the very competent, determined, good, all-round Blackpool XI rattled Spurs as no team did during the whole of last season, and this week they will be reflecting they need only the Blackpool poise to hold a high place in the First Division.' This was perceptive. Now aware of the levels of concentration that were required to compete with the best on a weekly basis, Tottenham upped their game. Even so, they still struggled, winning just nine points from the first nine games; solid but unspectacular. Suddenly, at the end of September, the team found its feet and the old Spurs emerged. They beat Aston Villa 3–2 at Villa Park to begin a run of eight straight wins. They put six past Stoke, Alf missing a penalty for the first time, explaining, 'Perhaps I didn't take quite so much care as usual. We were three-up at the time.' They underlined their credentials by beating Portsmouth – League Champions in the previous two years – 5–1 and then the culmination of the run saw them beat Newcastle 7–0. By now, the country was taking careful notice of Tottenham. The *Daily Mail* described being at the Newcastle match as 'a privilege . . . on-the-floor soccer, the short passing style one dreams of, constructive ability, speed, attack and first-class finishing. There is none of the first-time nonsense. Backs pass it to halves, the halves to forwards after defenders have been drawn.' The *Daily Telegraph* was equally effusive: 'Tottenham's method is simple. Briefly, the Spurs principle is to hold the ball a minimum amount of time, keep it on the ground and put it ahead into an open space where a colleague will be a second or two later. The result is their attacks are carried on right through the side with each man taking the ball in his stride at top pace, for all the world like a wave gathering momentum as it races to the far distant shore. It is all worked out in triangles and squares and when the mechanism of it clicks at speed, as it did on Saturday, with every pass placed to the last refined inch on a drenched surface, there is simply no defence against it.'

Rowe and his team had redefined the game. Ron Reynolds accepts that, 'The Championship team did revolve around Alf to an extent because they built from the back, a very unusual thing. Perhaps it wasn't fully appreciated then, but now we have these attacking wing-backs, and I suppose Alf was one of the first who was doing this, courtesy of dour Bill Nicholson, who looked after the space behind him. Alf was a kingpin of the side, he'd bring Sonny Walters into play so quickly – Sonny was very fast and if he got the ball, he went like lightning, so that was a good weapon. But Alf wasn't the only vital link in the side, there were others even more important. Ronnie Burgess used to bring Eddie Baily and Les Bennett into the game, which was vital. Ronnie was a human dynamo. Alf's work was mainly in front of him but Ronnie's was all around him, he got through more work than anybody.' George Robb believes, 'Tottenham became a great side through push and run, which was tailor made for Alf. There was no long ball from him, and he was one of the crucial members of the side, along with the likes of Burgess. Alf played a tremendous part in setting the passing pattern, which wasn't typical of the British game. It was a revolutionary side, very well-knit.' No other English side was playing the Spurs style, attacking with purpose from every position, combining with neat interpassing movements, striding up the field. Playing in triangles and with players always on hand to support a colleague, this was very much on the lines of the Hungarian model that Rowe had seen before the war. In the fullness of time, those styles were to mutate into the total football of the Dutch and the 'pass and move' style with which Liverpool dominated English and European competition. Alf saw the possibilities, writing that, 'There is no limit to where even a defender will go to attack. Maybe you have noticed how often I go upfield to cross a ball or even have a shot at goal. That a defender should not attempt to score a goal is something to which I can never subscribe.' Such an attitude seems common sense today, but forty-five years ago it was the kind of heresy that might see a footballer burned at the stake. Defenders stayed at the back, forwards at the front. That was the English way. But times had changed, the rest of the world were illustrating that there was another way to play. Tottenham were one of the first to take up the challenge.

Where Arsenal and Wolves were powerful, physical units, employing direct wingers, strong running half-backs, crunching tacklers and the long ball from the back, Spurs were more scientific. To those weaned on the traditional English virtues, their patience could be seen as ponderousness. Walter Winterbottom was exasperated by such reactionary views: 'When we played friendlies at home, we were out to develop our football on the style of the Spurs game, the inter-passing game. Just before Alf came into the side we beat France 3–0 at Highbury, playing lovely football, Wilf Mannion scything the ball around, and I had a score of letters from Arsenal supporters complaining that they wanted to see the high ball and the action in the middle. They didn't want this namby-pamby inter-passing stuff!' Spurs swam against the Luddite tide, proving that Brits – not necessarily even our most talented players – could play a sophisticated brand of the game. From Alf's point of view, the Tottenham style was made to measure: it gave him the space to redefine the full-back role. As Ron Greenwood says, Alf was 'A classic full-back . . . an expert defender, and that is not something which can always be said of the modern full-back, who has a broader role . . . Ramsey spent a lot of his time covering and was always on the goal-line at crucial moments, but he was also constructive and used the ball with the kind of accuracy which only comes from hours of practice. I have no doubt that he could have fitted into the modern game, pushing forward, overlapping, and I am quite certain he would have wasted very few of his centres.' Had tactical orthodoxy and his crippling lack of pace not prevented it, Alf would have loved to put such ideas into practice for they were already in the forefront of his mind – he did become the most zealous evangelist of the use of overlapping full-backs. Like most defenders, he wanted to get in amongst things at the glory end of the pitch.

As Rowe understood the importance of team building, he knew that the relationship between right-back and right-half was crucial. With Alf's penchant for getting forward, the right-half had to restrict his own attacking instincts. Ron Reynolds is clear that, 'What really made Alf so good at Spurs was playing with Bill Nicholson and Sonny Walters. The push-and-run style suited Alf perfectly. The number of times you'd see Alf with the ball, running back to his own goal, deliberately delaying the pass back to Ted Ditchburn, to give the winger chasing him the feeling that he had an opportunity to get it. Alf would then play it back, peel off towards the touchline and Ted would throw it straight out to him, giving him yards on the winger to bring the ball away. Alf would bypass Nicholson, who would then slot into the right-back position, because that was Bill's strength, while Alf went on to feed Sonny.' Though each was playing their part to the full, Nicholson and Ramsey did not always see eye to eye, as Ron Reynolds explains: 'There used to be out and out war between them on occasion, and there were times when Arthur used to leave them at it to argue among themselves. I think Bill was fed up with being by-passed so much and lumbered with the defensive responsibilities.'

For Alf, arguments went with the territory, George Robb adding that, 'Alf was a great theorist, liked to have his own ideas about the game. If he had an idea, he'd worked on it very thoroughly and was convinced it would be good.' He felt he knew exactly what needed to be done, how the game had to be played, and would not be deflected from that. As Brian Glanville wrote, Alf's 'thoughtful, scientific play set the tone for the whole ebullient [Spurs] team'. 'The General', as Alf was becoming known, was crucial in dictating the play. Yet for all that his play served his own ego, he appreciated Nicholson's presence, the more so after he came back from England internationals where Billy Wright refused to play a secondary role to the full-back. Without Nicholson's grit, his tireless running, his biting tackling, Alf would have been a luxury that Spurs couldn't afford, George Robb explaining that, 'If you had Alf playing, there was always a possibility that a really good left-winger would use the space he'd leave by going forward. So Alf certainly benefited from having Bill Nick in the side as the dominating, forceful ball winner who would cover for Alf. Alf did tend to leave space, so it was so useful to have Bill around.' Nicholson absorbed that lesson, for in management he teamed playmaker Danny Blanchflower with Dave Mackay, the man who made people play (Dave Sexton rates him the best all-round player that British football has ever produced) to similar effect. That was Rowe's legacy, that a team should slot together like a machine, run-of-the-mill minor components every bit as important as the glamorous outer casing. The lubrication for this footballing marvel was possession. That was Alf's game, as the BBC's Bryon Butler wrote in *Soccer Choice*: 'Possession was everything to Ramsey. He hated wasting the ball, and the cold precision of his passing up to thirty yards meant that he rarely did.' Always wanting the ball, he knew full well that without Nicholson he'd be sunk. Nicholson was a strong ball-winner; few forwards got much change from him. But once Nicholson had got it, Alf would want it, making it apparent that he considered himself better able to use it, his realistic view of things making the tactful approach redundant in his eyes. It's not hard to see how Nicholson resented Alf seeing himself as a cut above, but it was a fair assessment, however unpalatable. The doctrine according to Ramsey demanded that everyone be practical, accept their strengths and failings and work towards a common goal. If you couldn't do that, you weren't a professional. His philosophy was simple: 'By retaining possession of the ball, you are always poised for an attack. If you haven't got the ball, you must be on the defensive. If you retain possession, how can the other side attack and get goals?' This proved just how influenced he had been by the Continental and South American model, that he had been paying close attention in those few games where he had been exposed to other styles of play. Such an open-minded approach was highly unusual in the early fifties. Warming to the theme, he added 'That is why I favour a pass back to the goalkeeper if in difficulties. He is always in position to send the ball to an unmarked colleague and so keep his side on the offensive . . . there is no such thing as a defender or attacker. We are all footballers and members of a team. The aim of everyone should be to play good football and contribute something towards scoring goals.' And, the unwritten but obvious undertone went, if they couldn't do that, they should stop wasting everyone's time and get out of the game.

Even Spurs were human. Heavy rain in November and December threatened to disrupt their serene progress, the cloying ground holding up the pace of their passing game. It was indicative of Rowe's attention to detail that he noticed that in practice games the players had no such problems in finding their target. The difference? The pitch was sanded for match days. That was stopped and Spurs picked up momentum. Coming out of the trough of form which also saw them knocked out of the FA Cup at the first hurdle by lowly Huddersfield, they took nineteen points from a twelve-game run from late January into April, leaving the pack trailing far behind in their wake. With push and run flourishing once more in better conditions, only Manchester United remained in touch, but on 18 April, Cup Final day, the League was won, United ending four points adrift. As Jackie Milburn was putting himself between Stanley

Matthews and a Cup winners' medal, Spurs beat Sheffield Wednesday by a solitary goal, Duquemin administering the blow that relegated Wednesday after just one season in the First Division. The fortunes of the two promoted clubs couldn't have been more different. Tottenham were among the most deserving winners in history, for they achieved success with panache, intelligence and with an enviable economy of effort. The hard work was done on the training ground, so that on Saturdays the team were able to express themselves.

For Tottenham it was the realization of a long-held dream. As Arsenal had racked up the League titles just down the road, Spurs had never yet been crowned as the best side in the country. Finally, they were there, and a celebration was in order. All the staff were invited to a dinner at the Café Royal in London. Ron Reynolds was no exception: 'I'd been there for a year. I'd come up from Aldershot, from obscurity, really, and it was still a fantastic experience just to be with the likes of Alf, Ronnie Burgess and Arthur Rowe, these big names. It was all a bit daunting but I went along, we had the meal and afterwards there was a dance. Alf came over to me, and said, "I want you to meet somebody." He took me along and introduced me to Vickie, who was his fiancée then. They got married a little later. Within a matter of thirty seconds, he said, "You won't mind having a dance with her, will you?" Alf didn't want to dance, he wanted to talk about football to the people there, and so he lumbered me! She was very nice, but I was just a country lad, twenty-two years old, a bit out of my depth. I was practically speechless!'

Although by no means reclusive, it was rare for Alf to mix his private and professional life in this way. Vickie was always a devoted source of strength and support whenever Alf needed it and she became a keen follower of football – in *Talking Football*, Alf wrote that she 'never misses a match! Is this good? Of course it is. I'm all for any wife being interested in her husband's work – even if it is trying to stop a lot of super-fit athletes from scoring a goal!' Nevertheless, Alf chose to compartmentalize each aspect of his life, such that there was almost no crossover between the private and the public, hardly ever again mentioning his family in interviews. In time, this would prove to be eminently sensible, shielding his wife and daughter from an intrusive and, latterly, abusive media.

Winning the title is one thing, but defending it is quite another. Allied to the normal pressure the Champions have to deal with, Spurs knew that their system was no longer a novelty. In the TV age, with saturation coverage at home and abroad, a system cannot have shock value for long. If anyone comes up with so much as an original free-kick, it's immediately analysed by every manager in the League, looking to repeat or counter it. Forty or fifty years ago, the chances to monitor the opposition were few and far between, and you certainly couldn't watch them time after time on video in an effort to spot chinks in the armour, so you had a year's grace. Other managers now realized that Spurs' play was all about accuracy, playing the ball to marked colleagues who could then knock the ball back first time, taking a defender out. Spurs players weren't marked so tightly, defenders were in less of a hurry to commit themselves, sides fell back to defend, spaces weren't left for the Tottenham players to run into. Spurs could still get some mileage out of push and run but, if anything, they needed to play it at even greater pace and with more purpose. They opened the 1951–52 season with a defeat at Ayresome Park, but three straight wins suggested that there was no cause for alarm. Nevertheless, a spate of injuries, notably to Harry Clarke, destabilized them and played its part in one of the most surprising results of the season – a 7–2 defeat at Newcastle. The *Daily Mail*'s report remarked on a game which produced 'almost classic football for 90 minutes. The ball ran kindly for Newcastle but they were always the better side . . . the Spurs dressing room heard a great and philosophical manager saying, "You lads ought to be flattered to have seen a better demonstration of your own game than you have given this season." ' That was the problem. A few sides, though surprisingly not many, began to copy push and run, and these were sides that might have better players in key positions. Equally, they would have the enthusiasm born of innovation, where for the Tottenham boys push and run was old hat. Having climbed the mountain once, it was tough to start from the bottom again.

Rowe had instilled sufficient professionalism in his team to ensure they wouldn't simply lie down and die, and there were still some scintillating performances that recaptured the magic of the year before – a 6–1 victory at Stoke, good wins over Manchester United, Portsmouth and Bolton, the double over Villa – but they were infuriatingly inconsistent, losing eleven games compared with the seven of the previous year. Heavy pitches were again a major source of difficulty – between November and February they lost seven and won only one of twelve games, conceding their Championship in the process – and it was only an excellent run-in (eight wins and four draws from their last dozen games, and form that recaptured memories of their halcyon days) that kept Tottenham in the upper reaches of the table. They finished runners-up, four points behind Manchester United, ahead of Arsenal on goal average. That was some consolation, since not only did they finish above their reviled rivals, it meant the players shared £440 in prize money, the Arsenal lads getting £330.

After their all-conquering performances of the previous year, second place, however, was not good enough. Rowe insisted that the pitch at White Hart Lane be torn up and re-laid in an attempt to recapture the majesty of their free-flowing football. But their problems had deeper roots than the grass on which they played. The team was ageing, they were picking up more injuries which were taking far longer to heal, and the replacements weren't forth-coming. An early sign of the problems ahead came on the first day of the 1952–53 season when WBA went to London and won 4–3. And that after Spurs had been gifted a goal: Alf took a penalty and smacked it against the bar. He leapt out of the way of the rebound to allow one of his colleagues to try and get another shot on goal only to see the referee running back to the centre-circle and giving a goal, thinking Alf's kick had gone in! In spite of this, it was a poor afternoon for Alf, the *Daily Mail* reporting that, 'Ramsey and Withers were too often wrong footed by Albion's talented wingers.' This was becoming a theme. Although Alf was rarely beaten by his winger, they were being instructed to push up alongside him, keep-ing him in his own third of the field, nullifying his attacking threat. At a stroke, it put paid to that most productive move that he and Ted Ditchburn had evolved, based on Alf's experience in Brazil: the throw out to Alf as he wheeled away to the touchline. Now the left-winger scarcely left his side.

The finest teams become used to getting their own way. At their peak, Liverpool must have won something like 75 per cent of their games before a ball was kicked, certainly at Anfield. Teams were intimidated by their record, their presence, their players, and would often surrender to the inevitable. It wasn't until cracks began to appear towards the end of Dalglish's reign that teams began to feel they had a chance – the FA Cup Final defeat against Wimbledon was the first small breach in the dam. As they weakened, other sides scented blood, the chance for revenge, and raised their game, compounding their problems. Liverpool began to fret over their inability to impose themselves and entered a comparative spiral of decline which has yet to be entirely reversed. The same problem afflicted Spurs in 1952–53. Games became a struggle, points were lost to teams that would not have lived with them a couple of years before. Even Alf resorted to a little gamesmanship to try to lighten the load, as Tom Finney remembers: 'We played them in a Cup-tie at Deepdale and we drew 2–2. I just went in the dressing room after to have a word with a few of the Spurs lads. The replay was the following week and Alf turned to me and said, "You'll not be bothering to come down on Tuesday, then!", just dismissing our chances. It was a very exciting game, but he was right. They won 1–0.'

The Cup was light relief from a League programme that saw Tottenham stuck in a mid-table rut. As well as Preston, Tranmere were beaten 9–1 in a replay, Halifax seen off 3–0, and then three games were required before they limped past Birmingham. The reward was a semi-final with Blackpool at Villa Park. Still lacking their erstwhile fluency, Spurs slugged it out, Duquemin equalizing after Bill Perry had given Blackpool the lead. Bennett became a virtual passenger for the last third of the game following a blow in the face, but Spurs held firm. With a minute remaining, extra-time was on the cards, giving them the opportunity to regroup following the loss of Bennett. Perry broke clear down Tottenham's right but the immaculate Ramsey coolly dispossessed him. With seconds remaining, most players would have hoofed it fifty yards and waited for the whistle, but that was not Alf's way. Setting himself to slide the ball back to Ditchburn, he slipped, the ball ran short, and Jackie Mudie nipped in to score and send Blackpool on into the Matthews Final. Tottenham had still never reached a Wembley Cup Final, and the blame seemed to centre around Alf.

Again he refused to accept it, arguing, 'It was the right thing to do at the time and I would do the same again.' In *And The Spurs Go Marching On . . .*, Eddie Baily explained how Alf saw the goal: 'Alf took all the stick for us not making it – on TV and the radio, in the papers all over the weekend and for years afterwards . . . he took it all marvellously, and he needn't have done, really. There was no better student of the game than Ramsey. He could go over a match and tell you everything that had happened in it . . . he did just that at Villa Park, where we must have been the most miserable bunch of players in football history. Without any recrimination or attempt to shift the blame he told me where I had gone wrong on that goal . . . how I, having conceded a free-kick and stood there disputing it, argued with the referee that I had not handled the ball. Then how Blackpool rushed the kick to Bill Perry on their left wing, who in turn was challenged by Ramsey . . . then that back pass . . . I left a gap. And, as he always was, he was right.' That Baily should accept a portion of the blame says a lot about him; that Alf should try to shift it says more. He was still insecure for all the two dozen England caps he had at home, was still incapable of admitting to anything but the most blatant error lest it should dent his confidence. For all that Baily was wrong to argue with the referee, that was not the cause of the goal – it would have been had Perry got the ball and cracked in an unstoppable shot from thirty yards. Errors of play and of discipline are made all over the field and it is the job of the team to recover from them. If Alf had defended correctly, if he cleared the danger, there'd have been no goal and no problem. After all, he was a defender, whose very job it was to be safe and secure, to snuff out danger. When Bert Williams had been brilliant for England against Italy, Alf had not praised him but simply argued that he was doing the job he was paid to do. At Villa Park that day, Alf did not do his and Spurs paid the price. It was an error symptomatic of their season, illustrating how they had allowed the opposition to catch up with and then pass them. Their play had not been further refined, Alf's close on-field relationship with Ditchburn was being turned in to a weakness. He knew attackers were looking for him to play the ball back to the keeper, and yet he persisted. His play had become predictable and, however well you do something, once the element of surprise is gone, you leave yourself open to attack. Alf was punished for it. The season was over and so was push and run.

All in all, 1953 wasn't a great year for Alf Ramsey . . .

7   6–3

When the England party had returned from Rio in July 1950, it was
obvious that the domestic game had to change or they would continue to fall behind. If Walter Winterbottom cherished hopes that
our First Division would see the light, he was quickly disabused of the
notion. The eternal verities of a high ball in to the centre-forward, a
long hoof upfield and a cavalry charge, remained the staples of our
football. What made matters worse was that Tottenham were making
it clear that any team who used a little more thought could mop
up the honours and, at the same time, were emphasizing the fact that
a traditional England team could not compete on the sophisticated
international stage.

England had the players to do well – Ramsey, Wright, Finney,
Lofthouse, Milburn, Matthews – yet, forced to play the typical English game at club level, there was just not the time for Walter Winterbottom to instil new and better habits in the brief moments they had
together: 'We'd assemble on the Monday, have some light training,
obviously you couldn't do too much on the Tuesday with the game
coming up, and then we played the international on Wednesday. It
was ridiculous.' One further problem assailed the Englishmen. In
1950–51 they managed just six internationals, two of which came
in May. Of the six, three were Home Internationals, useful match
practice but little else since it scarcely gave them exposure to other
styles. To make matters worse, as Tom Finney complains, 'There
could be four or five months between England games and there'd
be a lot of changes – in a team that you thought had done quite
well, you suddenly find five or six changes made. That was when
people realized that Walter wasn't in charge of selecting players,
because no manager would chop and change like that. With England
there was no feeling that you were part of a team building towards
something.'

That's not to say players didn't have pride in playing for their
country. There was no prouder man than Alf in November 1950
when, in the absence of Wright, he was asked to captain England

against Wales at Roker Park. The *Mail* reported, 'England's players are all happy that Alf Ramsey has been chosen deputy captain for Billy Wright. The Spurs full-back is very popular. I feel sure that the team will pull out that little extra today to help Ramsey in his difficult task.' England won 4–2, Eddie Baily scoring twice. To an extent, this responsibility, proof that he was accepted as a key member of the England set-up, was the making of him, Winterbottom confirming that, 'He was a good captain, that was the time he started to really show his ability.' The players were happy with him too, Tom Finney adding, 'He was an ideal captain, very methodical. He studied the game a lot and knew so much about it.' Even Billy Wright, the briefly deposed skipper, had praise for Alf's performance: 'He encourages his colleagues . . . and in every way he is a remarkable character whose contribution to the game has definitely helped to improve the standard. For all round accomplishment I think Alfred Ramsey of Tottenham Hotspur and England deserves to rank among the most remarkable of them all . . . a man who both on and off the field has tried his hardest to further interest in the academic side of the game.'

Alf captained England the following Wednesday when Yugoslavia were the visitors to Highbury, though it seemed, briefly, that he too might miss the game. Playing for Spurs on the Saturday in their 7–0 win over Newcastle (imagine England today playing on consecutive Wednesdays but the players going back to their clubs for the Saturday!) Alf picked up a couple of knocks. Fortunately he was deemed fit, in a side that already showed three changes. It was as well that he did come through, for Yugoslavia were strong opponents. Indeed, they became the first foreign side to gain as much as a draw in England, the game finishing all square at 2–2. (England had been beaten at home by the Republic of Ireland, who won 2–0 at Goodison Park in September 1949, but few saw them as 'foreign' opposition.) It was a tribute to the Continentals' persistence that they got a draw, for they were 2–0 down with five minutes to go to half-time (Nat Lofthouse had scored twice on his debut; he then missed England's next four games). The Yugoslavs pulled back a goal just before half-time, but as the second half wore on, it seemed England were easing to a comfortable win. With a quarter of an hour to go, a cross came in from the left. Bert Williams called for the ball but Alf darted in and, in trying to hook the ball out to his right-winger to start an attacking move, played it into the path of Zivanovic, who equalized. In trying to be too clever, Alf had created danger where there had been none – perhaps that explains his indulgence of similar lapses made by Bobby Moore in England colours.

The match was followed by a banquet. As England captain, Alf was required to make a brief speech, the first he'd ever made: 'I was extremely nervous . . . when the ordeal was over I had to admit to [England left-back Bill] Eckersley that I'd far rather take a penalty at Wembley than go through such an experience again.' And why shouldn't he be petrified? After all, Alf was just an ordinary working-class man of basic formal education. Nothing had prepared him for standing up at a banquet before many dignitaries. When the shock of all those faces trained on him was compounded by his own innate shyness, it's not surprising that this was a formative experience.

The football field was still Alf's home, but he was not daft enough to think he could play for ever. He knew he had only three or four years left as a player, and realized he needed to make provision for the future. He was keen to remain in football. With his thoughtful approach, it seemed obvious that coaching and management offered great potential, but he understood that that would take him out of comparative anonymity and into public life. Even now, as captain of England, he was finding himself on a bigger stage, and it was something that disturbed him – he was a professional with a job to do and all the peripheral frills got in the way of doing it properly. In *Talking Football* he addressed this other aspect of the game, further illustrating his serious turn of mind: 'Invitations to read the Lessons at Sportsmen's Services are growing every week and I enjoy attending them. Somehow, however, I always seem to get the task of reading difficult chapters . . . [in the evening] I usually have a long read, for, like Billy Wright, I have found that serious reading has helped me to develop a command of words so essential when you suddenly find yourself being called upon to make a speech. People, remember, are inclined to forget that speech-making may not be your strong point. With this in mind I always try hard to put up some kind of show when asked "to say a few words".' The idea of him settling down with an improving volume is attractively Jeeves-like, and it did help, providing some of the basic skills which enabled him to solve the problems thrown up later by the Bertie Woosters at the FA with the same skill and alacrity as Wodehouse's famous manservant.

Essentially, Alf was repeating an earlier pattern from his life. As a young footballer, he hadn't the instinctive flair of a Finney, and instead worked on the basics of the game, turning himself into an utterly dependable passer and an exceptional reader of the play. As George Robb notes, 'I think he definitely felt that you should work to achieve what you were capable of.' Alf had the kind of mind which would always delve into any activity to the nth degree. He was a master of detail, excellent at going to the root of a problem and coming up with a serviceable solution. He was self-conscious regarding his Essex accent (the same speaking voice that Jimmy Greaves has turned to his advantage), the more so since this was an era where perfect BBC enunciation was seen as the ideal. Provincial accents were scarcely heard in public life beyond the music halls, where the likes of Max Miller made it part of their act. Otherwise, anyone in public life was expected to speak like Noël Coward. As soon as Alf opened his mouth, he was giving evidence of his roots. In a class-conscious society, that gave many the opportunity to put him down, to dismiss him as a working-class oik before they'd even bothered to listen to what he had to say. However annoyed he might be with such an attitude, he knew he could not change it, was realistic enough to decide he had to play by the rules. He worked on his vocabulary, giving him a start, and, as George Robb recalls, 'He mixed all right with the bigwigs and the boys in the dressing room.' Ultimately, he would need elocution lessons to help him speak the way the bosses did, so he could command respect from the off. These attempts at self-improvement did not make him a different man, but they did give him extra confidence as he approached public life.

Retirement was still some way off in 1951. With Billy Wright's return to the England side, Alf went back to the ranks, with a degree of relief, able to escape the glare of publicity. At the end of 1950–51, England had a tough fixture against Argentina at Wembley. England eventually overcame the South Americans 2–1, but only after a great struggle. In defence, the Argentineans simply dropped off the England attackers, funnelling back, always having spare men available, conceding space to England everywhere but where it mattered, in and around the penalty area. Still comparatively unfamiliar with the tactic (one which would help blunt Spurs), the Englishmen ran into dead ends time and again. Alf, though, enjoyed the freedom to come forward that such blanket defence offered and he created England's winner, planting a forty-yard free-kick on Milburn's head, the knock-down finding Mortensen, who scored. The game was enlivened for the crowd by the exploits of goalkeeper Rugilo, an

Alf Ramsey, England international, prior to
a game against Northern Ireland in 1951 (*Colorsport*).

Early days: at Southampton (*top left; Popperfoto*); at White Hart Lane, with Bill Nicholson in the background (*above; Popperfoto*); and (*left; Hulton Getty*) ever the perfectionist, keeping his eye on the ball in training.

(*Right*) From the penalty spot Alf puts away England's opening goal in a 2-2 draw with Austria in front of a packed Wembley, November 1951 (*Popperfoto*).

(*Above*) Drinks in the boardroom at Portman Road with Ipswich chairman John Cobbold, as Alf is appointed England manager, October 1962 (*Hulton Getty*). (*Below*) Four years later, Ramsey prevents George Cohen swapping shirts with an Argentinian following the acrimonious World Cup quater-final (*Popperfoto*).

The build-up to the World Cup Final. Fans throng Wembley Way and pack the stadium, 30 July 1966 (*all Hulton Getty*).

The kick-off (*left*); the ball crosses the line? (*above*);
the celebrations begin (*below; all Hulton Getty*).

(*Above*) Bobby Moore gives Alf the choice of kissing the
Jules Rimet Trophy or Nobby Stiles.

(*Below*) England's immortals. Back row: Harold Shepherdson, Nobby Stiles, Roger Hunt,
Gordon Banks, Jack Charlton, George Cohen, Ray Wilson, Alf Ramsey. Front row: Martin
Peters, Geoff Hurst, Bobby Moore, Alan Ball, Bobby Charlton (*both Hulton Getty*).

early version of Colombia's René Higuita. Alf was not amused, however: 'The international football field is no place for [such] clowning . . . our friend Rugilo, I shall always contend, went just a little beyond good taste.' Alf did not spare his colleagues either, attacking their profligate finishing, as he had done in Brazil: 'Mastery of the ball is not the sole basis for soccer success any more than is speed. What, I reason, we have to do is sprinkle our game liberally with them both, and, above all else, learn to shoot more accurately and quickly.'

Wright was dropped for the game against Portugal ten days later, and Alf got a final taste of leading his country. England won 5–2, Alf lining up behind Bill Nicholson for the only time in an England jersey, the difference between club and international football made brutally apparent. Although Nicholson scored after just 25 seconds, it wasn't a happy game for him, and the *Daily Mail* penned his international obituary: 'He was woefully inaccurate with his passing . . . not the deputy for Billy Wright.' Wright returned to the captaincy immediately, but there was never any question that Alf's place was in jeopardy. With thirteen consecutive appearances behind him by the outset of 1951–52, he couldn't be blamed for looking ahead to the 1954 World Cup. He remained at the hub of England's side – that much was clear when Austria came to Wembley, a game he described as his greatest international. The Austrians had a powerful reputation and were employing the same positional fluidity for which the Hungarians were famed. So impressive were they, Winterbottom actually got permission to call the England 'possibles' together for an extra training session at Maine Road. Tactically, there was one battle that had to be won, as he realized: 'Their left-half, Ocwirk, was tremendous at coming through and shooting from distance. I happened to speak to Billy Wright some time before the game and asked him if he'd mind playing inside-forward instead of wing-half in order to counter him – he'd played there for Wolverhampton, so there was no problem and he was keen to do it, being able to mark this fellow and play an attacking role. We picked him there and there was an unholy row from the chairman of Wolves, he made statements in the press saying players ought to play in their club positions, it would mean that the club manager would have problems with the player when he came back, and so on. This business of not being adaptable was absurd. Later on Bobby Charlton played inside-left, outside-left and centre-forward and in the middle for England, because he was such a good player, but there was no reason other players couldn't do that.' The English love of pigeonholing continued to hold back progress, but Winterbottom did what he could. England fell behind and were in more trouble when they won a penalty. With Finney missing, Alf had the responsibility, but could hardly have imagined having to take one in a more crucial situation – England's unbeaten home record depended upon him. The *Daily Mail* recorded the tenseness of the situation, saying how lucky England were to have 'ice-cool hero Alf Ramsey, who has so often been tested in this sort of situation and never found wanting . . . the painful silence as Ramsey slowly ran up to the ball was broken by the biggest roar I have ever heard from an England crowd as the ball, surely and truly hit, sped into the corner.' Alf was a master at taking penalties, the *Evening News*' John Oakley writing: 'He used to just virtually push the ball into the net, he never blasted the ball.' Back on terms, England pressed for another goal. It came courtesy of the brief practice session the team had managed before the game. Billy Wright wrote that, 'Mr Winterbottom decided that Ramsey should place the ball for Lofthouse in this game. Why? Because Nat Lofthouse could "climb", a great advantage when one realised that the tall Austrian defenders were particularly commanding in the air. For hours, Alf Ramsey and Nat Lofthouse practised the move. I have rarely known Ramsey to be completely satisfied with his efforts and, although early on he was placing the ball on Lofthouse's napper eight times out of ten, Alf, we all knew, would never be content until he could do it ten times out of ten.' The work paid off. Winning a free-kick out on the right just inside the Austrian half, Alf put the ball down, looked for Lofthouse and placed it unerringly on his head. In the event, Austria nicked a late equalizer with a penalty but, as the *Mail* reported, 'England, in retaining their unbeaten home record against foreign teams, gave a glorious fighting display at Wembley that completely rehabilitated the reputation of English international football, threadbare since our World Cup defeat.'

That rehabilitation looked complete when England flew into Europe for games against Italy, Austria and Switzerland. The tour was preceded by a get-together in Eastbourne which allowed the players to work for a week without interruption, a week which Alf described as 'among my most pleasant memories'. Fully established, he could relax and enjoy the company of his colleagues, offer more suggestions in team meetings and exploit his ability to the full. That week in Eastbourne was time well spent – England were unbeaten on their European tour. Their closest game came in Florence, the

Italians coming back from an early setback to earn a 1–1 draw, Alf again having cause to lament the Latin temperament: 'The most unpleasant international match in which I had ever taken part. After the game, as usual, there was the usual, "Well done, old boy" pats on the back for us from some of the Italians, but surely the time has arrived for these fellows, so charming off the field, to be told not to leave their good manners and sportsmanship in the dressing room when they trot on to the pitch, especially when the match happens to be an international. Do these sound harsh words to be used by an England player? They're intended to be, for like my colleagues, I do not stoop to dirty tricks or foul play.'

On to Vienna, for the rematch with the Austrians who had given England so much trouble at Wembley six months before. Bearing in mind their performance there, and that they had beaten Scotland 4–0 in Vienna, many felt England were in for a hiding. Alf graciously pointed out that the pressmen were 'quite entitled to their opinions', but didn't share them. England had prepared thoroughly, learning much from their earlier encounter. They had had the benefit of almost two weeks spent working in close proximity, bringing about an improvement in team play. To draw the sting from the Austrian attack, England retreated into defence for the early exchanges, quietening the crowd and frustrating their opponents. With tactics akin to Muhammad Ali's 'rope-a-dope' surrender against George Foreman, they allowed Austria to punch themselves out, only attacking on the counter and at pace. Lofthouse gave England the lead but Austria hit back immediately, converting a penalty given when Dienst hurled himself to the floor. 'As England players,' Alf remarked, 'we did not, of course, protest, but I shall always say that . . . if the laws of the game had been correctly interpreted, [Dienst] would have been warned by the referee for ungentlemanly conduct . . . to me more important than winning a game is to play it in the best possible spirit and obey the rules.' At half-time it was 2–2, Sewell scoring for England, Dienst for Austria. England persisted with their new tactics and, as the game wore on, the Austrians grew tired and increasingly frustrated as England grew in strength and confidence. Lofthouse won the game, running 45 yards before scoring the goal that made him the 'Lion of Vienna'. The tour wound up with a 3–0 win in Zurich, confirming that England could live with the very best providing they made proper preparations. They returned to find nothing had changed and that henceforth, Winterbottom would see his players for the statutory two days before an international, a clear indication that priorities lay with the clubs. Until that problem could be resolved, England's chances would always be limited.

The gap that was growing was illustrated in the summer of 1953. England had had their usual perfunctory diet of four internationals – the Home Internationals and a visit from Belgium, beaten 5–0 at Wembley – had used seventeen players in them and had had little time to work together. To follow that, they set off for South America to play in Argentina, Chile, Uruguay and the USA. Such an extensive trip was almost unheard of outside the World Cup, but looking ahead to the 1954 tournament in Switzerland, even the FA could see that it would be worthwhile meeting some of the competition. For Alf, a good series of matches was imperative for, like many of his Spurs colleagues, he had lost the edge from his game and a few newspapers were talking openly about him reaching the end of the road. Just twelve months from the World Cup, now was not the time to falter, especially as the precarious nature of his position was underlined when he was left out of an admittedly weakened FA XI that played Buenos Aires at the start of the tour, Blackpool's Tom Garrett deputizing. It was a good game to miss, as the FA side went down 3–1, Billy Wright explaining, 'Those Argentinos gave us the most harrowing experience of our soccer lives. Their football was a delight to watch, a headache to halt.' The game was soured when, just prior to half-time, Cecconato, the inside-right, developed a limp – at this stage, regulations in friendly games stated that if a player was injured in the first-half, a substitution could be made. As he hobbled to the side of the field, Mendez, perhaps the quickest player in South America, burst on to the field in his place in an obvious, but successful, piece of gamesmanship. The mistrust that existed between the two nations continued to mount.

Three days later, the full international took place at the River Plate Stadium. A violent thunderstorm erupted an hour before kick-off, flooding the ground. The rain stopped just before the game was scheduled to commence and, with a packed crowd in place, there was no prospect of postponement. In conditions more to their liking, England settled and shook the home team, so much so that the home crowd called for an abandonment, which duly came after 23 minutes. That still gave time for a vivid illustration of the differences between the two continents, as Wright explained: 'The men who a few hours before had imagined they were going to send us dizzy with their artistry now began to whine like spoilt children whenever we sent them flying with a shoulder-charge or brought them down with a tackle. The Latins began to toss their elbow around rather carelessly. Ankle-tapping and shirt-pulling, both of which had been conspicuous by their absence in the previous match, were employed a good deal by the Argentinos ... [they] are aces at dishing out defeat, but obviously cannot take one on the chin in return.' The *Daily Mail* was as forthright in its condemnation, stating that had the abandonment not come 'the match could have ended in a riot'. The Englishmen weren't enthralled by the behaviour of their hosts, Walter Winterbottom remembering that, 'Crowds in South America became a problem. They'd pelt the bus with oranges in Argentina, which rather upset some of the players, who didn't know what to expect next!' Although Alf wasn't the po-faced, humourless man of legend, like many of his colleagues he failed to see the funny side of such behaviour. He was a correct man, abhorred rudeness and thought guests should be treated with respect. He was not enamoured with the South American approach to life nor, in some ways, to football.

Things didn't get better in Chile. Although England won 2–1, the behaviour of the other side upset them. With England a goal up, Lofthouse struck a shot which hit Farias in the face. He collapsed and several Chileans attacked Lofthouse, the English reserves coming to his rescue beneath a shower of oranges. Order was finally restored and the Chileans 'fought' – 'I mean that literally,' wrote Wright – to get back on terms. Alf had a good game and England came away with a useful win but also a valuable lesson, according to Wright, one which would have an impact in years to come: 'If you want to beat these fellows the only way to do so is by using the ball first time. A player who tries to dribble past these South Americans stands a good chance of being brought down or having his shirt tugged. Using the ball first time is the only answer to footballers who do not readily understand or interpret the rules quite as we do.' Having endured physical attacks on the field, Alf was laid low off it by an attack of mild dysentery, another nail in the coffin of his distaste for the South American way. He recovered to play in Montevideo against Uruguay, silencing the critics with a masterful performance, back to his very best. The same was true of the team, the *Mail* enthusing, 'Not for a long time have the England team played so well but with so little luck ... Uruguay are the best team in this part of the world, but their fouls and attempts to pull opponents down by jersey holds and flying tackles offended even the home crowd.' The 2–1 defeat was an unfortunate end to their stay, but they atoned by beating the USA 6–3 in New York, the pitch set up on a baseball diamond! The tour proved the sense of having the team together for several weeks. The more they trained and played together, the better England performed, a lesson that took another twenty-five years to permeate.

Heading into 1953–54, Alf began to suffer the niggling injuries that come to players approaching their 34th birthday, and these helped cost him caps against Wales and Northern Ireland. He was available for a game against a Rest of Europe XI that took place in October, in which England's proud home record was under threat. In a pulsating game, England found themselves 4–3 behind when, in the dying seconds, they won a penalty. Up stepped Alf – there could have been no better choice, for there was no one in the country more determined to preserve English pride. The *Daily Mail* reported that, 'In a hushed Wembley Stadium, with thousands halted in their scurry to the exits, Alf Ramsey banged in a goal from the penalty spot 25 seconds from the end to save England's record.' English supremacy had, supposedly, been underlined, though as Walter Winterbottom explains, 'In actual fact, we were isolated. We felt that if we played our own brand of football we were the kings of the game, and this carried on for many years and of course it meant us getting more and more lost in the wilderness.'

In November, the Hungarians came calling on their way to the 1954 World Cup. They'd recently played in Sweden and Walter Winterbottom had flown out to spy on them, accompanied by press-men intrigued by talk of the Hungarians' breathtaking skills, rumours that were sweeping the Continent. Winterbottom remem-bers, 'Sweden got a draw, I think, but the press were laughing, saying that our game against them would be a cakewalk! I couldn't believe it, they couldn't read that game. Sweden were a hard-tackling team, the normal European style of play, where Hungary played beautiful football and had a number of near misses. It was obvious that if they clicked they could murder any team. The Hungarians had almost the same team that had won the Olympics in 1952 in Helsinki, and the players all knew one another. They all played in Budapest, training week in week out as a national team, playing against club sides at home and abroad, so they were constantly together, knitting to perfection. We had time with England to rehearse a few restarts, such as throw-ins, corners and so on, but they were rehearsing movements in play. They were masters of the early ball, the wing man playing the ball across long before he got to the goal-line, with players running in *en masse* at the other side – it was sickening! It was so well rehearsed and played. We never had that chance.' A point which Tom Finney echoes: 'There was no continuity with England where, if you think of the Hungarian side, they played together not just in internationals but in games against amateur teams, where they'd win 26–0, or something. The point was they could try things out with their full side.' There was still room for optimism, though, as George Robb – unfortunate enough to make his one and only England appearance in that game – concedes: 'The Hungarians were an excellent side individually but they worked as a team so well. They were quick – Alf wasn't tremendously so, and so he was troubled by them. But we expected to win. I'd seen them in 1952 when I was in the amateur side at the Olympics, and I saw that same Hungarian side win the Final, and you could see then they were great players. But we felt we were at home, we'd always done well at Wembley, we should win, but we'd got to watch them.'

Home advantage is always important, but England's unbeaten record was a much exaggerated state of affairs, as though we were some island fortress – typically jingoistic but wholly unrealistic. Since the first international had taken place in November 1872, England had played host to a foreign nation, or select XI, on just twenty-three occasions – a season's worth of matches in our Divisions One, Two or Three. There had been draws against Yugoslavia, France, Austria and the Rest of Europe XI, and the 'defeat' against Ireland, to go along with nineteen wins; impressive but hardly awesome. And those four draws had come in England's last seven home matches, so clearly the competition was getting fiercer. Defeat was a matter of time, as Tom Finney accepts: 'We had to carry the mantle of never being beaten at home, but of course the dam was going to burst one day, and it burst very forcibly upon us with the Hungarians. That was one of the greatest awakenings for the British game. We'd never seen players coming out twenty minutes before the game with a ball each, exercising, passing, doing tricks with the ball. I was selected for the game but was injured and went to comment on the Hungarians – you couldn't say anything about your own side in those days – for the *Daily Express*. It was the first time I'd been in a press box, and all the writers were saying, "It's all right doing these tricks before the game, but wait till it starts." That was a fairly good English side too: the forward line of Matthews, little Ernie Taylor,

Mortensen, Jackie Sewell, Robb, then you've got Dickinson and Wright, Harry Johnston, Alf, Eckersley, and Gil Merrick in goal. It was a good side, lots of experience, but what exposed us was the deep-lying centre-forward, because it was so new to us – we didn't play many internationals then, there was no European Cup or anything like that, so we didn't know what the Continentals were doing! The Swiss had played it just after the war, and they'd pulled Neil Franklin out of position by going deep. If he didn't go with him then the Swiss fella had the ball and could use it in space. So against Hungary, Harry Johnston was left in no man's land.'

The facts of England's 6–3 mauling are well known, Puskas, Hidegkuti, Bozsik, et al tore England to pieces, though England were not the only team so humbled – in the World Cup of 1954, Hungary beat West Germany 8–3, Korea 9–0, Brazil and Uruguay, both 4–2. What Hungary did most of all, and most valuably for the sake of our game, was to warn people of how fast and how far we were falling behind. Some of their play was astonishing – Hidegkuti scored from just inside the box after 45 seconds; Puskas, with amazing close control, sat Billy Wright on his backside before firing in from an acute angle, the pass coming from Czibor, nominally the left-winger, playing out on the right; Bozsik slammed a shot past a forlorn Ramsey guarding the goal-line from twenty yards out; Puskas lobbed a delicate ball in from the left edge of England's penalty area to the right edge of the six-yard box for Hidegkuti to score. Some of the play was mesmerizing, the *Mail* telling a shocked public that the Hungarians 'set the pattern for our football of the future . . . now perhaps our soccer will be remodelled, not only at national level but at club level . . . an England team were run off their feet, outlasted for stamina, humbled in every art of the game . . . like an amateur boxer taking on Jack Dempsey.' There were no excuses save one, articulated by Alf: 'Do not forget that three of their goals came from outside the penalty area. That could have been prevented.' One in a series of clumsy statements, it suggested that England had been unlucky, yet Alf knew that Hungary could have scored more goals had they needed to do so, could have upped the tempo and quality of their play further. Nevertheless, he felt they should have been made to work harder to get the goals, as George Robb explains: 'He always said afterwards that had Ted Ditchburn been in goal, two or three of those long-range goals wouldn't have gone in. Equally, Alf would have made that point to say that as a back line, he wasn't going to be held responsible for goals that went in from twenty-five yards. That was down to the half-backs!' Alf's professional reading of the situation was that no goalkeeper should be beaten so comfortably from such distance; harsh words for Gil Merrick, who remained England's keeper into the World Cup, though Winterbottom adds: 'Merrick was my disaster, nice fellow, strong, good at club level, but for England he sometimes lost his nerve – against Hungary I felt they were stoppable shots, but he got nowhere near them.'

But apportioning blame for a goal here and there was quibbling at the margins of the debate. The truth was England had been shown up all over the field. Defeat by Hungary at Wembley – followed by a 7–1 mauling in Budapest the next year – was a national humiliation on a scale which ranked with the USA defeat. That game could be put down to bad luck on the day, but the Hungarian débâcle could not be dismissed. Our game had been shown up as antediluvian, inadequate, out of touch. With our domestic game still wedded to the past, it was many years before our standing in the world game was to be recovered. Central to that renaissance was a stocky but immaculate little man, a perfectionist, obsessive about detail, a man who had played his thirty-second and final game for England at Wembley that November afternoon. For Alf Ramsey, there would be no more caps. But the England glory was still to come.

8 Living on Borrowed Time

In professional football, there's no more implacable enemy than time. A manager lacks it, especially if things are going awry. In a match, if you're winning, time seems elastic. If you're losing, time races away. As a player, no sooner are you making your debut than it seems that people are ready to pension you off. Alf's efforts to ward off the attentions of Father Time have been discussed, but changing your date of birth can never be more than a cosmetic exercise. Eventually the ravages of the years will have an effect and the evidence will be there for all to see.

Returning to Tottenham for the 1953–54 season, Alf could bask in the glow of a highly successful England tour of South America where he had been singled out for praise. It didn't prevent him putting his normal effort into pre-season training, but it boosted his morale. Approaching 34, he must have fancied himself to go to the World Cup and have three or four more years in Division One. Since Matthews had won a Cup winners' medal at 38 that year there was no real reason why he should not carry on playing. He took similarly meticulous care of his health: 'I am not over-fond of liquor and have at the most one drink on a Saturday after a match. Never in the week do I allow myself such a "luxury". So far as smoking is concerned, I gave it a trial for two years. From 1942 until 1944 I smoked an occasional cigarette, but I stopped when Southampton signed me as a professional because, no matter what anyone else may say to the contrary, I found smoking upset my wind and I certainly feel all the better for giving it up.'

It was soon apparent though that it was easier to play well in a good England team than in a Spurs set-up that was beginning to self-destruct. Three seasons on from the Championship year, Rowe still fielded basically the same team, but they were getting on – Ditchburn was 32, Alf 33, Withers 31, Nicholson 34, Clarke 30, Burgess 36, Walters 29, Bennett 35, Duquemin 29, Baily 28 and Robb 27. They were playing a kind of football which placed a premium on both intelligence (of which they had plenty) and stamina (which was on the wane). Not only that, the team was stale. With the exception of Robb, this was virtually the team that had won the Second Division. Not only does a team need new blood from an athletic point of view, it also needs the stimuli of new personalities, new ideas, fresh perspective, an opportunity to pose different questions – Alex Ferguson's recent reinvention of Manchester United is a case in point. The Tottenham side had none of that variety and, consequently, 1953–54 was colourless. Alf was as guilty as anyone, Ron Reynolds pointing out: 'On the field, every ball he played back to me he expected to get back, and of course there'd be arguments if I considered there was something better on and didn't give it to him! He wanted it every time, he felt that he was making all this effort running to the touchline and he wasn't getting the ball. He wouldn't see that it was the same thing all the time, it was stereotyped and that, as the goalkeeper, you had a view of everything in front of you, which might give you better options.'

In the League, Spurs were unable to mount any serious challenge and looked as though they might even flirt with relegation. It was a worrying period, surgery was required. Alf began to suffer – returning to play for Spurs against Sheffield United the Saturday after the Hungary game, he was on the wrong end of a 5–2 scoreline and, according to the *Daily Mail*, had 'an anxious afternoon against left-winger Derek Hawksworth. Hawksworth made four of United's goals.' The team was beginning to creak, and although they got to the sixth round of the FA Cup, losing 3–0 to eventual winners West Bromwich Albion, there was no disguising the fact that the push-and-run stars were coming to the end. Alf could feel which way the wind was blowing and, in February 1954, began to coach non-League Eton Manor on a part-time basis, George Robb explaining that, 'It wasn't unusual, it was part of the pattern. I think with most pros at that time, as you came to pack up playing, you didn't really have any other career to go to and so you wanted to stay in the game if you could. Alf was shrewd enough to get on the first rung of the managerial ladder.'

At the end of 1953–54, Ronnie Burgess, that colossus of the Spurs half-back line, finally bade farewell to the club after eighteen years and 298 appearances, returning to his native Wales with a transfer to Swansea City. Rather than sounding the death knell for Alf's career amid the break-up of the team, this might have signalled a new lease of life, since Rowe had no hesitation in appointing Alf club captain. Just as with England, Alf showed his true mettle when commanding the troops, though it didn't always make him popular, as Ron Reynolds confirms: 'Alf didn't suffer fools gladly, but he was the type of individual that thought everybody was a fool, he couldn't always differentiate!' – a man quick to anger and slow to forgive, this stemmed from his absolute passion for the game. George Robb reflects that, 'He always believed that a captain should *be* the captain on the field. There might be a case where he would be criticized for doing something, making a change, but it wouldn't worry him. He'd say that as captain, it was his right, his duty to do that. Alf wouldn't stand any nonsense, so that was a good thing for a potential manager. If he thought someone wasn't pulling his weight during a game, he'd let them know! He wasn't disinclined to reproach somebody. In team talks he was more forthcoming, putting his own ideas forward.' But ideas alone could not stem the tide, as Ron Reynolds contests: 'That was perhaps Arthur's main weakness, allowing that great side to get old at the same time without bringing in new blood until it was too late. I don't think push and run was rumbled as much as the fact that Arthur didn't bring in new players early enough – he had Harmer, Marchi, McClellan, Dyson that he could have brought in much earlier, we had Alf on the right and Willis or Withers on the left when we had Henry and Baker doing great things in the reserves, and who could have come in. By the time he was starting to ring the changes, Arthur's health had deteriorated, there was some in-fighting at the club and it all fell away.'

In 1954–55, Rowe realized drastic action was required. Mel Hopkins came in at left-back, Tony Marchi took over from Burgess, Ron Reynolds got in ahead of Ditchburn, and there were other changes in the offing, one of which affected Alf's entire future. Building a new side took a toll on Rowe's health, and he accepted that he needed a strong right-hand man on the coaching staff. Although Jimmy Anderson had been a tremendously loyal servant of the club and was Rowe's assistant, he did not see him as a suitable replacement, given that he had not played at the top level. For some time, Rowe was considering appointing Alf as his assistant, a matter that did not reach the ears of the players, though George Robb accepts that, 'Arthur would look ahead, and it doesn't surprise me that he was considering installing Alf as his assistant manager. Jimmy Anderson had been there since he'd been a boy, since 1908, or something like that, and Tottenham had a loyalty to him. Equally, they weren't a tremendously ambitious club at that time and wouldn't have booted anyone out to create a vacancy, however highly they might have thought of Alf.' Ironically, a vacancy *was* just around the corner, but circumstances conspired to take that from him. It was apparent that Bill Nicholson was ailing at right-half and had to be replaced. For some months, Rowe had been tracking a replacement, a young man from Northern Ireland, plying his trade at Aston Villa. Danny Blanchflower was eventually prised away from Villa Park in December 1954, shunting Nicholson into retirement. A valued member of the Tottenham think-tank, Nicholson stayed on, playing in the reserves, but it was obvious that at the end of the season, he'd be off.

The arrival of Blanchflower was of crucial importance to Spurs' future, Rowe seeing him as the man around whom he would rebuild the team, but there was no immediate improvement. Spurs struggled so badly that they barely escaped relegation. Looking to the Cup to lighten the dark skies, they'd come past Gateshead and Port Vale and were drawn away to York of the Third Division (North) in the Fifth Round. On a snowbound pitch, York prevailed 3–1, causing Blanchflower to write, 'The atmosphere was thick with remorse on the way back to London, the worst I had ever known in a football club.' It was the end of the road for Rowe, Blanchflower adding, 'When his team faltered and the whole unreasonable reaction set in, he was appalled at the ignorance and violence around him. It drove him back to the depths of a quiet desperation.' It wasn't unlike the traumas Alf would face in 1974, but where he was a more robust character, Rowe was laid low by his shattered nerves and fell ill. He was forced to resign as Spurs manager, Anderson stepping into the breach. That meant that there was a vacancy for a right-hand man and, since Nicholson's playing days were behind him, he was in the right place at the right time. Alf's hopes of staying at Spurs in a coaching capacity were dashed, for there was never going to be room for him and Nicholson. Instead, he had to look to play on and then make alternative arrangements.

The arrival of Blanchflower meant that Alf's playing days were up too. A fixture in the team before Danny reached London, it was obvious that the balance between the two was askew, their styles too similar. As George Robb explains, 'When Danny came, they were both attacking players, which did tend to leave a few gaps on the right-hand side. They just accepted that would be the case and that somebody else had better come across and cover!' To Nicholson, watching from the sidelines, that wasn't good enough. He knew Alf wouldn't change his game – he'd partnered him through five seasons and knew his game inside out – and that Blanchflower was also doing what came naturally. But Danny was the future, Alf the past. When Alf picked up an injury in March, he missed several games, including good wins against Sheffield United and Cardiff. His days were numbered. He got back into the team, but after two games he was dropped.

These were turbulent times at Tottenham, as Anderson ruled the roost in a very different manner to Rowe, George Robb noting that, 'Arthur knew how to get on with the players, he was friendly, on good terms. Jimmy was not.' Ron Reynolds adds, 'Alf had done great things for Tottenham but things started to go wrong at the club. It was at the time that Anderson was manager and Nicholson was appointed coach. We were going to Hungary on a close-season tour. To everybody's surprise, only one first-team player wasn't included in the party, and that was Alf. It was a bitter blow for Alf, and all the players agreed it was a rough trick to play on him, turfing him out like that.' He knew the end was in sight, knew Tottenham would not have a coaching job for him, knew his association with the club was coming to its close. He was disappointed, more with the offhand manner in which they dealt with him than in their decision to replace him – that was an occupational hazard. But to treat him so shabbily after years of dedicated service was unfair. Sensibly, while Spurs played in Hungary, Alf chose to boost his CV further with a bout of coaching in Southern Rhodesia. His services were retained for the following season, but when the trial games got under way in earnest, he was not selected, a piece of information not lost on the rest of the football world. For Alf, it was time to come to a decision. Did he try to get his place back at Spurs? That would be a brave but foolhardy choice. Did he ask for a transfer, accepting that like Burgess he would have to move down a division or two? That held little appeal for one who had played with distinction for England and Spurs on the great stages of the world. Or did he decide to take the realistic view, admit that his best playing days were behind him and go on to the next phase of his life, football management? As ever, pragmatism triumphed. By 8 August 1955, he had met with the directors at Ipswich Town and told the press, 'I'm all for joining Ipswich as manager.' The following day, the move was sealed. The Tottenham board agreed to release him after 226 games for them. The move was made easier since Alf decided he did not wish to go as player-manager, but would hang up his boots to concentrate on the job in hand, a typical gesture according to George Robb: 'I don't think being a player-manager would have suited Alf. He liked to be in a position where he could tell people, face to face, what they were doing right and wrong. As a player-manager, you're making your own mistakes on the field, and it's not easy. I think he said, "Right, I've finished playing, now let's move on." Even so, I was surprised he went to Ipswich because at the time they were nothing, really, and they didn't seem to have too much potential.' In August 1955, there weren't many who would have disagreed with that assessment. Alf's might have been the lone dissenting voice.

9 Preparation, Preparation, Preparation

In August 1955, few saw Ipswich Town as anything other than a small-town club with small-town ambitions. They were there to entertain the footballing folk of Suffolk, have a Cup run now and again, but satisfy themselves with a place in the lower divisions. They'd come into the League at Gillingham's expense in time for the 1938–39 season (not the greatest timing) and had done little to impress. Their finest hour came with promotion as Champions of the Third Division (South) in 1953–54, three points clear of Brighton. Sadly, exposure to the Second Division was too much for them and they were relegated the following year. Existing on gates that were typically around the 13,000 mark, there was little money to spend in those far-off days when gate receipts were a club's only real source of income. Having squeezed as much as he could from the sparse resources, secretary-manager Scott Duncan, who had been with the club since November 1937, when they were still in the Southern League, moved aside in the hope that a new manager might take the club further. Walter Winterbottom says, 'Duncan was a remarkable fellow. I'd been with him when he was manager at Manchester United before the war. I contracted a spinal disease that meant I could be fine one week and have a great game and then be unable to walk the next, but he tried to sell me to Blackburn Rovers knowing I was unfit! He was lured to Ipswich for quite a lot of money.' Ipswich's money was well spent, for Duncan was central in their elevation, his contacts within football helping secure the requisite number of votes at the League's AGM on 30 May 1938. Duncan wanted to stay with the club and so retained the position of secretary, leaving the way clear for the club to recruit a younger manager, one starting out who would be able to concentrate on football matters without having to bear the administrative responsibilities.

Such a progressive step meant that Ipswich was the ideal proving ground for an ex-pro trying to find his feet. Expectations were realistic – the Second Division was the ceiling of Ipswich's ambitions – and the club had a good atmosphere, a friendly place run by the

Cobbold family, whose money had been made locally in the brewing industry. As Joe Mallett explains, 'When Alf went to Ipswich, the people used to think in terms of building a club. You could go in and get all the club sides – first, second and third teams – right over a period of time, where now only the first team matters, and there's scarcely time for anyone to put that right!' The Cobbolds had a great reputation in that regard, allowing their managers to have a decent run in the job – Ipswich have never been a sacking club. The setting was also right. Alf was a country lad and there were similarities between rural Ipswich and the Dagenham of his childhood. He was not the cosmopolitan, big city sort (Gordon Boreham is adamant that in Dagenham they were 'Essex people, not Londoners') but instead enjoyed the quiet life, so he could relax and recharge his batteries. In its comparative isolation, Ipswich was the kind of club where a manager could make mistakes without the consequences being too grave. Under the spotlight of the press, every move would be scrutinized, every error magnified. In Suffolk there was no such pressure. That helped him ease himself into the public eye gradually. Alf accepted that he would be an important face in the community, but Ipswich was not a football hotbed like Liverpool or Manchester and so he would not be the centre of attention, a real blessing. Even so, he tried to make friends with the local press, understanding it would be advisable to get them on his side. They responded in kind, the *East Anglian Daily Times* reporting that 'Mr Ramsey's views on the press and football are such as must gladden the heart of a reporter. "Football and the press are all tied up together." That is his view and one cannot visualise a paucity of football news from this former England captain to whom newspaper men are definitely not "necessary evils." ' How things can change . . .

However lowly Ipswich may have been, it was a step up from playing, a move into an office job after years on the shop floor. The most famous, or infamous, manifestation of this move up the ladder and the changes it wrought in Alf's life came in the form of the elocution lessons he took to remove his accent. His new voice, the clipped, studied tones that made him sound not unlike Chris Eubank, was satirized and reviled – the techniques involved left him open to lampooning, the precision and leaden pace of his diction making it apparent that here was a man desperately trying to say the right thing, the right way. Some thought it pretentious, others that it was a risible piece of social climbing, that it was a betrayal of his working-class roots. These charges were ridiculous. Alf was anything but pretentious, regularly stopping off for a bowl of jellied eels and a cup of tea at Tubby Isaacs' bar on the way home to Ipswich when he was England manager, never looking to eat in swanky restaurants, nor stay in the glitziest hotels. Like anyone else he enjoyed a good meal and wanted a pleasant holiday, but that's no evidence of someone getting above themselves. He never attempted to cultivate a social circle drawn from the upper echelons of society, but instead remains happiest among football people. As for attempting to pretend he had no working-class background, that too is nonsense. In *Talking Football* he made no secret of his past, embellishing it perhaps, but there's no crime in that. And he could scarcely be called a class traitor when, for all his roots, he'd never been part of working-class life, didn't go to pubs or working-men's clubs, but kept himself to himself. The key point is that Alf was a man of his times, professionally ambitious, socially uncomfortable. He'd lived through the Depression and, if it hadn't really touched him in the way that it did people in industrial communities, he'd learned its lessons. He knew the value of money and the importance of the class system. He'd no great education, had left school at 14 like virtually all his contemporaries, hence his determination to forge a career in the field where he was best equipped to succeed – football. The equation was simple: better education = more comfortable = better acceptance by the directors = more freedom to work = better at the job. He was perpetrating an elaborate con trick, putting one over on directors, making them believe that here was one of their own and that he could be trusted.

It wasn't a question of wanting to pretend he had no working-class roots, more that it was advantageous to slip free of them. He was moving in different circles now, in the board rooms, dealing with the comparatively aristocratic Cobbolds (when asked what would constitute a crisis at Ipswich the response was 'a shortage of sherry in the board room') and, driven as always by his streak of perfection-ism, he did not want to be found wanting. He wanted to be able to deal with them, to not be embarrassed by the gap in status – if you want to know the importance of that, remember how the High Tories spent years sneering at John Major because of his supposed 'lack of breeding', his poor background, his accent, his education. And that in the allegedly classless 1990s. How much worse must things have been in the 1950s? Alf knew that football management was his big chance, his way out of a return to working life, to opening a pub or working as a salesman for a company glad to have an ex-footballer as a trophy. He knew he could handle the footballing side, but other things might bring him down, so he vowed to do all in his power to nip such problems in the bud, Joe Mallett remarking that, 'Alf always wanted to be the top man, he was the boss, which was a good part about him. He tried to do it correctly. He was meticulous in everything – taking elocution lessons was just typical of him.' If he needed to hide behind a carefully cultivated façade, then so be it. For all that, hard work can never make up for a limited vocabulary or an unsteady grasp of grammar, best dealt with in childhood. Consequently, Alf still spoke with the mangled syntax of John Prescott, but without any of the bluff charm, that having been ironed out by his elocution lessons, which improved diction at the cost of spontaneity.

Alf was a product of the pre-World War Two, 'I know my place' world, but was by no means typical of it. Many contemporaries would turn down promotion simply because they felt it would cut them off from their friends. That was Alf's era, they were his people, but he was different. A friendly enough chap, he never followed the herd, had his own ideas, his own standards and loftier ambitions. He wasn't worried about losing friends, since he wasn't naturally gregarious. A loner, he could survive in his own company, and that of his wife and family. There was no brake on his ambition. He had nothing against his working-class background but knew that it might betray him, so he simply blanked it out as he'd blanked out Alf Freeman after that disagreement in Southampton. How many others of his era could not, would not or had not the wit to do likewise? George Robb feels, 'He was from a working-class background, and I think all the way through he was thinking to himself, "I can do better than this, I can do better", without it being too obvious. You'd never say he was after something. In his own way, he'd look to improve himself just as he did his game.' Alf had turned himself into a top-class player by application and by hard work. He had conquered his nerves by a feat of will, he would now conquer his accent by similar dedication.

Let there be no doubt that in order to fulfil his goals, he had to conform. Less than a year before Alf took over at Ipswich, Aneurin Bevan made a speech at the Labour Party conference: 'I know that the right kind of leader for the Labour Party is a desiccated calculating machine who must not in any way permit himself to be swayed by indignation. If he sees suffering, privation or injustice he must not allow it to move him, for that would be evidence of the lack of proper education or of absence of self-control. He must speak in calm and objective accents and talk about a dying child in the same way as he would about the pieces inside an internal combustion engine.' Alf was only involved in football, but Bevan's remarks could apply to any leader in any walk of life. People looked down on labour leaders, political or union, because they spoke like factory workers or miners, they weren't the sort of people that one trusted to run anything – they did the work, but it was the men in the nicely tailored suits with the beautiful speaking voices that should take charge. Nonsense, of course, but perceptions and prejudices were strong. Equally, the British (especially the English) were swayed by a devotion to the stiff upper lip. Open displays of emotion were evidence that you came from the lower orders, that you could not be trusted. For one as committed as Alf, it was hard to conceal his passion for football, but it was a sign of the times that he had to do so. That was the world he lived in, hence the inscrutable expression, the clipped answers to questions, the wary responses to probing. Alf didn't like to give anything away because he could not trust himself. If he could cut a conversation short, it was safer. Westerns were his favourite film genre, and he learned a lot from Gary Cooper: 'yup' or 'nope' was often as much as could be prised from him. He had to be reserved and correct because that was what the public wanted, an attitude still almost a decade away from serious challenge when JFK and The Beatles breached the wall of protocol that governed public life. By then Alf was trapped in the straitjacket that elocution lessons – and the appropriate 1930s etiquette and manners that went with them – provided.

Another reason for his desire to blend in was his lack of professional qualifications. With the coaching bug sweeping the nation, most putative managers now had some kind of badge to their name, though some still ignored that convention, as Walter Winterbottom admits: 'Alf didn't want to go through the coaching scheme. There were a lot of players who didn't want to be embarrassed by taking examinations and tests, which was natural – they felt they were First Division players, why should they be examined? It was an idea which filled them with horror! Alf wasn't too keen on that, but he was a student of the game. I got him to come with me to the public schools, such as Charterhouse, where he did some coaching, and they were also keen to have him talk to the boys afterwards, and he did well at that, which made it apparent to me that he had a good future in the game.' His lack of interest in gaining a badge had much to do with a deep-rooted insecurity – examinations weren't something he'd faced in the past and he feared them. He knew he didn't need any coach to tell him how to play the game – neither did Shankly, Busby or Clough – but was fortunate that Ipswich were open-minded. He owed a lot to them, a debt he repaid with interest.

There was little raw material to work with when he first set foot in Portman Road, but Alf was content to make the best of what he had. He had a novel approach too, one others would do well to copy: 'It would be useless my deciding before I have even seen the players that I am going to adapt them to Continental, the old Spurs type, or indeed, any particular type of football, and yet that does not mean to say I have not got my own ideas as to how football should be played.' Later on, he recalled, 'I had no plan for Ipswich when I went there. In fact the first thing I had to do was to forget my set ideas on how football ought to be played. My experience had been in the First Division. I soon found that what I faced at Ipswich was very different. In fact the club put on a trial match for me to see what talent I had available. At half-time my wife turned to me and said, "Let's go home." The trial, by comparison with what we had been used to, was as bad as that.' One trialist was a Scot who had just come to the club. Jimmy Leadbetter was central to Ipswich's future, but, initially, he was worried about whether he *had* one: 'Scott Duncan signed me a couple of months before Alf came. If you get signed from another club, you take it you're going to step into the team, there was no squad system then, so it was a bit worrying to have a new manager come in before I'd kicked a ball!'

Alf could find no place in his line-up for Leadbetter, though perhaps he should have. His first game in charge saw Ipswich go down 2–0 at home to Torquay with 'as poor a performance as one can recollect at Portman Road' according to the *East Anglian Daily Times*. Even so, Alf had already brought in some innovations, the local paper commenting on 'three distinct types of corners: a short pass to an inside-forward, the usual lob, and a fairly fast drive into the goalmouth.' Having taken charge ten days before, Alf had had little chance to work with his players and limited his work to set plays; an intelligent approach. In a move that was symptomatic of his methodology, amid a storm of local protest he gave the same side a chance to atone in the next game, reasoning, 'The team certainly cannot play any worse than they did on Saturday but I simply must give them a fair crack of the whip . . . if I had thought in terms of dropping players I should have had to drop seven or eight, and remember I had no glowing reports from Carrow Road [where the reserves played].' The *East Anglian Daily Times* reporter made the prescient observation that, 'I feel somehow that Ipswich's new manager is not going to be swayed by anything he reads or hears.' His methods were proved sound when, on the following Wednesday, Ipswich thumped Southampton 4–2, though Alf pointed out, 'The defence must be tightened up and we have got to get more devil into the attack and indeed into every department.' He was right not to get carried away, for performances remained variable: they could as easily beat Swindon 6–2 as lose 3–0 to Brighton. Everyone needed time to adjust, not least Alf himself, according to Leadbetter: 'He'd played for England, and coming to Ipswich was a big change! We had quite a few players of "mature age", so it was a bit of a shock for him. There was no money either.' Alf's view was, 'I had to see how I could use whatever talents they had to the best advantage. That is where tactics must begin for any manager.'

His tactics were having an impact. When they beat Aldershot 3–0 in late September, the *Daily Times* drooled, 'Ipswich can produce football to match the best . . . [they] tore the opposing defence to shreds.' In sixth position, three points behind Northampton, there was cause for optimism, though Alf accepted promotion was unlikely. He was looking two or three years ahead, looking to mould the side. A string of decent results led him to greater ambition by mid-October, admitting that, 'I think Ipswich are good enough to finish in the top three and have a good chance of winning promotion.' He was right to be cautious, for the Third Division (South) was tough to get out of – only the Champions were promoted. By then Alf had sorted out his first priority, getting the defence to work as a unit, the *Daily Times* noting, 'The play of the defence showed just how much the influence of the manager Mr Alf Ramsey is making itself felt. Covering is becoming automatic and after the game a very knowledgeable journalist told me he had not seen a better planned or more methodical approach in the Third Division for many years . . . much stronger in defence than in attack. Only now are we beginning to see the fruits of the hard work put in by the manager and players at Portman Road in long training sessions.'

Alf was a stickler for the basics. Some of his players lacked quality, but there was no reason they couldn't pass a ball accurately over short distances. He brought in voluntary training sessions in the afternoons, and a number took advantage, perfecting their play. He continued to refine Ipswich's use of restarts, made notable use of short corners. Rowe and Dodgin had seen the value of novel moves and that was a tactic Alf followed. More than anything, he followed Rowe's maxim of simplicity: 'The simple thing is usually the best thing and [wing-half Neil] Myles does his jobs both in defence and attack with the absolute minimum of fuss. His football is not always noticed because he is not flamboyant but he cannot often be faulted and nine times out of ten the passes he makes are accurate.' He might have been talking about Roger Hunt ten years on. Alf's central philosophy emerged very early on in his managerial career: know your job, do it right, work hard, the rewards will come. For all that, he knew Ipswich lacked a spark – they might not concede, but the problem came in scoring, a problem that was to dog his sides.

It was then that he pulled the kind of masterstroke that was the hallmark of his time in Suffolk. Jimmy Leadbetter had made no impression, save getting one appearance in a 1–0 win against Bournemouth in early October, after which he'd been dropped. 'I wasn't one of Alf's first choices, so I had to prove myself in the reserves. Halfway through the season Alf came and asked me to play outside-left, which I hadn't played since schooldays (I was an inside-forward). He just said, "Go home and think about it." I had a wife and child, so you're out to get your money to pay the bills, and you got a bit more in the first team, so I told him I'd give it a crack! I never thought I'd be playing on the left wing, I wasn't fast enough. That was the first thing I said to him, but he knew that well enough. He told me that it was what the ball did that counted: "You don't have to run by the man, you can pass it." That was my game, I liked to pass the ball accurately.' With that one switch the foundations for Ipswich's ascent were laid. With Leadbetter coming into the side at Christmas, fresh impetus was handed to the promotion push – QPR, for example, were humiliated 4–1, the *Daily Times* reporting that Ipswich won 'without taking their hands out of their pockets'. Yet victory didn't always win praise from the manager, Jimmy Leadbetter recalling, 'We played Northampton away from home and we gave them a hammering, 5–0; Tom Garneys got a hat-trick. At the end, Alf gave us a real telling off and we were sat there wondering what we'd done wrong. But Alf knew that if anything needed changing, if you weren't doing something right, it was best to point it out when you were winning.' It seemed he even had control over the weather, for the local press reported, 'Mr Alf Ramsey had been hoping all week for rain and when it came just before the start his tactics were planned and ready to be put into operation – Ipswich were hitting the ball hard from man to man . . . a battle of movement which left their opponents helpless and frustrated.' This was almost push and run, if less sophisticated than Spurs' version. Nevertheless, Ipswich were a side that was coming together. They were tight at the back, Leadbetter had offered precision, Tommy Parker was scoring freely, but with a tiny squad, injuries were always likely to cause problems. Having gone top after beating Aldershot on 4 February 1956, Ipswich then took eight points from seven games, at the time when closest challengers Orient won seven in a row. As had always seemed likely, Ipswich were found wanting at the death, the limits imposed on them making it impossible for them to make promotion – they finished third. Looking ahead, Alf brought in goalkeeper Roy Bailey from Crystal Palace and signed right-back Larry Carberry as soon as he completed his National Service in Bury St Edmunds – Alf knew better than most that Army sides could be a good source of talent.

Disappointed to miss out, Alf was not downcast, for he knew his time had been well spent and that Ipswich weren't going to be far away in 1956–57. But there were storm clouds on the horizon. Alf was unhappy with Duncan's continued involvement in day-to-day affairs. As far as he was concerned, this was unwarranted meddling. He was manager and anything connected with playing matters was his preserve. He found it hard to understand Duncan's position, a difficult one, as Jimmy Leadbetter concedes: 'It was only natural Duncan would want to have something to say because he'd been there for years. He'd been responsible for getting Ipswich into the League, so the club was important to him, it was a personal thing. He was a nice old fella, but a new manager always wants to change things. And Alf always knew exactly what he wanted.' It left them in an awkward position, one which threatened the club's future. The good work Alf had put in hadn't gone unnoticed, and an offer came his way just as the new term began. Jimmy Seed had resigned as manager at Charlton and they wanted Alf to take his place, offering him a contract. Alf declined their offer on the proper grounds that he had a contract with Ipswich and could not be induced to break it. (Wouldn't that be a refreshing attitude today?) It brought home to Duncan and the Ipswich directors that they had a good man on their side, and that it would be a tragedy if he were to go elsewhere. Duncan accepted, reluctantly, that he should take a back seat and content himself with administration.

Ipswich made a dismal start to the new season, winning only one of nine games, taking four points. With gates slumping to 10,000, many were quick to write an obituary on the season, but as Leadbetter points out, 'We weren't too disappointed because we knew we had a good side. We just used to say, "If we can win all the rest of the games, we'll still go up!"' Few outside the club were so sanguine, ignoring an injury crisis. So negative were reactions, Alf had to speak to local reporters, assuring them that, 'I have got a very tired team but I can assure the supporters that the team spirit is excellent. They had a tough game at Walsall [where they lost 2–0] and played very good football up to the eighteen-yard line. One of the goals against us came as a result of a bad defensive mistake, the other just a hundred-to-one chance that just came off. The luck will turn but we cannot afford mistakes and chances up front must be taken.' Luck had not smiled on them, but Alf was disguising the fact that the team had yet to get going, boosting morale inside and outside the camp by bending the truth. He knew there wasn't much wrong that a good win wouldn't put right, and that now was not the time to castigate the players. The corner was finally turned when Coventry were beaten 4–0. Three days later, Brentford went down by the same score, sending the *Daily Times* into raptures: 'Ipswich's two goals in 50 seconds was an all-time record . . . Brentford were outplayed in a bewildering first half . . . Ipswich played thoughtful football against the League leaders.' Shortly afterwards, Ipswich won six in seven games, including a 6–0 win over Torquay that was to have enormous consequences, but just before Christmas they were still eight points adrift.

Alf's canny knack of getting the best out of the transfer market was also being revealed, Bailey and Carberry becoming regulars, Carberry coming in for special praise: 'Time after time he was applauded for his cool constructive football. He is essentially a "Ramsey product" and the manager must be delighted with his discovery.' As crucial was the return of a forward who had spent Alf's first season out on loan at Stowmarket. Thrust back into the side, Ted Phillips was rapidly making an impact, and by the turn of the year had scored twenty-nine goals in twenty-three games, including three hat-tricks. A narrow defeat against Second Division Fulham in the Cup illustrated the progress they'd made, and the side knuckled down to the run-in. Savage blows were dealt when Tommy

Parker, top scorer the previous year, had to retire through injury, and when Tom Garneys was forced out of the last thirteen games a void was left that Phillips did much to fill.

With such misfortune the task seemed too much, but Ipswich took eleven out of twelve points going into the last game to give themselves a chance. A point behind Torquay, the situation was simple. Ipswich needed to win at fourth-place Southampton and hope that Torquay might draw (they had an inferior goal average) or lose at struggling Crystal Palace. To return to the Dell in triumph was excellent motivation for Alf, but it was a tense occasion, according to Jimmy Leadbetter: 'It was a hard game, but Basil Acres got a cracking goal and I nicked one too, so we won 2–0. Afterwards we sat in the dressing room waiting for Torquay's result to come through, because they'd kicked off about forty-five minutes after we had. It was terrible, we had all these rumours coming through that Torquay had won, then we found out it was a draw. We went up on goal average! It was a big thing for all of us. Coming home, getting near Ipswich, the train driver was pulling the whistle all the way, and we had a great reception.' Back in Ipswich, fans had begun gathering at the station a couple of hours before the team got in at two o'clock the following afternoon. By the time they arrived, 3000 people were jammed in there, among them one veteran supporter brandishing cardboard cut-outs of the team. Alf was the main attraction, and the local press spoke of him being 'half-pummelled towards the coach by eager supporters. Finally the Police had to surround him to get him to the coach . . . "Good old Alf," chanted the crowd.' At the celebration that followed, some have alleged that Alf was found under the table singing 'Maybe It's Because I'm A Londoner', but Leadbetter nails the myth, adding, 'I'd have loved to have seen it, mind!'

Alf's mind was already on the Second Division and what he could do to avoid a repeat of Ipswich's previous venture there. Their greatest asset was solid defence, the foundation of their success, something which gives any team a chance. His preoccupation was strengthening the team, building a solid squad on a shoestring budget, a matter made more urgent by the loss of Parker and the retirement of Wilf Grant. Trading on Ipswich's new status, Alf was able to bring in Derek Rees and Reg Pickett from Portsmouth, Brian Siddall from Bournemouth and Bobby Johnstone from West Ham. These were signings typical of Alf's policy: Pickett and Siddall brought experience, Rees and Johnstone youth; all were cheap, all had a lot to prove. Alf gave them the platform and advice, but success or failure was down to them. Bringing in useful footballers from the scrapheap was an intelligent way to work, for the players knew they owed everything to Alf and would give their utmost. They found it a privilege to work with a man of such repute and were inspired by his interest in them. He built a terrifically loyal playing staff and maintained good team spirit.

They knew they'd come to a place where hard work was valued highly as soon as they were thrown into pre-season preparation, Jimmy Leadbetter remembering, 'That was the most important time, when we did a lot of road work to get fit enough for the season ahead – if you missed out on that, it took you quite a long time to get back, to get fit to play. Then when the season got under way we played with the ball quite a bit, not as much as we liked, maybe, but we had a lot of five-a-sides. Alf knew that a body can only take so much. Supporters used to ask why we didn't train eight hours a day, but if they'd come down with us for half an hour, they wouldn't be able to talk! You have to do some training, but once you've got fit, you have to save yourself for Saturday. Alf had been a player, he knew that.'

Facing Blackburn at Ewood Park was a tough opener, but a goalless draw was ample proof that Alf had assembled a unit that could hold its own. This was a real achievement, for the Second Division was a tough assignment. Many of the teams Ipswich were facing had had recent experience in the First Division – Charlton, Cardiff, Huddersfield, Sheffield United, Middlesbrough and Liverpool had all played there in the previous four seasons, while other big clubs such as West Ham and Blackburn were keen to end longer spells in exile. Add to that ambitious outfits such as the Haynes-led Fulham, Stoke and Derby, and it was obvious that there were few easy points to be had. Disillusion came when Barnsley won 5–1 at Oakwell, but Ipswich were rarely embarrassed in higher company. Much of their strength was born of a determination to learn from their mistakes, Alf noting that, 'I like to find out why a goal has been scored against us. There is always a reason if you have an organised defence why you lose a goal. Someone has done something wrong and although you can't expect perfection you can at least discover where you failed and try to correct that fault.' Ipswich weren't often caught out the same way twice, and gradually settled into a nice pattern. By Christmas, short of a catastrophic slump, they were safe. Thoughts turned to the Cup and, following a win at

Crystal Palace, where Bailey starred against his old club, Ipswich were given a visit to Old Trafford, on 25 January 1958, to take on the Busby Babes, the reigning League Champions. It was a genuinely thrilling prospect, another marker to help judge how far they'd progressed. They went in good spirits, an unbeaten run of eight games putting them within three points of a promotion place. Nor were they overawed by United, taking the game to them before succumbing to the inevitable, a Bobby Charlton goal just before half-time. As the *Manchester Evening News* pointed out, even then it was 'no pushover for United ... [Ipswich were full of] splendidly footballing ideas', the *Manchester Chronicle* adding that 'their defence was magnificent'. Jimmy Leadbetter recalls, 'We were very unlucky. I hit the post twice, we could have beaten them, but then with five minutes left Bobby Charlton hit one that just flew past Roy Bailey!' The *Evening Star* summed up the reverse: 'In attack, the United carried field guns where Ipswich could only muster rifles.' The field guns were soon silenced, for this was the last time the Babes played at Old Trafford.

Elsewhere, the footballing world continued to turn. Ipswich were knocked off their stride by the Cup defeat and managed only seven points from nine games to fade to mid-table obscurity. Yet it was a reflection of the optimism engendered by the early season promise that eighth place in the Second Division should be looked on with disappointment. Goalscoring had been the problem – 68, when Champions West Ham had managed 101, third-placed Charlton 107 – and this was a situation that needed rectifying. True, Phillips had been restricted to just eleven appearances – and eleven goals – but Garneys was beginning to lose his touch. If Ipswich were to progress, a replacement had to be found. But Alf faced other challenges. Scott Duncan finally retired from active service at Portman Road, and Alf took on the mantle of secretary-manager. This gave him additional administrative duties, chores he could have done without, perhaps, but at least it gave him the absolute control he had craved since his arrival. Taking advantage, he brought in several new faces – Peter Berry and Jimmy Belcher from Crystal Palace, Dermot Curtis from Bristol City and Arsenal's Len Garrett – though they were not successes in the mould of Bailey and Carberry. Although the four cost no more than a few thousand in total and could hardly be expected to set the world on fire, none made more than 42 appearances for the club. Ironically, it was Curtis' initial good form that paved the way for Alf's most successful foray into the market. With four goals in his first three games, Curtis received a call-up for the Republic of Ireland, leaving Ipswich short in attack once more.

Alf had been keeping tabs on the form of a young Portsmouth striker by the name of Ray Crawford: 'I'd come out of the Army and got in the team, but I broke my ankle in 1958 and by the time I was fit, we had a new manager, Freddie Cox. He called me in one day and said Ipswich wanted me, Alf Ramsey wanted me to go and watch them. They were playing Orient and they were bloody awful, so I went back to Freddie and told him I wasn't going there! He told me I'd got no future in the team so I decided it might be best to go. I saw them play Fulham and lose 3–2, but I thought they were really, really good and that changed my views. Alf was a gentleman, immaculately dressed, well spoken. He told me what he wanted, how they played, but really I was only interested in playing first-team football; things were sour at Pompey and I wanted to get out. He said he couldn't guarantee me a place but that he was sure I could force my way in, and after about a month, when Dermot went to play for Ireland, I did.' At £5000, Crawford must rank as one of the greatest bargains of all time. It was his twenty-five goals in thirty games that kept Ipswich afloat. Assailed by injury, they struggled and ended up sixteenth, though so congested was the division, two more wins would have seen them eighth. As Jimmy Leadbetter points out, 'The Second Division was a very hard league, harder to play in than the First in some ways. In the First Division there's more intelligence, anticipation is better, where in the Second Division, you get some very good players but you also get hacked a bit more, kicked up in the air and no questions asked! It took us time to adjust.'

Things were moving, though. In the summer of 1959, Liverpool put in a bid for Ted Phillips which, in the past, would have been accepted with alacrity. Under Alf, there was no question of his best players going anywhere, evidence of his single-minded approach. Ron Reynolds notes: 'Alf was a perfect example of a top-class player adjusting his outlook when he went into management. Danny Blanchflower said that he could never be a manager, and he was right, because he wouldn't want to do things that managers have to do. In those days managers didn't even have to let a player know that another club was in for him – Danny hated that, whereas Alf was ambitious and made the necessary changes. He did the same on the field – he understood the value of a solid defence even though he'd been an attacking full-back, he knew the importance of team work even though he'd been a loner.' In those days, players were bound to their clubs for as long as the club wanted them. While it may have been unfair to the players, it did give the manager the opportunity to build a team, opportunities often denied today. And although Alf could see the iniquities of the system, he'd lived through it himself, so why shouldn't his players have to do the same? He was happy to help his players move on if he no longer wanted them, but if he needed them in his team, they were going nowhere.

It was as well that he held on to Phillips, for Ipswich were soon on the verge of a breakthrough. With the addition of centre-half Andy Nelson (an £8500 steal from West Ham) the team was taking shape. Ray Crawford remembers, 'When I first went there, that system he had wasn't so obvious, but when I got in the side, you saw the wingers dropping deeper. I don't think he quite had the players he wanted to play that system, and my going there was part of the change towards that – he'd got Jimmy Leadbetter already, but he had to build gradually. Alf brought in some others, like Roy Stephenson in 1960. Then it seemed to fall into place.' That system was the root of all Ipswich's success. In 1960 most English club sides were still playing a fairly rudimentary version of the game, particularly in the lower leagues. There had been new tactics intro-duced to the game, such as push and run, Manchester City's Revie Plan, and some sides were moving towards 4–2–4, but many fol-lowed the tried and tested 3–2–5 formation. Innovation was at a premium, a narrow-minded view which hurt the English game in the wider sense but which inspired more thoughtful managers. Any-one with intelligence could see that by doing something different, they'd catch the opposition cold. Ordinarily, a side would take the field knowing exactly how the other team would play, what the individual duels would be out on the pitch, exactly how the game would pan out. It was simply a question of which side played the better on the day. If you could throw a spanner in the works by putting players in different positions, the opposition would be in turmoil – who would the defenders mark, where should the half-backs go? Alf was in the perfect position to exploit the window of opportunity that existed, reinforcing a point he had made regarding Winterbottom's approach with England: '[Tactics] can be the basis of success for teams and players if sufficient interest is taken and the talks treated with the seriousness I think they always warrant.' More to the point, at Ipswich the only way success could be earned was by some tactical masterstoke. Without the money to bring in supreme natural talents, Alf had to maximize the talents of the honest professionals he had at his disposal. Leadbetter was a prime example. Intelligent and a good passer of the ball, but with the pace of an injured snail, there was no point asking him to play like Cliff Jones. Instead, Leadbetter became the playmaker. Subsequent success illustrated that you didn't need a team brimming with genius if you had a solid tactical foundation to build from and filled your side with players of intelligence, men willing to work and learn, men of character.

The focal point was Leadbetter, the converted outside-left: 'I was supposed to be the left-winger but I wasn't playing that game, I was pulled back, collecting balls from the defence – the other full-backs wouldn't come that far out of defence to mark me so I had space to move in. As I went further forward, I could draw the full-back out of position. He wouldn't stay in the middle of the field marking nobody, he felt he had to come with me. That left a big gap on the left-hand side of the field. That was where Ted played. He needed space, but if you could give him that and the ball, it was in the back of the net. With the lighter balls they play with nowadays, Ted could have scored from the halfway line because he could hit a ball! He didn't always know where it was going himself, he had such swerve on it. Many a time the goalkeeper would go to the left and the ball would fly off to the other side! I enjoyed feeding people like Ray and Ted. It was a pleasure to give them the ball!' As Alf's former Southampton colleague Joe Mallett comments: 'When he went to Ipswich, he deployed two players in deep positions, because as a player he had found himself in great difficulty when he had to look for his winger. If the winger went deep, he wasn't sure whether he should go with him or stay at home. If the winger at Ipswich went deep, he had a lot of space to run with, to run at the full-back, which was exactly what Alf didn't like to face as a player. He thought of his own deficiencies and built his team accordingly. This was revolutionary at the time, because wingers all stayed in the attacking half, alongside the full-backs.' In Leadbetter, Ramsey saw so much of himself. Alf had been a better player – his collection of caps illustrated that perfectly well – but the two shared many character-istics. Both were slow, verging on the ponderous, but mentally each was razor sharp, quick to spot an opening, fast to react. Each had worked hard and become influential passers, their lack of pace forcing each to think deeply, concluding that crisp, timely and per-fectly measured passes could do far more damage, far more quickly than running with the ball. Leadbetter became the embodiment of Alf's own pet style of play.

Such a new tactic took time to come together, the Ipswich lads struggling to come to terms with the new style of play. Ray Crawford recalls, 'Jimmy used to get in trouble for playing everybody onside! He was so slow he'd get left behind. Big Andy would come out, leading the full-backs to play offside, he'd turn round and twenty yards behind him would be Jimmy, because he'd been on the post for a corner!' But as 1959–60 wore on, it became apparent that Alf was on to something. Ipswich managed four more points in the League than the previous season, scored sixteen more goals and conceded nine fewer. Ipswich were going places, though as Jimmy Leadbetter concedes, 'I thought that the Second Division was as far as Ipswich could go. They were nice supporters, but Ipswich isn't London or Liverpool or Manchester, there wasn't that kind of money available.'

Season 1960–61 is remembered as Tottenham's golden year, when a side of speed, skill, artistry and industry seared its image on to the consciousness of every football supporter in the land, a season when their 'Double' had a glorious inevitability about it. For those looking for the unpredictable, they were to find it in Suffolk. Alf believed that his team could gain promotion, but sensibly he kept his own counsel, refusing to heap pressure on his players. He brought in John Compton from Chelsea for £1000, Billy Baxter from Scottish junior football and, crucially, outside-right Roy Stephenson, who cost £3000 from Leicester City. Again, there was little obvious reason to get excited by these captures, but Ramsey knew exactly what roles he wanted them to fulfil. With the side now used to its 4–2–4-cum-4–4–2 formation, he knew they would be solid – they could have as many as eight men working back – and tough to shackle when they had the ball. 'Ramsey's Rustics' would take some stopping, he knew that. Training was kept light-hearted wherever possible, the players simply left to enjoy their football. Ray Crawford looks back on those days with great fondness, since it seems unreal compared with life at the top today: 'We used to change in what we called the cricket shed at Ipswich, there was one great big bath for all of us, the trainer came in in the morning with armfuls of kit, dropped it on the floor and we dived into it to get what you could! It'd be great in a TV comedy now! Old Jimmy Forsyth took the training and he had a gammy leg! Training was running and running, a bit of shooting practice, maybe a five-a-side or a full-scale match sometimes, but back then it was mainly running. Wednesday was out on the road for ten miles with Jimmy and his peg-leg, and while we were running, Ted Phillips would disappear and go scrumping or something silly – Ted was the comedian.' Jimmy Leadbetter adds that, 'Alf wasn't what you'd call a tracksuit manager, he let Jimmy take training but obviously he told him what he wanted us to do. He loved being out among the boys on the training field. He loved playing against me, because he was faster than me! We had five-a-sides and he'd play as right-back opposite me. The boys used to say he loved walking by me! He was still a good player too.' Tactics aside, Alf's greatest gift to the Ipswich squad was team spirit. It's a nebulous ideal, not something that can be quantified, not responsive to any magical formula, hard to create, easy to dispel, but Alf was a master of the art, an exceptional man-manager, as Leadbetter agrees: 'A lot of people on the outside didn't understand him, but to us he was the tops. He was very considerate. He knew I was a married man, for instance, and he'd tell me to get off home if anything had happened there, to look after my family, where other managers think they own you, they couldn't care less about anything else. That doesn't make you a happy man. Alf believed that if you were happy at home, you'd be a happy footballer and you'd play your best, which is true.' These were sentiments echoed by Roy Bailey: 'If he'd asked them, even our wives would have played for him.' Families were encouraged to participate in the club's success, and Alf made it a point that they be included in any celebrations, Christmas get-togethers and so on. It all fostered a family environment, one where each looked out for their friends.

They got off to a great start, nineteen points from twelve games setting them on the right road. The quality stemmed from simplicity, each player knowing the job he had to do, each recognizing his value to the team, none wanting to let his team-mates down, all working for a common cause. As Crawford explains, 'Alf liked team-play, liked to let the ball do the work. In training, he talked about the difference in getting from A to B by running with the ball and by passing it, proving how much quicker you could get there by passing the ball. He wasn't keen on individuals, they didn't fit in with his plans. I'd get the ball but I always wanted to lay it off to the winger or the wing-half, then I'd go off into the box and wait for Jimmy or Roy to get in the box for us. That was the sort of unselfish play he looked for. Alf was behind our success. He didn't rant and rave after matches, he'd not say anything to you, because in the heat of the moment people can say things that aren't very helpful. On the Thursday while we were training, Alf would pull every player that had played the previous week to one side, one at a time, and go through the game with him. Within five minutes he'd discuss everything you'd done, make suggestions about things you could do better. I had a lot of energy and mobility, but Alf said I'd make the wrong runs – I'd give the ball to Jimmy and then go off down the left wing for a ball back. Alf would say, "It's all right doing that, but who's going to score the goals? Why not just give Jimmy the ball and then get yourself in the box?" Or he'd say, "Do you remember when you turned on the ball on the edge of the box and you had a defender with you? Wouldn't it have been better to trap it, just hold it and wait for support and lay it off to them?" Little things like that made you a better player and us a better team.' Alf's memory for detail was legendary: 'He knew the game,' Jimmy Leadbetter says. 'We'd be talking and he'd say, "Remember that game, that pass," and start running through the game in detail, and it would be from two or three months ago! If there were any tactics, it was in our way of playing. It was never a question of saying, "We'll mark so-and-so tight." Where coaches dictate things more now, then we were allowed to play. You'll see a coach standing outside the dug-out now shouting at his team. I couldn't see Alf doing that! He'd be embarrassed to do that, both for himself and for the players, he wouldn't show them up in public. He'd never try to make you look small in front of other people. If he had anything to say to you, he'd have a quiet word with you on your own, suggesting you try to do something, nothing nasty at all. And he got tremendous respect for that. He set an example and the team behaved properly because of that. He was a model. Even if the cameras could get to him, his face never changed, you wouldn't know if we were winning 4–0 or getting beat 4–0! Because he backed us in public, we wanted to play for him. If you did your job, you could get to know him, you'd get his respect and you'd find he was a very warm, generous man.'

By Christmas, the Ipswich bandwagon was still rolling along, successive wins over Plymouth, Orient and then Norwich twice in a row yielding sixteen goals, as Phillips and Crawford scored at will. Promotion seemed on the cards, but Ray Crawford recalls that 'promotion and relegation never dawned on players like it does now, with all the media talk – then you played your games, and then, come Easter time, if you were up there or down the bottom, that's when you started to look at those sorts of things. Alf never put pressure on you, he never talked about having to win this or do that. He just let you play.' With such an easy going atmosphere surrounding the club, it was easy to survive their most serious setback of the year. Drawn away to Southampton in the third round of the Cup, they encountered a side that had, for the first time, made an effort to combat the Ipswich strategy. Ron Reynolds had moved on to the Dell and was part of the think-tank that operated there: 'We'd been to Ipswich in September and got away with a draw, 3–3. Alf perfected an excellent method which staggered us the first time we came across it. Before the Cup match, there was a pre-match talk among the senior players (Cliff Huxford, Tommy Traynor, myself) and the manager, Ted Bates, because they tore us to shreds in Ipswich. Anything that came out of defence went through Leadbetter, picking up balls and throw-outs from the goalkeeper, in a deep position, much as Alf had when he was a player. Regular as clockwork, he'd feed Ray Crawford, who'd detach himself from the centre-forward position, come back and pick it up, lay it back, then the through ball would go to Phillips the inside-left. Ted Bates wanted to block this move. Cliff Huxford, the left-half, would literally have kicked his grandmother into the stand if he'd played against her, but our right-half, Dick Conner, loved to attack and that had been the problem in the League game. Ted wanted to switch them, but if we'd told Dick we wanted to switch him because he couldn't look after Phillips, there'd be uproar. I suggested we kid him along, saying that he'd be better in a forward position without defensive responsibilities. When Ted suggested that to him, he said, "Don't you think I can mark Phillips? I'll show you what I can do." We won 7–1, and Dick had a great game. Three weeks later we had them at home in the League. Ted had the same meeting to ask us what we wanted to do. I felt that Dick had proved his point and he wouldn't mark Phillips again, so we were on a hiding to nothing. We went out and Phillips should have had four in the first half, but we finished up with a draw. That was a tremendous strength that Alf played to, and nobody could really combat it.' It was an equal strength that Ipswich should be so resilient: unlikely pacesetters, a reverse as serious as that at Southampton would have burst the bubble for many a lesser side. As Jimmy Leadbetter points out, Ipswich were made of sterner stuff: 'They really hammered us, but we just carried on like nothing had happened. That was the mark of a good team. At half-time it was 6–0, they were hitting balls from all angles and they just flew in the net. Alf couldn't say anything. We were all tensed up, and if he had said anything it could have a bad effect on us afterwards. But we came off at 7–1, so the second half we got a draw! But we were just determined to get back and the following week we beat Bristol Rovers 3–2.' Alf did make a tentative attempt to strengthen his defence following the humiliation at the Dell, as Reynolds confirms: 'After that Cup game, as I passed the visitors' dressing room, Alf came out. He walked along with me and it was as near an invitation as any player could get to join them – I think there was talk that Roy Bailey was going back to South Africa at the time, and Alf was asking me how much I liked Southampton, was I enjoying my football, that Ipswich would be in the First Division next year, enjoying a better standard of play and so on! But I was settled.'

Alf's confidence that Ipswich would get promotion wasn't misplaced. Seven wins in eight games through February and March confirmed Ipswich at the summit, though as Ray Crawford explains, there was no reason to get excited: 'We came to Easter in '61 and we had Middlesbrough at home on Friday, Huddersfield away the next day then Middlesbrough away on the Monday. Alf took us away before that weekend, but there was never any mention of promotion. When I look back, it was so laid-back. If anything, the supporters got worked up while we didn't. Nothing was different, there were no get-togethers or extra meetings. We just turned up at quarter-past two, the kick-off was at three, and that was it. Nothing changed.' That was the key, for it would have been very easy for the players to get carried away with their achievements, to suddenly realize where they were and to freeze. After all, this was lowly Ipswich Town, a team who had only been in the Football League for sixteen seasons. Yet they were at the top on merit, as Huddersfield's left-back Ray Wilson, a regular opponent, admits: 'In my mind, Alf was already far ahead of managers of that time. Playing against them was incredible. We'd scratch our heads coming off, you'd have had the ball 85 minutes and come off losing 4–1. It was tactics, purely and simply; the man was in front of everybody else. He had one or two kids, but most of the side were people who looked like has-beens, journeymen who came together at Ipswich, like Jimmy Leadbetter, who must have been 60 then! But he was magnificent. We had the right-back follow him everywhere and he'd end up in their box leaving 50 yards of space, so the Ipswich lads would just knock into there, Phillips and Crawford would get after it, pick the ball up, the centre-half doesn't know where to go, and they're through. The only reason they made it was the system. None of the other clubs could see it, and they got away with it for years.'

Promotion was clinched on an emotional afternoon at Portman Road by beating Sunderland 4–0. Two goals up at half-time, Alf went on the public address system to ask the supporters not to run on the field at the end when promotion was secured; a measure of his confidence but also an indication of arrogance, an inability to foresee defeat that would cost him dear in the future. For the moment, there were only celebrations, things getting even better two days later when a 4–1 win at the Baseball Ground meant Ipswich went up as Champions. They'd scored 100 goals – Phillips 30, Crawford 40 – won 26 games and accumulated 59 points. Worthy champions indeed, though as Spurs took the Double, Ipswich received little coverage for their magnificent achievement. Pre-empting the patronizing coverage meted out to Barnsley by thirty-six years, what mentions they did receive were of the order of 'plucky little Ipswich will have their first – and only – season in Division One next year', Jimmy Leadbetter now able to laugh at 'the paper talk that was full of Sheffield United, who went up with us. Nobody talked about us. They forecast they'd do well, but that Ipswich would go straight back down. We read the papers like everybody else, so we said there's no way we're going down! But to win it, we got the shock of our lives!'

10   Champions of England (Again)

Promotion to the First Division was the biggest thing that had happened to Ipswich Town. With an apparently ragbag side, most felt Alf would need to spend if they were to have any hope of surviving. Instead, he maintained faith in the squad that had won promotion, proving that he valued loyalty above all other qualities, and that that loyalty was a two-way street. Only inside-forward Dougie Moran was brought in, for £12,300 from Falkirk, and he was scarcely the charismatic name that fans and press were hoping to see unveiled. Some assumed, understandably, that money was simply not available, others that Ramsey had gone mad, still more that he'd accepted he'd done all that he could with Ipswich and would be looking to move on during the course of the season, his managerial credentials well and truly established. The truth was more prosaic. He knew what he wanted to achieve, how he was going to do it, and concluded that he didn't need new players; better to stick with footballers already well drilled in the Ramsey way rather than bringing in big names, perhaps with big egos, who might undermine team spirit and be unable or unwilling to conform. It was a philosophy with which his players agreed, Jimmy Leadbetter explaining, 'It was about trusting each other. We didn't go out blind just to enjoy ourselves and entertain the crowd. If you could do it by entertaining people, then do that by all means. But we were there to win. Our minds weren't full of tactics. We had a system, he expected us to play to it. There's nothing worse than a manager who says, "Don't do this, don't do that." It just confuses players. There were certain rules, things we didn't do in defence. We wouldn't play square balls because there was a chance of an opponent nipping in on goal, but other than that, we just played our football. If you're playing, you should have a football brain, you should be able to use the thing! That was what Alf thought. If he put you out there, you knew you could play in the position he gave you. He was brilliant at that. John Compton was a wing-half but he made him play at full-back. As a wing-half you've always got somebody behind you, but as a full-back, you've not got anyone there. John slotted back easily, he was always in the team, but we couldn't see how Alf knew he could play there! You'll see managers bringing in players from other clubs and they don't fit the style of play. It's not the player's fault, it's the manager who picked him. Alf would never tell players to do this or that, he always wanted you to play your natural game, and before you realized what you were doing, you were fitting into the team pattern, and it came naturally to you. He was a great one for putting players into their best position so that they could believe in what they were doing. He was quiet, thoughtful, it was a pleasure to play for him.' Having played in most positions himself, Alf knew what was required from each role on the field and regularly drew on that experience.

Alf also knew how the First Division worked. Looking back a decade, he remembered that the established sides paid little heed to the newcomers, did not expend energy in spying on them, in working out their methodology, in combating their tactics. Instead, they took it for granted that their greater abilities would help them crush the interlopers. He knew they'd view little Ipswich as cannon fodder, a team promoted out of its depth. With their revolutionary push-and-run tactics, Tottenham had run away with the League before anyone had noticed. The same opportunity existed for Ipswich – though the Championship might be beyond them, their unique game plan would serve them well, he was confident of that. A goalless draw at Bolton was a promising start, but, paradoxically, it was a defeat at Burnley that led them to feel the First Division held no terrors. Champions in 1960, Burnley were highly fancied to relieve Tottenham of their title. In a thrilling game, they eventually beat Ipswich 4–3, but Alf was moved to call it 'the best performance I have ever seen from any Ipswich team since I have been connected with the club'. The spirit was good, the side equalized on three occasions, but a fourth was beyond them, Jimmy Leadbetter recalling, 'The goals were going in, the game was back and forth. They got ahead towards the end and we kept saying to the referee, "Hold on, play till we get another!"' A week later, Ipswich got revenge, hammering Burnley 6–2 at home, Leadbetter pointing out that, 'We had a good team, a nice moving side, we all felt confident in it because we backed each other. Whatever position you were in, there was always somebody there to help you.' At home, Ipswich were well nigh invincible, helping them augment their fairly meagre wages with a little extra. According to Ray Crawford: 'We believed in ourselves, we thought we were a good team and just wanted to get on with it. We all did the football coupons and at the time you could do the fixed odds at 40–1 for four homes. There were a couple of foregone conclusions like Arsenal and Manchester United to win at home, and the dodgy one was us to beat West Ham, but we were confident about that. We all had a tenner on us, we beat them 4–2, and we won good money. At home, we thought we could beat anybody, we knew what we could do.'

With Leadbetter running the show – 'the basis of all Ipswich's success' according to Alf – they were up with the leading pack before anyone noticed. They continued to refine their basic style, and were attacking with pace and vigour. Alf's view was, 'We believe in striking quickly from defence. A team is most vulnerable when it has just failed in attack. If I had to suggest an ideal number of passes I would say three. It is difficult to generalise on such a fluid game as football, but generally the second pass out of defence I would regard as the most vital.' With such a move in 1966, Geoff Hurst became immortal, but back in 1961–62 it was earning dividends for Ipswich. The root of all their play was doing straightforward things well, simple and quick, Leadbetter adding, 'Alf's idea was the less number of passes you take, the less chance there is of making a bad pass. It's better to make three good, simple ones, because if you try to make ten, as sure as anything you'll make a mess of one of them! You should be in a position to shoot with the third one. You could do that then because of the way teams played. It was hard to counter it – they had the centre-half and the full-backs, who worked on a swivel, with the right-back covering if the ball was down the left or vice-versa. That was the only cover you got, so if you could beat your full-back, your forwards had a good chance. Now, with sweeper systems and four or five men at the back, it's much harder.' Ipswich were fortunate that this was still the pre-TV age, there was no *Match of the Day* to expose their tactical secrets. Very often a team would have no idea what was going on when they first encountered Ipswich's peculiar method because they hadn't bothered to study it. George Cohen was at Fulham and vividly remembers 'Leadbetter laid so deep, I didn't know who the hell I was supposed to be marking. He pulled me out of position and started pumping the ball over me to Crawford and Phillips, and they had two goals before we knew where we were. At half-time we decided I should stay back and let the winger look after him, so we went into a 4–4–2 without knowing! Substitute Phillips and Crawford for Hurst and Hunt and you have the England set-up.'

People began to take notice of Ipswich once they'd thumped Manchester United 4–1, Alf even indulging in a little joke after Ted Phillips had scored twice: 'He has the best two feet in the game; the best I can remember. He doesn't know one from the other either.' At the turn of the year, they were third, three points behind Burnley and showing no sign of flagging. Perhaps fortunate to go out of the Cup early on (Burnley and Spurs went all the way to the Final) Ipswich were able to concentrate on the League. Fewer games meant fewer injuries, crucial for a club with the slenderest of squads, and they were lucky to have a basic eleven that played week in, week out – Roy Bailey, Larry Carberry, John Compton, Billy Baxter, Andy Nelson, John Elsworthy, Roy Stephenson, Doug Moran, Ray Crawford, Ted Phillips, Jimmy Leadbetter all managed thirty-seven or more League appearances in the season. They had a wonderful understanding, absolute faith in their colleagues and complete respect for Ramsey. He was able to dampen down excitement with his own icy demeanour, keeping everything in perspective, never looking too far ahead, happy to keep things ticking over. He put no pressure on his players, making it clear that if they gave of their best and did not make silly mistakes, that was all that could be expected. It was easy to keep things calm because it never looked as though Ipswich would quite make it to the top – after thirty-seven matches, they were in second with the same points tally as Burnley, but Burnley had three games in hand, more than enough opportunity to put daylight between the two. Alf insisted that his men keep plugging away, picking up points, looking for the best possible finish to the season, always hoping Burnley might slip up. One might have thought that to have any chance of taking the title, they'd need five straight wins, but a point was lost against both Arsenal and Chelsea. Yet Burnley were crumbling still faster. It began to dawn on the media that Ipswich might yet win the League, and reporters were sent to cover their games in depth. The 2–2 draw with Chelsea gave *The Times* the chance to file this backhanded compliment: '[Ipswich] defy explanation – they do the simple things accurately and quickly; there are no frills about their play and no posing. They are not exciting; they do not make the pulses race. Simply, they are eleven men doing their job professionally, blessed with a rich team spirit, backing each other, covering each other's faults and playing to their strong points . . . maybe, after all, there is virtue in the honest labourer.' Their final game was at home to Aston Villa in front of 28,932 supporters. Victory would give them 56 points and force

Burnley to win both their remaining games to win the title on goal average, but they had to wait 72 minutes for a breakthrough, a Ray Crawford header easing the tension, the game made safe four minutes later with another Crawford goal. At full-time, the news filtered through that Burnley had been held by Chelsea. Ipswich were Champions, *The Times* confirming that they had 'accomplished the impossible, beating the best that money could buy, cocking a snook at tradition and proving for all time that team spirit and the basically simple tactics of their manager, Mr Alfred Ramsey, probably the one great genius the game has produced in recent years, are an unbeatable combination.' For his part, Alf was so elated he said he felt like 'jumping over the moon', becoming perhaps the first footballer to coin the phrase. According to his chairman, John Cobbold, that evening following the game, he found Alf sitting alone in the stand after a gin and tonic or two, taking in what he had done. He took off his coat, gave it to Cobbold and 'ran a lap of honour with me as the only spectator. It was a bloody marvellous, intimate moment. People say Alfred is cold. What tosh! He is a very private man, but has enormous warmth.'

It was that personal warmth that had inspired his players to perform the seemingly impossible, yet for all that Alf tried to tell the world that it was a victory for his players, it really was his triumph. The *Daily Times* noted that 'without him one feels that the whole edifice would come tumbling down about our ears and that might well be so, for he has coerced, encouraged and kidded players, who, before they fell under his spell, were not outstanding individuals ... blind faith in the rightness of the manager's ideas, unselfishness on the field and real friendliness for one another have been big factors.' Ray Crawford echoes those sentiments: 'Players win things for you, but the job of the manager is getting the best out of them. Everything Alf had, he squeezed the last ounce out of it: the ground, the facilities, the supporters, the players. He wouldn't be dictated to – the local press would pick a team on a Wednesday, but Alf wouldn't pay any attention. He stuck with the players and they stuck with him. We used to go out together as a team on a Wednesday to play in the darts league to raise money for charity, about fifteen of us! If a player can't do what you ask them to, it's no good shouting and bawling at them, they can't do it. Alf never asked you to do something you couldn't. He'd never embarrass you. I think we were all decent players and Alf knew that. We'd mostly been at clubs that didn't appreciate what you could do. Alf believed in us and we were probably pleased that he took an interest in us, taught us something, that he managed to get the best out of us. There were no big boys. I'd been kicked out of Portsmouth, Leicester didn't want Roy, West Ham didn't want Andy, Roy Bailey couldn't get a game at Palace, apparently he made lots of mistakes, but Alf used to tell him what he was doing wrong and helped turn him into a good goalkeeper. But he'd tell you without getting your back up, he didn't have a go, he just talked to you normally; it was all constructive. We all owed Alf something, which is why we looked up to him. The way he worked and conducted himself brought the best out of us. We had a good team spirit, he welded us together as a team. He had the sense to look beyond the flashy players who the newspapers raved about and look at what the more ordinary looking players could do.'

The team spirit was a strength but there was more to them than that, as Tom Finney says: 'I went to see them playing away at some of the big clubs, and they won by being methodical about their play. Alf had certain players available and he'd given a lot of thought as to how he could best use them all. Leadbetter was looked on as an oldish player, a bit slow, but he was a good user of the ball and Alf devised a system that allowed him to do that. It was a fantastic achievement, but I don't think it was properly recognized. Perhaps the press wanted the likes of Arsenal and Manchester United and Spurs to keep winning, but it was just an incredible thing to do. Ipswich were a backwater team, nobody gave them any hope, but Alf signed the right people to do it. Irrespective of who wins, to come out top after forty-two games takes a lot of doing, you have to have consistency, and he did it with no money. I think it confirmed that you didn't need star players if you had a good system. If you can get star players to do what you want them to do rather than what they want to do, that's very important, but it's not always possible.' Finney's point about the lack of acclaim is a good one. Certainly the London press weren't happy to see a faceless, characterless team such as Ipswich steal the title away from their beloved Spurs, their Blanchflower and Mackay, Greaves and Jones. But it was a magnificent performance, possibly the greatest in the history of League football. Where Tottenham spent almost £100,000 just to bring Greaves back from Italy, Alf had spent less than a third of that in creating a Championship side. That was real football management, easily the equal of Brian Clough's performances with unfancied players at Derby and Nottingham Forest, for at least

Clough had the benefit of being at clubs with tradition. Before Alf arrived at Portman Road, Ipswich had nothing. More than that, he had taken his club through the divisions with barely changing personnel – Bailey, Carberry, Elsworthy, Phillips and Leadbetter became the only players ever to have won First, Second and Third Division Championship medals with the same club. Of course, there was an opportunity to succeed – Manchester United were still recovering from Munich, Wolves were in terminal decline, Tottenham were ageing and had one eye firmly on the European Cup, Shankly and Revie had yet to rebuild Liverpool and Leeds – but opportunities have to be taken. While around them faltered teams based on great individuals, Alf had performed alchemy, taking the basest of metals and turning them into gold – his reputation in the country was so strong that he topped a *Daily Mirror* poll searching for the next England manager. His tactical acumen had foiled the finest brains in the English game, Bill Nicholson and Danny Blanchflower among them, as Leadbetter explains: 'Tottenham thought they had us taped. Alf told me that Blanchflower would come over to me and leave the full-back to mark Ted. Alf asked me what I wanted to do and I said that I'd do what I always did, kid on I was a winger and let Danny mark me. Danny loved going forward, loved having the ball, he had no time for running about trying to get it, he wanted it to his feet. Anyway, he came over and said, "I'm playing full-back against you, Jim!" I started dragging him down the field and after a while he said, "Bugger this! I'm not playing this! I'm going to play wing-half again." So we won the battle.'

Yet within a matter of months, Ramsey the alchemist looked more like a con man who had beaten the rest with a footballing version of the Emperor's new clothes. Starting their defence with the traditional charity shield game, against Tottenham, Ipswich were soundly beaten, 5–1. Bill Nicholson had brought his full-backs inside to pick up Phillips and Crawford and let the half-backs take care of Leadbetter and Roy Stephenson. It was a ploy that was to be repeated up and down the country, though at the time it didn't give Alf much cause for concern. 'I still don't think our tactics were wrong,' he said. 'We failed as individuals.' It was a seminal statement, exposing his entire philosophy. We succeed as a team, we fail as individuals. Alf and his players all failed in some degree, in part because success has a habit of bringing its own peculiar problems. Ray Crawford had scored thirty-three League goals in the previous season and earned an England call-up: 'I wanted to leave at one point – I'd played for England and I'd heard all this talk about the wages players were getting, the maximum wage had gone, and I wanted a better contract. The club wasn't prepared to give it me so I asked for a transfer. Alf said it would be brought up at the next board meeting, but it was dismissed and that was it – he thought £30 a week was fair enough, when Johnny Haynes was on £100! In his view, he was right because he felt I was in a team, and without Jimmy to cross the ball or Andy Nelson to win it, I couldn't score any goals anyway. Success does bring problems, but if you're a strong manager, you can control that, certainly then more so than now, what with all the agents involved in the game. You were close to your manager – we saw Alf virtually every day, we knew he was there keeping an eye on us. You always felt you were playing for your place, especially on Tuesdays when the first team played the reserves and Alf would be there watching everything. The real trouble was, the next season, it caught up with a few of the players – the younger lads were OK but some of the older players struggled, there were injuries and Alf didn't have strength in depth because Ipswich couldn't afford it. Alf couldn't make changes to the side when he wanted to. If he'd been at Spurs or Arsenal he'd have won the League again because they had the resources. There's no doubt that he was a mastermind, but at Ipswich we struggled because we were stuck with what we had.' Not only were some of the players ageing, they'd achieved everything they ever could in the game. Alf had to ring the changes, as Jimmy Leadbetter concedes: 'We were getting a bit older together, and that's when you've got to bring some younger boys in. As a player, you're quite happy to keep playing, but the manager needs to look at the whole team. No disrespect to Alf, and I don't know what money was available, but the manager needs to make changes to keep the team fresh. There were a lot to make.'

Financial constraints made life difficult, as did his loyalty to men who had been with him for six or seven years. When Alf was forced to leave Leadbetter out of a European Cup game, he found it an enormous wrench, admitting, 'This was a terrible moment. After all Jimmy has done for this team he took it well, better than I did.' The very loyalty that had been the source of Alf's success would now make it harder for him to take the club onwards. With a stubbornness bordering on the reckless, he argued, 'We know the element of surprise has gone but we are not changing our tactics. We will defend our League title the same way we won it.' Week in, week out, it was obvious that other sides were now wise to Ipswich's game plan, while its fulcrum, Jimmy Leadbetter, was struggling. As Ray Wilson points out, 'It was only when they'd won the First Division that people set out their stall to stop the system. Then they were knackered.'

Ipswich had relied so heavily on their tactical formation that, once rumbled, they had little to fall back on. Alf recognized the problem but in offering a solution made it obvious there was little he could really do to resolve it: 'You must have an alternative method of attack for when your key men are being well marked or are off their game . . . when Leadbetter finishes, as some day he must, I wouldn't look for another player to replace him in the same role – I doubt if I could find one . . . youngsters must be brought in gradually and taught to blend into the set team and the set pattern. I am often aware as I watch our opponents that while they may have talent they have not got such a rigid plan as we have developed. And I am sure that it is because we have had better understanding and have made better use of our perhaps more limited capabilities that we have won the success we have.' A rigid plan is fine for a time, but rigidity becomes a stereotype, and while your players can be sure of what their team-mates will do, so too can the opposition. Alf knew this only too well, but trying to survive on gates of around 20,000 meant there was no money for new players and the new ideas they could help introduce. At the same time, some accused him of neglecting the reserve and youth sides at the club. There wasn't a clutch of young lads ready to step into the first team, though given Alf's reluctance to move aside his tried and trusted players, he might not have brought them in until forced to. Whichever way he turned, he knew he'd face trouble.

An end to his problems was just around the corner. By the end of September, Ipswich had eight points from eleven games and were struggling. So were the FA. Following England's moderate performance in the 1962 World Cup, Walter Winterbottom stood down as manager leaving a vacancy that proved harder to fill than many had imagined, despite the fact that they received fifty-nine applications, including one from a convict. The FA then approached Alf. Leaving Ipswich was never going to be easy, for he had formed close relationships not only with the players and officials, but with the supporters. When Ipswich were offered the use of Wembley for their European Cup games, for example, his response was 'It would be like kicking our fans in the pants if we took those matches away from them,' adding, 'Who could work for a finer club than this?

Money isn't everything.' Having considered the FA's offer throughout October – when Ipswich played four, drew two, lost two – on 25 October, he agreed to take up the post, though he said, 'I am torn by loyalty to the club to whom I owe everything.' These were not mere words, but a true statement of his feelings. After all, he hadn't applied for the vacancy, feeling it inappropriate to do so when he was still under contract. But the fact that he'd need to start almost from scratch with Ipswich, albeit from a far better position than the one he'd inherited in 1955, must have made it easier for him to go, however indebted he felt. The players were stunned by events, Ray Crawford remembering, 'We didn't realize he was in line for the England job. We were really pleased for him but sorry to see him go. We picked the local paper up and read it there first! Reg Pickett said to me, "If he wins the World Cup, it'll be Sir Alf!"' He did not leave at once, however, but made it clear that he wanted to see Ipswich clear of the danger zone and work in tandem with a new manager to show him the ropes. The gesture of solidarity was a genuine and affecting one, but perhaps it would have been wiser had he made a clean break, for as Jimmy Leadbetter notes, 'There were a lot of disturbances that year, Alf getting the England job, players getting injured and moving away, some of us were getting too old, it was hard to concentrate on your football.'

One light note amid the gloom of their League form was the progress made in the European Cup. Drawn against Malta's Floriana in the preliminary round, Ipswich won the away leg 4–1, but still attracted 25,287 for the rather academic second leg. The team did not disappoint, winning 10–0, Ray Crawford scoring five. Alf's reaction was typically pragmatic: 'Having it so easy was rather difficult in some ways. There must have been a temptation for my players to try to be clever – the sort of thing I detest.' Their reward was a tie with AC Milan. Jimmy Leadbetter recalls the first leg in the San Siro with some amusement: 'The media didn't give us a chance, but Milan didn't take any risks! They had us waiting on the field for ten minutes before the kick-off – Alf was going to call us back in. When they finally came out, they got all the photographers behind our goal. When they won a corner, they all moved out to the side the corner came in from and flashed their flashlights at Roy Bailey! He couldn't see anything!' Ipswich went down 3–0, scarcely an embarrassing reverse, but the *Daily Mail*'s Brian James recorded that, 'Ramsey's graceless but honest side [were] beaten as much by their own starkly exposed deficiencies.'

The return leg was the biggest ever game to hit East Anglia, and another big crowd packed Portman Road. With a three-goal deficit to claw back, there was little chance of victory, but they prepared in the same manner. Ray Crawford remembers, 'The kick-off was 7.30, I think, and we just had to turn up at quarter-to seven as normal. My car broke down, I didn't arrive until ten-past seven, twenty minutes before kick-off! There were 25,000 in Portman Road, but Alf was just like normal: "Where you been, Ray?", very casual. I told him, he just said, "OK, you'd better get changed, then." So laid-back, it calmed you down, there was never any song and dance.' The consummate professional, Alf always expected his men to do their job whatever the circumstances. On the night, they did him proud, beating the eventual European Cup winners 2–1, with 'gallant galloping football' according to Brian James.

Fitness and form had returned and as Britain entered the severe winter of 1963, it looked as though Ipswich would be safe, a situation helped by Orient's atrocious form. A new manager had been recruited too, Jackie Milburn arriving at the club in good time to take up the reins from Alf, who had an old score to settle. According to Milburn: 'The first thing he did was to tackle me really hard and I went down. I had been fouled at Spurs eight years earlier and had got up in a terrible rage and pushed over the man nearest to me – who happened to be Alf Ramsey. I'd forgotten all about it until then ... but the way Alf looked at me, I knew he hadn't forgotten it. Alf had a tremendous, fantastic, magnificent memory.' For all that the two had played for England together, they found it hard to work with each other. As Ray Crawford says, 'Jackie and Alf were like chalk and cheese. Jackie was a lovely man, but he wanted to be with the lads. Jack wanted to have a fag, a drink in his hand, his foot on the ball and be one of the boys. He wanted to come down the café with us all, order the drinks and bring fifteen cups of tea over to us, join in. Alf knew the difference. He knew when to get out of the way, he ruled from a distance. He had his rules and regulations, but he was never there to put them in force in person. We respected him. He ruled the club, ruled John Cobbold the chairman, kept him in order! Jackie's problem was he was a good coach, he ran really good training sessions, but he wasn't an Alf Ramsey, wasn't a manager. The first thing he said to me was, "You'll not be here long." It wasn't malicious, but I thought it was a funny way to start. Obviously he wanted money to strengthen the team, and he thought I was the one they'd get the cash for. I suppose that helped Alf make his mind up about England, because Ipswich were a minnow club, really, they couldn't compete with the likes of Arsenal or Manchester United.'

For his part, Milburn was shocked to find just what he'd let himself in for. According to John Gibson's *Wor Jackie*, Milburn soon decided that, 'Ipswich were a First Division club with a Fourth Division team. We had no youth side and not a scout on the books . . . starting literally from rock bottom [in May 1963 when Alf had left] I wheeled and dealed and ended up flogging centre-forward Ray Crawford to Wolves so that I could buy Gerry Baker, Joe Broadfoot, Frank Brogan and Danny Hegan for peanuts . . . time was always against us . . . for me it was all too much . . . I was affected dreadfully . . . I would sit in a darkened room, brooding for hours . . . I started drinking gin like it was going out of fashion. The side of my face even began to swell to grotesque shapes through worry after matches . . . Alf Ramsey had warned me that I needed new players but the money was limited. In 18 months I clocked up nearly 40,000 miles by car in my search for signings, to say nothing of all the train and air journeys . . . what was nice was that when Bill McGarry eventually got them promotion he thanked me publicly for laying a good foundation for the club, and three Ipswich directors did the same in front of everyone when they came to Sunderland for a match.'

The implication is clear. Alf had built a club without the necessary foundations and in a sense that's true. Some might say that Ipswich couldn't afford to channel resources into a youth side, but as Dario Gradi has shown at Crewe, small clubs can't afford *not* to have such a set-up. From day one, Alf had immersed himself in the first team. He'd spent plenty of time watching reserve games, but he left their training and the scouting to others, Ray Crawford pointing out that 'he thought people should do their job. If somebody recommended a player to him, then he thought they should know what they were talking about – he spent £12,000 on Bobby Blackwood, which was a lot of money to Ipswich, without ever seeing him play.' That degree of trust in one's employees is laudable and dangerous. In fairness to Alf, had he not concentrated so much on first-team matters, it's hard to believe that Ipswich could have got out of the Second Division, let alone won the Championship – certainly not in such a short space of time. An ambitious and talented man like Alf was not going to fritter away his career in the Third Division (South), and so he had to get on with the job. He was lulled into a false sense of security by Ipswich's serene and injury free progress in their first season in Division One, and should have made greater provision for back-up players than he did, but on a shoestring budget that was always going to be tough. And for all the problems and distractions of 1962–63, he did keep them in the First Division with four points to spare, even if they were relegated the following year.

Perhaps the fact of the matter was that once he became secretary–manager, there was too much work to do. Alf loved getting results every week, that was the be-all and end-all of his footballing life. By focusing on that, it was inevitable that he could not spend enough time on the bigger picture, and the club's long-term future had to suffer. In that light, it's obvious he was not a great *club* manager. This was not surprising, for club management revolves around administration and finance, areas that he was not qualified to deal with. For all those failings though, you must also accept that it was Alf who put Ipswich on the map, who gave the club its greatest triumph and who made life easier for all those who followed him to the club. He was a superb *team* manager, one of the very best – he excelled at getting the best out of his players every Saturday, pieced together a pattern of play that would accommodate the disparate talents at his disposal. At heart, Alf was a player's man, loved being with them, working with them. Leaving Ipswich at the end of April 1963, he was now about to discover what he might do with the best the country had to offer.

11   Revolution Not Evolution

International football in England was heading for its most crucial days, years in which it must come of age, odd for a country that had been involved in the international game since 1872. Nevertheless, England had long been little more than a fringe player on the world scene, its refusal to acknowledge FIFA's pre-eminence preventing the FA from taking a central role in the wider development of the game. It was only in the aftermath of the Second World War that the home nations returned to the fold, and, of course, only 1950 when England first played in the World Cup. Showing a remarkably forgiving attitude, FIFA rewarded England with the greatest gift at its disposal. In 1960, it announced that England would host the 1966 World Cup, the valuable adjunct to which was that they would escape the rigours of qualification. From then, all was geared towards producing an England team that might do well, even win the Jules Rimet trophy. We had long since accepted we weren't the rulers of world football: our humbling at the hands of the USA and Hungary and unfortunate campaigns in both 1954 and 1958 had seen to that. Post-Puskas, in 1954, a shell-shocked side had reached the quarter-finals before losing 4–2 to Uruguay, who were then themselves dismissed by the same scoreline by Hungary. Four years later, a promising English side had been decimated by the Munich distaster, Duncan Edwards, Roger Byrne and Tommy Taylor, all vital components in the side, snatched away by the snow and ice. Viewed in that light, there was no shame in securing three draws in the group stage against Brazil, Russia and Austria, but England then went out to Russia in a play-off. We now had a rather more realistic measure of our standing in the world game, expectations lowered. No matter, we must still put on a good show in 1966.

England qualified for the 1962 series, to be held in Chile, without much difficulty, and flew out with hopes of reaching the latter stages in spite of an imposing qualification group that included Hungary, Argentina and Bulgaria. There were no traumas such as those of 1958 when the Munich disaster had robbed Winterbottom of the spine of his team, and preparation, though far from perfect, was a vast improvement on the comedy of errors that dogged the 1950 campaign, the team flying out a fortnight in advance, even squeezing in a friendly with Peru. Winterbottom's side contained some highly skilled footballers, players such as Ray Wilson, Jimmy Armfield, Jimmy Greaves, Johnny Haynes, Bobby Charlton, Gerry Hitchens, Bryan Douglas and a youngster who had only just arrived on the scene to replace the injured Bobby Robson, Bobby Moore. The year leading up to the 1962 World Cup saw England play twelve internationals, meeting opposition as diverse as Italy and Mexico, Austria and Peru. Accepting that English football had to adapt, Winterbottom had greater scope to experiment with tactics, broadening the horizons of his players: 'In 1962 we played 4–2–4, but it was a pliable system and we did play 4–3–3 at times when required, or even 4–4–2. Gradually we were adapting our system so that we could switch within a game. One thing we never did play was the sweeper, which we still never have, even though I reckoned it was a damned good system – but it was impossible to do that with the time we had. But we had played 4–2–4 before the Brazilians made it theirs. We'd give an inside-forward a defensive role to go 4–2–4; we beat Scotland 9–3 in 1961 with that style. Sometimes we tried to play with two centre-forwards, looking for the full-backs and the wing men to be interchangeable, using the overlap. A wing man like Douglas would have a responsibility to defend, while Jimmy Armfield would have licence to get forward. So we were very flexible – we had attacking wing-halves and would let them float through – we tried to encourage the alternation of a player up front and behind, players from midfield breaking through. We were just coming to that style in the late 1950s, early 1960s. Things were changing, but it was a slow process because of the conflict with the clubs. When West Germany were preparing for the World Cup in 1954, their manager, Sepp Herberger, got all their clubs to adopt the sweeper system, and they agreed. Can you imagine Cullis or Busby or Shankly agreeing to play the system I wanted them to play? The co-operative spirit elsewhere is quite amazing – Brazil suspend the league for six months! Is it any wonder they make progress nationally?'

England struggled through the opening round, losing to Hungary, beating Argentina and drawing with Bulgaria, but all was not well. The players were annoyed with journalists who they felt wanted England to fail; the attacking fulcrum of the England side, Greaves and Haynes, were not operating with the required potency; and the squad divided into cliques and was ill at ease, Bobby Charlton suggesting the team 'became dilapidated' and lacked heart. Others noted the skilled but mercurial Haynes and Greaves might have been better replaced by George Eastham and Roger Hunt, an interesting observation in the light of the controversies that would rage around Greaves four years on. With Haynes captain, his place was never in doubt, while Greaves was so natural a goalscorer it seemed unthinkable England might take the field without him – no committee would have the nerve to drop him. They were our individuals, the men with the skill to unlock the securest defence, successors to Matthews, Mannion and Finney. But what this failed to acknowledge was that if two men were responsible for English creativity, opponents need only block them out to render England impotent. With little threat coming from elsewhere in the team, their poor early form meant they were left with a troublesome quarter-final against Brazil, who'd started well but weren't the awesome force of 1958, and had lost Pelé to injury. England travelled hopefully, but as Brian Glanville explained in *The Story of the World Cup*, 1962 was 'the World Cup of Garrincha, the World Cup of 4–3–3'. England were beaten 3–1, bemused by Garrincha's virtuosity, baffled by Brazil's formation, revised from the carefree 4–2–4 in order to preserve their ageing players. By the time England returned home, the upper echelons of the FA had begun to worry that England might disgrace itself in 1966. Only in 1938 in France and 1954 in Switzerland had the host nation finished outside the top three places, and England looked some way from that. That fatuous cry of desperate administrators everywhere rent the air: 'Something must be done.'

Walter Winterbottom had decided to stand down. He had been favourite to succeed Sir Stanley Rous as Secretary to the FA, but internal politics kept him from a post for which he was eminently suited, Denis Follows taking the job instead. Nevertheless, he was given the chance to offer his thoughts on a successor. Journalist Ken Jones recalls, 'I met Walter at Lilleshall after the World Cup and we were speculating on who would take over, and I don't think Alf Ramsey's name was mentioned.' Winterbottom felt the choice was an obvious one: 'There's no real link between the skills you need to run a successful club and those that you need to run a national side well. I felt we needed a good coach and we went for Jimmy Adamson, who'd been with me with England, so we could maintain some continuity, but Burnley weren't keen to let him go. There was a similar problem with Dennis Wilshaw, who had been a player with Wolverhampton. Denis Follows was in charge of the process and I said to him that one man who could do the job would be Alf. The one thing I insisted on was that the new man shouldn't have to put up with the selection committee. We'd changed it to focus on what I wanted, but they could overrule me! We'd tried to put a young side together: playing Wales in 1959 we had the young-est forward line ever fielded – Connelly, Greaves, Clough, Charlton, Holliday – and they played well and drew 1–1. We had the same team against Sweden and I tried to tell the committee to be prepared for a poorer performance because these were young lads getting experience. We lost 3–2 and the next time they made five changes! You couldn't fight them – other countries like Sweden, and even Argentina, still had committees, so you couldn't say we were the only ones left. You can only make major changes such as that when a new man comes into the job, because then everyone starts afresh. I told Follows that Alf wouldn't take the job under any other circum-stances.'

Winterbottom's attitude was shared by the players, who didn't know whether they were coming or going at international level. Ray Wilson broke into the side at left-back in 1960 and remembers, 'It was a big problem. The side changed so rapidly. The selectors had no squad, they picked players who were in form. There's some sense in that, I suppose, but to survive at that level club form doesn't come into it. There was an amateur attitude from the selectors, rewarding players who'd done well for their club by giving them international caps. Very few got a fair amount of caps. But we never won anything. The world game got more professional and you had to be more professional about it. The FA was amateurish – we never entered the World Cup because they thought we were too good for it. It seems to me the best thing to do if you're that good is to enter and keep winning. It's in the books that Italy won it twice in the thirties, that Uruguay won it, not that England were best. We'd just invite the winners over, maybe beat them and send them home. But we won nothing and they had the World Cup. Then when we went in we got an eye opener. You can't afford to be left behind, it happens very quickly – look how we controlled Europe with Liver-pool and Nottingham Forest for ten years, and how long it's taken us to get back into contention after the ban. The FA was run like a little club, people who wouldn't know a ball from a tomato picking players, and that's awful.' The time was right for seismic changes to be made, but how to prise power away from those who enjoyed wielding it?

Ironically the FA backed themselves into a corner. It was common knowledge that Winterbottom was forced to coach a side he hadn't selected while still taking the flak for its inadequacies, as though these were failings of his own making. As the tone of newspaper reporting moved from the deferential to the accusatory, no sane man would expose himself to vilification without having control of his own destiny. Far from being the pinnacle, the job of England manager was a poisoned chalice, and for all that Adamson and Wilshaw may have had sound personal reasons for turning it down, they had better career ones. They had seen the evidence of 1962, could see England were a long way behind many of the teams on show. They understood that the manager would be under the microscope for the next four years to a far greater degree than Winterbottom ever had, they knew that piecing together a cohesive and settled England squad was impossible given the prevailing circumstances, and saw the struggle as an unequal one, one they could not win. Nor were they alone, for it became clear that successful club managers such as Bill Nicholson – a former England coach, still basking in the glory of the Double and back-to-back FA Cup wins – and Stan Cullis were not interested in taking the job either. And once England had been held to an unimpressive 1–1 draw at Hillsborough by an undistinguished French side in the first leg of a first-round European Nations Cup-tie under Winterbottom's caretaker management, the post held even less allure. The FA were running short of options at a time when the nation would demand an appointment in which it could believe. They were selecting the man to take us into the 1966 World Cup, our best ever chance of winning it. The public would not be fobbed off with a placid yes-man.

Ramsey was not a last resort, certainly not in terms of his ability. He had proven himself to be a high-class footballer, something which Ray Wilson felt was important: 'Walter was of the old regime. He'd no great professional background, partly because of the war. He knew the game well enough, but at international level I think the guy who runs the team has to have played at that level. International players are a little special, not just because they are able to play, but because they cope with the occasion, the pressure. You have to have been there in order to communicate with them; you automatically get respect.' Alf had shown that tactically he was exceptionally astute. For all the problems he left behind him at Ipswich, his achievements were incomparable. He had all the qualifications an England manager needs, yet there was hesitation in approaching him – it wasn't until September that contact was made, just after an intriguing interview conducted by Brian James had appeared in the *Daily Mail*, one which read like an application form: 'England should appoint a manager on exactly the same basis as a club appoints a manager. He must be allowed to pick his team alone and to decide how players will play ... I think an England manager must make up his mind what players he has and then find a rigid method for them to play to. If any player, no matter how clever an individual, is not prepared to accept the discipline of the team's method then I can see no advantage in selecting him ... [people say] Matthews, Finney, Carter and so on – they never needed a plan. Well, I played with many of these players and I would say England's team was good then, but it would have been many times better if we had also had a rigid plan. Remember many of the "great" players were in England's 1950 World Cup teams. But the fact is even then they couldn't score against the United States or Spain ... under the present system it must mean a poor England team or poor club teams ... most I feel want club to come before country and this is understandable. You would have to prove to me that a successful national side brings one extra spectator through the club turnstiles ... [for the World Cup in 1966] we won't have to travel or get used to foreign food or suffer heat we are not used to. This must count for a lot. But the League will have to help. Perhaps we could shorten the season to give the England party time to play together and be rested before the World Cup really starts ... if we can work out something like this, something to give England proper time for preparation – I think we can win.'

It's a fascinating piece which suggests Alf believed events were moving in his direction. He knew as well as anyone that the FA were short of candidates and that his name would be near the top of the list. The conversation with James offered the opportunity to set out terms, making it impossible for the FA to backtrack on them. He was almost daring them not to appoint him – if, after this well-argued and eminently logical dissertation on how the England team should be run, they chose not to invite him to take over, the public would know why. Given that in his subsequent career Alf and the public rarely saw eye to eye, it's ironic to reflect that his appointment to the job was the result of collusion between himself and the fans. Yet that was the case. He became the public's choice as England manager, riding high on his manifesto of radical change.

After years of wielding untrammelled power, decades spent as important men running the game and treating the manager as little more than an irrelevance, the committee's end was near. There would be no more influence with newspaper reporters grubbing around for exclusive snippets of information on forthcoming sides, no further opportunities to posture and pose. They were relegated to the sidelines, redundant, impotent. As Tom Finney points out, 'He wouldn't have accepted the job had he not been allowed to do it his way. You've got to do that in today's game. Probably that was the most important thing he did.' The FA recognized it was time to back down and summoned Alf to Lancaster Gate for an interview.

He did not retreat but stipulated the terms on which he might accept the appointment. Financial considerations were secondary – he was reportedly given an annual salary of £4500, not dissimilar from that he was receiving at Ipswich. What mattered was that he be left to do the job as he saw fit. Certainly the FA had the power to fire him should they wish, but while he was England manager, things would be done his way. Whatever reservations they had – and there must have been many given they were consigning their historic role to the dustbin – they decided that Alf must be given the job. As if to further underline the desperate nature of their situation, he did not accept the offer there and then but instead asked for time to consider it, little more than window dressing, stamping his authority on the situation, making it clear to the FA that they could not do without him. There were reservations. His loyalty to Ipswich has been addressed, but he knew that he could not stay at Portman Road for the rest of his days. He had already outgrown the club, it was a matter of time before he had to move on. In pure footballing terms, he was ready for the challenge, but did he really want to be thrust into the public domain? As Ken Jones points out, life in Suffolk was nice and relaxed: 'At Ipswich, most people seemed to get on with him and the circumstances helped. It was a friendly place, the Cobbolds were good company, people enjoyed going there, so the atmosphere was good. At Ipswich, he was looked on as quirky more than awkward, there weren't problems with the press.' Equally, the press weren't particularly interested in him. Despite winning the Championship and thereby writing one of the great stories in football history, newspaper proprietors were still only interested in Arsenal, Spurs and Manchester United. And the only team that was in sharper focus than they were was England. That prospect gave him much food for thought.

Ultimately there was only one decision. *The Times* went so far as to suggest that he took the job from a sense of duty, and there's a lot in that. Like most of his generation, Alf was a great patriot. He'd been drilled in the virtues of the British Empire, spent his childhood in a nation that had just fought one world war, his adolescence in a nation preparing for another, and his early adult life fighting for his country. He was the personification of the dutiful citizen, one who, to paraphrase JFK, asked only what he could do for his country, not what it could do for him. Of course he had personal ambitions – it's impossible to be a successful manager if you don't have a big ego – but Ramsey genuinely felt that if the call came from the country, he must heed it. He saw our reputation was sinking and felt he had something to offer in its repair. George Robb points out, 'He played in the defeats against Hungary and America and I think that he'd decide that that kind of thing would never happen again, there'd have been plenty of resolution there, I think! I think perhaps he wanted to put the record straight!' The importance of those two reverses cannot be understated, for it taught Alf that the quality of your play means nothing if it doesn't get the required result – England played well against America, but who cared about that? They'd lost. Entertainment was fine, but first get the result.

With his powerful self-belief, Alf may have felt that he was the only man for the job, the only man with the necessary determination to defeat the FA and then the rest of the world. On 25 October 1962, he accepted, with the proviso that the appointment would not become operative until 1 May 1963. Winterbottom would take the England side for the game against Wales in November, Alf's first game in charge would be the return against France in February, at which time he would still have leave to manage Ipswich. The sense of relief was palpable. The *Guardian*'s Eric Todd felt, 'If he receives the support and respect to which he is entitled from officials and players, he will not be found wanting.' Brian James added that here was 'a man with the character of steel'. The most important statement, however, came from FA Chairman Graham Doggart: 'The selection committee, as such, is finished.'

At a stroke, Alf had removed the most important obstacle between himself and winning the trust of his players. As Ray Wilson explains, 'You'd think you'd had a good game but you always wondered whether, if one of the committee had a favourite at his own club, you might be out next game! Alf changed all that, made it much more professional, so the players knew what he had to do, who we had to play for. He didn't make himself popular for that, but that's the only way you can run it.' As sole selector, Alf made it clear from the outset that, 'There will be no place for any player no matter how great his ability who is not prepared to show determination and will to succeed ... I don't worry what people say of me if I believe I'm right. But I will always try to protect my players from what I consider unfair criticism. Never let your lads down or let them be hurt.'

More than most, he understood that his first job was to restore confidence, at a very low ebb following the poor showing against the French. He addressed that immediately by making the point, 'I believe in England and Englishmen, as well as English football.' A crucial declaration of the creed that would see him through to the World Cup, it was a neat U-turn from his summary of our game in the *Daily Mail* a month earlier: 'Times continue to change and we must adapt with them ... one of the things England has lacked recently has been players of the ability of Ernie Taylor. He was great ... he could make others play well ... and he could beat an entire defence with one good pass. There are not enough players like that today, although Haynes has done everything for Fulham.' Perhaps he was doing some of his footballers a disservice, for there were a number of cultured players around, but it was a pointer towards where he was heading. We don't have the individuals of a Brazil, so we must make the best of what we have, application, organization, persistence and courage. If these could be used in a framework that allowed someone of Haynes' talent to flourish, England might too, but any success would be built on the bedrock of solid values.

Ramsey's appointment offered scope for debate. He was known to be thorough, meticulous, painstaking in his attention to detail. It was recognized that he was at his best when in among the players on a daily basis. How would he react to meeting up with them just eight or nine times a year? Would he be able to introduce a tactical plan in such circumstances, asking his team to play in ways alien to them at club level? Ken Jones makes the point that, 'Having watched what he'd done at Ipswich, I felt it would be very interesting to see what he would do with the best players in the country. In fact, he did very little in the sense that he was no coach. He had a way of playing in mind and picked players who could fit that, to do exactly what they did for their club.' There was more to the job than mere selection, and evidence that the winds of change were blowing through Lancaster Gate came before Alf took over. Prior to Winter-bottom's final game, the FA introduced a drive for greater fitness. When players had finished training for the game against Wales, they were taken off to White City for an exhaustive medical check-up. It was decided that such tests would take place at every fixture so that dossiers could be built up on each player to monitor their condition from month to month. It seems a trivial measure today, but six months earlier, England had travelled to Chile without so much as a doctor in tow.

Ironically, since Alf was not officially taking control of England's affairs until May, the selection committee was still in charge for the game against France in Paris that started his reign. Alf picked the side along with Doggart, Sid Collings, Joe Mears, J.P. Richards and Denis Follows and managed three days with the players prior to the game on 27 February 1963. The circumstances could hardly have been worse: thanks to the appalling winter in England, most players had managed only a couple of games since Christmas, so they were hardly in the best condition. It was an inauspicious beginning. Using five forwards – John Connelly, Bobby Tambling, Bobby Smith, Jimmy Greaves and Bobby Charlton – England went on the attack from the outset. Some early chances went begging before the French took the lead in controversial circumstances, Alf complaining, 'Our goalkeeper received a kick in the ribs when the first goal was scored. He bravely carried on and it may have affected his performance after that.' Ron Springett did not have one of his better games, and they were 3–0 down and apparently out of the competition by half-time. Alf refused to be downcast and pointed out that had England taken their chances they'd be level. He asked the players to maintain their effort and believe, as he did, that they could still get a draw. They pulled it back to 3–2, only for Springett to allow the ball to bounce off his chest and into the path of an oncoming forward. At 4–2, the fight-back was extinguished. The game finished 5–2, *The Times* forced to lament, 'One had thought that there might be a rebirth of an England side . . . English footballers have stopped [thinking] at the critical moment . . . where England goes hence-forth is anybody's guess.' Alf was not amused, though he was gracious in defeat, allowing that, 'France were the better team on the evening.' He kept his players in the dressing room for half an hour to discuss the game, a break from his normal pattern forced on him by the short time he could spend with them. He stressed that while individuals had played well, the team had not – we succeed as a team, we fail as individuals. Jimmy Armfield, England's captain, recalls his first impressions of life under Alf: 'He wasn't a man of many words, but when he spoke, you listened. He was very forthright – that game was on an icy pitch, they were a good side, but we just had a bad day right through the side. After the match, he came up to me and said, "Do we always defend like that?", which put it in perspective – we weren't going to defend like that again. It was a good way to start in a way, because the only way was up from there.'

There weren't many observers who took the defeat as phlegmatically as Armfield did, though his approach was sensible. With England bundled out of the Nations Cup at the first hurdle, it meant that they would not play another seriously competitive fixture until the World Cup three and a half years later, an almost insurmountable obstacle. It was that, rather than the disappointment of losing (no one really took the Nations Cup seriously in this country until at least 1980), that worried the football correspondents. But as Armfield rightly says, it gave Alf the chance to experiment, free from the need to win competitive games. Had England progressed through to the semi-final stage in Spain in June 1964, the public would have expected them to win. Defeat in those circumstances might have damaged morale, forced Alf into picking a side focused on winning there rather than in 1966, the date uppermost in his mind. Alf was probably fortunate to have a clear track ahead of him.

Sensibly, he did not make radical changes. Harold Shepherdson had worked as a trainer with Winterbottom for several years and he kept Shepherdson on the team, even when, in his secondary role as baggage man, he lost Alf's suitcase on the way to France. Shepherdson reflected, 'Bless him, he took it as an accepted part of his baptism as an international team manager.' This was not the behaviour of the humourless disciplinarian that was already appearing in caricatures, but this willingness to allow people to earn his respect won that of his squad. Changes were required, notably in defence. For all that the selection committee had a say in the game with Scotland at Wembley in April, it was obvious that Alf was bent on getting his way – Springett was replaced by Gordon Banks, Ron Henry by Gerry Byrne, Brian Labone with Maurice Norman. Lining up in a 4–2–4, things showed a slight improvement. Though England lost 2–1, they looked altogether more secure, calling to mind Alf's summary of Ipswich's strengths: 'We believe in first, a concentrated, well-organised defence in which every man must know how he is expected to play in relation to his team-mates. And secondly we believe in striking quickly from defence ... that is the basis of our football ... if I went to another club I wouldn't try to create another Ipswich. I would again study the players I had got and try to create another method. But I would still insist on speed out of defence on to attack – most managers these days would agree this is essential to beat concentrated, retreating defences.' Alf had the patience to start from scratch, knowing it was a far harder job at international level given the constraints of time and the fewer games played. He concluded pretty swiftly that he needed a certain kind of man in his team, a player who would accept Ramsey's supremacy without question and would do the job required of him. One player who did not seem to fit the bill was Johnny Haynes. For all that he'd praised Haynes' performances at Fulham – and Haynes was an absolute master when it came to distributing the ball accurately and imaginatively, traits that Alf always admired – he never pulled on the England shirt under Alf. He had missed the early internationals in 1962–63 following a serious accident, but by the time Alf took charge he was coming back to fitness. He'd flown out to Paris with the England party to watch that French defeat and, on the way home, his friends were calling for his recall, suggesting that after such a thrashing, England could not do without him. Never one to let anyone pick his side for him, maybe Alf wasn't going to give these critics the satisfaction of seeing him recall Haynes. More likely, Haynes was omitted for sound footballing reasons. Still not 30, although he returned to play beautifully for Fulham, some felt that he was never the same player again, not the influential figure around whom Winterbottom had built the side. Questions had been asked about his temperament following his disappointing World Cup in Chile, the more so since he had failed too in Sweden. These were harsh accusations – in 1958 he was drained by a long season in which Fulham had just missed promotion, while in 1962 he was not the only failure in a troubled series. Still, he'd had two opportunities on the world stage and had failed to deliver, so why should he take a third World Cup by storm? Some felt like *Rothmans*, that 'he sometimes seemed less than tolerant of those not so gifted', Brian Glanville observing in 1962 'a thin-skinned petulance about him which seemed to permeate the team'. This would have been the clincher. Alf wanted team men, those committed to the cause, selfless individuals willing to take responsibility. He knew he needed a player of Haynes' quality, but could not convince himself that the £100-a-week man was the answer.

Alf didn't only want good players – and pretty well every player he picked *was* a good player – he wanted players that would run themselves into the ground; winners, men who would do anything to save England from defeat. As Jimmy Armfield recalls, Alf was keen to show his men just what he wanted from them, right from the outset: 'Alf was a bit of a one-off, much stronger than people thought, very resilient; he knew the game, knew players. He had a great ability to read people. I don't think he liked frills, in spite of the fact that he was a sophisticated, ball-playing full-back himself. When we played Scotland in 1963, I gave a goal away. I could see him walking towards me at the end of the game, he didn't need to say anything! I said, "I know, I know." Alf said, "Don't do that again," meaning, if I did it again I wouldn't be playing any more. He understood that everybody made mistakes, you didn't do it on purpose, but he insisted that you had to learn from it. The cardinal sin was to do it again. There was never any doubt where you stood.' In that Scotland game, England lost to a team down to ten men, Caldow breaking a leg after just five minutes, *The Times* observing, 'England now were grave, uninspired, slow-thinking, pedestrian and ungainly . . . it was the artist against the stevedore.' Alf could scarcely be blamed for these deficiencies, but his anger in defeat was genuine enough. One well-meaning committee man approached him to say that at least we'd only lost to Scotland, that it wasn't a World Cup game or anything important. Fixing him with a cold stare, Alf is said to have replied, 'I'd sooner anybody beat us than the bloody Scots.' One of the selectors compounded this felony by telling *The Times*, 'Don't forget, we only lost 2–1.' Alf's reaction is not on the record, but it doesn't take much working out.

The new regime began in earnest on 8 May 1963, the first game after Alf's appointment became operative. The visitors were Brazil, World Champions. Changes were made in personnel, the most notable being the return of Ray Wilson at left-back: 'Fortunately I missed his first couple of games where they got beat, and Ron Henry and Gerry Byrne played. Talking to Alf, if either of them had had really good games, I might not have got back in. We had a chat later on and he didn't particularly like me, thought I was noisy, arrogant, a big mouth – he'd got that impression when I'd played against Ipswich so much in the Second Division. I don't think he liked my attitude, which was strange because I was fiercely competitive, that's for sure. But he did tell me he'd made a bad judgement personality-wise, and that was something I took on board, not judging somebody before you really know them. It was very different from Walter's time, you knew straight away who was running the shop. When we played Brazil, Huddersfield were playing on the Monday against Swansea, so I didn't get to London until late. I reported straight to the training field and Alf made a beeline for me, coming to meet me. He asked me what suited me, how I wanted to play, how I preferred to use the ball. He was just giving me enough rope because then he said, "You'll play like I want you to play," putting one over on me, which he'd do. I had a really good game that day and after that we never had any problems, we got on fine.' Interestingly, Wilson had barely played in the First Division, since, as he says, 'Players weren't allowed to go anywhere then. I was with Huddersfield, they were in the Second Division and that was it. Johnny Byrne played for England when he was at Crystal Palace in the Third!' Having won his first England cap with Southampton and others with Spurs while in Division Two, Alf knew that the issue was how you played your football, not where. Wilson played his football superbly. He'd started out in the game as an inside-forward and wing-half, which meant he was extremely quick and excellent on the overlap. His experience as an attacking player meant that not only could he spot opportunities to get forward himself, but he was equally adept at reading opponents' intentions and was quick to close them down, utterly decisive in the tackle. One look at Wilson at close quarters convinced Ramsey that here was a fundamental cog in the machine.

Even a weakened Brazil offered a stern test, but a 1–1 draw gave a hint that the side was responding to Alf's demands for defensive organization. He'd been good as his word when he promised he wouldn't recreate Ipswich with better players, but persisted with a conventional 4–2–4 line-up. Although England performed better at the back, they let themselves down when Brazil scored with a swerving Pepe free-kick that Alf had warned them about. Already he was stamping his absolute authority on the side, at pains to make it clear that, had they – and Banks in particular – paid heed to his instructions, they might now be celebrating a win over the South Americans. For all that, it was England's forward play that was lacking, *The Times* complaining, 'The English forwards gave the impression of people thumping their heads against a brick wall . . . when,

Sir Alf takes steps to ensure he is not misquoted (*Express Newspapers*).

(Left) Standing in the mist at Lilleshall, 1968; (Below) drinking Coke in the sun in Mexico, 1970 (both Popperfoto).

(*Above*) Attempting to rally the troups before extra-time against
West Germany, Leon 14 June 1970.

(*Below*) The beginning of the end – Colin Bell, Francis Lee and Sir Alf leave
the field after the West German defeat (*both Colorsport*).

(*Above*) Always happiest with his players, Alf concedes a goal during training at Roehampton, April 1971 (*Hulton Getty*); decidedly less at ease with the media, prior to that month's fixture against Greece (*below; Colorsport*).

(*Above*) The boys in blue, Les Cocker, left, and Harold Shepherdson, right (*Colorsport*);
(*Below*) In discussion with Derby's Roy McFarland, November 1972 (*Hulton Getty*).

Poland's goal at Wembley, scored by Domarski, 17 October 1973
(and subsequent tension on the bench; *inset*) that effectively signalled the end
for England's World Cup qualification hopes and of Sir Alf's reign (*both Colorsport*).

Relaxing at his local, Sir Alf's not bitter (*Express Newspapers*).

oh when, will they find the brainwork to make the vital openings where it matters, inside the penalty area?'

Some answers to that question seemed to be forthcoming on England's summer tour, where they visited Czechoslovakia, East Germany and Switzerland over a period of almost three weeks. Given the opportunity to work with his players at length, Alf didn't underestimate the importance of this trip, introducing a team doctor for the first time, Dr Alan Bass. As they embarked on the expedition, few expected fireworks but hoped Alf might be able to begin moulding a side. By early June, his reputation as a miracle worker seemed secure. The first opponents were Czechoslovakia, World Cup Finalists a year earlier. A far cry from the shambolic performances to date, England worked as a unit, *The Times* making the important point that it was a 'team victory which brings a happy start to their tour ... a well-planned win, tactically, with a retreating defence and a quick riposte in attack.' Ray Wilson agrees: 'We had a magnificent tour in 1963. We were a good side away from home, better equipped to play away. We never gave anything away. We did find attacking difficult at home, it was hard to break down sides who'd defend. But I'd have fancied us against anybody away from home because we got a fair amount of goals simply because we attacked quickly on the break.' Keen to ring the changes and give all his squad experience, Alf left out goalscorer Greaves and introduced Hunt for the match with the East Germans. Hunt obliged with a goal in a 2–1 win that was more comfortable than the scoreline suggested but which left Alf raging that 'our passing was erratic and careless'.

This passing game was vital, for it was used to unleash the wingers – Charlton and Terry Paine – who Alf saw as crucial in getting round the back of packed defences. Preparation was thorough too, Ray Wilson explaining that, 'There was always a lot of difficulty getting players together throughout the season, so the tours were important. You gel more when you're touring. Alf did manage to get us more time together – when Walter was manager lads might not be able to turn up until Tuesday for a Wednesday game. There was no time to work on tactics or anything like that then. But on that tour, we worked out some of the basics.' Enjoying this unexpected honeymoon with the press, Alf was also very approachable and let slip little nuggets of information on the tactics, as well as pointing out that he was concentrating some efforts on turning Bobby Charlton into the linchpin of the team, making him work harder in training and on free-kicks. Against the packed defences now routine in international football, creative free-kicks could be the difference between winning and losing. Alf saw Charlton as the focus of his side very early, even when he was still ploughing a furrow out on the left. All managers have their favourites, players who appeal to some instinct, prejudice or belief, and Bobby Charlton was clearly Alf's star, a player he indulged even when struggling to find his best form.

The tougher games behind them, the Swiss game in Basle became an end of term party. Having lost all three games in Chile – a feat they'd repeat in England in 1966 – there was no fear that England would crash to an embarrassing defeat, but the convincing nature of their win took everyone aback. Winning 8–1, Charlton scored a hat-trick, Johnny Byrne two, Bryan Douglas, Tony Kay and Jimmy Melia one each, in an effervescent performance. *The Times* was forced to concede that, 'The wisdom of using one's reserves at the right moment was shown clearly . . . here was an England side buoyant, full of confidence and on its tiptoes – looking to the future . . . a most unexpected tour has ended. May we hope that the tide which has been channelled so successfully will be continued next season and beyond to 1966 and the World Cup. But maybe that is too big a dream.'

Maybe Alf was carried along by that same wave of optimism. Within weeks, he had made it clear that, 'England will win the World Cup in 1966. We have the ability, strength, character and, perhaps above all, players with the right temperament. Such thoughts must be put to the public, and particularly to the players, so that confidence can be built up.' The importance of positive thinking is well documented, but to some, this was a step too far, as Ray Wilson recalls: 'If I have anything agin Alf, it was sitting in the house listening to him say, "We shall win the World Cup." I thought, "Christ, what do you want to say that for?" If you want to put pressure on players that's how! Obviously he knew something we didn't.' That pronouncement is one of Ramsey's most famous, and deserves consideration. It was a brave move. He knew it would be stored away in newspaper cuttings files, ready to be dusted off each time England faltered. If they should fail in 1966 – and few backed them to do well, let alone win it – it was tantamount to a suicide note. There were sensible reasons for the move, because he was trying to create a climate of confidence such as had existed at Ipswich. Games, especially important ones, were won as much off the field as on it. For too long, since November 1953, English football had laboured under a cloud of doom, the absurd over-confidence which had existed replaced by a trough of despondency, an unwillingness to believe that we could ever climb to the summit. That came down from the press and the terraces and could erode belief among the players. It was an attitude that had to be transformed, a mood to be dispelled.

Alf had been exhilarated by the quality of some of England's football. For all his apparently placid nature, beneath the façade he was very emotional, likely to get caught up in the joyous nature of England's play and react accordingly. He knew one good performance against a weak side did not constitute much, but it had pointed a way ahead, shown him that England had players who could compete with the best. Get them to a peak and get them to believe, and you had something. Like most successful managers, there was something of the con man in him. He had the precious ability to make players think that whatever he said, however outlandish it might sound, must be true. Where players at Liverpool or Derby believed implicitly in Shankly or Clough, the England boys followed Alf out of the respect he commanded as one of football's great thinkers. If he believed in the players, they should believe in themselves. And because Ramsey was no hyperbolist, because he was so reserved, his statements carried more weight. In years to come, Malcolm Allison would make similarly bizarre sounding statements, but they would be ignored, brushed aside as mere 'Malcolmisms', hot air designed to capture the headlines. Alf Ramsey, modest, sedate and thoughtful, only said things after careful consideration. He wasn't one to exaggerate. Whatever point he made must be worthy of attention. So for all the pressure he might be exerting on the team – though, in reality, the pressure was mainly on himself – he was boosting their morale. Henceforth, every time a man was selected for England, he could think, 'Alf must reckon I'm a World Cup winner.' To that could be added the caveat, 'This is a once-in-a-lifetime opportunity, don't mess it up.' The squad he assembled was a credit to the nation on and off the field.

It was as well that England performed so creditably, for there were aspects of the job that weren't so appealing. When in July players and managers were reporting back for duty at their clubs, Alf was left at home in Ipswich with little to do but think about the forthcoming itinerary, what matches he might watch, which players might break through. He suffered withdrawal symptoms from the day-to-day involvement in the game that he had enjoyed since 1946. He was at his happiest with the players out on the training field and suddenly that luxury was denied him. Jackie Milburn found him a pest at this stage, since he 'visited the ground regularly, which didn't really help'. With Milburn trying to stamp his authority on Ipswich, he didn't need Alf continuing to turn up and confusing the issue. The isolation remained the hardest thing for Alf to bear, an absence that made it all the more difficult for him to deal with the administrative irritations, the need to report to the International Committee on progress, the difficulty in forcing the FA to book the right kind of hotels at the right time; petty issues which preyed on his mind. Left to his own devices, Ramsey would fret (recall how his row with Bill Dodgin at Southampton festered while he was injured). Ironically, for one dismissed as aloof, he disliked solitude, as Alan Mullery, himself something of a loner, averred: 'I liked to go off and watch television on my own in the hotel lounge and often I would be startled to see Alf sitting silently beside me. He doesn't like to see anyone alone.' Instead of stewing in his own company, he wanted to be among colleagues, getting on with the job. Perhaps it was the fact that he was so divorced from a normal working pattern, had so much time to dwell on criticism, both perceived and real, that his relations with the press soured so badly.

There were three more wins in 1963 to take his record to six in a row. Wales were overcome 4–0 in Cardiff in an unimpressive game remarkable only for the controversy surrounding the non-selection of Johnny Haynes, who Alf had watched closely in the early games of the season – Eastham was finally preferred. Haynes was finished. In a Home International against a nation whose players were very familiar to him and his players, his pre-match practices were not allowed to slip, Gordon Banks writing that Alf 'analysed the Welsh team in such detail that I think we could have played them with our eyes shut and still have won'. The next fixture saw England beat a Rest of the World side 2–1, marking the centenary of the FA. With Haynes passed over again – a decision made easier by the good run of results – Alf chose to give Bobby Charlton an opportunity in a free role, coming through from deep. The *Guardian* reported that this was 'the finest display from England for many years . . . England played almost with greatness', although such praise was exaggerated. Although England defeated a side including Yashin, Schnellinger, Masopust, Kopa, Law, di Stéfano, Eusebio and Gento, with Seeler and Puskas coming on in the second half, they'd beaten great individuals, not a cohesive team. England were making progress, underlined in an 8–3 win over Northern Ireland, Wembley's first floodlit international. Not only were England winning, they were winning well, Greaves and Bobby Charlton scoring at will, the defence shielding Banks, who dealt confidently with anything thrown at him, Walter Winterbottom noting the influence that a great goalkeeper can have on a side: 'Gordon was a real goalkeeper. Unflappable. One of the best we ever had. Never worried about anything at all. If you have a good goalkeeper you can have confidence in your team.' Delighted by England's dismissal of the Northern Irish, Brian James of the *Daily Mail* wrote, 'The graph of progress that has marked England's past six games shows them climbing still . . . control in defence, the speed and decision in attack and the precision of passes that link both.' Billy Bingham joined the chorus of praise, arguing, 'We were beaten by the best team in Europe. England have now got a system and the players to suit it.' It was a system based largely on the use of gifted wingers, but a system nonetheless, Alf explaining, 'What appealed to me most was to see the development of understanding in the team. We built play up in our own half and then attacked quickly and directly from there.'

Alf's stock was high, perhaps as high as it ever would be. He'd inherited an apparently depressed and depressing side devoid of direction and had transformed it into a fast-moving, highly motivated outfit. This was unrealistically optimistic, but it was the accepted wisdom. In reality, Winterbottom had done much to change the English attitude to the game and had laid solid foundations. The disappointing results between Chile and England's summer tour had more to do with post-World Cup blues and the uncertainty over Winterbottom's successor. The upturn was in part due to Alf's methods and selections, partly because certain opponents were weak, and largely to do with the fact that appointing a new man anywhere tends to bring with it a breath of fresh motivation. Alf had made a promising beginning, no more, though as Jimmy Armfield says, 'The team was going through a bit of transition in '62 and by the end of '63 we had quite a good side together. Any manager is only as good as his players, and Alf was fortunate that we did have some good players of the right age maturing together in 1963 – Banks, Wilson, Moore, Greaves, Bobby Charlton.'

It's indicative of the tightrope that the England manager walks that following six excellent results, he was savaged after one failure. Fretting for five months between games, Alf took his side to Hampden Park in April needing only to draw to win the British International Championship. Using Hunt and Byrne up front, England misfired and lost to an Alan Gilzean goal, thereby sharing the tournament with Scotland and Northern Ireland. Few worried about that, but the *Guardian* wasn't alone in wondering if 1963's good form had been a mirage: 'The manner in which their attack ambled and blundered through the opening period and subsequently showed no indication of being capable of beating a well-organised Scottish defence was pathetic.' Exulting in victory, Celtic's chairman Bob Kelly let off a stinging volley of criticism aimed squarely at Ramsey, never a man who had endeared himself to the Scots, his calm self-possession the embodiment of all they loathe about the English. Attacking the control that Alf had over his players, he concluded, 'Ramsey pulls the strings and the players dance for him.' There was truth in this, but was it the negative approach that Kelly pretended? An international manager gets little time with his players. Not only is he getting to know them, often they're getting to know one another, for they can be drawn from seven, eight or, as in the game against Scotland, nine different club sides – this was certainly the case in the 1960s, when the available talent was spread more equally. Under those circumstances, players cannot combine with the instinctive naturalness that they would each Saturday: Charlton didn't have Law, Norman didn't have Mackay, Hunt didn't have St John. Those pairings knew one another inside out, knew precisely where they'd be, where a pass should go. For England, there was no such luxury – the right-wing combination of Armfield and Paine had managed just five competitive games together in ten months, so how could they create an understanding? After the Northern Irish win, it was 143 days before England would take the field again – little wonder momentum was lost. Any relationships established in November would have withered, attitudes changed by the different club disciplines. In such a situation, the only sensible answer is to impose a plan on your side, school them in it and hope that they can make it work. Over time, a team that starts from a framework can develop its own fluidity, its own sense of identity, but everything has to start somewhere, and few things look elegant in prototype.

So much for tactics. There was a streak of pragmatism behind Alf's insistence on players obeying him. Up to the 1950s and into the 1960s, football management was a comparatively secure job, certainly compared with today. It wasn't unusual for a manager to be at a club a decade or more, perhaps only leaving when it was time to pick up his pension. As the media became more strident, as supporters came to demand more, and as directors became hungry for money and glory, teams no longer existed to play football. They existed to win. It was up to the manager to produce the required results. Three or four lousy results and his job was under threat, so it was little wonder managers wanted to take as much control of team affairs as possible – I take the flak, you do as I tell you. Sport is unlike anything else, it's live, it's chancy. Other entertainers, actors or musicians, have a script to work with, songs to sing, but with sport, nothing is written down. There are ideas, thoughts, plans, but nothing concrete. Who then can blame a manager for wanting to write the script in advance? If his livelihood depends upon it, who can criticize him for putting his players in a straitjacket, seeking to reduce the element of risk or luck? If the team fails, the manager's the scapegoat. Why shouldn't he try to dominate the team, get them to do his will? After all, if Moore or Banks made costly errors, Alf might be out of work, but his successor would still select Moore and Banks. This climate of fear ushered in the era of dogma – if a manager was to take the rap, it had better be for his own mistakes rather than somebody else's.

Some suggest that as early as April 1964 and the Scotland game, Ramsey was looking to jettison the flair that had characterized his first year, but that's a superficial view which stems from the selection of Hunt ahead of Greaves. Hunt had been a success in Leipzig the previous summer, had had an excellent season for Liverpool and offered a different option, but few have viewed him rationally down the years, Alf's critics seeing Hunt as a symbol of all that was wrong with his teams, his appearance on the team-sheet proof that Ramsey prized sweat over skill. But how many poor players did Bill Shankly tolerate for long, how many mere artisans have managed 245 goals for a club in a ten-year career spent mostly at the highest level? Hunt was a top-class footballer, be in no doubt about it. If he didn't have Greaves' genius in front of goal – and who did? – he made up for it elsewhere, taking the pressure off his partner, making unselfish runs into space, showing himself for the ball, able to control it and make it stick, however poorly hit the pass. Hunt never hid, while others, including Greaves, did, as Walter Winterbottom confirms: 'Alf wanted determination – he was determined himself. The flamboyant players might have a good game and then occasionally just didn't want to know. Jimmy was sometimes like that, which was infuriating because someone of his skill, his quick movement, ability to nip in early on chances, ought never to have a poor game, but when he starts to hide and you can't find him, then that's bad for the side, and of course in those days, you weren't able to make a substitution. Alf wanted to be absolutely sure of the fellows that he had, that they would give their utmost.' To that can be added the question mark over Greaves' time in Italy. His comparative failure there had much to do with his inability to settle on a personal level, but it also made many wonder if he was quite the same force when faced with the tightly locked Continental, rather than the more accommodating domestic, defences. Greaves never won a Championship medal, leaving some to ask if his style hindered the team. The Greaves saga was to rumble on for years but one point bears consideration. While Greaves was scoring, Alf didn't leave him out of the side other than to give other players international experience, something he could not do by way of substitutions. At Hampden, for example, his preference for Hunt was an experiment – Hunt didn't become a regular for another twenty months and a seminal game in Madrid – and an early indication that in order to succeed, Alf felt he needed solid teamwork. It was not a shredding of the 4–2–4 formation that had served him so well through the six-game winning streak. After all, what sensible manager changes a winning formation unless he has to?

In spite of a workmanlike but scarcely inspiring 2–1 defeat of Uruguay at Wembley in May, the Scottish reverse looked like a blip. Nevertheless, Alf had to take some abuse for the failings of the England side, the *Daily Telegraph* recording that he and his side were 'booed and slow-clapped by a crowd whose patience had been tested beyond the limit by slow-motion football'. In a foretaste of what was to come, Alf complained of 'soul destroying football by Uruguay and [that] some of the England players did not feel they had been in a game'. The South Americans had nothing on their mind but defence and had frustrated England, who lacked the invention to overcome them, in spite of a forward line that included Charlton, Greaves, Paine and Johnny Byrne, who scored both goals. Some dismissed the performance as a bad day at the office, that England had been caught on the hop by the negative play of their opponents and would be better prepared next time, but others wondered if 4–2–4 was the way ahead. Much would be revealed by the summer tour that took in Portugal, Ireland, the USA and Brazil, where England would take part in a four-team 'Little World Cup' with the hosts, Argentina and Portugal.

The tour offered the chance to bring in new faces. This was particularly important to Alf, since it wasn't mere footballing ability that interested him. He liked the chance to assess a man's character, to see whether he would fit into the squad, to decide if he would run, run and run again for his colleagues and country. Ray Wilson's view is typical: 'He was loyal, honest and if his players were like that they were OK. He had a lot of players come in the squad at one time and another, some massive stars who will be so for all-time, but there was none who tried to run the shop, nobody who thought they were bigger than anybody else, and that has to be put down to Alf. He got people who would mix. If anybody wouldn't, they'd have a couple of times in the squad then disappear. There were no cliques, and I realized later that he was picking a team, not particular about whether they were the best players, but putting together guys who would have died for him.' Some changes were enforced – Armfield dropped out of the reckoning for a time through injury giving George Cohen the chance of a run in the side – others came naturally, Liverpool's winger Peter Thompson forcing himself into the side having taken the First Division by storm.

Following the Uruguay game, there was an opportunity for the squad to get together to do some general work before they embarked on their arduous schedule. However much players revere the chance of playing for England, if you bring them together in mid-May after a long, tiring season, there's going to be a desire to relax and let off steam. Ray Wilson recalls that, 'We broke the curfew, but it was pretty innocent. We met on the Thursday at Hendon Hall and came in in dribs and drabs, all coming from different parts of the country. We had the evening free and Bobby Moore said there was a guy he knew opening a new restaurant and we were invited down. Me, Bobby, Jimmy Greaves, Bobby Charlton, Gordon Banks, George Eastham and Johnny Byrne all went along. It was harmless, but looking back we should have gone and had a word with Alf before we went out and asked him if it was OK. We were only a bit late, an hour or something, nobody was drunk or anything like that. When we got back, our passports were lying on our beds so we knew that Alf knew we were late. He never did anything about it for a while, but he was very quiet the next day, so we knew we were in for something. After training a day or two later, when we were already in Estoril, he said, "You can all go now, except the seven of you who would like to see me." He pulled us all together and he did give us some stick, that's for sure. If he'd thought he'd had enough players, he said he'd have gone out to Lisbon without us and that was that, but that he couldn't do it, that we should learn a lesson. Then of course Johnny Byrne scored a hat-trick and we won in Lisbon, so we felt like saying, "Are we out next Thursday night, then, Alf?" But we didn't dare! He'd have been pleased with that!'

It was a pretty innocent night out but it became a turning point. It's overstating it to say that Alf was pleased that his men had broken the curfew, but it provided a golden opportunity to lay down the law, to show what would happen if anyone overstepped the mark in future. He was incensed that his authority had been flouted, but was clever enough not to fly off the handle. Having checked the rooms and found the players absent, it would have been easy, and tempting, to wait in the foyer and give them a rollocking there and then. That would have been chancy though. If the players had had a drink, someone might answer back, a small local difficulty might escalate, someone crucial to his plans might say something that could not be forgiven and rule themselves out. That would turn a minor row into a major incident, forcing Alf to explain to the press why, say, Bobby Moore had been thrown out of the squad. That would have had two massive consequences – England would have lost a great player but, more important, the nation would have been let down by its representatives while under Alf's watch, a stain on his reputation that would have been hard for him to bear. By registering his displeasure, the players knew they were in the wrong and the incident was kept under wraps. Letting the players stew also appealed. They had committed a terrible sin, they had failed their country. Let them worry for a day or two, let the magnitude of their mistake sink in. Keep them guessing, wait until they felt suitably contrite, then admonish them so that their overwhelming emotion would be one of relief that it was out of the way, not anger that their manager was treating them like children after an innocuous night out. After all, in Moore, Wilson, Greaves and Byrne, there were some forceful characters who could stand up for themselves, and Eastham had taken on the Football League in order to win freedom of contract. They weren't easily cowed, so timing was all. It was testimony to his gifts as a man manager that he got it right.

Alf was no fool. He wasn't going to sacrifice five world-class players, certain starters for 1966, just to impose discipline. How could he replace Banks, Moore, Wilson, Greaves and Charlton? If the five had been Waiters, Flowers, Milne, Wignall and Hinton, might they not have slipped quietly from the squad? His distaste for their antics was genuine, but he needed them in his team. That made his disciplinary measures all the more impressive, for they worked superbly, winning him yet greater loyalty from those he attacked, all grateful that he hadn't dumped them, aware they couldn't get away with it again. And, as Wilson points out, the reaction was positive, a 4–3 win with goals from miscreants Charlton and Byrne firmly putting the episode behind them, moving Brian James to comment that the display was, 'A vindication of all Ramsey believes . . . England were playing for more than mere victory. They were playing to tell Ramsey's critics that they too believe.' It seemed 4–2–4 was back on the rails, a feeling reinforced when the Irish were beaten 3–1 in Dublin. In America, Alf looked to settle a few old scores, Gordon Banks writing later that, 'Alf got quite worked up in his team talk before this game, played on a dustbowl of a pitch in New York. He told us how he had never been allowed to forget that he was one of the England team beaten 1–0 by the United States . . . he warned us against complacency and said we would not be allowed to live it down if we failed to win.' Those repeated comments down the years about the American defeat would have burned within Ramsey, adding steel to his character each time it was brought up. There would be no repeat of that fiasco. Hunt scored four as England registered a 10–0 win, their biggest victory since 1947, when a similar scoreline in Lisbon was run up by a team that included Swift, Wright, Franklin, Matthews, Mortensen, Lawton, Mannion and Finney – good company. Through his first year, Alf had weathered the inevitable setbacks and created an England team that was successful and often attractive. Looking over the eleven games since they had gone out to Czechoslovakia the previous year, England had ten wins and forty-seven goals, making the defeat in Scotland look all the more isolated.

The win in New York had been good for morale and had pleased Alf no end, his delight so great it allowed him to make the arch comment: 'I thought the Americans looked very good with the ball,' a backhanded compliment given that they had barely seen it in the ninety minutes. Logistically, though, the trip to New York turned their tour into a nightmare. George Cohen remembers: 'We flew from New York to Rio and played Brazil thirty-six hours later, which was the wrong thing to do. You don't get over flying at 45,000 feet in that time, you need to be there a week to get your bearings.'

Jet-lagged and exhausted they may have been, but Brazil were taking no chances against a team that had held them at Wembley a year before. According to Ray Wilson, 'We were sat in the dressing room for a couple of hours before they arrived. We were told that the kick-off was something like, say, 7.30, and at 9.30 they still hadn't arrived! If that had been after 1966, when his reputation was complete, I think he'd have called it off and we'd have gone home.' Perhaps it was anger that fuelled them, but England tore into the Brazilians once the game did eventually start, Johnny Byrne having a shot cleared off the line in the first minute. A minute after half-time, the score was 1–1, and Alf thought, 'We were beginning to stretch their defence and push the ball through. I felt we had a chance of victory.' But it was inevitable that England would wilt. 'It was a shame,' says Ray Wilson, 'because we'd played really well, but then Pelé came through strongly in the last half hour and they finished up winning 5–1. I was disappointed with the score because we didn't play that badly. In fact, when we got back to 1–1 I thought we'd cause some problems, but once they got a second and a third very quickly, we did collapse a little. We'd just flown from America, it was about three in the morning our time. I think we all fell asleep in the second half, because it was about five o'clock in the morning for us!' Alf was as thrilled by Pelé's astonishing ability as any, saying, 'One man did it all . . . what happened tonight is something you can't budget against,' but he recognized it was the kind of performance Pelé could turn on at will. You had to budget for that. He accepted that his players were not at their peak, and looked to mitigate the loss and repair morale by arguing that it was a freak result, but it was evidence that England needed to change. Brian James in the *Daily Mail* suggested that, 'England halted what is still the world's greatest team only to be finally humbled by the world's greatest player . . . in a cruder, more brittle manner, we borrowed enough of Brazil's system to persuade watchers we have learned most lessons.' Yet that was taking the wrong lesson. England had travelled to South America in imperious form, playing the 4–2–4 system and playing it well, only to be heavily beaten. The timing was unfortunate, perhaps. Had England played the Brazilians two or three days later, things might have been more even, but the Brazilians had done enough to illustrate that there was a gulf between the two nations, that if you tried to play Brazil at their own game, there would be only one outcome. Three of their goals came from remarkable free-kicks, things which Alf had warned the players about but which they were helpless to prevent. Who in England, Bobby Charlton apart, could emulate such devastating play? You could not go at Brazil head to head, because the English game – the northern European game – did not produce such footballers. If you were serious about beating them, you had to stop them from playing.

After that mauling, Alf knew the players were mentally and physically shattered, so he gave them a break. This was an interesting volte-face, since in New York he had had a disagreement with Moore over the amount of training the team were doing. Moore approached him on behalf of the side to complain they were being worked too hard, though he got pretty short shrift from the manager, Ray Wilson explaining that, 'Alf was open to suggestions, but I'm not sure he took a lot of notice of them! He'd listen, he'd put on his studious face to show he was taking it in, and then I don't think it would register! I can never remember him letting anybody make a choice for him, at any rate.' But he did recognize that some of the players were suffering, notably George Cohen, who played no further part: 'I remember being ill after the Brazil game. I saw Alan Bass and he took me for a walk, for some tea halfway up Sugar Loaf mountain, because I just couldn't play again, it was too much for me.' Five changes were made for the game against Portugal, which England drew 1–1, Roger Hunt scoring his seventh goal in five internationals.

The final game was against Argentina, who had already made a deep impression on the English party. They'd seen them 'tear Brazil to bits', according to Ray Wilson, playing a highly flexible 4–4–2 cum 5–3–2 formation (having played 4–2–4 against Portugal in their opening fixture). In that Brazil–Argentina game, the watching Englishmen almost found themselves at the centre of a riot, Johnny Byrne allegedly pointing out the fact that Brazil were losing to an already disgruntled section of the crowd. Alf had to lead them to a place of safety behind one of the goals, but not before he was struck in the small of the back by a half-eaten apple flung at him by a spectator. After the fireworks of his previous visits to South America, he wasn't keen on their manners, but this was nothing compared with the behaviour of the Argentine footballers, which stretched his patience almost to breaking point.

Having had so many options in their earlier games, Alf couldn't decide on the formation the Argentines would put out. Avoiding defeat would win the 'Little World Cup', so Alf was certain that they would not display much attacking intent. But how would they play? To salvage a much needed win, Ramsey put out what was the first-choice side, minus Cohen, but they never threatened a side mar-shalled by Antonio Rattín. Playing 4–3–3, described by most of the English press as a 'no-risks formation', Argentina strolled through the game. Ray Wilson remembers, 'They never came out of the penalty area. It was like playing Ipswich, we had the ball for 85 minutes and lost 1–0. I remember the game very well because Rattín refereed it. He was incredible. That game set Alf against them, but we did learn something from it. They were very physical, they were gangsters, really. Rattín was awesome, a big man, and he was every-where, sticking his nose in – if the ball was a foot away from where it should be for a free-kick he was in there, complaining. It was painful. It was a shame, because they were a good side.' Brian James was equally incensed: 'If you do not give a damn about the game and are prepared to leave entertainment to music halls you can win anything . . . Argentina have simply taken logic and pushed it to the limit. Their policy lays down that "if they do not score, we do not lose" . . . only in their wildest moments of heady recklessness were they prepared to open out.'

An England team that had arrived full of hope slunk away from Rio in disarray. The advances of the previous year were forgotten, Pyrrhic victories over similarly backward nations lacking in the sub-tleties required in international football. And despite complaints about Argentine cynicism, no one could pretend that they couldn't play, Brian James adding the coda: 'The question ceased to be whether England could get a goal. It became whether we could get the ball . . . [the players] have seen how they trail in their grasp of the game's basic skills, how their passing is accurate only to a yard when it must be precise to an inch.' Alf conceded 'there is still a tremendous gap between us and them but not a gap that can't be bridged', though he added the characteristically myopic, 'I thought we were much the better team.' Perhaps in terms of values, perhaps in terms of being the only team willing to play according to the Corinthian origins of Association Football, but not in terms of tech-nique nor organization. We were way behind.

That tour became a long, dark night of the soul for Ramsey. In hindsight, his first year as England boss looks an aberration, a time when he indulged himself, picking the best players rather than building a system. He'd used thirty-one different players in his first seventeen internationals, anathema to his avowed policy of conti-nuity. As Danny Blanchflower wrote in the *Sunday Express* '[He] might very well know what he's looking for, but it seems to me he certainly doesn't know how to find it.' It was a rebuke that wounded Alf – most criticism did – but it had a point. The encounters with Brazil and Argentina confirmed England weren't advancing. So low had Alf sunk that Ipswich reportedly offered him his old job back after they'd been relegated. But he was not going to give in without a fight. A sound beating can be the springboard towards success and Alf was no slouch when it came to learning from his own errors. Brazil had shown that, for individual flair, they were in a class of their own. That was fine. Alf accepted we could not compete with that, in the short term at least. What did come as a shock was finding we lagged behind the Argentines in terms of organizational disciplines, a traditional strength. Argentina became the bogey men, the team to be feared. In England, Alf felt Brazil would struggle simply because it is so difficult to take the game and culture of one continent on to another and win – England had suffered that in 1950. But Argentina had the flair of the Brazilians and the organization of the Germans, the best of both worlds. They would provide stern opposition indeed when one added into the equation their liking for physical confrontation.

The Football Association's *World Cup Report* of 1966 pinpointed the '64 tour as crucial to England's future. 'The experience gained by the players was of tremendous importance to them,' it declared. 'They had their first insight into the type of defensive football played by Argentina. It was their initiation to eight-man defence, and England lost that game, after having three-quarters of the play territorially, as a result of one defensive error.' If it taught the players something, it gave Alf a profound insight. He had seemed to believe that England's strength lay in its forward play. Argentina had shown that strengths were less important than weaknesses, that the successful teams camouflage them effectively and then turn them into strengths. As Brian James pointed out, if you don't let in a goal, you don't lose. And if you know you'll keep a clean sheet, it takes the pressure off your forwards, who need take just one chance to win. Alf concluded it was his job to eradicate errors from England's play.

He had already been at work on the defence – Banks, Cohen, Wilson and Moore were in place, with Norman equally strong. Looking at that backline, one wonders how it could be improved. And therein lay the answer. The back four and the goalkeeper weren't the problem, it was the players in front. With their 4–4–2 or 4–3–3, Argentina's defence could be augmented by two, three or four players from the midfield, giving a potential eight defenders. In England's 4–2–4 that was impossible. On the flanks Charlton and, in particular, Thompson weren't the kind of players who spent time tracking back. Their job was to get the ball and run with it. And the idea of asking Greaves or Byrne to come back deep into their own half was ludicrous. England's two midfielders were often Gordon Milne and George Eastham, though Eastham was more an inside-forward and thus stronger in attack than defence. Moore, an old right-half, might step up from defence to help out in midfield, but in making three in the middle, that would leave a hole at the back. Midfield was the powerhouse, the area for the playmaker. But if you had only two players in there, there was no room for a holding player, a Nobby Stiles. So who won the ball in the first place? 4–2–4 was fraught with problems, leaving you potentially outnumbered all over the field, suitable only for teams blessed with genius, as Brazil had been in 1958. And England weren't that lucky.

It was all very well putting eight past Switzerland and Northern Ireland, or four past Portugal, Wales and Czechoslovakia, but you were unlikely to meet them in the World Cup Final. Come 1966, the games that mattered would be won 1–0 or 2–1. And England weren't geared to getting those results, their game was too expansive. It meant changes in style and personnel, though quite what those would be remained unclear. Ironically, England's greatest, perhaps only, success of the 'Little World Cup' had been Peter Thompson, whose very presence as a winger was part of the problem: 'I got off to a fabulous start, we won 4–3 in Estoril and I got rave reviews. It was a change to play for Alf, he was such a quiet man, but you listened to every word he said. I was used to Bill Shankly, who used to rant and rave and scream and shout, and you'd ignore him, but Alf was the exact opposite in every way. In Brazil, I had a great series, they picked an XI from those four, which were perhaps the best four teams in the world, and I was in it, they were calling me the White Pelé! The start of the next season, I had four terrible games. Shankly had me in after that and said, "The White Pelé? You're more like the White Nellie!"' That inconsistency, the perennial criticism of individuals throughout the English game, was a failing Alf couldn't indulge, and yet Thompson had become his most potent attacking weapon. Finding the right balance would be the most pressing problem of the next two years.

But Alf accepted the time for change had come. With Armfield on the injured list, he needed to appoint a new captain, the leader who would take them through to the World Cup. For most, there was only one contender – Bobby Moore – but Alf continued to delay. Moore had incurred his wrath in May, and Alf was slow to forgive. The first international of the new season came in October 1964, with a visit to Belfast. Moore was selected and he and Alf had a long discussion about the captaincy. Alf made clear just what he wanted, the standards of behaviour he would expect from a man who was, after all, his representative on the field. As a former captain and as a great admirer of Billy Wright, he held strong opinions as to what a captain should be, ideals he should live up to, revolving around duty and loyalty. Ramsey remained unconvinced about Moore, and as Ken Jones notes, 'It was an odd relationship between them. In the beginning Bob and Jimmy Greaves were guilty of mickey taking. Alf knew it was going on behind his back.' That would be tough for him to take, for as Walter Winterbottom points out, 'He was exceedingly sensitive and found it difficult to accept any kind of personal remark.' He was being let down by men who, for all their gifts, he was doing a favour. Without him, they wouldn't get any England caps and would be nothing in the game. Alf was looking after the players far better than in the past, was regularly sticking his neck out, trying to make life more congenial for them – after the tour of 1964, he thanked the players for their efforts and then thanked the FA officials 'for having the good sense to keep out of our way', making his priorities very obvious. Perhaps this was intended as a joke, his stonefaced delivery leading people to take every word he said seriously, but even if it was supposed to be funny, it had businesslike undertones. To be repaid by being made the butt of childish humour wasn't good enough, nor was it just. To be fair to Moore and Greaves, there was no malice involved, it was schoolboy fun, mimicking a stern headmaster. But no matter, it was insubordinate, and Alf wondered it if revealed a lack of application. So strait-laced himself, so relentlessly devoted to football and to England, he found it hard to grasp that a player might be light-hearted in his spare moments but deadly serious once the game got under way. Jimmy Greaves revealed the gulf that existed between him and his manager, writing, 'It was much more cavalier, more fun with Walter, a more relaxed atmosphere . . . I had the same respect for Alf but the fun did go out of it.' Fun? When had Alf promised fun? A point he was to make most forcibly to Allan Clarke in 1969. Flying out to South America, five or six of the party were in high spirits according to Moore, one of whom was the newcomer Clarke. Alf asked him if he was enjoying himself. ' "Yes, Alf. Great, thank you," came Allan's reply, perhaps with the slight uncertainty of a new boy,' according to Moore. ' "You don't fucking enjoy yourself with me. Remember that," ' was the response. Alf saw playing for England as the pinnacle of a footballer's aspirations. They should be ready to do anything to achieve it, and if that meant doing as they were told then so be it. Alf allowed them to relax when he felt the time was right, so they should behave in an appropriately sober fashion at all other times.

He was willing to be persuaded that Moore could change his ways, for in the light of Jimmy Armfield's serious injury, it was clear that Moore was the only man to succeed him – his 'one of the boys' persona meant that he knew what the players were thinking, how they felt, their hopes and fears, emotions that Alf wanted to know all about. He made Moore sweat so that he wouldn't take the position for granted, but there's little evidence that he had anyone else in mind. For, in October 1964, who else was an apparent certainty for the World Cup? Greaves wasn't captaincy material, nor was Banks, marooned away from the play in goal. Cohen wasn't established, Wilson too feisty, Norman too reserved. Moore aside, Bobby Charlton was the only option. Alf was already looking at him as the heartbeat of the rejuvenated team, so he didn't want to saddle him with additional responsibility. Moore had to be the man, though perhaps too much was made of it all. Ray Wilson doesn't reckon 'a captain on the field is that important. I got on with my job, Jack was a talker, we all knew what we had to do. It's not cricket where the captain makes all the decisions. It's more an off-the-field job in football, liaising with players and manager, representing the club or the team. When I played, all the changes I can remember came from the sidelines, not the captain. If we had anything to say we'd talk it over with Bobby, and he'd go and see Alf, but that was generally things off the pitch.'

Like Alf, Moore wasn't stupid. He understood that 1966 offered an unparalleled opportunity for English footballers to carve their name in the annals of the game. Like Alf, Moore was an Essex lad, he'd grown up in Barking, on London's sprawling doorstep, knew what fame and fortune could bring. He was ambitious, he'd tasted the limelight with England and West Ham, and he wanted more. He wanted to be captain of England and was astute enough to recognize this was his chance. He would do whatever it took to convince his manager that he was the man. Eventually Moore was so on message that he was able to write this eulogy to Ramsey in his 1969 book *England! England!*: 'There is a message sewn with invisible stitching inside every England cap. It sears into the brain ... "just remember you are here to play for me, for England and to do as I say" ... the author of those words, which are a rule and a command, is, of course, Sir Alf Ramsey, the architect of England's fabulous re-built image.'

Moore and Greaves, another Dagenham product, were working-class boys made good, just as Alf was. But where Alf's youth had been spent in the service of his country and then in a professional game that paid little more than £10 or £12 each week, Moore and Greaves were well paid and with the freedom to move around as they wished – Greaves had been to play in Italy, with all its financial implications. Where in Alf's day players were seen and not heard, Moore and Greaves dwarfed their managers in terms of popularity. They were superstars, they had plenty of cash, they were accustomed to doing things in style, they enjoyed their privileged lifestyles. Ironically, it was also to their advantage that they could be themselves, play the cocky Cockneys and be further adored as ordinary, down-to-earth blokes, who liked a drink and a laugh. Alf must have seen some of his younger self in them, for he was a product of the same environment. He surely regretted that he couldn't be as easy going as them, that he hadn't had the same rewards, possessed such confidence at their age, simply because he was born at the wrong time. Alf was 'Basildon man' in terms of ambition though not with the flash, loadsamoney connotations of today, whereas the likes of Greaves and Terry Venables were more that way inclined. There had to be a certain, unspoken, tension between the two camps, simply because they couldn't understand one another's viewpoint. Alf had served his country in the war and took his patriotism seriously, whereas some youngsters seemed to see playing for England as little more than a personal stepping stone. The class system was starting to open up too. After The Beatles and Michael Caine's success in *Alfie*, accents were no longer a hindrance but a positive advantage, and Greaves made the most of that. It was the first evidence of a generation gap between himself and his players that would cause problems. For the present, however, Moore, though always remaining friends with Greaves, did rein in his playboy instincts and became detached from the pack, Alf's ideal captain.

Rebuilding began in Belfast, but Alf had to move gradually. His side lined up as 4–2–4, but now Charlton had moved into Eastham's slot as midfielder-cum-inside-forward and Terry Paine on the right wing could play a withdrawn role in the Leadbetter mould. It wasn't 4–3–3, but it was a step in that direction. England won 4–3 but played poorly. In a veiled reference to unrest in the camp, the *Mail* noted that 'ninety minutes of shambles in Belfast ought to be enough to end the eighteen-month reign of amiable Alfred. England's team manager should and must feel angry enough to become Ruthless Ramsey . . . a more depressing performance than any beating of recent years.' England had been four up at half-time and Alf was furious with the slipshod performance in the second period. At the end of the game, he launched into the team, asking, 'If you can't cope when you are four goals in the lead what's going to happen when you are a goal down?' Such outbursts remained rare, for he believed them to be counter-productive, producing resentment rather than *rapprochement.* George Cohen says, 'Alf was very quiet, to the point. Coaches – in business not just in football – often strike up a different tone to their voice, they lecture you, but Alf didn't, he'd just have a conversation, make suggestions.'

The greatest benefit of ridding himself of the selection committee was that it allowed him to develop a squad, to maintain continuity in the face of bad performances. After the Northern Ireland game, the committee would have reconstructed the defence, but Alf kept faith. When rebuilding a team any sensible manager starts with the back line, which only improves by playing together, so Alf gave them every opportunity. For all that, England's next international against Belgium was an eye-opener. Played at Wembley, England got a 2–2 draw but, as Peter Thompson remembers, 'They absolutely murdered us. It had a real effect on Bill Shankly. He said, "I've never seen a team play like that in my life." Ten of that side played for Anderlecht and we were playing them a couple of weeks later in the European Cup. Before the game he got us all together and he called them rubbish. He said, "Thommo played like a genius against them, they couldn't stop him." I hadn't had a bloody kick, but I started to think maybe I hadn't done so bad! The captain wore glasses held on with rubber bands, so Shanks said, "The best player's a blind man, if it rains he won't see you, we'll win 3–0." That was how Shankly motivated players, where Alf would just say that if we played to our best we would beat anybody. Everyone really respected his tactics, where Shankly left that to Bob Paisley a bit. Shanks was a great motivator but I wanted to play for Alf just as much as I did for Bill Shankly.' Again, though, England looked out of their depth tactically, and according to Tommy Smith it was Liverpool that showed the way ahead: 'Shanks was a bit apprehensive and that's when I started sweeping up, but I had number ten on my back to kid Anderlecht. Shanks wanted me as "Ronnie Yeats' right leg". That was the start of the solid back four in this country. It wasn't until later that Alf Ramsey, who I've a lot of respect for, started to put that together. Bill Shankly was the first to go for a 4–4–2.'

Certainly the Liverpool line of Lawler, Byrne, Yeats and Smith was a solid unit, but England themselves were just months away from the same style. Alf struggled through a couple of internationals, his team decimated by club calls that made it hard for him to build as he wished, before arriving at a get-together in February 1965. Even then, the likes of Bobby Charlton, Venables, Milne, Thompson and Banks had to cry off because their clubs wanted them in training prior to Cup-ties on the Saturday. Although it was hugely frustrating to lose so many of his leading footballers, it allowed Ramsey to get to know a few of the lesser lights and to experiment with a full trial game against the Under-23 side. Alf unleashed a 4–3–3 and was delighted with the results.

In April when England fought out a 2–2 draw with Scotland to win the Home International series, Ray Wilson, having missed four matches, was back in the fold: 'I got a horrendous injury in my third game with Everton in August 1964. I tore the muscles in my groin off the bone, and I got to the stage where I thought I wouldn't play again. It was weeks and weeks getting worse before they sent me for X-rays and found the bone was calcifying inside the muscle. By the time I got back against Scotland the team had changed completely. One to six was: Banks, Cohen, Wilson, Stiles, Jack Charlton, Moore. That was Alf's system coming together. You have to be sound to win anything and the longer you play together, the easier it gets. People talk about full-backs playing well together, but now you don't have anything to do with one another, you're so far away. Later on I played with Martin Peters in front (he was very good defensively) and big Jack alongside, and we were both mouthy players. It's very important that players talk, and we had it down to a fine art. We never broke, we used to keep the back four solid. We'd never tackle unless they were getting near the penalty area, we backed off, and the other lads just put people under pressure to the stage where it became more and more difficult for them to squeeze a ball through. If the defender goes in then, you've a chance, where if one of the four tackles just inside your own half and misses, it's mayhem, because one of the others has to come and cover. That creates spaces somewhere else and it's like knocking dominoes down. But we wouldn't break, and because we'd been together for a while, it became solid, natural. That's the basis of any side – not necessarily for the most entertaining side, but if you're looking to win things, it's pretty important. Newcastle were wonderful under Kevin Keegan but they finished up with nothing because they weren't solid at the back. It was another change from Walter's day. I do think Walter felt England ought to play good football, whereas by then Alf just wanted to win.'

The sudden arrival of Stiles and Charlton raised eyebrows, but it was the greatest single step forward to winning the World Cup. What committee would have selected them? This was Alf at his very best, understanding the importance of team building over the merits of the individual. Stiles was too easily dismissed as a little terrier, snapping at forwards' heels but with nothing creative to offer. Anchoring the midfield, Stiles was not a direct replacement for Gordon Milne, who previously wore the number 4 shirt, for Milne was of a more attacking bent. Instead, Stiles' arrival showed that Alf wanted a greater degree of solidity in his midfield. His productive club partnership with Bobby Charlton was important too, notice that Charlton would soon be given the freedom to roam. Bobby's older brother Jack was deemed too old at 30 to be making an international debut – he'd only just got into the First Division with Leeds, ending as a Championship runner-up in his first season there – but with Maurice Norman reverting to a full-back role at Spurs, Alf needed a full-time centre-half, one who would not be overawed by the challenge of 1966. Most observers felt their elevation to the team was evidence that Alf was desperate, hoping for a miracle. It was nothing of the kind. He had found the blend. He had his defence in shape and he'd done it by reverting to basic principles of hard work, as George Cohen points out: 'After that 1964 tour, I think he was trying to form a defence. Elsewhere he had Bobby Charlton, of course, and Roger was always going to be around because he was the sort of player Alf liked. He got people he knew he could trust, people who knew the game lasted ninety minutes, whatever the score. He liked players who'd take a bad knock but still get up and play, the player who was absolutely knackered but would draw himself up for the next run. He could see through a person's character, which gave him a big edge on lots of other managers. He could see those who hadn't got the ability or the application he was looking for. He knew those who'd tackle back, who wouldn't shirk, who'd do what he wanted from a player.' That was underlined in Belgrade, when another pivotal figure was introduced, young Alan Ball of Blackpool, Alf assuring him that, 'This is the first of ten caps you'll get for England and by that time we'll know how good you are.' The *Guardian* praised a 'magnificent performance by England's defence' in a 1–1 draw, but the building blocks were slowly being cemented into place across the team. Banks was his goalkeeper. The back four was secure. Nobby Stiles was in the holding role. Alan Ball was making his way as possibly the most important player in the side, one who made it finally possible for England to play 4–3–3 with confidence, a man who could do creative and defensive work in midfield, could double as a winger, would run himself daft for an England cap. That left the forwards, the problem area, not helped by the absence of many Liverpool and Manchester United players from the 1965 tour to Yugoslavia, West Germany and Sweden, robbing Alf of Bobby Charlton, Roger Hunt and Peter Thompson. Thompson, though, was beginning to fade out of the picture, as he admits: 'I was an individualist at Liverpool. Shanks wanted me to get down the wing, to beat the full-backs, to keep the Kop happy, but I was never as comfortable playing with Alf. I did get off to a good start, my first half a dozen matches I was always getting great reviews, and it looked like I'd play sixty or seventy times for England, but it went a bit sour. I wasn't doing that well, I wasn't sure of a place, my sixteen caps came over six years, so it was a bit in and out.' This was further evidence that individuals had no place in Alf's side if they could not conform to the plan he was evolving. He had come to believe that the only way England could win was by fastidious preparation, having a set way of playing so that each individual knew his job, and a novel tactical method that might catch opponents unawares. You could either accept that, or call it a day, as Jimmy Armfield remembers: 'Tactically, he was astute. He believed in the basics, making the best of what he had. When he first talked of 4–3–3, a lot weren't too sure, including some of the players. My attitude was to see what happened first. We got into a rhythm with it and handled it well, because prior to that we'd had 4–2–4 with two wide men, but Alf thought we had to move on and you had to move with him. It helped that we all liked him and trusted him. I know he wasn't everybody's cup of tea, he'd never have got a job in PR, but he stood up for his players, and we liked him for that.' Bobby Moore agreed with the assessment, writing, 'He was always at his happiest in the company of his players, his own people. Left alone with us, he could relax, share in the jokes. He always bought the drinks.'

4–3–3 made its bow in Nuremberg. Stiles was absent and replaced by Ron Flowers, but the basic pattern remained. Ball was in midfield with Flowers, Mick Jones of Leeds got a game up front with Eastham, Temple and Paine alternated between orthodox wing play and a deeper role supporting the midfield. It was a makeshift side, but England won with plenty to spare, the 1–0 scoreline hardly doing justice to their dominance. Albert Barham of the *Guardian* reported that 'Their defence has served them splendidly and surely here Mr A. E. Ramsey's World Cup problems are all but solved . . . there seems a long way to go before Helmut Schoen gets a World Cup team together.' Once Sweden had been beaten 2–1, Stiles returning from club duty, the press were uniform in their approval, Barham's report summing up the feeling: 'How refreshing this tour has been with many World Cup team questions seemingly answered.' Few seemed to have noticed England's new system, testimony to the methodical manner in which it was introduced. Alf had taken a year to implement it, doing a lot of work on the training fields of Lilleshall. This dramatic switch proved conclusively that he was not the inflexible dogmatist, and that he wasn't always as sure of himself as he seemed. He was wise enough to adapt. The only worry came via Alan Ball, a fixture in the side. Playing in an Under-23 game in Vienna in June, he was sent off for dissent. Alf waited until the day after the game, then, 'He took me aside and talked to me like a father. "Look here, lad," he said. "You're going to have to face up to a lot more problems like this, especially if you want to keep on playing in international competition against the Continentals. And there's only one way you can win. Sometimes, it's true, decisions are bad decisions – but you must learn to accept them."' If England had one trump card over the Argentineans, Alf felt it would be their refusal to get involved the way Rattín had done in Brazil. Ball would be an important member of the side, but an asset could quickly become a liability if he were to be dismissed in a World Cup match.

Alf was now satisfied that a version of 4–3–3 gave England the best chance of winning the World Cup – even the scorelines, 1–1, 1–0, 2–1, were right. He was delighted to see that no one had yet picked up on it in the media and was keen to keep it under wraps and retain the same element of surprise that had made Spurs and

Ipswich so dangerous. The next few results were mixed – England drew 0–0 in Cardiff and beat Northern Ireland 2–1 at Wembley, but in between they slumped to a disappointing 3–2 defeat at home to Austria. The press reaction was predictably shrill, the progress of the summer forgotten. Against Wales, Eric Todd of the *Guardian* had questioned Bobby Charlton's role: 'What R. Charlton's part in the plan of campaign – if any – was supposed to be, I have no idea. Link man? More like a member of a chain gang.' Todd's colleague, Albert Barham, was even more dismissive of the Austrian defeat, claiming, 'On last night's performance they would never have qualified [for the World Cup].' Alf was able to take these criticisms more philosophically than before. He had the backbone of the side in mind. The trick now was to find attacking momentum. Bobby Charlton was not used to the central role as yet and would take time to find his feet. Alf indulged him for he knew that he would be central to the campaign, offering the kind of creativity that had been absent since the days of Haynes, but in a different fashion. But Greaves' form had dipped alarmingly, though it was later revealed this was because of a bout of jaundice. That was cause for concern, for it meant there was a real chance he might miss out on the World Cup. The options up front weren't great – Hunt was a possibility, but no one else had revealed themselves to be a natural goalscorer in the Greaves mould. With 4–3–3 though, the responsibility for scoring goals could be shared around the side a little more – Bobby Charlton might burst through, for example. Alf was relaxed about England's chances in 1966. The only worry was that others might lack that conviction. It was time to show the world just how good England were.

12 Brain First, then Hard Work

The early results in 1965–66 dented public confidence in Ramsey. But the manager was happy enough. It was what England did in July 1966 that would determine his success and failure – the Jules Rimet trophy wasn't awarded for performances in October 1965. And the team was coming together. He had eight names in the forefront of his mind – Banks, Cohen, Wilson, Stiles, Jack Charlton, Moore, Ball, Bobby Charlton. The problem was one of formation and attacking personnel. Alf's planning had been complicated by Greaves' illness, though if he made a full recovery, he'd be in the side. Where the uncertainty lay was in Greaves' strike partner, and a winger. Ramsey had concluded he wanted a 4–3–3 formation. He needed to give it a further trial, to help familiarize his players with the system and to find the final playing pieces.

England played in Madrid on 8 December, against a Spanish side that had qualified for the finals by defeating the Republic of Ireland in a two-team group. They were strong opposition and would offer a stiff test. Or so it was thought. In fact, England registered their first victory in Spain with the easiest of wins, 2–0 barely telling the story. 'We absolutely toyed with them because of the system,' recalls Ray Wilson. 'Their full-backs didn't know who to mark, they were standing there, ball watching, and we ripped them to bits.' Ramsey employed his first-choice defence and a midfield of Stiles, Ball and Bobby Charlton bursting through from deep, shuttling from one penalty area to the other. Up front, Hunt, Eastham and Joe Baker worked well together, Baker giving England the lead early on before injury forced his departure after twenty-five minutes. He was replaced by Norman Hunter; Hunter slotting into midfield, releasing Bobby Charlton and Ball to help the attack. The *Guardian*'s Albert Barham caught the mood, writing 'that's much more like it England', while Jack Charlton argued England could have won 6–0. Harold Shepherdson wrote, '[Alf] had gradually built the formation up to 4–3–3 [and] exposed it in blinding, brilliant fashion before the world's most critical observers in Madrid.' For once, no one was getting carried away. England looked world beaters. Although the personnel wasn't right – Hunt had run himself ragged and scored the important second goal, but Eastham had been less impressive – the system was sound.

Alf then cloaked the system in secrecy, reverting to a more traditional formation for an ungainly draw with Poland in Liverpool in January. When that was followed by an equally drab game with West Germany the following month – England won 1–0 at Wembley with a goal from Nobby Stiles – the knives were out again, the balmy days in Spain forgotten. The *Guardian* complained Bobby Charlton was wasted and unhappy and that 'imagination itself is fearful of what will happen to England if they produce this apology for football in the World Cup . . . a travesty of football as once we knew it . . . one of the most painful nights I have spent watching England.' Ray Wilson accepts that people were finding it hard to come to terms with England's evolving style, adding, 'I can understand there being some opposition because it was a different type of game and we played best away from home. And we had a few northern lads in the team, which didn't help in London!' The crowd were unimpressed, booing the team from the field, but, again, Alf took the appropriate lesson, telling his players that, should they turn in a similar performance and win the World Cup with it, those who complained now would soon be turning cartwheels. The German game was significant. Not only did England beat a highly organized side, they'd never been under threat – that was important, for a home defeat would be psychologically damaging. Fortress Wembley remained intact. George Cohen points out, 'Alf knew the opposing team very well. He never sent you into a game without knowing them, which is why we conceded so few. He'd put it over very calmly. He was forceful in that he'd accentuate points he particularly wanted to make, but he was never over the top, which we appreciated. We were treated like adults, made to realize there would be disciplinary measures taken against those who didn't act the right way on and off the field.'

Any new player coming into the side came under scrutiny, but that was particularly the case with the forwards. The rest of the side was settled but there was concern about Alf's policy up front. Geoff Hurst was given a try and was quickly welcomed into the fold: 'Alf was always at the hotel to meet you, said "Thank you for coming" when you arrived and when you left, he was always pretty formal, very polite. I got my first cap against West Germany, although Nobby wore number 9 and scored, but he didn't play centre-forward. That was just Alf trying to confuse everybody.' Hurst's arrival was a godsend. He and Hunt looked the part alongside one another, Hurst giving England the chance to vary their play, knocking in high balls to make use of his power in the air, as well as the through balls they'd been trying to give Greaves and Hunt. Although both got their fair share of goals, that was not the be-all and end-all of their game, as it was for a natural finisher like Greaves. Instead, they had to offer other attributes to justify their selection and were unselfish as a result, creating space, tracking back, hurrying defenders, making runs off the ball, laying the ball off for midfielders. Despite scoring once, England seemed to have promise in attack to go with the cast-iron defence. But this was not enough for most observers, who demanded that England look to play a more open, aggressive game. The side went to Hampden in April and beat Scotland 4–3, even Denis Law admitting that the score flattered the Scots. The press were thrilled, Albert Barham in the *Guardian* reporting that it was a joy 'to see two no-nonsense inside-forwards, two outside forwards moving far and wide objectively and R Charlton his usual, happy, thoroughly efficient self.' England were a far more potent attacking threat in that style, but look at the goals against. For all that Scotland tried harder to beat England than any other nation, they were not a great team and would not be at the World Cup, yet they'd managed to put three past Banks. That was the telling statistic, not the four England scored. If the Scots had found gaps, what would Argentina do? And their finishing was far superior. Not even the most blinkered optimist would expect England to score four against Argentina, whatever their formation. In going for goals, England's balance was fatally disrupted, the defensive capabilities of the midfield undermined. This win proved once and for all that 4–2–4 would be of no help to England in a World Cup that would be won by the side that conceded fewest rather than scored the most. Still the doubters complained: the object of the exercise was to score goals, wasn't it? That was indisputable, but it ignored the fact that a 1–0 win was as valuable as a 5–4. If you shut out the opposition you'd come out with at least a draw where, in looking to score five goals and taking risks at the back, you could lose 6–3. Winners get the prizes even if the entertainers get the glory. Alf, a quiet, modest, self-effacing individual, wasn't interested in glory. He was interested in putting the record books straight.

The World Cup was just weeks away and for all that tactics were resolved, personalities weren't. Since the 'Little World Cup' Alf had been looking for character as much as talent. Stiles and Jack Charlton came in, Ball made his mark and Hunt had established himself. Hurst was ready to gatecrash the party in case of Greaves' continued absence, but there were a couple of places up for grabs. The midfield was not yet cast in stone, particularly as Alf appeared uncertain whether or not to give the place to a conventional winger such as Paine or Connelly, or an old fashioned wing-half. That was underlined when Yugoslavia came to Wembley and Ramsey selected both Paine and another debutant, Martin Peters. Peters, soon to be lumbered with the tag 'ten years ahead of his time', was a modern footballer, as were Hurst and Moore. This was a significant development, one which can be laid at the door of Walter Winterbottom, who had overhauled an outdated mentality: 'We were getting senior players to become coaches and they were starting to get into management, people like Ron Greenwood for instance, and this meant that players were more aware of that side of things and ready to accept coaching. There had been a feeling that a man was born with skill and didn't need coaching, they'd deny the value of coaching, but this was starting to change. That in turn helped Alf with the England side. Coaching had been denied its proper place in the game for far too long.' Where footballers had seen themselves as having one primary role – I defend, number eight creates, number nine scores – Peters and his ilk were multipurpose footballers, and Ball was in the same mould. Tactically disciplined, they were able to use their intelligence, defending when necessary but breaking forward to support the forwards when possible. And for all that Peters was a quiet man, reticent and reserved, he was another determinedly ambitious character, committed to making the most of his talents. Few paid much attention to his elevation against Yugoslavia, seeing it as match practice for a squad member, but Ramsey had more in mind for him than that, a point reinforced when Peters came close to scoring on several occasions. This was his trump card. A good reader of the game, he could spot opportunities early, and had the priceless ability to ghost into the penalty area from deep, arriving unmarked and able to nick vital goals. At five feet eleven inches, he was strong in the air too, giving England an additional threat at the far post if Ball could produce crosses from the right. At a time when Alf had decided that the goalscoring onus should not be placed solely on the front two or three, Peters' arrival was extremely timely.

One of the changes had been the concentration on players from a few clubs. When England lost to Scotland back in 1964, nine clubs were represented. Now, the first team might see six or seven sides involved. It was still a good number, but it disguised the use of club relationships in key areas. In the midfield there was a Manchester United combination, Nobby Stiles tackling, foraging, winning the ball and then instinctively feeding Bobby Charlton, knocking simple balls into areas where Charlton wanted it. Now, with Peters and Hurst coming into the team, there was a West Ham link too, building from Moore at the back – the value of that combination would be obvious before the summer was through. Those combinations aside, Alf was trying to create club familiarity, as Winterbottom notes: 'Alf's main achievement was realizing the impossibility of building a side out of a team as they do in Brazil or Italy – in 1982, Italy had eleven out of their twenty-two from Juventus, building solidarity from a club. This allows the players to have instinctive awareness of what each one may do in any situation. Alf understood he could not do that because no England manager can – leaving aside any Continentals, our League teams are servicing five nations. It isn't feasible to get the unity you require from a group like that, and so Alf was quite right in insisting on achieving it by virtue of a settled England squad and side. He also realized that the way our clubs played was not the way England needed to play, and so he couldn't draw on a particular team's style, couldn't play like Tottenham or Manchester United; he had to develop an England form of play.'

With the Yugoslavia game and a 2–0 win behind them, England's players adjourned for a month before reconvening at Lilleshall on 6 June – it must have amused Alf that his final preparations would begin on the anniversary of D-Day. He approached Lilleshall confident that progress had been made, sure of the players that would take England to victory, convinced that 4–3–3 was the way forward. Even his striking problems seemed to be resolving themselves with the successful, goalscoring return of Greaves in the Yugoslavia game. England would never have a better chance of winning the World Cup than this, a belief he impressed on the twenty-seven players who arrived there. He pointed out that the next two months would require utter dedication, but that the rewards would make any sacrifices worthwhile. Finally, he added, 'Gentlemen, if anybody gets the idea of popping out for a pint, and I find out, he is finished with this squad for ever.' There would be no second chances. Ray Wilson didn't think he was bluffing: 'He was his own man. I wouldn't have liked to have crossed him, I wouldn't have liked to have made fun of him. He had this thing where he kept a barrier up between us. That dropped occasionally when he'd had a drink or two, if the game had gone well and he'd come down to our level. But you knew who was in charge.'

Again, it was a function of the characters he had on board that there was no problem. George Cohen admits, 'Lilleshall was worse than a POW camp, it only needed a moat! It was a long way to the nearest pub, so nobody bothered. We had everything there, we knew we were there for a purpose, it was a momentous thing, nobody was under any illusions as to how important it was and everyone reacted in the correct way. I'd had a very serious knee injury towards the end of the season so that interrupted my momentum and I believe I didn't have a great World Cup because of it. So I had to train hard under Les Cocker and Harold Shepherdson, they worked me like mad after training. I loved training, but when it was over I could barely stand! But I understood the value of it, and I respond to discipline anyway, so I didn't mind. You have to accept that young people are going to look for fun of some kind, but the idea was that while you were with Alf and the squad you were expected to behave like adults. Alf thought, "Surely I'm not asking too much?" and he was absolutely right. His view was: They've got the rest of their lives to do what they want; for the course of their England careers, they should do the right thing.' Younger members of the set-up, such as Geoff Hurst, agree: 'It's difficult to be away under Alf's strict disciplines for a month but, personally, I came into the side late and I was more concerned about doing myself justice to look too far beyond that. It was still twenty-seven players at Lilleshall and I wanted to make it to the twenty-two, so I didn't see it as a problem, it was a great adventure – if he'd said six months at Lilleshall, I'd have been happy. It's not a hardship when you're on the verge of the World Cup at home. Alf had worked out the right characters who would cope with it. We didn't have players who questioned Alf or the circumstances. Alf had the knack of easing out those players whom he felt might have been detrimental to the party; anyone he felt wouldn't have operated properly under those conditions was removed.'

Lilleshall was a period of sustained hard work. The squad was divided into four training groups run by Ramsey, Shepherdson, Cocker and Wilf McGuinness. George Cohen remembers, 'There was always fun and games in the five-a-sides and Alf would always, always join in. He liked nothing more than a kickaround with the guys.' The days were regimented, players occupied from nine in the morning to nine in the evening – breakfast together, followed by training, then lunch followed by recreational games, afternoon tea, dinner, a film and bed. Keeping the players locked away from the outside world, Alf needed to keep them busy all the time, though as Ray Wilson points out, he needn't have worried: 'Players didn't get into trouble in those days, because that's how people were, and we didn't have the money to throw around that they do today. We used to get £2 a day expenses! If you think about it now, the lads that didn't make the twenty-two went through thirty days of hard work for nothing in terms of money. Then, if you were in the final squad and didn't play, you didn't get paid. We got a bonus of £22,000 when we won it and it was going to be something like £1500 if you played and £500 if you didn't, but we decided to share it equally. There was a good team spirit, but there was at club level as well then. How many clubs are there now with six or seven lads who've been there for ten years? When I went to Everton there were lots of lads who'd been there all their lives, because there was no point going anywhere else, the wages were the same and Everton were a top club. You don't get that now, so it's very difficult to get that sort of bonding.'

At Lilleshall the players were forced to pound away on the playing fields to reach a peak of fitness. They were mentally pummelled into shape, forced to accept without question the disciplines and strictures of the team plan. As Ray Wilson explains, 'Being at Lilleshall was like doing National Service again! It was gruelling, but it was good. The way we played, we did work hard. The spell at Lilleshall was pretty fearsome, and that was after a League season. That's why we were so good at competing, we were fitter than most teams. Whether we used to bore them to death, I don't know, but in the last half hour we'd generally overcome most sides. Alf set his stall out to do what he wanted, we were in the middle of nowhere, and we either got on with each other or not. There was a lot of sense in it, much better than being in the centre of London. It was essential that we had to be fit and ready. We really worked hard. By the end, we were looking forward to the tour. It was so boring, twenty-seven virile men in their twenties, and the only enjoyment they get is playing tennis! And we must have seen about three million films at Lilleshall. People think it's a glamorous life playing football for your country, but it really is boring! So is the touring. People say to me, "You've been all round the world, Ray." But I've been nowhere – you get on a plane, get on a bus, go to your hotel, get on a bus, go to the ground, play, come home! 1962 in Peru made Lilleshall look wonderful. All the mountains around us, just a little tin mining village in the middle of the Andes, but there was nothing to do, we couldn't go anywhere, you can't walk around for hours on end looking at the sights because it wears you out. We just got sent down to the grounds to play the games. We ended up watching French films with Spanish subtitles!'

Clearly, there was no room for prima donnas, individuals, those not prepared to toe the line. The squad became something akin to an Army unit, Jimmy Armfield remembers, 'I had a bad injury in 1964 and when I was fit again Alf brought me back into the squad for '66, so he was loyal to us. The unit stayed intact for a long period and I think that was one of the secrets.' Jack Charlton has writtten that, 'Ideas had to come from Alf, you couldn't suggest anything. We had ploys, Nobby would shout something to me, next day Alf would come along and we'd try it out.' This was partly because of Alf's sensitivity to questioning but largely a matter of discipline. Nothing should undermine the manager's supremacy, none could question his tactics – what would he have done with Cruyff and Neeskens or Gullit and van Basten? Discipline was all, but as Peter Thompson explains: 'The players idolized him, listened to every word he said. They respected him and that was enough motivation for anybody. Back-room people are always important. Alf would go out training, but Les was the trainer, Harold was on the coaching side. They had a very important part to play, but the decisions, the tactics, that was all Alf. That was where he got everyone's respect.'

After such intensive work, the players were straining at the leash, keen to escape the confines of rural Shropshire. On 21 June, they assembled in London for a brief tour, but five of them had been left behind. On 17 June, the final day at Lilleshall, Alf had reduced the squad to the twenty-two he would submit to FIFA. Johnny Byrne, Gordon Milne, Keith Newton, Bobby Tambling and Peter Thompson were the unlucky ones. Thompson wasn't too surprised: 'The disappointment came towards the World Cup in 1966. I had two really poor games and I was so disappointed with myself, but where Shankly would lay into you, Alf never made any criticisms. I had a terrible game just before the World Cup and he came over and sat beside me, touched me knee, said, "Very disappointed" and walked away. I was nearly crying because I wasn't used to that, it was so difficult to take. I was so disappointed to miss out on the final squad, because that would have been the pinnacle of anybody's career, a World Cup at home, and Alf preferred three other wingers to me. Then as soon as the World Cup was over I was back in the squad!' The three wingers Ramsey picked showed just how determined he was to pursue 4–3–3. Connelly, Callaghan and Paine were all fine players, but they weren't the out and out entertainers that Thompson was. Thompson accepts that, 'Alf only wanted results, and that was why I didn't fit in – at Liverpool I'd beat six men and cross it into the crowd, the Kop loved it, but it was useless for the team. Shankly would say, "Christ, that was brilliant, but could you cross it on to the pitch next week?" Alf wouldn't put up with that. He wasn't interested in entertainment. Ian Callaghan was more direct, probably did more running. Individualists are on or off, and he felt method players would give him something every time, where I might have a poor start and lose my confidence, or I might have a great game. He couldn't be sure. It was sad to go out of the squad, because we'd been so close. When we were at Lilleshall, we were all a part of the World Cup squad, we were getting free suits, free this, free that, our cars were full of stuff. Just before he announced the players to miss out, a firm came with white macs, and we were trying them on. Then Alf announced the twenty-two and we all sat down with him – he wanted us to stay in training in case anything happened to the others in Scandinavia, because he didn't have to confirm the squad until 3 July. I was disappointed, Bobby Tambling was nearly in tears, but Alf just said, "I'm so sorry, I've had to make a decision and I feel that the twenty-two I've picked will do the job for us and win the World Cup. Any questions?" Johnny Byrne said, "Can we keep our macs, Alf?"!'

For those who missed out, it was the biggest disappointment of their careers. Perhaps they all knew they weren't in Alf's first XI, but to be in the World Cup squad, at home, on the verge of history, to have a chance of figuring in one of the games, that must have seemed a real possibility. To have that snatched from them was cruel indeed. The only man to have suffered as they did was Ramsey himself. His was the ultimate responsibility, to close the book on the greatest dream any professional can have. He didn't have to think too long about who would drop out – Keith Newton, who had been Ray Wilson's most recent deputy, was the most surprising omission (though he'd get his chance to play in a World Cup four years later), Liverpool's Gerry Byrne, fully conversant with a 4–4–2 system at club level and a man described by Tommy Smith as having 'more bottle than anybody you could meet' after playing all but three minutes of the 1965 Cup Final with a broken collar bone, replacing him after a three-year absence from the England side – but breaking the news was hard. But there was no option. Five had to go, so they might as well go sooner rather than later so that he could deal with the job in hand, preparing the twenty-two, now whittled down to Gordon Banks, George Cohen, Ray Wilson, Nobby Stiles, Jack Charlton, Bobby Moore, Alan Ball, Jimmy Greaves, Bobby Charlton, Geoff Hurst, John Connelly, Ron Springett, Peter Bonetti, Jimmy Armfield, Gerry Byrne, Martin Peters, Ron Flowers, Norman Hunter, Terry Paine, Ian Callaghan, Roger Hunt and George Eastham.

The first warm-up was in Finland, a game in which Alf caused a major surprise – Moore was left out. Ken Jones thinks, 'Alf played a little game with Bobby. He dropped a hint that he was thinking seriously about Hunter – not many of the press bit on that, Bernard Joy did, and ran it in the *Evening Standard* – and he did that to gee Bob up. I don't think he ever intended to do without Bobby.' It had the desired effect, Moore writing, 'From that day on I never expected to be in an England squad until the letter from the FA dropped through the letter-box. Alf was driving it home to me that there are always enough players for any team to get by without one player.' It was a point not lost on the rest of the squad. If the captain could be dropped, so could they. The result was a clinical performance against Finland, Peters, Hunt and Jack Charlton scoring in a 3–0 win. Alf deployed his 4–3–3 line-up using Ian Callaghan as the winger, with Ball, Peters and Charlton in midfield, but it was apparent that this wasn't the answer to all the problems. The midfield three combined well, but to have just one winger left the side unbalanced. In Oslo three days later, it was a different story. Moore was back, as was Greaves, and Alf played two wingers, Paine and Connelly, though Paine was in the withdrawn, Leadbetter role. Paine, who had made all his England appearances as a Second Division player, was an old-fashioned winger who liked a big target man to hit with his crosses from the right. He was less suited to this deeper position and it was increasingly apparent that, like Connelly, Callaghan and Thompson, he was fighting a losing battle in trying to hold down a regular England place. Wingers were to be used only in specific games against a certain kind of opposition, sides that offered little attacking threat, such as Norway, who were hammered 6–1, Greaves reminding everyone just who was England's premier forward with four, the *Guardian* noting 'Out of chaos came football of a quality that has eluded England for so long.' The strange thing was England had fallen behind and looked a poor side for much of the first half until Greaves went on the rampage. He had been the spark that put England back on track. He was England's key man. Ringing the changes to give all the squad a game, Bobby Charlton was left out of the game with Denmark. England won 2–0, but it was a game which had huge repercussions. Hurst had been paired with Greaves and looked utterly at sea, disrupting Greaves' game as well as his own, Ray Wilson admitting that, 'The two of them worked hard but they got in each other's way; they didn't gel.' This didn't exactly throw England's plans into chaos, but it posed interesting questions. It was unthinkable that Greaves would not play, so Hurst had to miss out. This illustrated that Ramsey remained flexible to the last. The squad was officially announced immediately prior to the Denmark game and Hurst had been given the number 10 shirt, he was first choice, not Hunt, as is often assumed. The Denmark game made it clear to the England camp that the choice now was between Greaves and Hurst for the second striking role, not Hurst and Hunt. Greaves might be the greater goalscorer, but it was Hunt who gave England balance, who fitted in best. Greaves would start the World Cup, but it was he whose place would be under threat if things did not go well.

Things were going well elsewhere, for as George Cohen remembers, 'While we were in Scandinavia, Alf nipped over to Sweden to watch Brazil play in a friendly. He came back, and in one of his training sessions said, "I've seen the Brazilians play and I can tell you that you will not have to worry about Brazil in these finals. They will not progress." He mentioned their ageing defence, the fact that people would get through the middle, would stretch them. He was adamant we wouldn't have to worry about them. We believed him, and that was a great thing, because Brazil had it won twice in a row, they were favourites.' Ramsey was not joking, for his acute judgement was backed up by Pelé, who wrote later that the Brazilian Federation took victory for granted, much as England had in 1950, hence their chaotic preparation: 'When winning is guaranteed, there is no need for the complicated organisational plan that carried us to victory in 1958 and 1962.'

There was time for one last piece of drama in Katowice, where England played their final friendly with Poland. Ken Jones recalls, 'Alf sprang Martin Peters on us – he had a couple of caps, he hadn't been at all prominent in the build-up. He read the team out, mischievously pausing before the eleventh player, "Number 11, Martin Peters." There was a gasp in the room, and Frank McGhee, who got on well with Alf, said, "Alf, can you explain what role Peters will be expected to perform?" Alf said, "No, Frank," got up and walked out with a smile on his face! Some people took that the wrong way, some of the reporters felt he was being awkward, but it was the way the England manager should behave. Yet so many wanted to put him down. He was organizing the team in very much the way people do now, and there was resentment about that structure. A lot came from the older guys, who'd had a comfortable relationship with Winterbottom and the FA. They could go to committee members and get a hint of what the team might be, but now only Alf knew the team. But Alf was right – if you look back to Graham Taylor's last days, he got into the habit of having debates with football writers! He liked to hold tutorials as if he were a guru dispensing football wisdom, the press were getting at him, but I could not understand what the hell he was doing, getting involved in the first place, asking for trouble. After the game, fine, you should offer some explanation, especially if you've lost, but the manager shouldn't be expected to give indications of what he intends doing before the game!'

The arrival of Peters was shocking. Everyone expected that, in this final game, Alf would put out his first team. The defence was as expected, Stiles, Ball and Bobby Charlton were selected, Greaves and Hunt. But instead of the anticipated place for Connelly, Martin Peters, a midfielder, was selected. This, even more than the exposition of tactical flair in Spain the previous December, was a performance designed to strike fear into the rest of the world. Previously, the 4–3–3 formation had seen England deploying a fairly traditional outside-forward on one flank. This team had no such player. Indeed, it was scarcely 4–3–3 but, as Nobby Stiles pointed out in his autobiography, 4–1–3–2, a hybrid, a line-up that wasn't going to concede much. It was designed more for the rigours of the second phase of the competition. In a group with Uruguay, Mexico and France, Alf felt England would progress to a quarter-final with either West Germany or Argentina. Either side would be tough and would herald a shift in emphasis. Qualification would see England having to beat sides of lesser quality, and be more aggressive. The knock-out phase would, paradoxically, be less about winning, more about not losing. In those latter stages, Alf believed that chances would be few and far between. Rather than going looking for them, England's best chance of victory was to be on their guard, to ensure that we did not offer any. Our trump card seemed to be Greaves, who could conjure goals from thin air. With Greaves in the team, if a chance came, he'd take it. If the rest of the team could engineer a clean sheet, England would, eventually, overcome.

Banks was as good as any goalkeeper in the world. A back four of Cohen, Moore, Jack Charlton and Wilson was solid. With Nobby Stiles playing almost as an advanced sweeper in front, they had extra cover, they knew Nobby would harry the advancing forwards, giving them time to take up position. Peters and Ball were both tireless runners, well versed in defensive duties, creative users of the ball when they had it. Bobby Charlton could roam the middle but would never be allowed to forget the need to track back when the opposition had the ball. That he did magnificently – if you look through photographs taking in the action in and around the penalty areas in England's World Cup games, whether they're attacking or defending, Charlton is always there. In Hunt, Alf had another workaholic, always making it easy for the midfielders to find him. Greaves was the thoroughbred, a man who might touch the ball three times in a game and come off with a hat-trick. And the greatest player in the side? The surprise formation, just as it had been with Ipswich.

All the time Alf had been switching between 4–2–4 and 4–3–3, he knew full well that the latter system offered greater potential. But he was never happy to rest on his laurels, he wanted to fine tune further. One winger meant greater emphasis on the full-back on the other flank getting forward – some had already commented that when Paine played on the right, Wilson left gaps behind that could be exploited. The midfield too was undermanned, particularly creatively if Stiles was to play as, essentially, an extra defender. That needed to be addressed. In the end, it was. At the crucial moment, he sprang 4–1–3–2 on the world. And he did it in Poland, in Katowice, as difficult a ground to travel to as any in Europe, a stadium where nobody would be able to see the birth of the 'wingless wonders'.

Ramsey had selected Poland as final opponents, informing the team, 'This will give you all the chance to know what things will really be like in the World Cup . . . the Poles will be all out to beat you, and prove that they should have been in the World Cup,' adding that there was no honour in defeat and a draw was barely acceptable – they must win. The experiments were over. Results meant everything. In that spirit, England gave a display of perpetual motion, each player knowing he had been given an opportunity to cement his place in the team. The new formation worked well and England won 1-0 thanks to an early goal from Hunt – twelve goals from thirteen caps, a ratio that did not pale alongside Greaves' forty-three from fifty-one. Alf had two goal-hungry forwards at his disposal, as good a bet as any to snaffle up one of the rare opportunities that would come their way, but most satisfying was the military precision of their rearguard. Ray Wilson looks back on the game as a turning point: 'We looked a good side. That was the first time, as we were coming back, that I thought to myself, "We've got a chance, we really are a good side." We were just blending together. If you don't lose, you think you're never going to. Everything was so comfortable, they never got a look in.' Geoff Hurst, now relegated to the sidelines, was equally impressed: 'Alf repeated his comment that we would win the Cup. If a manager at a club says that, players might think it's a bit strong, might snigger at it. There was none of that with England. I don't think we all necessarily believed it, but there was nobody questioning his statement publicly or privately. As a unit, we felt that we couldn't be beaten. He had a great knack of not just picking international players, but picking a team, not necessarily the best players, but a team that would play together, players with character. To ascertain that in the short time you had together with England was a remarkable talent.'

By this stage, even the newspapers were beginning to think England would not disgrace themselves. They had won seven in a row, their best streak since 1949–50, though that had been ended in the 1950 World Cup by the USA, not the happiest of omens. They returned to London on 6 July. Rather than keeping the players in training, Alf released them for a couple of days, giving them the chance of a brief rest both mentally and physically, a decision he later regarded as perhaps his best of the whole competition. They returned, suitably refreshed, booking into Hendon Hall Hotel for the duration. After years of preparation, several false starts and numerous experiments along the way, there was only one question left unanswered. Would England fulfil Alf's promise and win the World Cup?

13   4–2

The eighth World Cup opened on 11 July 1966 at Wembley Stadium, when England met Uruguay. South American opposition had rarely been kind to Alf, so the draw might have fallen more kindly, but to win the Cup all opposition had to be faced. It was therefore good to start with a tough opener against the 1930 and 1950 Champions. In spite of the greater optimism engendered by their tour, few thought England would emulate them, no surprise given their dismal track record – fallers at the first in 1950 and 1958, unconvincing quarter-finalists in 1954 and 1962. We'd even managed to lose the Jules Rimet trophy when it arrived in England – the trophy that had survived the Second World War hidden under a bed in France was stolen as soon as it went on display. Would this be the only time an Englishman lifted it?

Uruguay didn't pitch their ambitions particularly high. As Ramsey surmised, they fell back, making his selection of Connelly sensible, replacing Peters and offering a more aggressive 4–3–3. The tactic failed, though Connelly couldn't be faulted – it was three Englishmen against eight Uruguayans, with little support coming from the midfield of Charlton, Ball and Stiles. Alf stressed the importance of avoiding a damaging defeat, so they were loath to push forward lest they be caught. George Cohen confirms, 'It was obvious they'd come to stop us – most of the time Gordon was the only one in our half. We didn't over-commit because to lose would have been disaster. We had Ray or myself within easy reach of Jack, because we were quick, then Bobby would just move in front or behind Jack as the situation arose. It was never a flat back four because anybody that gets caught flat deserves to get beaten. We played off one another, so if one slipped up there was cover. The press gave us stick, but it was a game where we did all the work and, most important, didn't lose.'

Very quickly, it descended into dismal stalemate, Hugh McIlvanney complaining that although 'the Uruguayans were very well endowed with the finer techniques . . . it seemed increasingly sad as the evening wore on that such a richness of basic talent should be turned to such negative purpose ... the fear [was] that the lack of outstandingly creative players was a fundamental deficiency that would ultimately cripple the English challenge. Organisation and tactical discipline are necessary to ensure that a side gets the full reward for its skills but they must never be seen as a substitute for real talent.' The game petered out, an obvious 0–0 long before the end. England won sixteen corners, had fifteen shots on goal but rarely threatened, the *Mail* thundering, 'England have had Greaves, Charlton and Hunt trying to score. If they cannot succeed, who can? The only alternative that can be found among England's twenty-two is allowing Hurst a run in place of Hunt,' an observation that ignored the evidence of their incompatibility in Denmark. Most observers were disappointed with England's impotence, but it illustrated a lack of understanding of the world game, as Ray Wilson confirms: 'If a decent side limits their ambitions to a 0–0, if they don't concede early on, it's not that hard to do it. Things have changed a little in this country, we seem to be a little more educated now, but back in 1966 the supporters had been weaned on the football just after the war, where everything was wide open. I'd been in the game from 1950 as a kid and nobody talked about tactics. The manager would say "go out and enjoy yourselves" and that was it. If anybody came up with a system, you'd no chance. The supporters would say "it's not like it used to be" but sides who set systems ruled the game – Chapman did it, Tottenham did it. City had the Revie Plan, and I remember as a kid hearing managers say the centre-half should follow Revie everywhere, which was stupid. All Revie did was go deeper and deeper, get the ball and spray it, with the centre-half stood leaving great gaps. The supporters wanted action all the time. If I got the ball in my own penalty area at Huddersfield and tried to play a one-two, there'd be uproar: "Get it down field"! Crowds didn't understand what was going on when teams came to defend, they'd never seen it before.'

Alf had prepared his players, shown them how it worked in South America, but that didn't prevent frustration boiling over, Stiles swinging a punch at Pedro Rocha away from the referee's sight. To many, Stiles wasn't an ideal choice, Brian Glanville writing that, 'Whatever his inspirational function, [he] gave nothing in creativity, and seemed in these games, when goals had to be scored, no more than a testimony to Ramsey's penchant for counter-attacking football and at least one "hard man".' But that was to overlook his value to team morale. That 'inspirational function' was paramount. He was part of Alf's defence, a defence that had to be watertight and had to play together. More, Stiles had become a talisman, the physical embodiment of the manager out on the field. While others chose to see Moore as Ramsey's protégé, cool, unruffled, cultured, it was Stiles who best represented him – tough, resourceful, tigerish, desperate to win, passionate about his country, willing to make every effort to see his side home.

It was fair to say that the game confirmed one of Alf's prejudices, that to run with the ball against South Americans was a waste of time. You couldn't progress. If they didn't take the ball, they took the man, as Billy Wright had complained in 1953. To defeat them you needed crisp passing. For all the disappointment though, this was the ideal first match, tough, bruising – Ball picked up a slight injury – which brought a sense of realism to proceedings, an antidote to the lavish opening ceremony that preceded it. Had England played the weak French and won 3–0 in a carnival atmosphere, the country, even the team, might have got carried away and lost the plot. Uruguay reinforced that utter professionalism would be the key. The low-key nature of the display dampened expectations nicely too, reducing the pressure on players restored to the ranks of the also-rans.

The great and the good rushed to have their say on the destiny of the World Cup following this benchmark game. The venerable Vittorio Pozzo, Italy's victorious manager in 1934 and 1938, felt 'This was a bad England team. They did not look like scoring tonight.' The Brazilian press agency added that England had 'a very good defence but the attack does not think well. As an adventurous and winning team it is not very good.' Finally, *Sports Informations Dienst* from West Germany issued some famous last words: 'England will not win the World Cup.' Among this harvest of gloom and doom, the most important comment was lost. It came from Greaves: 'There can't be a fitter team in the tournament. Those Uruguayans were big and strong but they went before we did.' The work done at Lilleshall would be vital before the competition was out.

Few took account of the strain placed on England by the emotion of playing the opening game, the tension that built up as their nation watched expectantly. Alf realized that his players needed a break, and the next day they went out to Pinewood Studios, where a Bond movie was being shot. An enjoyable day and a long lunch took the edge off things and the players relaxed, Alf inadvertently adding to the mood when thanking Sean Connery for his hospitality, pronouncing his name 'seen'. Greaves apparently responded by telling Moore, 'That's the funniest thing I've ever shawn.' The party returned to Hendon Hall refreshed, but Alf was still tense prior to the second game, with Mexico, as John Oakley relates: 'Alf was taciturn, didn't like to give anything away. They were training and Bernard Joy, who was with the *Standard*, went up to talk and, just to set the ball rolling, said, "Everybody fit, Alf?" Alf snapped back, "Why the hell shouldn't they be? Of course they're fit!" His instinct told him the press were trying to make a story out of nothing, when Bernard was only saying hello! Alf was a quiet man, liked to keep things to himself. You'd ask what the team was and he'd say, "Well, I'll be picking it soon." He was a bit frustrating – perfectly pleasant most of the time, but he said nothing!' More aggressively, Alf asked Danny Blanchflower, by then a full-time journalist with the *Sunday Express* and critical of England's play, 'What gives you the right to say what you like?' Already he was, unwittingly perhaps, storing up trouble, exacerbated by his attitude to the FA, Jimmy Greaves writing that, 'He treated many of the councillors with an abruptness bordering on contempt.' But why worry about making enemies on the way up if you weren't coming back down? All that concerned him was Mexico, who had fought out a dull draw with France, who were then beaten by Uruguay. A win would almost certainly put England into the quarter-finals. Time to move up a gear.

Mexico were not of the same quality as Uruguay, but they held similarly limited ambitions. With Ball unavailable, Alf reshuffled. He persisted with 4–3–3, but replaced the right-sided Ball with Peters, who played much of his football on the left. To maintain the balance, Connelly was left out and Terry Paine given the winger's role – he was unfortunate enough to get a knock on the head and played through the game more or less concussed, a passenger. The die was cast from the off. Mexico kicked-off and lumped the ball forty yards forward to Banks. While the goalkeeper picked up the ball, the Mexicans formed up into a defensive blockade. For much of the first half, it looked as though England would be repeating the trials of five days previously when, suddenly, Bobby Charlton burst through from the midfield and cracked an unstoppable shot. It was quite unlike any other goal he ever scored – more than a thing of beauty, it was a shot of rage, of primeval fury, unleashing the pent-up frustrations of an entire team. That one flash of brilliance, of blinding colour, transformed England and the tournament. And that was the beauty of England's system, constructed so as to allow its greatest player the chance to win games. George Cohen comments, 'Bob used to get chewed off by the crowd at Wembley on the wing, and I don't think he was as suited to playing out there. Like Best, moving into the middle gave him freedom; they both had explosive acceleration, beautiful balance, which gave them a chance when there wasn't one.' It was a crucial strike, as Ray Wilson admits: 'We'd played all these games away, there was space, and it was pretty easy for Jimmy and Roger, but it just didn't work at home. The Uruguay game was typical, a goalkeeper and ten defenders. For a good while Mexico were a real problem, until Bobby got that goal which released the tension. We hadn't had many chances previous to that.' Charlton's goal did not draw Mexico out of their shell and the game meandered, Hunt adding a second fifteen minutes from the end, snapping up a chance after Greaves had forced a save. As a spectacle it disappointed, leading more to doubt England's credentials, but that failed to recognize they'd done their job. Mexico had been beaten, qualification virtually assured – had they won 8–0, it still wouldn't have put them any closer to the trophy. Ramsey's men were disciplined, well schooled in doing what had to be done with the minimum of fuss and exertion. To go all the way, another four games would have to be won in a fortnight, so it was wise to husband one's energies. It might not have been glorious, but it was realistic.

The early stages of the competition did drag – three games in twelve days prior to the quarter-finals wasn't a hectic schedule for players versed in the Football League, so it fell to Alf to maintain morale. Some time was taken up with training and with watching other games from the competition – all were piped into their hotel so they could watch whatever they chose. This was popular with the players, as it soon became clear that no one could intimidate England. Brazil were in disarray, out of the competition before England's group was completed, Pelé kicked out by Portugal. Argentina and West Germany looked good, but their ill-tempered game at Villa Park indicated brittle temperaments. Of the rest, Portugal and their brilliant forward Eusebio looked most threatening, North Korea most entertaining, especially when they dismissed Italy. The more England saw, the less they had to fear. To escape football, there were visits to the cinema, which as Jimmy Armfield reveals were used to remind everyone who was boss: 'Alf loved cowboy films. We'd be sat around in the hotel and he'd say to Harold

Shepherdson, "Harold, I think we'll go to the pictures," and he'd stand up and we'd all be rushing around getting our things together. Alf would be off down the road and we'd be chasing behind trying to catch up. After the film we'd come back and have to discuss it.' On one occasion, the squad had its revenge, according to Ray Wilson: 'We were going to the pictures, there were three or four to choose from, and one of them was a Hitchcock. Alf liked him and hadn't seen this one. Alf asked us which one we wanted to see, and seven or eight of us told him we'd already seen the Hitchcock and voted against it. There were more votes for the other films, but Alf got up and said, "Right, we've made the decision, we'll go and see the Hitchcock." So we had to get up and go, which was useless for us. We sat down in the cinema, a bit disgruntled, and the film came on. The first time the villain came on to the scene, we all got up and said, "This guy's done it!" So we never had any problems after that!'

Something as trivial as a visit to the cinema was considered a vital part of team building by Alf. Even five years later, when Roy McFarland had come into the squad, group outings were still an established part of the routine: 'We were at Hendon Hall, we'd eaten, and had a team meeting. When he'd finished, he said, "Right, we're going to the pictures, boys. There's a cowboy film on. It's *Hang Hem High*. No, it's *'Ang Hem 'Igh*." We all burst out laughing. He said, "I'll get it right in a minute, boys. *Hang Hem High*." He must have tried it at least half a dozen times and we were just cracking up. In the end Alan Ball said, "For fuck's sake, boss, it's *Hang 'Em High*." Alf just said, "Right then, boys, let's go." He could laugh at himself. That togetherness was important. With Alf, like with Cloughie, if you went to the pictures, everybody went to the pictures. If you went to a show, everybody went, there were no exceptions, unless you were ill. We had to do everything as a group, and that was part of the education, part of being in Alf's family, you had to join in.'

Such unity of purpose was crucial in 1966. The final qualification game was with France. Uruguay and Mexico had already played out another 0–0, leaving Uruguay top with four points. A draw or a win would put England top, a 2–0 defeat would see the French through in England's place. Paine was left out and Alf played his third winger in three games, Ian Callaghan, in an otherwise unchanged side. To have flirted with so many wingers seems promiscuous, but Alf was clearly keeping his cards close to his chest. Although the obvious

205

move would have been to restore the fit-again Ball, that would have exposed the 4–1–3–2 formation too early in the day. And though Alf did not take the French lightly, he knew England would not succumb 2–0 and would progress. Better to keep the formation under wraps and give Ball time to recover completely. It was another shrewd decision. Forced to play an open game in the search for the win, the French didn't pose the same difficulties, and while Banks had more to do than hitherto, he was rarely threatened. Hunt scored his second goal of the competition just before half-time in an uneven England display which lurched from the lethargic to the sprightly, Ken Jones reporting in the *Daily Mirror*, 'There were times when England suggested they had found the spark,' a hint that they were coming to a peak at the right time.

Stiles had picked up a caution for 'rough play' prior to the game's great controversy. With England moving serenely on, Stiles was late with a tackle on Jacky Simon, Ray Wilson admitting, 'Nobby's tackle looks horrendous when I see it now on film. He looks so unlike a footballer. When kids read about him or parents talk about him, saying he was a little animal, they mustn't be able to believe it. He looks like Woody Allen!' George Cohen's reading of the situation was, 'Simon got the ball and tried to sell Nobby a dummy, Nobby went straight through him. It didn't look nice but it happens in most games, it wasn't malicious.' The felony was compounded when the ball reached Callaghan who centred for Hunt to score, as Simon writhed in agony. The game was wrapped up 2–0 but shortly after, FIFA's Disciplinary Committee confirmed Stiles' booking and 'requested the Head of the English Team Delegation to warn Stiles that if he were reported again, serious action would be taken'. By the time this had been filtered through the FA, the message to Alf was, 'Is Stiles necessary? Can't you leave him out?' His response was simple: 'If Stiles doesn't play, England won't play.' George Cohen adds that, 'I've since heard that Alf told the FA, "If you require me to drop Nobby Stiles, I'll resign." To be honest, far worse tackles were permitted during the World Cup: there were some diabolical tackles against us from Argentina, in particular, there was the ill-treatment of Pelé, all of which lead FIFA to standardize the laws and conduct of the game. In South America, it wasn't unusual for referees to be jostled, and that was outlawed, as was some of the harder European tackling.'

The debate rumbled on. Some at Lancaster Gate felt that England should be whiter than white, the more so as hosts. The ideals of fair play and decency needed to be upheld. Alf quizzed Stiles, reporting that since Stiles assured him it had been an incidence of mistiming rather than deliberate foul play, there was no case to be answered. Alf could neither stand nor understand the FA's attitude. Football was a physical game, a contact sport. It should be fair but also hard. That was Stiles. No further questions. From a player's perspective, Alf's stance was ideal, Geoff Hurst believing, 'His priority was his players at all times, and we responded to that, we had the highest regard for him personally and professionally.' Ken Jones believes, 'That bond between him and the players was probably the most powerful element in the success.' Throughout the furore Ramsey took the greatest care to ensure that Stiles didn't become depressed by the situation and, the day before England's game with Argentina, he took the unusual step of telling him that, 'You might like to know you will be playing tomorrow.' From there, Alf asked Shepherdson to seek out Stiles and, according to Shepherdon's autobiography, 'talk to him like a Dutch uncle. I told him that he owed a great deal to Alf, who had stood by him against very strong newspaper criticism, and that if he did anything silly, he would be letting down the man who had faith in him.' While there was never any question Alf might let down one of his beloved players, it was important that Stiles played. He'd had a miserable time in the qualifiers, for there'd been no obvious role for him where opponents offered no threat. In the knock-out phase, he'd be vital. The controversy worked in Ramsey's favour, bonding the squad in the face of external criticism, leaving them more determined. Ray Wilson suggests, 'Hoddle is similar in many respects to Alf, very loyal to his players. He's a strong man, the way he's stuck by Gascoigne, much like Alf did with Nobby.'

There was a siege mentality about the camp, encouraged by Ramsey's own extreme reaction to adverse comment. Few writers offered England much hope of further progress once they were paired with Argentina and, in fairness, it's easy to see why. England had stumbled through, though as Alf pointed out, 'I had no idea the pressure would be so severe. The players haven't been allowed to play with any freedom because of the emotional pressure, but having qualified they will have that freedom.' Even so, they'd offered little evidence that they could break down Argentina's resistance or overcome free-scoring teams like Portugal and West Germany. Tom Finney remembers, 'After the qualifying groups I was very confident England would do well, so much so that I took a bet on them winning, and I'd never done that before! They were 10–1 I think, which shows how few people thought they could win it.' Few shared Finney's optimism, but to express it in public was tantamount to treason where Alf was concerned. He seemed to find it impossible to understand that ours was a free press, that journalists were not propagandists, apologists for his team, but were expected to report on what they saw, that if they felt England weren't up to it, they had a right and an obligation to tell their readers. Those who upset him – particularly if they criticized his players – were rarely forgiven, Ralph Finn a case in point: 'Alf ceased to know me. When he was manager of Ipswich I first noticed that his normal aloofness had grown even more distant. And [as] manager of England, he did not recognise me . . . I hated being made to feel this way.' But people with such certainty of purpose as Ramsey both inspire and alienate in equal measure.

Alf couldn't worry about upsetting the press, for his mind was elsewhere. There were three days between the French game and that with Argentina, and a major problem had presented itself. Greaves had picked up a nasty leg wound that required three stitches. He was out, Hurst would replace him. This problem also proffered an opportunity. England's forward line had been misfiring and Greaves had looked out of sorts – had it not been for Charlton's moment of inspiration against Mexico, England might even have played three games without a goal. Alf had toyed with the idea of making changes, as had the press. They wanted Hunt's head, but Alf wouldn't provide it. Hunt had scored three of the four goals and was an important cog in the machine. Hurst and Greaves didn't hit it off, and to throw the two together at such a time was too risky. Alf maintained that had Greaves not been injured, he'd have dropped him anyway. Had he done so, it would have been an extremely brave decision, one open to misinterpretation given the well-reported differences in outlook between him and the Spurs forward – falling in the quarter-finals would have been deemed failure and would have been blamed on the Greaves decision. Now, he was presented with the chance and could escape censure if it didn't pay off – equally Hurst was relieved of the pressure that would have gone with replacing a fit Greaves. It was an important move, as Jimmy Armfield notes: 'We weren't convincing, but Alf had the nous to put Hurst in. Alf did listen to people, then did his own thing – I remember having a conversation with him and Harold, saying I felt English teams were more comfortable with the bigger centre-forward rather than a smaller man like Greaves. He was clever enough to reapply himself, to change tack. He had a bit of luck, but you need that. The main thing was that his key players down the middle kept their form and he was clever enough to build round that.'

After the grim qualifiers, people were looking for thrills against Argentina, but that was never on – this was England's third meeting with Latin America, and each had been about attrition, neutralization, stalemate, making one chance count. England need have no fear as long as they applied Ramsey's principles in the 4–1–3–2 formation. Yet Argentina were favourites and looked on as highly advanced: fawning dissections of their play raved about a sweeper, pacey overlapping full-backs, a defensive barrier thirty yards out that smothered attackers and provided a springboard for attack. But didn't England do likewise? England were modern, noisy and effective, the perfect machine for the age of the 'white heat of technology'. It wasn't a clash of styles, but a clash of cultures, and it was here Ramsey hoped to prevail. Against West Germany, Albrecht had been ordered off for repeated dangerous play, the team and coach trying to force the referee to retract his decision. FIFA warned the team to play in a more sporting manner or risk expulsion. The Argentines *were* volatile, but they were unlucky to be playing in Europe. In South America their conduct was part of the drama, football as bullfighting. In northern Europe the reverse was true, histrionics were frowned upon while heavy tackling was part and parcel of a man's game. This would act to England's advantage if they kept shape and discipline. Alf was aware that the crowd had a part to play. The press turned Argentina into pantomime villains, Rattín in particular – provocative treatment of a proud man, whose disdainful approach was echoed in Eric Cantona's dismissive body language. The crowd responded by hounding them at every turn, crucial in the psychology of the game, helping turn the screw by booing every tackle, foul or not. It would be stupid, though, to suggest the Argentines were more sinned against than sinning, for there was a genuinely nasty side to their play, George Cohen remembering, 'There were some very late tackles: the pat on the shoulder that turns out to be a wrenching of your ear; getting hold of the short hairs on your neck, which is particularly nasty; spitting in your face. And when an attack broke down and you were running back into defence they ran alongside and raked their studs down your Achilles tendon. It was diabolical.' But like any good manager, Alf turned it to his advantage, informing his team what would be required of them – 'Well, gentlemen, you know what kind of game you will have on your hands today' – stressing that if England kept their temper, Argentina might self-destruct; ice-cool Bobby Moore maintaining discipline on the pitch. To reduce the risks, Stiles man-marked Ermindo Onega, and Ball was detailed to prevent left-back Silvio Marzolini getting forward, to stifle their threat. As Tom Finney notes, 'Alf was one of the first to study the opposition in depth, to get a clear idea of how they played and how to defeat them.' Argentina was a perfect example – since 1964, when he'd been spooked by Rattín in particular, his team had advanced in leaps and bounds. They knew everything Argentina might do, including blow up. That was important, as England had an inferiority complex where Argentina were concerned, Ray Wilson admitting, 'I thought they'd be the problem. But we'd got into the habit of playing Alf's way. In 1964 we pushed forward all the time, which suited them. We didn't do that at Wembley. We played more or less the way they did. It must have been a bloody awful game to watch, but we played to strict instructions. We were as good a defensive side as anybody then. Everybody had a job to do. If you're wanting to entertain and always lose in the quarter-finals, that's easy. We lacked a certain flair at times, but we were effective. Alf had his way of playing, but we weren't just a defensive side and I think the goals for and against will match up with most managers throughout the world. They weren't all 1–0 games. And the world game became much more defensive, everybody taking the bat off Italy. But the game with Argentina got the crowd going, they started to get behind us, and that was encouraging.'

A game which McIlvanney described as 'not so much a football match as an international incident' started with a frenzy of activity, England winning four corners in four minutes, but it soon settled into the niggling pattern for which it's remembered. Ramsey asked his men to play one-touch football, knowing that running with the ball was futile, the player with it certain to be chopped down. Many commentators remarked on the number of names taken by the referee, Rudolf Kreitlein, but only four – the Charltons, Artime and Solari – were cautioned. But it was the dismissal of Antonio Rattín that gave the game its place in infamy. Not unlike Diego Maradona in his determination to be in the thick of things, Rattín spent the thirty-six minutes he had on the field shadowing the referee. Rattín felt it was his job not only to run the midfield but to referee the game too. Wherever Kreitlein turned, there was Rattín, towering over him, peering down at him with ill-disguised contempt. George Cohen is still bemused thirty years on: 'They were a very good side, technically brilliant, but they deteriorated into a mob when things didn't go right. If they felt the referee was biased, things got out of hand. But Rattín tried to run the competition, he harassed the referee on every possible decision, and he decided he wouldn't have it, quite rightly. If anyone had to get sent off it was him I was glad to see go, because he was an outstanding player, and by leaving the pitch he didn't do his side any good.' Ray Wilson adds, 'Their problem was Rattín. They seemed to get more satisfaction out of niggling, shirt pulling, nasty stuff, than playing. If they'd played, they could have been a massive side, they were wonderful. But we were ready for them and they didn't cause many problems.' When Kreitlein's patience snapped and he ordered Rattín off, he wouldn't go. The Argentine delegation raced to the touchline in protest, Onega spitting in the face of FIFA commissaire Harry Cavan. The game was held up for seven minutes before order was restored. It was just the breakdown in discipline that Ramsey had foreseen.

Subsequently, England took flak for not tearing apart ten men, Glanville writing, 'A side more sophisticated and imaginative would surely have turned the man over to ruthless advantage.' But that was unfair. Argentina fell back much as Uruguay had, though England were now better equipped to face it, as Ray Wilson explains: 'We'd a forward line of smallish guys and I think it benefited us when Geoff came in, it gave us an option. Because when teams defend very heavily there comes a time when you have to give sharing balls, knocked into the area from deep, looking for knock-downs, for chances to be made that way. Forty yards out, eleven facing you, it's very difficult to squeeze balls through, so you need to knock some in the air, where Geoff was very good. Jimmy and Roger were similar, but they suited us away from home because the other side's got to come and have a go, and if you break, you've got spaces to pass the ball into, which was ideal for them. At Wembley there was no space.' Hurst agrees, adding, 'Alf was keen on the balance and there certainly was a better balance with a bigger presence at centre-forward. You need a bit of luck – sometimes an injury to key players enforces changes and it can be for the better. In Mexico in 1986 we started poorly then lost Bryan Robson and Ray Wilkins, and though they were both good players I felt the balance looked better.

It happened in '66, and we started to play better because the balance worked. The team was significantly different to the way we'd started.' And to underline that the 'wingless wonders' weren't without width, George Cohen points out, 'Alf wasn't averse to wingers. He really used Alan Ball in that way when we went to a 4–4–2 after he brought in Geoff – we had two strong front-runners, we needed width to get the balls in for them, because they were both good target men. No point wasting their aerial combativeness.'

That new dimension got the crucial goal. With thirteen minutes left, Peters knocked a ball in, perfectly placed and weighted for his West Ham colleague Hurst to drift between two defenders and glance a header home. Such a goal would have been impossible against Uruguay, but it was justice for Hurst, who had taken a battering: 'They played in an aggressive manner, trying to kick us out of it, where had they been content to play football, they might have had a better result. It was very difficult to play as a front player!' Argentina fought back but where ten men is no problem defensively, creatively it's often fatal. 1–0, England through, Alf's ideal score. The difference was temperament and discipline. Ball had been sent off in England colours the previous year but now kept his head. Nobby Stiles might have been seen as a liability, but as Alf said in the dressing room, 'You know I don't usually mention individual names. I think today, however, I would be reflecting what you all think by saying how proud we are of Nobby's professional performance.' At the decisive moment, the basic training at Lilleshall had paid off. No one snapped under provocation.

Ramsey was under no illusions how hard it had been. At heart, he was still the schoolboy sent off for dissent, passionate about the game and the way it was conducted. Argentina were cynical manipulators, he had no sympathy with them. As George Cohen recalls, 'Alf was incensed. He was a very experienced player, he knew about heavy tackles, man-to-man combat. He understood and recognized all those nasty fouls, things that may not have been obvious to the ordinary spectator following the ball – Alf was following us! At the end, this guy came up to swap shirts, so I said OK, I felt once the game was over, it was over. By the time I had it over my head, the guy could see Alf coming and tried to pull it away from me before Alf got there! He got as far as the sleeve when Alf arrived and said, "You're not changing shirts with *these* people." By then the sleeve was three feet long!' After Alf had run twenty yards to prevent him swapping shirts, the Argentinean wheeled away and swapped with Ray Wilson instead! But it still wasn't over. Referee Kreitlein needed police help to get away from the Argentineans, several of their players barged into England's dressing room looking for a fight, another urinated in the tunnel. Almost immediately, Alf was called away for a TV interview: 'England played to win, and win we did, which was important. We are afraid of no one. We still have to produce our best football. It is not possible until we meet the right type of opposition, a team which come out to play football, not as animals, as we have seen in the World Cup.' His face was taut, the strain of the previous two hours etched on it, but he was plainly livid, nothing could mask that. He was weighing every word, desperately trying to find some formulation that could express his distaste without letting England down, striving so hard, he almost developed a twitch. And he had every right to be angry. Never mind what happened on the pitch, the opposition behaviour afterwards *was* unforgivable. He felt he'd suffered one way or another at the hands of the South Americans and their different attitudes since 1948. This was an argument too far, though he had no idea that his use of the word 'animals' would be so provocative, having ramifications down the next four years as a continent united against him (twenty years on, for Argentines, the 'Hand of God' seemed revenge for '66. Would even Maradona have used such spurious justification against any other team?). The immediate problem arose when FIFA asked the FA to discipline Ramsey for the 'animals' remark. Alf issued a limited apology. His humour was little improved by a letter to *The Times* from Lord Lovatt, who wrote, 'Any unbiased critic would agree that the Argentina XI were quite definitely the best footballers. England . . . have got through to the last four by a lucky disqualification and the crippling of two Frenchmen in an earlier round. Is it too much to hope that when the might of England plays little Portugal tomorrow, Eusebio . . . is not given the Pelé treatment by Ramsey's defensive players who boast that they have not conceded a goal in all the matches played? Having seen them in action, I am not altogether surprised.' Sent from the Guards Club, this approach infuriated Alf. His England were hard but, to his mind, scrupulously fair, and their record bore scrutiny in this fiercest of tournaments. And regarding the 'Pelé treatment', it had been Portugal who kicked him out of the World Cup, so this was scarcely a credible argument, symptomatic of the amateurish stupidity that had reduced England's standing. He had taken them to a semi-final, their best ever showing, against a side that breached the spirit of the game, not just in his view, but that of FIFA too. They fined Argentina the maximum 1000 Swiss francs, suspended Rattín for four games, Ferreiro and Onega for three, and told the Argentine FA to put their house in order or face expulsion from the next World Cup. Hugh McIlvanney backed them: 'The Argentineans must discipline their delinquents or accept that they are a threat to the competition which the other entrants cannot tolerate.'

None could deny that Ramsey could be insensitive and behave clumsily at times, but few this side of the Atlantic disagreed this time. He'd been angered most by the way his players had been put at risk by Argentine foul play – he was defensive of his men and hated to see them hurt, hence his response, Hurst adding, 'He's very passionate about his country and about his team. On reflection I'm sure he'd like to withdraw the "animals" remark because it's ill-advised, it's almost a diplomatic incident at that level!' Sir Michael Cresswell, British Ambassador in Buenos Aires, needed a special police guard in the aftermath, so badly did the Argentineans take to Alf's statement. Oddly, it was a statement that was needed, if not couched in such terms – perhaps that's why he felt it politic to keep his mouth shut in future. European and South American football had been growing further apart in their interpretation of the laws and spirit of the game, in refereeing and in play. Rattín would never have been sent off had the game taken place in Mexico, yet an Englishman might have for what we considered tough tackling. The odious events of this World Cup brought matters to a head, though it wasn't the first vicious game (recall Brazil v Hungary, the Battle of Berne in 1954, and Italy v Chile, a game of two sendings off, a broken nose and explosions of violence in 1962). Tension built during the West Germany–Argentina and Brazil–Portugal matches. The two continents looked incapable of meeting on the football field. Action was finally taken to harmonize the laws, with mixed results, but things began to improve after that horrible day at Wembley.

The magnitude of victory was lost amid recriminations, but not on Ramsey. The England players were finally allowed a few drinks to unwind. And though no one said it, they knew the toughest hurdle had been overcome. 'We started to believe, we'd got to the stage where we hadn't let anybody down,' says Ray Wilson. 'The worst thing would have been if we'd lost in the qualifying group, but we got through – if we hadn't, we wanted turning over because Uruguay were the only side there; France were awful and you'd have paid to have them and Mexico in your group. I thought if we got to the knockout stage, maybe the semi-finals, even if we'd got beat, we wouldn't have let anybody down – that's your problem at home.' Portugal were their surprise opponents, Eusebio supposedly replacing Pelé at the top of the game, but after Argentina everything seemed easier. And as Ramsey pointed out in his briefing, Portugal were good but the North Koreans had scored three past them in the quarter-final, so their defence was suspect. Would Greaves be back to exploit it? He was still short of match fitness, but it wouldn't have mattered. The side had matured. It would not change. Greaves asked if he could return home to recuperate, but Ramsey refused. He wanted to keep the unit together, like musketeers. Greaves' request to go home left Ramsey to note his suspect temperament – not a team player.

There was a row over the venue. It had been intimated that if England got through, their semi would be at Goodison, but that wasn't cast in stone. In the end, the committee made the pragmatic decision to leave them at Wembley – their semi would draw 90,000 where the West Germany–USSR game would only get 40 or 50,000. Money won, England stayed at Wembley to Ray Wilson's delight: 'We didn't want to move. Wembley suited us because were ever so fit. Early games there, I always got cramp – it's so spongy because there's not many games there. It always felt enormous.' Some saw this as part of a conspiracy to give England the Cup, especially after the Rattín incident, but though decidedly average in qualifying, England were at this stage proving themselves as good a team as any. Their passing was crisp and precise, if not yet incisive, but they would improve in play, as they did against Portugal. Ramsey thoroughly briefed them on each player, especially goalkeeper José Pereira, who he felt was vulnerable. As to Eusebio, the whole defence looked to blot him out, making him shoot from distance, retreat, pass sideways, keep him on his weaker left foot. But the final responsibility was Stiles', and George Cohen believes, 'Nobby had his best game for England, he did a terrific job on Eusebio. He got so fed up he gave up, went on the wing. Eusebio was six inches taller, four yards faster than Nobby, yet Nobby shunted him all over the place, shadowed him, pushed him into dead ends. But when Nobby had the ball, he used it well. He always looked for his mate Bobby Charlton; they had a great understanding of where each other was.' That club understanding came to the fore again in a game finally decided by Charlton. For months people had argued over him, should he have the freedom Ramsey gave him, was he that kind of player? It was risky, for Charlton was a player of mood, of form, one of few that Ramsey tolerated. But he was also a 24-carat-genius, England's guiding light. As Jimmy Armfield notes, 'We had a trump card – every great team has one, and we had Bobby Charlton. Alf found a role for Bobby which suited him, and that was good managing.'

West Germany had beaten the USSR in the first semi-final so England knew who would be waiting in the Final. The right perform-ance was also required to remove the taste of the Argentina game, just as Portugal wanted to exorcise the Brazilian game from public memory. Perhaps that's why the two sides produced a beautiful exhibition, a joy to watch, quite unlike most semi-finals. The Soviet news agency Tass termed it 'a spring of clear water breaking through the murky wave of dirty football which has covered recent matches in the championship.' Their strengths were at opposite ends – Portu-guese attack, English defence, a balance which favoured England. They took advantage on the half hour, Hunt running down a long ball from Wilson, forcing Pereira to scramble it clear to the edge of the box. Bobby Charlton, coming from the midfield, met it crisply. 1–0. It remained that way until eleven minutes from time when Hurst broke into the box, steadied, and saw Charlton on the run. A simple pass into his stride, 2–0, almost a carbon-copy goal. England conceded a penalty and endured eight frantic final minutes, but clinched the game 2–1 to reach the World Cup Final, Ray Wilson recalling, 'Portugal suited us; it was the best game we played in. That was always the case with them. They couldn't play any different, they got on with it. They were entertaining, they'd some great players, they'd come and have a go at us, which gave us a chance – it was like playing away. By the Final, we'd nothing to lose, even Alf relaxed, because nobody had tipped us to get that far!' He allowed them one drink that evening, but no more, claiming, 'We've got a final on Saturday, and then when we've won it, I shall make sure you're permanently drunk.'

The semi-final was won on Tuesday. The next four days saw a national debate on the future of Greaves, when the big worry was Moore, who went down with tonsillitis immediately after the Portu-gal game. Had Dr Bass not been with the team at all times and so caught it early, he could have missed the Final. That was kept under wraps and the controversy allowed to rage around Greaves. It raged around Hurst and Hunt too, Hurst remembering, 'I was aware

Jimmy was fit, but I don't recall feeling under pressure. He was the great goalscorer, it was unthinkable that if you wanted to win the World Cup, Jimmy wouldn't be in the team. That was a really major decision for Alf to take, because Jimmy was a genuinely world-class player. To leave him out in a game with no substitutes, and selecting instead a player with seven caps, who hadn't started the tournament, was a very brave thing to do. What would have happened had we lost and Roger and myself missed a couple of sitters? Alf would have been hung, drawn and quartered! Alf had a very strong character, essential for a national team manager when 50 million people are telling you who to pick. It's easy to get side-tracked, but Alf wasn't.'
He now had a team that functioned superbly in every department. They'd concede little and pinch the odd goal, the ideal recipe. That was Ramsey's strength, his disregard for names. No other England manager has dared to leave out the 'star player' even if he disrupts the side – look at Hurst's comment on Robson and Wilkins in 1986. Equally, Walter Winterbottom persisted with an out-of-sorts Haynes in 1962, and there were times under both Taylor and Venables where the omission of Gascoigne would have benefited the side. Ramsey understood *team* play. And as Ken Jones adds, the team didn't want changes: 'Bobby Charlton told me they felt it was the right decision. The way the team had started to work suited Bobby; Geoff and Roger taking people away, Bobby bursting through. There were stupid comments that Alf didn't like Greaves' type of player, but the one thing he respected above all else was ability.' Ultimately, there was no decision – England played their best football without Greaves and though Alf agonized, understanding the repercussions if it went wrong, he had to stay loyal to Hurst and Hunt. And with Greaves returning from injury, who could tell if he'd last 90 or 120 minutes? To his eternal credit, Greaves has never criticized nor blamed Ramsey.

Geoff Hurst, centre of the storm, recalls, 'Nothing changed in terms of preparation. I can't even recall when Alf told me I was playing! You'd think that would stick in your mind, but it was so low key. I'm sure Alf told everyone privately and asked them to keep it quiet – Martin was told in the cinema the night before the game. That was the only change, so players might sleep well.' It worked, Stiles enthusing, 'We were practically free from tension because of the way Soccer Svengali Alf Ramsey had prepared us for this moment . . . we were the puppets and he moulded us for the job both mentally and physically!' On the day of the game, at eleven, the twenty-two filed into the lounge at Hendon Hall. Alf went through the opposition – Beckenbauer's bursts, the speed of Held and Lothar Emmerich, the overlapping Helmut Haller, hammering home that the player with the ball was to be supported at all times. Ray Wilson described how the system would provide: 'We went through their team but we made no changes. Alf had nothing to say to us at the back, because we marked zones, not players, which is why we talked so much. If anyone got into my area behind me, Jack would give me a call. Whoever was in your area, you were responsible for picking him up.' The formation took care of things, with the proviso that Bobby Charlton had to keep an eye on Beckenbauer, given similar instructions by Helmut Schoen. Beckenbauer told David Miller, 'Charlton at that time was the best player in the world, and he also had lungs like a horse. I never remember being so exhausted as I was at the finish.' According to Moore, Ramsey did 'not suffocate us with an abundance of detail. His philosophy [was] "Why should we worry about them? Let them worry about us!"' For the benefit of the press, Ramsey added, 'This is a very fine German team and the only thing I can say is that it helps that we know their players and their style perhaps better than any team in the tournament. But for England to win must mean that every Englishman plays better than he has ever played in his life. I believe they will.' England expects . . .

So did the players, George Cohen admitting that, 'We felt we were coming to a peak. We'd beaten West Germany twice in a year, home and away, so we felt we could beat them, even though they were good players. So were we. We knew they'd compete and not give up. They were known to us, I knew Held and Emmerich. Held was a sprinter who never got his head up, you could run him into blind avenues, Emmerich was skilful, had a great shot but no speed. They interchanged, but as long as you got down on them quickly you could cope. Just read the game. They never gave me any trouble and I understand that Schoen told them to make sure I didn't get forward. I made them work for it, and in stopping me they stopped themselves. By putting Beckenbauer on Bobby, they lost their creative genius, which was a mistake. Beckenbauer was a truly all-time great player, as was Bobby, and they were busy looking after each other.' That's the crux of the game. England had an excellent system, but a system alone wins nothing. What England had was intelligent footballers who could adapt and implement. Football is not a static game played out on a blackboard, it's one of movement, of thrust and counter. England had the players equipped to do that.

But few sides as good as the '66 team have had such a bad press. They're dismissed as lucky, workhorses, destroyers of the noble art, but that's nonsense. They did add endeavour to ability, but ability was the bedrock. Stiles and Moore were almost interchangeable by the Final, allowing Moore to step forward and make use of his range of passing. In midfield the positional play of Peters and Ball was exceptional. Both popped up in unexpected places, but neither sold the other short. And Ball was effervescent, playing so much in from the wing, but also contributing to work in the engine room; the flexibility of 4 – 1 – 3 – 2 allowing Ball and Peters to support the attack along with Bobby Charlton, making five forwards (seven if the full-backs were up with the play) or eight defenders. Hunt and Hurst were remorseless chasers of lost causes, relentlessly dragging defenders all over to expose the German sweeper. From the outset, England looked to make things happen. That made it all the more shocking when West Germany went ahead after thirteen minutes, a poor header from Ray Wilson from a hopeful punt by Held falling straight to Haller, who shot past Jack Charlton and Banks. George Cohen remembers, 'Ray was an outstanding full-back, so it was so rare for him to make a mistake. But it was a character thing again: to be responsible for giving away a goal when there was no danger, at home, in a World Cup Final, would be a crushing blow to many people. Ray was an old stager, he just said, "That was a bloody stupid mistake, I won't make another one," and got on with it.' England were resilient. Six minutes later Moore took a quick free-kick midway inside the West German half, floated it towards the penalty spot where, in a replay of his goal against Argentina, Hurst lost his marker and headed home the equalizer. Another club combination.

England then held the balance of play without making many clear chances, Charlton's defensive responsibilities and the attentions of Beckenbauer preventing him becoming a threat. But the ascendancy was clear, Stiles pushing further forward than previously. With seventy-eight minutes gone, Ball took a corner. His cross came out to Hurst on the edge of the box. Hurst's shot ballooned off Höttges and, just as Wilson's header had fallen kindly for Haller, this dropped invitingly for Peters to club it past Tilkowski. With ten minutes to go, England retreated from the halfway line with a pass back to Banks to a chorus of boos from the crowd, who began to chant 'we want three'. It was true that English crowds were wedded to constant action, but tactically they had no idea of how to win internationals. If only England had killed a little more time. In the last minute, Jack Charlton was penalized for pushing, the ball was driven across a crowded box and Weber stabbed in an equalizer. 'It was devastating when they equalized,' Ray Wilson reflects with a grimace. 'I didn't think it was a foul, the referee was naïve when the German lad backed into Jack. It ricocheted and it was like slow motion. I remember it hitting somebody, I turned and Seeler stepped across me, then backed off. I had to go again after the ball. Weber slid in and knocked it over my outstretched leg. And for the whistle to blow straight away was awful. I thought they were favourites then, you always feel that. We battered them in the last half hour, one or two chances were missed, we overran them. They were really tired but when we scored, they had to come forward. But if it had finished 2–1, it would have gone down in history as a pretty dour game. The equalizer and the third goal means it's remembered as a great game, but I wasn't sure about that over the ninety minutes. And Geoff wouldn't have had his hat-trick and Kenneth Wolstenholme might have been out of a job!' Geoff Hurst, probably the greatest beneficiary of that equalizer, accepts, 'The Germans never give up, are never out of it. Normally, having scored in the dying seconds, you would expect them to go on and win it. But because of the characters Alf had assembled, we shrugged it off, got on with it again. Alf came on and simply said, "We've won the World Cup once, now go and do it again." Just a one-liner. He didn't need to lift us, he'd done his job by picking the right team.'

It sounds simple, but this was the culmination of two years' hard work since the 'Little World Cup'. Alf had the men he needed on the field, knew they'd do the job. He was lucky that substitutes weren't permitted. How tempting would it have been to swap Hurst for a fresh Greaves, especially with 100,000 people baying for his entrance? It allowed him to maintain his formation, plugging away for 120 minutes, not losing faith, following the German way. With substitutes, there's a temptation to tinker, but in 1966 they could only keep going. And they did. Where one would have expected the Germans to come out full of life, they were flat, England buoyant. Ray Wilson was surprised: 'We were much fitter than them in extra-time. They were gone, they created nothing, they spent themselves in the last ten minutes of normal time.' Words that George Cohen echoes: 'At the end, we could keep going on where they were finished – had there been ten more minutes of extra-time, we'd have scored another couple. When Alf came out at full-time, he said, "Look at the Germans, they're finished." And they were all lying on the floor. Alf made us stand up to show them how fit we were. Alf knew that however tired we were, we'd get through extra-time. Schoen said later that we had the right blend, the battlers and the great players that make teams work. He was very complimentary.' The World Cup was won on the playing fields of Lilleshall. Within a couple of minutes of the restart it was obvious England would win on points, but could they administer the knockout blow?

On 100 minutes they did. Stiles hit a long pass down the right. Ball, who had run several inches off his legs already, set off, caught it and crossed on the run. Hurst swivelled, thumped a shot off the bar and, according to the linesman, over the line. There was a howl of protest from the Germans, but the goal stood. In a way, it's a shame it did, for it took the shine off England's win. They were lucky it was given – it wouldn't have been in Munich – for how could the linesman decide? He was level with the six-yard box at the time and couldn't see for certain, so had to give the benefit of doubt to the defending team. His decision was incorrect. But as Beckenbauer has been gracious enough to concede, 'England were the better team, over ninety minutes and then in extra time. There's no argument. They deserved the trophy.' Had the goal not been given, England would have regrouped and scored again. England would have won the World Cup anywhere in Europe in 1966, and might have won it more impressively away from home. To do it on another continent is tough, but in Europe, England were supreme. Geoff Hurst merely underlined their supremacy with the final kick when he sledgehammered the ball past Tilkowski after a quick ball out of defence from Moore caught the Germans over-committed. Alf's ideal goal.

As the ball nestled into the net, the English bench exploded. The World Cup was won. But one man sat quietly in his seat. Ramsey did not leap up, did not dance, did nothing but keep his eyes fixed on the field. As Ken Jones relates, 'It is true that at the end, as Hurst battered the fourth goal in, he said, "Sit down, Harold, I can't see." But it was an indication of his attention to detail – he didn't see the ball go in because he was watching Overath tracking Hurst. He had tremendous respect for him, and while everyone was out on their feet, he was watching him run forty yards to try to get back at

Geoff.' Alf was typically prosaic when he said, ten years later, 'Players and trainers had been grabbing at me and pounding me on the back. It was difficult for me to get to my feet. Although I don't think I would have started dancing around anyway. Since then though, I think Englishmen have become more emotional, and if it happened today I might jump for joy.' Rather than dancing, maybe he was simply letting the enormity of what he had done sink in, savouring the moment. Three years earlier no one had taken his promise seriously, but now he had delivered the World Cup. Because of his work, and that of his players, no one could laugh at England any longer. They were World Champions, a feat all the greater since it was built on our strength, passion and commitment, and on character that had been tested to the limits of endurance by the last-gasp equalizer. It was a very English victory. And the secret? In the words of Bobby Moore: 'He made us proud to play for England.'

Victory restored pride in the country too. The pound was under threat at the time and Britain's influence in the world was crumbling; Harold Wilson travelled in vain to Washington to ask Lyndon Johnson for help. In such circumstances, the World Cup provided relief, Cabinet minister Richard Crossman recording in his diary: 'I must record a big change in Harold's position . . . tremendous help for him that we won the World Cup on Saturday . . . when I told [my wife] over lunch today that the World Cup could be a decisive factor in strengthening sterling she couldn't believe it. But I am sure it is. It was a tremendous, gallant fight that England won. Our men showed real guts and the bankers, I suspect, will be influenced by this, and the position of the Government correspondingly strengthened.' Sterling survived another sixteen months before being devalued. If England's football team had helped restore, however briefly, the standing of the nation, that was all Alf could ask for. We were still GREAT Britain (which to many meant England), a world power; Suez the only recent blot. But times were a-changing, our influence waning. Our music, our culture and our movies maintained the illusion that we were important. The World Cup win bolstered that. 1966 had been a patriotic crusade, but decently so, perhaps the last such in this country. We wanted to win, were proud to be English, but if the team floundered, the world didn't end. We had a grumble, but it wasn't a catastrophe. Since then, our authority has collapsed; Englishness is celebrated with a spurious sense of superiority, of having to show the bloody foreigners. In '66 we were too close to a war for that kind of odious nationalism to come through, but later our thugs chanted 'two World Wars and one World Cup' at German fans. We were thankfully free of all the 'football as war' metaphors because there was still too much real blood on the collective psyche, the memories of lives lost in real warfare still too vivid a memory to be sullied. Not so today – if you look at a sizeable minority of English supporters, even those with no interest in finding a fight, you find a very belligerent sense of nationalism, a dislike bordering on hatred of foreigners, a Little-Englander complex that is fuelled by the Europhobic newspapers (some of which are owned by an Australian with American citizenship) which proclaim 'Rule Britannia' at every opportunity. It's behaviour that makes some Englishmen and women hope England lose because they want no part of *that* country. In 1966 it was very different. English nationalism was dignified. The personification was Alf Ramsey, a man of integrity who left the lap of honour to his players and walked away from the glory saying, 'It's your day'. As Stiles and Moore held up the Cup at one end of the ground, at the other Ramsey was making his way down the tunnel. Ray Wilson feels, 'It was typical of the man that we should have the lap of honour. It was pretty good of him. He'd think, "I've done my job." He'd be off then on the gin and tonics!' George Cohen adds, 'Everything today is self-promotion. That certainly wasn't Alf's way of doing things.'

On the balcony of the Royal Garden Hotel, where a reception was held after the game, Alf looked genuinely delighted. Had he done more of that, identified himself with the win à la Ron Atkinson or Tommy Docherty, he might have won the nation's affection as well as its respect. It's sad that because Alf was no extrovert, he wasn't really identified with the triumph in the way that some of the players were. He wasn't loved like Busby or Shankly. He could, though, have done more to persuade people: the day after the Final, he had a brief altercation with Ken Jones, one of the few reporters to back him: 'I went to Elstree, there was an ATV lunch there that had been arranged. Alf got out of his car, I congratulated him and asked if he had five minutes. "No, Ken, it's my day off, I've been working for the past nine weeks." So had I. There was a sharp exchange, but those moments were rare.' To the public, they were typical – another story did the rounds that he was congratulated by reporters who had been less appreciative. His response was said to be, 'Are you taking the piss?'

But why should he be good in public? It's not everyone's ambition to be on TV. For some, it's an unwanted by-product of the job. So it was with Alf. He had to put up with it, but he didn't like it. He appeared unnatural on the screen because he was, he was forcing himself into a character that was not his, simply to get through what he saw as torture. And again, the elocution lessons were thrown back at him as provincial accents began to dominate – the irony of that was that the man who produced The Beatles, the lads who'd supposedly turned the tide, was George Martin. He was almost a contemporary of Ramsey's and, in order to get on in the world, he too had taken elocution lessons. But where was the criticism of that? The Beatles laughed at his posh tones, but it was good humoured – the attacks on Ramsey were not, they were vicious and malign. He wasn't part of the swinging sixties, Ray Wilson noting, 'He always seemed much older than us players, but he was a relatively young man, only 46.' Alf didn't fit in, and that posed problems. For the moment, though, he was vindicated. He had been reviled by the popular press, but he had triumphed. As Jimmy Armfield says, 'A lot of players he selected, people didn't always think they were the best for the job, but the only proof in the end is results. There is no other proof in football, so Alf was right.' That only added to his immense self-belief. Who could question him now?

As is so often the case, the World Cup winners came from seemingly nowhere to take the crown, the team that best sorted out its defence in advance triumphing, the pressure off the attack. And goalscorers are creatures of form – Hurst was the man in '66, Muller in '74, Kempes '78, Rossi '82, Romario '94. Since 1966, how often has the Cup been won by expansive, exciting, joyous football? Brazil in 1970. That's it. For better or worse, football has become more cagey, clinical, industrious, tactically absorbed. Alf felt the way the wind blew earlier than the rest and built his team accordingly, something for which he is castigated. But if England hadn't won, Argentina would have. And would that have been better? England weren't as dour as legend has it. They were sophisticated passers with four world-class footballers – Banks, Wilson, Moore and Bobby Charlton – and several others pushing for inclusion in a World XI – Hurst, Ball, Peters. As Tom Finney says, 'You don't win the World Cup with a lot of duck eggs, do you?' It's impossible to deny that the late sixties were a time of fear in the game, but did Alf usher that in? Was it his fault? The Italians had already introduced *catenaccio* defence, after all. And Alf did not fear defeat, he just loved to win. There's a difference. He felt, like most professionals, that you only enjoy the game if you win. Perhaps he was unlucky to manage England at a time when two of the best known football writers were Danny Blanchflower and Hugh McIlvanney, both renowned for their love of the beautiful game; Blanchflower for his 'entertain at all costs' philosophy, which sadly failed in terms of results when he put it into practice a decade later. He and Ramsey were poles apart, irreconcilable. Blanchflower was harsh on his team, saying, 'They were as defensive in intent as any team in the competition,' a reaction not only to the football but perhaps to Ramsey's offhand manner with him ('I don't give interviews to players,' he had said in 1962 when he got the England job). But Blanchflower conceded that the problems came when clubs tried to adopt 4–3–3 or its hybrids without players of sufficient quality. It was a system that only works with players of the calibre of Bobby Charlton, Peters, Moore, Stiles and Ball, and few had players that good. As Alf had said long ago, look at the players you have, formulate a system from that. Don't impose one.

For winning the World Cup, the squad received the bonus of £22,000 which they split twenty-two ways rather than by a sliding scale depending on appearances. It reinforced the camaraderie, as Ray Wilson agrees: 'I know success bonds you together, that's obvious, but when I do meet any of the guys from 1966, whether they played or not, there's a feeling that you were in something together, similar to being in the Army, that closeness. Sometimes I can go a year or two without seeing anybody, but when we do meet up it's as though we were together yesterday. Alf did a lot of that by getting the right lads involved.' Alf picked up £5000 but, as he said, 'I can still only eat three meals a day. It is what I'm doing that counts.' Victory was its own reward. Musing on his achievement and on the future, he speculated, 'It would be rather fun to again build up from scratch like I built Ipswich and England. We were the fastest and the strongest side in the World Cup but I do not think we can ever match the individual techniques of the Latin-Americans or the Latin-Europeans. We are built differently. We play a different kind of football.' Responding again to questions about his self-contained demeanour, he said, 'I am sorry that I present this [unruffled] picture to everyone but it is not intentional, I assure you,' admitting that he was 'a little worried' when manhandled by colleagues after Hurst's third goal! The day after the game, the squad came together for the final time. Alf gave a speech thanking them all for their efforts, and they disbanded. The greatest month in English football was over.

14 3–2

Once again, Alf had reached the peak – 1951 with Tottenham, 1962 with Ipswich, 1966 with England. On the previous occasions, triumph degenerated into anti-climax. But this was England, only the best was enough. Yet the drawback with success is it makes a rod for its own back. You have to maintain it, but you're there to be shot at, you become the benchmark that all aim to beat. The difficulty is reinvention. When you start from scratch, you know what you have to beat. At the top, how do you tell if you're getting better? And can you accept taking a temporary step backwards in order to go two forward in future? As Peter Thompson notes, 'In 1966 we were two steps ahead, but as an individualist I found it a bit boring. But they won it. People criticize him for doing away with wingers, but he won the World Cup that way. The problem was that club managers followed the example, and two or three years later there was a shortage of wingers – Shanks stuck by myself and Ian Callaghan, but Alf decided he didn't want us.' But would wingless wonders win in 1970? At Ipswich, Alf had employed wingers – one conventional in Roy Stephenson, one withdrawn in Jimmy Leadbetter. He'd been flexible enough to ditch that, deciding a multipurpose side was required to succeed in 1966. But who would threaten in Mexico in 1970? Could England simply maintain faith with the system and insist it would prevail? Tough questions, but Alf was a systems man through and through. He'd stick to 4–1–3–2 or 4–4–2.

The next challenge was the European Nations Cup. The Home Internationals were used as qualifiers over the 1966–67 and 1967–68 seasons. Alf had taken a warning shot from Football League President Len Shipman, who made it clear they'd helped as much as they were going to by giving him access to players in 1965–66. Now it would stop: 'For a change the clubs will want first call on the players' services.' This was a bleak background, but of little consequence initially. Loyal as ever, the World Cup winners played England's next three games – a 2–0 win over Northern Ireland, a

0–0 with Czechoslovakia and a 5–1 win over Wales. The first change came in the Wembley showdown with Scotland, when Greaves returned in place of Hunt. He might have wished he hadn't, as England slumped to a 3–2 defeat. This was England's first game since Alf had become Sir Alf in the New Year's Honours, which he accepted in typical fashion: 'This honour reflects on the whole team. It is a wonderful tribute to all British soccer.' Maybe the Scots didn't think it was a tribute to them, for they gave a fierce display. Jack Charlton broke a toe, Wilson was injured too, but Scotland deserved their win, which they felt made them morally the new World Champions – if that was the case, they lost the crown a month later when the USSR won 2–0 at Hampden.

The game was of little importance – England had four points, Scotland five, a deficit that could be clawed back. But had a year been wasted? No new faces in undemanding games. Was this building to 1970? A couple of games against Spain and Austria in May allowed Alf to play Peter Bonetti, to give Alan Mullery and Brian Labone games in place of Stiles and Jack Charlton, and John Hollins and Norman Hunter a turn in Peters' shirt, but this was half-hearted at best. Of more use was an FA tour of Canada in the summer. Many first choice players were unavailable allowing Alf to observe some youngsters at close quarters, players like Hollins, Mike Summerbee, and Paul Madeley. The FA XI was joined by Borussia Dortmund, Sportklub Vienna, Leon of Mexico, a Russian Select XI, and Standard Liège in a tournament to celebrate Expo '67. All the teams stayed at Loyola College, which was cramped to say the least – there were three washbasins and six showers in each corridor of eighteen residents. Ramsey was livid, complaining, 'The arrangements are ridiculous and totally inadequate . . . but we are all in this together.' His concern for the players was laudable, but he retained the tendency to speak without thinking – this was a no-account tournament lasting a few days. Why worry about the facilities, why antagonize your hosts? Ken Jones recalls another example: 'This guy stuck a microphone under his nose and said, "Sir Alf, we're going to give you five minutes of CBC time." Alf didn't break stride. "Oh no you're not," and carried on walking.' The FA beat Borussia Dortmund 3–2 in the Final, but Alf had had to endure another mishap in training, Harold Shepherdson writing later that he moved on to the ball 'to have a bang against makeshift goalkeeper Ray Wilson, when he kicked the ground and almost broke an ankle . . . dear old Alf made light of this, his latest problem, which left him hobbling about with the aid of a stick ... "I hit the ball correctly. It is just that the ground was too high!" [claimed Alf].'

That injury could have been a problem, for Alf was planning to fly from Canada out to Mexico to begin taking notes on the conditions that would confront England in 1970. He got there and reflected, 'There are three major problems facing us – altitude, extreme heat and the rather worrying threat of boredom ... it would be ideal to take the team to the Pyrenees for a three-week stay to get acclimatised. But this seems out of the question with the growing number of club commitments facing players.' Those commitments were causing problems – six internationals in 1966–67, four more to February 1967, whereafter the number would be determined by progress in the Nations Cup. The only significant change to England on the field was the replacement of Stiles with Tottenham's Alan Mullery who, though a year Stiles' senior at 26, offered England an additional option. Mullery's tenacious tackling made him a valuable first line of defence, but to his ceaseless running he added a greater range of passing and the ability to pop up and score important goals. Consequently, England's formation was refined to a more conventional 4–4–2, which actually offered Peter Thompson a way back against Northern Ireland at Wembley. The team failed to fire, won 2–0 against a team short of Best and Dougan, and got a roasting from Ramsey for their casual approach. Changes were still few and far between, despite increasingly loud calls for them following England's indifferent performances since winning the Cup. That was inevitable, for it's hard to repeat that intensity in irrelevant friendlies against Spain, but even so, didn't we have youngsters ready to play? George Cohen accepts Ramsey was cautious, but sensibly so, in his opinion: 'He looked at your form, your experience. If a younger player, maybe a better player was coming through, he'd still think, "Just a minute, he may not be used to the crowds, he may feel the pressure if I put him in too early." Alf would consider every aspect. You had to do an apprenticeship.' And when a player broke through, according to Moore they always got a pep talk along the lines of, '"I've seen you play, do what you usually do, don't worry about what's happening at the club, even if you're having a bad run – you're here to play for England because I want you to, so do as I say."' This was further proof that the system would remain and that he'd look for players who would fit it without needing to adjust. It was sensible as far as it went, but as Ray Wilson adds, 'Once we won the Cup, most international sides started playing exactly how England had, which is why things started to level out a bit for him; it wasn't new.'

There was still enough mileage in it to get England to the final stages of the Nations Cup. They'd overtaken Scotland and got the draw at Hampden that took them on to a two-leg quarter-final with Spain, reigning Champions. Bobby Charlton gave England the win at Wembley but one goal is a slender advantage to take to Madrid. On the day of the game, England were thrown into crisis when Hurst picked up an injury. At 1.30 the players had a briefing at which two plans were outlined, one with, one without Hurst. By 5.30 it was clear Hurst was out. Hunter came in and England went 4–2–4 with Bobby Charlton, Hunt, Peters and Ball all pushing forward. England subdued Spain in the first period and went on to win 2–1, Peters and Hunter scoring, though once England were ahead, Ramsey sent out instructions to slow the game down, Hunter made a fifth defender and Hunt was left up front alone. It paid off, but wasn't it a little negative? Didn't it give Spain the initiative, one which a better side might have grasped? England's possession football *was* superb, though, and the Spanish press described them as 'a true giant of world football'.

England arranged to play in Hanover on the way to the finals in Italy. Colin Bell was given a debut in midfield and Peter Thompson recalled, to his surprise: 'I hadn't even been playing that well for Liverpool. At Liverpool I was a bit greedy, I'd want to beat four, five, six men. I went a bit too far, probably, but that was me. Before the game, Alf said, "I want you to play exactly the way you do for Liverpool, but don't hold the ball." That was like tying my legs together, and I had a shocking game, I didn't know whether to hold it, run with it, pass it, or what to do.' This reinforced Alf's belief that you should only ask players to do what came naturally. Although Thompson remained in the squad, he was never a real contender again. It was a sad day all round, as England lost to the West Germans for the first time. The manager was not amused. Thompson remembers: 'Adidas were giving us £200 each to wear their boots. Just before the game the rep for Puma came in and said, "We'll give you £300 if you wear our boots." So we just cut the three stripes off and painted a Puma on the side. Adidas came back and said, "We'll give you more." So we washed the Puma off and painted three stripes on. In the end it was a mass of white, you couldn't see anything, so a lot of the players were given new Adidas boots – I'd always worn them so I'd got my own pair anyway – but a lot of the lads finished up with massive blisters and we lost. When Alf saw our feet afterwards he just said, "If anyone ever wears new boots for England, I'll never pick them again."'

England played Yugoslavia in the semi-final of the Nations Cup in Florence and were in good heart, with the return of key players such as Ray Wilson: 'I got injured and had to miss the game in Germany. I rung Alf to tell him, "If you want me for Yugoslavia, I'm fit." So I flew out to Italy to meet the squad. They were my last games for England – the start of the next season, we were in training and my knee collapsed, and that was me finished. We should have won that Nations Cup. We played Yugoslavia, an inferior side, but they sat back, never came out at all. We were never out of their half, but they scored on the break. Then we played Russia in the play-off and we absolutely paralysed them because they played football. That would have been lovely, to win the World Cup and the Nations with virtually the same side – it would have been proof that we were better than people give us credit for. People say we were dour, but we did score goals, and we gave most of our best performances away, where people didn't see us. This was before satellite television. We toyed with sides.' But the semi-final was a sign of the times. Yugoslavia accepted England were physically powerful and resolved to be equally robust. In a nasty game, some of the tackling was a disgrace, Ramsey complaining afterwards, 'England have been accused of being too physical but I have seen teams we could not hold a candle to in that way, and Yugoslavia is among them ... we're no angels but other countries get away with a lot against us ... I jumped out of my seat when Trivic fouled Charlton early on. I've never done that before.' Harold Shepherdson added, 'Luckily for [Charlton], one scything tackle just missed, otherwise I don't think that Bobby would ever have played football again.' Few had sympathy for England, arguing with some justification that a team that put men like Stiles, Hunter and Jack Charlton out on the field had done much to create that climate – and it had been Mullery who was sent off. Yugoslavia proved the world had learned from 1966, as Shepherdson was to concede: 'In this word of defensive football when only those who take the half chance prosper, it was a defensive mistake [from Bobby Moore] which cost us the match. But nobody got the blame from Alf.' European sides adopted blanket defence and games were now fought out in a packed area across the middle third, compounded in this game by leaving Hurst out and playing with just one forward, Hunt, in an unbalanced side.

Was Hurst saved for a Final that never came? Alf's system still allowed England to hold their own, but stalemates were more frequent. The 4–4–2 formation no longer unlocked defences with the same ease since opponents now applied the same double padlock England had. It was time for a rethink.

Perhaps Ramsey's public relations need to be revisited too. England didn't play just Yugoslavia, they played an Italian crowd, whipped up by disgruntled local pressmen who were furious they couldn't have the same access to England's footballers as they had to the other three nations'. To play amid such animosity can't have helped. But as Jimmy Armfield says, 'Alf didn't bother what the press, other managers, those at Lancaster Gate or anybody else said about him. He was unswerving. Once he'd won the World Cup it gave him a confidence that took him on thereafter and made him feel he knew best.' England defeated the USSR 2–0 in the third-place play-off, Hurst and Stiles restored to a better-balanced unit, though Stiles was booed at every turn. Ramsey leapt to his defence: 'There has been a vicious campaign against Stiles throughout Europe. Because he plays full out every minute of the game he is booed, although he takes much more punishment than most ... the public of Europe has been brainwashed in respect of English football. Let me remind you that we made the laws and that we play to them. At all times we insist on playing the ball. We do not play the man.' Unlike some, was the obvious inference. Defensive under questioning, Alf's responses sounded arrogant, even if that wasn't the intention.

Third place in Europe showed England were still a force but two years previously they were first in the world. They had slipped. The summer of 1968 was a time for some thought, following a further visit to Mexico to take in the Olympics and examine the data provided by British doctors on the response of our athletes to the climatic conditions. The team's style and personnel required a makeover. George Cohen's career was cut short at the age of 29, in 1968, by a serious knee injury. Ray Wilson was gone too. Stiles had been replaced by Mullery, Labone and Jack Charlton vied for the centre-half spot. England's legendary defence was finished. In midfield, Ball and Peters were still young but Charlton hadn't been at his best for some time. Up front, the punishing work done by Hunt was taking its toll. England's players had to work bloody hard. Application became more and more a watchword; fitness levels across the world game were improving. But a game built on sweat would surely struggle in Mexico. If it were to work, fresh legs and a fresh approach were required. Having a system is, as Ramsey proved, of benefit to a team, but sticking with it too rigidly is deathly. If the manager knows exactly what his players are going to do, then so does his opposing number, and counters it. Wherever they went, England were now faced by concentrated defences that would not leave their station. Draws were easy to get, but how could England win?

Having been derided as the man who dispensed with wingers, it's ironic that it was to them that he looked for salvation. Or rather, to players who could play that *and* a second role – not wingers in the Peter Thompson mould but wide players who could defend too. By nature, most wingers weren't that well equipped. With the advent of Alan Mullery, Ramsey was able to use Ball and Peters in wider roles rather than the fluid interchanging game they'd played in 1966. Even so, they had defensive chores and were expected to help in central midfield too, so they could not be relied upon for all the wing play. As midfielders, they were often marked too tightly to run at defences. However, new full-backs were emerging who could carry on the work done by Wilson and Cohen. These would overlap regularly, coming on to defences from deep, running at their opposing number, building up a head of steam, getting past them, combining with midfield and crossing into the forwards – vital against packed defences. This was part Ramsey wanting a system and finding the players, and part making the system fit his men. In Terry Cooper, Alf had a man ideal for the job, a former winger converted to marauding left-back. At right-back, he could call on Keith Newton, Tommy Wright or Paul Reaney, all of whom could do a similar job. Wing-backs had arrived.

Things rumbled inauspiciously on, with three draws against Romania home and away, and Bulgaria at Wembley, a game in which Francis Lee made his debut: 'Alf was very, very thorough. Before every game we had to watch a film of the team we were playing and then we'd laugh our heads off as he was trying to pronounce these East European names – one of the older lads like Jack or Gordon would pipe up and say, "Could you just repeat that name, Alf?"! I got in because he could see Roger was coming to the end and he saw me as a similar partner for Geoff. People used to say he was dour and defensive, but he wasn't, really, he took me on one side, told me I'd be making my debut, and said, "Don't worry, I just want you to do for England tonight exactly what you do for Manchester City, play a free role, go wherever you want and support Geoff."

That was a good start! I enjoyed my first game against Bulgaria, it was my life's ambition to play for England, so why shouldn't I enjoy it? Then I had a good run where things went well for me and Joe Mercer used to ask me if I could arrange to play for Manchester City like I did for England!' That was the sort of character Alf was after, one who would not be upset by the big time. Lee had been around the squad, been watched in training. Once Ramsey was satisfied with his attitude, he was in. Alf was criticized for not blooding youngsters more quickly, but Lee argues, 'He wasn't rebuilding because there was no need. I think he was lucky in that he could put six or seven names down right away, and then experiment with two or three positions, looking to get the squad right. Ball, Hurst, Peters were all going to actually improve from 1966 just on sheer experience, because they were still young men at that time. Why would you replace them?'

Suddenly, England clicked into gear with a 5–0 win over France in March 1969, Hurst getting a hat-trick. From nowhere, a team and a squad had crystallized – Banks, Newton, Cooper, Mullery, Labone, Moore, Ball, Peters, Bobby Charlton, Hurst, Lee, with excellent reserves like Colin Bell, Peter Osgood, Norman Hunter, Jeff Astle and Emlyn Hughes all looking to get involved. England's prospects for 1970 looked bright once more, yet the France game had started inauspiciously. Given the dearth of goals, many had been clamouring for the return of Greaves, who had not played in almost two years, in spite of scoring 73 League goals in the three seasons that followed the World Cup. Ramsey took his seat at Wembley to a chorus of boos, astounding treatment of the man who won the World Cup three years earlier but indicative of the lack of warmth the public felt for him. He complained later that he was being 'crucified' and that Greaves had asked to be left out – Greaves denied it, saying he did not want to be called up if he wasn't going to play. To Alf that was the same thing – if you considered being a squad member beneath you, you weren't sufficiently committed.

Had Alf given a little more time to his public image, these problems might not have cropped up with such frequency. Journalist John Oakley admits, 'Alf was a much maligned guy, he was a nice person. Alf wasn't nasty towards the press but I think one or two papers had stitched him up, and that upset him. And if things went wrong, he was worried he'd be misquoted. If he got to know you, he was fine. We had a game in Romania and had terrible trouble travelling there – I didn't get there until the middle of the second half, and some didn't make it at all – and afterwards we had a drink and he was very sympathetic; he understood he wasn't the only one with problems. If he was in company and didn't suspect you of foul play, he was amiable.' It's a sentiment with which Ken Jones concurs: 'Some people took the trouble to get to know him, others couldn't be bothered. It wasn't easy, but he wasn't opposed to criticism as long as he felt it was fair.' He was also caught out by the changing times, as Jones explains: 'Alf was never a personality as such, he wasn't an extrovert in any way. He was always immaculate, smartly turned out, and he expected that from the players. They used to travel in blazers or suits and the players got on to Bobby Charlton one day to have a word, to ask if there was any chance of travelling casual. So Bobby asked him, and Alf said, "I'll think about it." He walked away, stopped, turned round: "Bobby, we'll travel in suits." He was looked on as stuffy, very English. He was a stickler for traditions, a patriot, though not stupidly so.' But in the late sixties that was old fashioned, as was a public figure being shy and retiring. They should be brash like Allison or Clough. But Alf wasn't, as Jones adds: 'He wasn't a funny man, some people aren't. We got back to Heathrow from a game in Ireland and I ended up with Alf and Geoff Hurst in my car going back to London. I dropped Alf at Lancaster Gate, and as he got out, Geoff said, "All the best, Alf, see you at the next match." Alf turned and said, "Yes, Geoffrey, I'll send you a couple of tickets." It wasn't nasty, he was trying to be funny, and he couldn't really do it.' Alf suffered for that, adding to the paranoia that soured his relations with the press and with authority. It drove him into himself, making him ever more self-reliant – if things remained within his control, they would be done properly. If they went outside, disaster would result. It meant taking more work on, on matters of which he had no experience, as he had at Ipswich.

Because Alf wasn't loved, he had to get results to maintain his position. And after the French game, he could be satisfied he'd do so. It was at this stage things had begun to come together for 1966. History was repeating itself promisingly, reinforced when England won the Home Internationals with three straight wins. Francis Lee starred against Northern Ireland, winning only a rebuke: 'If you are the sort of player who gets big-headed with all this attention, I will drop you like a stone.' Wales were beaten 2–1, Scotland hammered 4–1, Hugh McIlvanney commenting, 'The unquestionable class of [the England] players was always liable to break out of the system and did so spectacularly.' People were starting to believe, referring to the high quality of the players, their technical expertise and their potential. This was the start of the great debate that lasted the rest of Ramsey's reign. England were producing a new kind of footballer, lads who had grown up with blurry TV images of Brazil in 1958 and 1962 and were trying to emulate them. Youngsters like Alan Hudson, Roy McFarland, Peter Shilton and Rodney Marsh were on the fringes of the England set-up. To some, this was a sign that England could throw off the shackles as McIlvanney said, could emerge a beautiful, exciting, talented team, fit for any stage in the world. Marsh was drafted into the Under-23 side and was 'in the original forty-four that was announced for Mexico a year or so before. There was a get-together at Lilleshall. I was surprised because I was still at QPR and in the Third Division. I'd scored forty-four goals and I think Alf looked at me as a flair player but perhaps thought, with those goals, maybe I can turn him into a Geoff Hurst type!' That was always the tension, between flair and team play. As Marsh admits, he perhaps wasn't ready for Mexico, but the fact that Ramsey wanted to change his game speaks volumes – Peter Thompson is one of very few who received that treatment, and he was an individual too. It's too glib to say Ramsey mistrusted flair, but what he did insist on was the harnessing of individual gifts to the pattern, as Bobby Charlton did. It is easy to entertain and lose, but Ramsey's first obligation was to win. As Francis Lee confirms, 'Nothing was ever good enough for the press, but Alf's answer was always the results. He knew how to set out his stall to win and wouldn't be deflected from that.'

Just how hard it would be to get results was illustrated in the summer of 1969 when England visited Mexico, Uruguay and Brazil. Almost on arrival, Gordon Banks was given the awful news that his father had died and Ramsey went out of his way to sympathize and help arrange flights home, emphasizing his affection for his players. Banks confirmed, 'I will always think of him as a warm, sincere and intensely loyal man, who is shy with strangers and who will not suffer fools at all, let alone gladly.' The tour opened with an easy 4–0 win over a Mexican XI, but with two substitutions now allowed (as they would be in the World Cup) Alf asked Ball and Peters to run themselves into the ground in the first half before replacing them. It was an optimistic tactic at best, undermined by injuries to Bob McNab and Jack Charlton in the second half. It also went against Alf's policy of consistency, for although substitutes were well versed in their roles, changes in personnel are inevitably risky, potentially disruptive. In the light of what was to come, it's worth looking at the role of substitutions. When Alf was at Ipswich, substitutes still weren't allowed in League games. Tactical substitutions were an innovation, an exciting, but difficult one. The manager had yet more responsibility. He couldn't simply tell his team what the opposition would do in the knowledge that this would cater, more or less, for the ninety minutes. Now he had to be flexible, had to react to changes brought about by his opposite number, or introduce new faces if things were going wrong, while still bearing in mind the need to keep a reserve for injuries. It was a new facet of the game and it took some adapting to, especially for a man approaching fifty, set in his ways and who believed so utterly in the value of rigid plans.

Drama came when Mullery was sent off for the second time in a year. The aftermath provided an example of the widening gulf between Ramsey and his employers, as Ken Jones recalls: 'Alf was extremely disdainful of those guys at the FA – he had a lot of time for Major Wilson-Keys, who was a grafter. If he went on a tour, he worked, but most of the others went for a holiday. A couple of the FA guys ducked out of going to Mexico because of the altitude and the health problems it might cause. Mullery was sent off, which was sensational in those days. They had a meeting when they met up with the FA in Montevideo and Alf was asked about the incident by Sid Collins, who was on the committee. Sid asked Alf if he could put his response in writing too. Alf said no and looked at Denis Follows, who was with them: "He's the secretary, he can let you have it in writing." '

The international with Mexico was a scoreless draw but was worrying when, at the end, Bobby Charlton and Mullery suffered bouts of vomiting. It was especially disturbing that Charlton was so badly affected, for as Francis Lee points out, England's strategy still revolved around him: 'Alf always played 4–4–2, which he believed in totally, wanted to make us hard to beat, and then rely on the quality players like Hurst and Charlton to score goals. He reckoned that was a good formula.' In spite of Alf's instructions to conserve energy, his players were suffering – by the end of the tour, Moore, who played all four games, would also collapse.

From Mexico, the team flew to Uruguay, Francis Lee recalling it vividly: 'The experience in 1969 was very good for us to get used to the conditions, just to get yourself sorted out, really. But in terms of the grounds we played on, and the travel arrangements, it wasn't ideal. Getting to Uruguay meant a horrendous flight: Mexico to Peru, on to Uruguay, took twenty-four hours, or something. We got there in the middle of the night, got up for training at ten, played the next day and won, and it was the worst preparation for a match you could imagine!' Such resilience underlined the quality in the side, ability often overlooked. As Lee adds, 'The formation was the real tactics of the side. So as long as you knew that, it was easy to slot in. We'd work on free-kicks and things like that, the West Ham boys linked well, good at dead balls, but apart from that we didn't do a lot of practising because we had a lot of talented players around who could do the spontaneous thing.'

The tour ended in Rio with a memorable display against Brazil. It started in typical ramshackle fashion, reminiscent of 1964. Francis Lee recalls: 'We were in the tunnel ready to go out and Alf said to an official, "Where are Brazil?" He replied, "You've started too early, go back in the dressing room, we start in half an hour." Alf said, "If that team is not out in the corridor shortly, there is no game, we're going home." Five minutes later they shuffled into the tunnel!' With England World Champions, Ramsey could assert an authority he lacked five years earlier. This time Brazil were caught on the hop. England took the lead but the rigours of the tour caught up with them. Refusing to make substitutions 'because of sentiment', according to Bobby Moore, England burned out and Brazil scored two late goals to win. Seduced by the possibility of a win at the Maracanã, Alf had not wanted to deny players the chance of being there when victory was sealed. Consequently, it slipped away. This substitution business was tricky. Despite the defeat, the tour had been invaluable. They'd learned a lot, particularly that, in the heat, football was now a thirteen-man game.

Evidence that the Football League had little interest in England's success came in 1969–70 – Ramsey was allowed just seven internationals, three in the Home series. Wanting to avoid morale-damaging defeats but needing to introduce new faces, it was a juggling act. Emlyn Hughes came into the side, as did Peter Bonetti, and Ian Moore got a game, suggesting that wingers might make a return. But that was a mirage – in spite of the strength-sapping climate, Ramsey felt lengthy preparation in Mexico would mean his full-backs could fulfil the dual role. Alf, though, could not hide a disturbing lack of creativity which threatened to dissipate the optimism of the previous year. Worryingly, Martin Peters and Bobby Charlton were out of sorts through much of the 1969–70 season.

Peters, perhaps jaded after a decade at Upton Park, only began to rediscover his form after a move to Tottenham, Jimmy Greaves moving the opposite way as makeweight. Bobby Charlton, after a decade of emotional highs and lows from Munich in 1958, through the rebuilding of Manchester United and on to the World Cup triumph and then the European Cup win in 1968, seemed drained, short of his usual enthusiasm for the game. With Busby stepping down as manager at Old Trafford, the turmoil that followed did little for Bobby's game either. While Colin Bell was proving an able deputy in midfield, Alf needed those two at their best. He was irritated by events, the more so when England were booed off the field at Wembley in January after a 0–0 draw with the Netherlands. His retort to press questioning was brusque: 'If you want me to win unimportant matches I will pick teams to do so ... surely they were slow hand-clapping the Dutch team?' As in 1953, England was suffering from the blinkered attitude that we should beat everyone in sight, but this Dutch team included Johan Cruyff, Wim Van Hanegem and Ruud Krol, it contained the backbone of the Feyenoord and Ajax teams that would dominate the European Cup from 1970 to 1973. A few months later, this didn't look such a bad result. Relations with the press were reaching breaking point. The atmosphere at conferences became as poisonous as at any time under Graham Taylor. Ramsey would pointedly ask, 'Have I been rude to you? Can anyone give examples? It seems to me I am treated with rudeness, you push these [microphones] in my face and so forth.' Another conflict of generations. Ramsey was the man from the past, where public figures were treated with deference, whereas now the news media was becoming increasingly aggressive, convinced of its divine right to ask any questions, however impertinent, and expect a reply. There were faults on both sides. Danny Blanchflower, writing on the eve of the 1970 World Cup, summed up the feeling among some of the press pack: ' "You would like to go over and wish him luck," a much-travelled journalist remarked, "but you know it's 10–1 he will humiliate you" ... how many of the humiliated, like Indians in the bush, are sharpening their spears and waiting for the dark of night to fall?' Ken Jones admits: 'Alf would be horrified to think anyone thought him rude, but he was clumsy at times.' With sports reporters, there were fewer problems, but as time went on, he had to deal increasingly with news reporters, on the lookout for a story, ready to manufacture one if necessary. This was alien to Alf. How could he be expected to cope alone? He needed a PR man, but dismissed the idea – 'Why should someone speak on my behalf when the person people most certainly wish to talk to is me?'

Ramsey was flexible enough to realize the team had to change, a spark needed to be found. Perhaps the system should have been looked at, but instead he looked at personnel. One young man hitting the headlines had been in the forty for the 1966 World Cup but hadn't had a look in since. Chelsea's Peter Osgood was on the way to thirty-one goals and an FA Cup winners' medal, spearheading their drive to third place in the First Division. Osgood was *the* name: 'I was around the Under-23s for a long while when English football was at its best, I think, with a lot of quality youngsters coming through. You knew Alf was in charge. He picked the squads, said this is the way we're going to play, then let the players get on with it. It was very frustrating in the late sixties. People always talked about me getting in the squad, then getting in the team, and it never seemed to happen. Eventually I got in against Belgium in February 1970 – I got a call on the Sunday from Dave Sexton, saying, "Ossie, will you go and join the England squad." I said, "You must be joking. I'm not going to carry the bags again! I'm fed up with it." Dave told me that Alf had said that if I went, I'd play. I went out to Hendon Hall to join up with them, and there were guys like Frank Worthington and Rodney Marsh already there. I hadn't even been picked for the squad, but I played and we won 3–1. Half an hour before the game, I'll never forget it, Bobby said to Alf, "Is it all right if we have a drink now, Alf?" and a bottle of brandy came out! This great England captain had a swig of brandy, so I thought if it's good enough for God, it's good enough for me! After the game, Alf just said, "Ossie, you've played extremely well today, welcome to our team, now go out and enjoy yourself," which was great. I went out with Bobby and a few of the lads, into this nightclub about 11.30, and it seemed a bit funny. After about half an hour, Bobby went up to the bar and dropped his trousers, so he was standing there in his boxer shorts. He'd realized it was a gay club! But it was a lovely introduction to the England set-up. I've always wanted to be one of the lads, whether at Chelsea, Southampton, or now in the local. I went into the England squad and they just accepted me right away. They knew I could play, it was marvellous to be in the company of lovely people like Mooro, Geoff, Ballie; they were winners and saw me as part of Alf's set-up that wanted to carry on winning things.'

The Home Internationals followed and Ralph Coates and Peter Thompson were each given an opportunity to play wide, again encouraging thoughts that England might play a winger, particularly when Thompson starred on a dour afternoon in Glasgow, Hugh McIlvanney railing against the 'scurrying defensiveness of England, whose sole intention seemed to be to suffocate the game in midfield'. This was part of their plan for Mexico, for Ramsey had decided that in the heat, midfield possession was all. In a tough group with Brazil, Romania and Czechoslovakia – and England had been unable to defeat any of them since 1966 – Alf concluded that in the first phase, discretion was required. Give nothing away, because to chase a goal in that heat would be asking for trouble. Control was essential, as was taking chances. Francis Lee lost one task for that reason: 'He gave me the job of taking penalties because I hadn't missed one in four or five years. I got the first one against Portugal in 1969 at Wembley on a very heavy pitch and my standing foot gave way as I hit the ball – it missed the photographers, it was that wide. Then we played Wales and got another and I hit the bar. After the game he said to me, "Frahncis [sic], I don't think that taking penalties for England is your vocation"!'

In one of few concessions to England, the League season ended early, getting the Home Internationals out of the way by 25 April. The players had a week off before the twenty-eight assembled for a fourteen-hour flight to Mexico City. This time there were no boasts that England would win the World Cup – a significant omission – but Alf did concede, 'It's a very strong party, most certainly a better party than in 1966.' Was the first XI better? Banks, Moore, Hurst, Peters and Ball had experience to go with ability. Bobby Charlton's form remained a worry, though he came through superbly in the tournament itself. But was the defensive unit – as a unit – as good? Cohen, Wilson, Charlton, Moore and Stiles had been the foundation on which victory in '66 had been built. Was the grouping of Newton, Cooper, Labone and Moore so solid, given Mullery was more adventurous than Stiles and didn't fulfil quite the same holding role? On that would hinge England's fortunes. The party comprised Gordon Banks, Peter Bonetti, Alex Stepney, Peter Shilton, Jack Charlton, Terry Cooper, Emlyn Hughes, Norman Hunter, Brian Labone, Bob McNab, Ian Moore, Keith Newton, David Sadler, Tommy Wright, Alan Ball, Colin Bell, Bobby Charlton, Alan Mullery, Martin Peters, Nobby Stiles, Jeff Astle, Allan Clarke, Ralph Coates, Geoff Hurst, Brian Kidd, Francis Lee, Peter Osgood and Peter Thompson. They were a determined group, as Geoff Hurst recalls: 'We had the backbone of 1966 and new players like Mullery, who took over from Nobby very well, and Francis Lee, who gave us more flair and variation in the last third. We'd broken the hoodoo by winning it, which was important, and I think we were confident we'd do well. We'd been able to prepare without worrying about results, which is a tremendous advantage. And we had something to prove – it's a big advantage playing at home, but it's unfair to say, as some did, that we wouldn't have won it otherwise. Over a four- or five-year period, consistently, I think we were the best in the world. I felt we were better in 1970 and we were the only team to compete with Brazil in their own back yard. If you look at Holland from 1973–1979, they were probably the best, but they didn't win anything. We were in a similar position for five years, but we did.'

The party arrived in Mexico on 4 May (their first game was on 2 June) and spent the next thirteen days at 7349 feet at the Parc de Princes Hotel in Mexico City, Neil Phillips, who succeeded Alan Bass as team doctor, suggesting they'd need a day in Mexico for each of the seven hours of time difference, so they had a leisurely first week. In the first of a catalogue of disasters, they found themselves sharing their complex with the Mexican squad, whose quarters weren't finished. Although Alf arranged for a separate dining room, it was irritating that his plans were going awry so early. They did light training at the Reforma Sports Club, a favourite among ex-pats, but as Peter Osgood says, 'For the first couple of weeks the conditions were a big problem. In the first week or so we had a mini-Olympics, throwing the javelin, throwing the cricket ball, hurdling, that kind of thing – Colin Bell won everything, he was so fit. It was a lot of fun and after the first couple of weeks you got acclimatized. You'd walk upstairs in the hotel and you'd be exhausted, then all of a sudden you were there, you'd got over it. It was very professional, the whole preparation.' As Osgood says, Bell was the fittest member of the party, but even the man nicknamed Nijinsky had problems: 'It was very hard to breathe, it was a week before you could think about training. You'd run ten yards and put your hands on your knees, you couldn't go for a one-two. It was frightening, like we all had asthma.'

To combat the problems of dehydration, Ramsey ushered in a strict regime. According to Francis Lee: 'We trained quite hard, we were locked up in the hotel, we didn't go out or anything like that, so the weight dropped off! Once the competition got going, a game

242

took so much out of you, all you wanted to do was recover for the next game. We never went out for the entire time we were there – he once gave us a night off at a golf club for a few drinks, and that was it. There was no going over the wall – I suppose now they'd have to be cells, not rooms!' Peter Thompson does remember a rare evening off: 'Just before the competition started he gave us a night off on the strict understanding that we were back at a certain time. Everybody broke the curfew – I stuck with Bobby Charlton because I thought he wouldn't get in trouble – but as we went upstairs to the floor we were staying on, Harold Shepherdson was sat there with a notepad, checking us in! We weren't too bad but a few were incredibly late and the next day Alf called a meeting. He was so quietly spoken, he said, "I gave you the night off, you've let me down, three or four of you I'll be speaking to individually, but I'm just going to tell you this now. The next time you step out of line, it doesn't matter how famous you are, I'm not going to bother to speak to you, I shall just give you your ticket home and thank you for joining us." Nobody did it again.' The most trouble Alf had regarding player behaviour thereafter came when Jack Charlton threatened to send him off for arguing during a game between the players and press – Ramsey on the side of the journalists for once – which the players won 9–0, Charlton's interpretation of the rules helping them on their way.

There were storms about to break and, predictably, they revolved around the local press. Alf had antagonized them the year before, complaining after the game with Mexico, 'There was a band playing outside our hotel 'til five o'clock this morning. We were promised a motorcycle escort to the stadium. It never arrived. When our players went out to inspect the pitch they were abused and jeered by the crowd. I would have thought the Mexican public would have been delighted to welcome England.' It was an unfortunately pompous conclusion to a series of legitimate points. But it was time to accept that other countries did things differently and if that wasn't to his liking, better to draw a diplomatic veil. Instead, Alf had made matters worse by throwing Mexican journalists out of the dressing room, forgetting it was accepted practice for them to be there. His zealous concern for his players spilled over and did them little good. When the Brazilians arrived in 1970, they went on a charm offensive, winning over a local population already predisposed towards them. At the other extreme, England adopted a bunker mentality. Admittedly, a fifty-year-old man would find the conditions taxing, the heat fraying his already short temper, but Ramsey did not take sufficient care of public relations. The result was a continent – already incited by memories of the 'animals' quote – united against him and his players. He was let down at times, it's true, as Peter Thompson describes: 'There was a lot of interest in us. Alf said, "The press are here from all over the world, we'll give the photographers an hour," allowing them to do anything they wanted. It went on and on, and after an hour Alf said, "Right, thank you, we're going to start training now." First of all we were going to run the length of the pitch three or four times to warm up. As we ran down the pitch, they followed us and as we turned round there was this bank of people and we couldn't get back. So Alf had another word, but it went on for ages and he lost his temper, and those were the photos that got used: "Wildman Ramsey"!' In the face of provocation, Alf was not the type to count to ten. But this merely compounded glaring errors in the preparation. England flew out their own meat (against Mexican law) and their own fruit, remarkable in a region renowned for producing it! Again, Alf was trying to ensure the minimum disruption to his players, but the Mexicans naturally took it as an insult, Francis Lee remembering, 'Alf was insistent on flying the food out, and I remember one Mexican newspaper saying that if you're thinking of throwing tomatoes at the English team, always wash them beforehand!' The fact England had a bus brought out rather than using those supplied was the last straw. Ken Jones admits, 'Alf made a mistake in not having people around him to handle things he shouldn't have had anything to do with. Alf wasn't good at that, wasn't sensitive to the locals, and it shouldn't have been left to him, he needed a good liaison officer. But he wouldn't have trusted one. He wanted to keep it tight, didn't want people around him, didn't want scouts and coaches, just wanted Alan Bass and then Neil Phillips as doctors, then Harold and Les Cocker who were essentially conditioners. Les would argue with him, Harold wouldn't, and perhaps he could have done with a bit more of that. But Alf knew what he wanted and usually got it.'

Such behaviour allowed the press to caricature him as a xenophobe, a Little Englander, even Bobby Moore writing, 'Alf didn't particularly like foreigners and he was vary wary of Mexico.' Hugh McIlvanney couched an attack in stronger terms: 'One of the most consistent elements in [Alf's] behaviour is a public lack of warmth towards anyone born outside England ... the criticisms that would be made of Ramsey for his tactics, his timing of substitutions and general handling of the team had infinitely less validity than complaints about his apparent attitude to people of other nationalities he encountered.' It's a serious charge, which suggests racism. Alf's attitude did leave much to be desired, but it was less rooted in racism than in patriotism and his marked lack of diplomatic gifts. He carried the feeling of superiority that the majority of English people of his generation carried – he grew up in the days of Empire when children were schooled that the greatest gift you could have in life was to be born British, preferably English. It was ingrained in him. And where many of his contemporaries had seen the world and met many different nationalities through the war years, Alf's only foray outside the country had been a brief posting to Palestine, so he'd had no real exposure to a foreign way of life. More accurately, his attitude to many foreign countries, notably the less well-developed nations of Latin America, was patronizing, redolent of English holidaymakers on package tours to Spain complaining about the lack of Watney's Red Barrel. He was so correct that being impolite would be the last thing on his mind, yet he could not help himself. His job must come first and if that meant ruffling a few feathers, so be it. Lack of familiarity with foreign reporters meant he didn't know whom he could trust, so he distrusted everyone – it saved time. Because he was an introvert, he was uncomfortable with strangers. He'd rather flee, but because he couldn't, his shyness made him abrupt, often upsetting people. And of course the language barrier didn't help. English journalists knew Alf better and accepted his idiosyncrasies, but abroad it could lead to trouble. Banks accepted that Alf was less than perfect: 'The Mexican press had done their worst to blacken our reputations both as footballers and private citizens. They had been antagonized by Alf's cold manner towards them and got their own back with a procession of wicked lies, exaggerations and innuendoes in their own newspapers.' These included claims that the players had indulged in orgies in local brothels and were thieves. Peter Thompson describes how the latter charge was concocted: 'We were warned before we went out not to buy any jewellery in the streets, not to go in jewellers on our own. But it was a trip of a lifetime and obviously you wanted to bring things back, so Alf arranged for a jeweller in Mexico City to come and see us and sell us stuff at wholesale prices. They put this stuff out, we had to pick what we wanted and then collect it when we got back to Mexico from Colombia. An Omega watch went missing. Alf got us all together and said we should put together and pay for it between us. Geoff Hurst said he didn't think we should because there'd been waiters and all sorts trying things on, loads of people walking round, that nobody was going to come out to Mexico, pinch a watch in the first week and carry it round all these different countries. Alf said that was fine, he understood our feelings: "I know nobody's taken it, I'll pay for it myself." The players then got together and paid for it, but it was obviously a bit funny.' This was a picnic compared with what was to come.

After a fortnight, the party flew out to Colombia. Dr Phillips concluded that the best way to beat the altitude was to play in Ecuador and Colombia, higher up, then coming down to Guadalajara for the group matches. England were staying in Bogotá at the Hotel Tequendama. As Francis Lee says, 'The first thing any football team does when it gets to a hotel is walk round the foyer and wait for the coach to shout out your room numbers, so we were all roaming around.' Peter Thompson, Bobby Moore and Bobby Charlton walked into the jeweller's, looking for presents for their families. Finding nothing to their taste, they walked out and sat down opposite the shop, Thompson recalling, 'We were laughing and joking because there were massive diamonds, earrings for £10,000. I walked ten yards to get some mail from the desk and as I walked back in, this woman came running out screaming and shouting about a bracelet that had been stolen, and Moore and Charlton were just standing there not knowing what to do. She said three men had come in, and within five minutes the foyer was full of police, cameras and reporters. It was a total set-up, because they were on the spot. We'd been warned something might happen, but we never thought it would be in the hotel. There was chaos. Alf was there, so I told him I was the third man, but he told me not to worry: "They're not after you, Peter, it's a set-up." They were after Moore and Charlton, two of the most famous players in the world.' Brazilian manager João Saldanha confirmed that his side had been subjected to similar treatment the year before – he had locked himself and the accused players in the store room until the police came to search them, in order to prove their innocence.

Ramsey immediately began to interrogate the shop manager, trying to knock holes in the evidence. Moore wrote, 'Alf handled it like an expert, and everyone thought it was done and forgotten.' The friendlies went ahead as scheduled. At 8500 feet, England beat Colombia 4–0, an impressive start, Ralph Finn noting in *World Cup 1970* that 'this was push and walk. Intelligent, accurate, man-to-man passing.' With the B team winning 1–0, it was a satisfactory day after the travails of the hotel fiasco. England flew to Ecuador to play at 9300 feet, fully 4000 feet above Guadalajara. Again England performed well, winning 2–0, with Brian Kidd staking a late claim for a place in the final squad with a goal. The B team beat Liga University 4–1 with an Astle hat-trick – Osgood had a poor game. England then had to fly back into Colombia to get a connection on to Mexico City – Ramsey had arranged to kill the time there with a screening of a western at the hotel. Peter Osgood remembers, 'We walked into Bogotá and next thing we knew Mooro had been arrested. He'd never have done anything wrong in his life, he was a superb man. It was just a big set-up.' But Alf was as calm as Bobby was. Even so, as Ken Jones says, 'Alf knew they were running a risk by going back in, but it was the only route. I don't think he thought for a moment it would happen. He couldn't comprehend it.' Moore was taken from the airport to the local courthouse while the players went off to the hotel. He was still there when the time came for England to fly out. Bobby Charlton offered to stay too, but Ramsey refused, and Moore was left in Colombia with FA Chairman Dr Andrew Stephen and Denis Follows. A thoroughly shaken manager was left to lament, 'You won't see a smile on my face until I see Bobby Moore. And I won't feel happy until I have found out how he is. This feeling has nothing to do with England or the World Cup. How can I drive the players in these circumstances?' Peter Osgood believes, 'It was probably lucky it was Bobby Moore not Bobby Charlton, because Mooro just took it in his stride. For three or four days it was upsetting for us all. If it had been anybody else, we'd have been up in arms, worried about the guy, but because it was Bobby and he was just so cool, so relaxed, it all seemed a bit unreal.' As Geoff Hurst adds, 'While Bobby was suffering in Bogotá, the rest of us were professionals and, whatever happened, we just got on with the job.' The only light relief came via Peter Thompson, Moore's room-mate: 'Alf banned all phone calls, but before he did, I was getting calls from all over. I got one from Sean Connery – Bobby moved in a different world from me – and when I told him Bobby wasn't there, he said, "Who are you?" I said, "Peter Thompson." And he asked me, "Are you his butler?"! Bobby was the man, he handled it smashing. I'd have broken down, but he accepted it and got on with life.' Moore was forced to go through a humiliating reconstruction at the shop on 27 May, but by the 29th a local judge offered him a conditional release and he returned to

Mexico, flying to Guadalajara where England had set up camp. There he was greeted by Ramsey, who threw off the stiff upper lip and hugged his returning captain. And for those who suggest that his motives were purely footballing, Ken Jones points out: 'I don't think he was ever more devastated than when Bobby got lifted, he was only worried about him.' But, as Francis Lee says, 'It gave everybody a lot more resolution, because Bobby had been framed and we were more determined to do well.'

Any previous lack of resolution is perhaps explained with regard to a lapse in team morale that occurred in Ecuador as England were ready to fly into Colombia and Moore's possible arrest. Peter Thompson remembers the slip vividly: 'Years before, we'd played in Germany and Alf always insisted on telling the players the team before anyone else, but the papers were always trying to get information to meet their deadlines. On this one occasion, he gave them the team on the promise that they didn't tell the players. Half an hour later, we knew the team, because the press had told us. Alf went crazy and got slated for his attitude after he tried to do them a favour! He didn't do it again until Mexico, where there's lots of problems with the time differences. He told the press lads the six that were dropped so they could tell their offices back in England, before he told us. The press rang England and local reporters were sent to the players' houses. David Sadler's wife rang him from England to tell him he wasn't in the twenty-two; I heard from my wife; we all knew before Alf told us, and that was really disappointing, a terrible way to find out. We went down for breakfast and there was a terrible atmosphere. We all knew the squad. The lads who were in were thrilled but they couldn't show it in front of us. It was awful. David Sadler stormed out, he got hold of Alf in the corridor and said, "I've been working with you for five weeks and all I wanted was to know from you what was happening. My wife's told me I was dropped." Alf just dropped his head. I think he was embarrassed as much as anything. We went back in to breakfast and before we started, he said, "I'm so sorry. I tried to do this properly, it's been years since I gave my team to the press, and I can only apologize to you." The press had gone round the wives looking for a quote, but I'd warned my wife not to say anything before I went out – it's easy to say something in a moment of anger and it's all over the back pages. Alf wanted us to stay out there, he said, "We came as a squad and I'd like us to stay as a squad." But only David and myself stayed. Shankly rang me in Mexico: "Thommo, I want you home on the next plane, that man has humiliated you, your wife, me, Nessie [his wife], the Liverpool supporters, everybody on Merseyside." But I'd done five weeks' work, we were staying in the Hilton, I thought I might as well get to see the World Cup in luxury!'

The six dropped were Sadler, Thompson, Coates, Shilton, McNab and Kidd – both wide players had been sacrificed, a significant move. It reflected Ramsey's loyalty, which was bordering on the self-destructive. Peter Thompson took his omission phlegmatically: 'I played at Hampden in April 1970 and got substituted, but all the papers said I'd been the best forward, so I was quite hopeful, but Shankly called me in and said, "There's no way he'll play you in Mexico." I thought I had a chance. Whether he picked me out of loyalty because I always turned up, I don't know, but he took me and then I got knocked back again. I wasn't bitter about it. Alf got a lot of criticism for it, but I always feel if I'd been good enough I'd have forced him to play me. If I'd stayed at my very best, like I did in 1964, he'd have had to pick me. I had a good run, I played eleven on the trot, and so if I'm honest with myself I can't criticize him. The few games I had after that, I didn't do that well. It wasn't as if I played fabulous and he just dropped me because I was an individualist, so I had no qualms about being left out. All through my career Alf's biggest criticism of me was that I didn't look up, which was true. I'd get the ball and off I'd go, and I couldn't change my style. He was always on at me to stop and find some of the players around me so that we could switch the play. I'd tell him I'd try my best, but once the game started I'd get the ball and disappear on my own – it wasn't me. In hindsight, it would have made me a better player, but I couldn't help it. At Liverpool, when Bill started talking tactics, he'd say, "You can go now, Thommo, because you never bloody listen," and I could leave. That wasn't how Alf played.'

If England denied themselves width, other than via the full-backs, equally odd was the fact that Jack Charlton (at 35) and, particularly, Nobby Stiles, who had little chance of playing, were selected. It caused the South American press to scoff, '1966 football will not win the 1970 World Cup.' Writing in the *Sunday Express*, Danny Blanchflower argued, 'The forces of nature are against us and Ramsey has decided to retreat in the face of them and muster his forces at the back. That way he believes England will make fewer mistakes – or pay less for their mistakes.' Blanchflower's colleague Alan Hoby was prophetic: 'Ramsey knows that, although acclimatised, his men won't be able to run and run – and then run again – as they did at home in the last World Cup. This would be lunacy in Mexico. He knows that in Mexican air even Ball and Colin Bell will have to pace themselves. He knows too that the ball, in such a rarefied atmosphere, emulates the maddest of hares on the ground; that it swirls and swerves in the air . . . he will cram the midfield with players. In modern football it is midfield domination which wins the great prizes . . . if England are to defy the cynics during their coming psychological and physical ordeal, Alf will have to perform like a puppeteer. He will have to ring the tactical changes – with flawless judgement.' Others questioned the lack of ball players in the side, but who was available? Alan Hudson was injured and others such as Frank Worthington or Rodney Marsh had not yet established themselves at the highest level. To throw them into a World Cup was risky and potentially damaging to them, something Ramsey took into consideration.

The return of Bobby Moore was a fillip prior to the first game with Romania. Peter Osgood remembers, 'I roomed with Geoff Hurst and Jeff Astle, and Astle is a funny, funny man. He brought a little record player with him and he had this copy of "Spirit In The Sky", which he just kept playing all the time. In the end me and Hursty broke it, but he kept us amused. The spirit in the squad was good and through that first month we were just looking forward to playing, which kept us going. We had a great build-up, results were superb, we were very fit, no injuries, so the time away wasn't a problem.' Ramsey escaped from the world with his players and, as Brian Glanville wrote, 'However tense and taut he might be with the world at large, Ramsey with his players was generally relaxed, friendly, avuncular, even humorous, cheerfully joining in the training games, never losing his authority but never wielding it in the paternalist manner of a Vittorio Pozzo.' Francis Lee adds, 'He was still a good player in the five-a-sides. You could always tell the lads who wanted a game, because they'd keep passing to him!' There were no selection surprises for the opener with Romania, the side that played Colombia and Ecuador taking the field, though not before Ramsey had criticized the pitch at the Jalisco Stadium in a petulant outburst, indicative of the mounting pressure. The game was no classic, but England were sufficiently commanding to ease through 1–0, Geoff Hurst scoring. They lacked real invention, but against a side physical to the point of barbarism – Newton had to be substituted after a savage tackle – this was no time for niceties. Much of England's game functioned well and the greatest concern was Banks', who noted, 'The ball comes much faster, more unexpectedly than it does at sea level and it's not sure to stay true. Sometimes it's going all over the place. Things I'd eat up at home I may find myself really scrambling to hold.' Francis Lee is less certain that conditions made that much difference: 'The keepers used to say the ball moved quicker through the air, but as a striker you couldn't tell whether it did or not. Overall, it was a tough game against Romania, but we were a better side and, although it was only 1-0, we were comfy winners.' The only cloud on the horizon was the constant abuse England had been subjected to by the locals, a problem they'd brought on themselves.

England's second opponents were Brazil, and there was speculation over team changes. Peter Osgood felt he had a chance of getting back in the side: 'We had a B side v the A side game, and the B team won 3-1 - I got a couple past Gordon, was nutmegging Nobby Stiles, it was marvellous. I was at the top of my form, the fittest I'd been in my life, working hard. I came on against Romania and played well. I was flying. Bobby Moore told me I was playing against Brazil and when Alf gave the team talk he said the team would be that which finished against Romania, which was great. But then he started talking about what Francis Lee was going to do, and I'd come on for him in that game. Bobby said, "Hold on, Alf, Ossie finished the game." Alf apologized to me - I wasn't even in the squad. It broke my heart, I went out that night and got drunk. I was only 23 and that was no way to treat anybody. I missed training the next day, the only one to miss it on that trip, I think.' Ramsey hadn't meant to upset Osgood. Rather it was an example of how he could be so preoccupied with a problem that all else simply slipped from his mind - Spurs players have recalled down the years how Alf once came out of the dressing room in such deep thought that he walked straight past his wife without recognizing her! And in Mexico, Alf had plenty to think about where Brazil were concerned - they'd already demolished Czechoslovakia 4-1. Meeting Ken Jones in the hotel after he'd seen the game, Ramsey said simply, 'They can play,' a classic understatement which made his admiration clear. He understood how upset Osgood was, but did he forgive? Osgood played against Czechoslovakia when Ramsey was desperate to rest his forwards, but did not play again until 1974 despite England's often chronic lack of goals and creativity in the intervening years.

Ramsey felt Brazil had a weakness in the air. He stressed that Wright and Cooper should get forward to provide ammunition for

Hurst, while Astle was on the bench. The game was of great psychological significance: if England could hold Brazil, in conditions to their liking, it would confirm that the World Champions would not let the crown slip without a struggle; if they were brushed aside, as Czechoslovakia had been, the game was up. England were fortunate in having five days to recover from the Romanian match, much of which was given over to relaxation. Peter Thompson remembers, 'They didn't let us go in the sun. Whether that was a mistake or not – because they had to play in it – I don't know. We were in this beautiful complex and we were sitting in the shade, it was a bit embarrassing. Bobby Moore went to Alf and said, "Is there any chance of any sun?" But Alf said, "No, it's exhausting." We had a meeting, and eventually Alf said, "You can have a quarter of an hour on your front and on your back." Harold Shepherdson had a stopwatch on us – we'd run out of the shade and lie down, then fifteen minutes later Harold would come out and shout "turn over". It was ridiculous, really, the Mexicans were laughing at us! Then fifteen minutes later, Harold would come out and tell us to come back in!' Rest was of paramount importance, but the night before the game, the squad got precious little, as Francis Lee recalls: 'It was a disgrace – there were about 4000 people out in the street, they got some old car wrecks and they were jumping on the roofs, banging them with sticks. We couldn't get any sleep.' That England were as popular as the plague was rammed home the following day – if the reception in the Romanian game had been aggressive, now it was positively hostile. The Mexicans were not simply anti-England, but pro-Brazil. Add the Brazilian contingent and England had few friends in the 69,000 capacity crowd.

1970 and that Brazilian side have become increasingly legendary with the years, so it's as well to remember that they were apprehensive about playing England. England had the kudos of being Champions, had played well in Rio the previous summer, and had proved conclusive winners over Romania. In a game played at noon in 98 degrees to accommodate European television, they made a bright start, Pelé forcing Banks to make *that save* in the tenth minute – had that gone in so early, what difference might it have made? As it was, England assumed superiority for much of the first half, Ramsey's insistence on precise passing paying dividends. England rarely lost the ball in the packed midfield and made chances, Lee coming closest. As he relates, 'We could have won – I missed a good chance, I went to volley it but finished up heading it straight at the keeper and it rebounded out. We clipped the bar; second half we missed a few.' But as Blanchflower wrote, 'Pretty even ... the Brazilians could get goals where we could not.' England continued to have possession in the second half, but the Brazilians became more urgent, menacing. At times, it seemed only Moore stood between them and a deluge of goals, Geoff Hurst marvelling at, 'The most magnificent display I've ever seen from a central defender. He raised his game to another level.' Eventually, a goal had to come. Tostao beat three on the left, including Moore, and pushed the ball across to Pelé, the defence open as Moore had been drawn across. Pelé held it a fraction, slid the ball to Jairzinho, who crashed it past Banks. Ramsey's reaction was commendably quick, bringing on Astle and Bell in place of Lee and Bobby Charlton, though as Peter Thompson recalls, they were barely ready: 'Emlyn Hughes was on the bench for the Brazil game, and he was sitting next to Jeff. It was so hot, just watching in the midday sun was tiring. Emlyn told me that Jeff was just nodding off when Alf told him to come on, so he was still half asleep when he got on the pitch.' Immediately Astle's height was used to advantage as he manufactured a chance which Ball missed, then Astle shot wide. For all that, England looked threatening, making the absence of wingers galling – had Thompson been on hand to feed Astle and Hurst, England might have salvaged a draw. As it was, they had to be satisfied with honourable defeat. Exchanging shirts at the end, Moore and Pelé agreed they'd meet in the Final, though Pelé was later less enthusiastic about England's football, arguing, 'One has to remember that England's defence was strong precisely *because* their attack was weak. With only two or three men in front it automatically gives the defence one or two more men.' When one recalls England's outstanding players were Moore and Mullery, Pelé has a point. Ramsey was disappointed but not downcast, for Brazil, far and away the best team, had no desire to meet England again. He allowed the players out for a drink, with an 11.30 curfew, while he picked over the bones of the game and surely realized that while England could compete, they could not overcome, not in Mexico. Moore had been asked whether the Brazilians were stronger than the Englishmen and replied, 'I could not say that I had [noticed] but this was largely due to the Brazilians' style of play. They dictate their own pace, slowing it and speeding it up when necessary, so that it is difficult to detect a higher degree of fitness unless, say, a match goes into extra time.' England were a good passing side (Lee recalls Ramsey 'preaching every day not to give the ball away because you couldn't get it back') but they could not dictate in that manner. It was not in the character of our football to do so, until Liverpool developed their style on the European model. Six years later, Ramsey conceded, 'The side I took to Mexico was a good one with a chance of winning, but I can admit now that I didn't really think we would win. It is difficult in South America with the high temperature and altitude problem. European teams are at a disadvantage, as was proved in the end. Even if we had reached the Final I don't think we would have held on to the trophy.' As Peter Thompson puts it, 'We went out early to acclimatize, but you're never going to feel comfortable in the heat and humidity.'

'When you got to playing a game it was very difficult because it was so hot, you sweated a lot,' says Francis Lee. 'Smaller guys like me lost seven or eight pounds, the bigger guys, like Brian Labone, as much as twelve pounds a game. When your body's subjected to that kind of punishment, it takes a good week to get right, to come back from it. The guys who did most work were up front, and neither Geoff nor myself played against the Czechs because it was so demanding, especially with a 4–4–2. He gave us a break looking towards the latter part of the tournament.' But this only reinforced the paucity of talent open to Ramsey. We required endeavour because we didn't have the skill of the Brazilians, Lee arguing forcibly that, 'People talk about us not playing with wingers, but if we'd had Jairzinho and Rivelino, we'd have played with bloody wingers. And if you've got three forwards like Gerson, Pelé, Tostao, then you play them as well! Not everybody played with five up front, people forget that about 1970.' England were not the only team beaten by Brazilian genius. Ramsey might have shown a little more imagination in his squad selection and it's possible to argue that the inferiority complex he carried over the South Americans superior technique blinded him to similarly gifted home-grown footballers, but, ultimately, he was faced with the same problem that faced Walter Winterbottom in 1953. The opposition were better. He tried to paper over the cracks with a suffocating 4–4–2 system that might well have won again in Europe, but he did so because of circumstances – look at your players, decide on a system. Broadly speaking, we still had the same players or similar ones, the hard runners English football produced. When faced by a nation demanding victory, what else was he to do? No pundit's nor supporter's job rests on the outcome of a game. His did. We can all dream of fancy footwork and thrilling formations with five forwards plundering goals, but Ramsey had a duty to fulfil. England weren't popular with certain sportswriters because they were dull, worthy rather than dashing, allowing McIlvanney to complain, 'What had to be admitted on all sides was that those who had seen [England] had rarely been in danger of having a heart attack from the excitement of it all . . . but football, despite the incessant parroting of the virtues of "professionalism", is not merely about results. It is also about style, about the way results are achieved, about pride.' Laudable sentiments with which many concur, but it ignored the central point. What is the England team for and who does it represent? The players? The Football League? The press? The 80 or 90,000 who go to Wembley? The millions of football fans who watch on TV? The millions more who pay no heed to football except when there's a World Cup or international? Ramsey concluded England represented just that. England, the nation, all of it, good and bad. He was as accountable to people who didn't know a football from a cabbage as those who went through the turnstiles week in week out. He had to win, that was all. Ramsey was not at fault as much as the culture that produced him.

By the time England played Czechoslovakia, Brazil had won the group with six points. England and Romania had two each, the Czechs none, so a draw would see them through. Confident his defence would provide the necessary clean sheet, Ramsey made changes. Astle replaced Hurst, Allan Clarke made his debut in place of Lee, Jack Charlton came in for Labone, Newton returned from injury, Bell came in for Ball. Inevitably, England stuttered, the changes destroying continuity, but they won, Clarke converting a penalty. The only alarm came when Banks misjudged a shot and was lucky to push it on to the bar, the altitude playing tricks. Danny Blanchflower mourned, 'A load of old rubbish . . . there is no way that Sir Alf Ramsey or anyone else can justify the present England tactics. He has found a way to destroy the game rather than glorify it . . . by doing it Ramsey makes a potentially good team look like a bad one. They survive despite their tactics – not because of them. The team has lost the sense of going forward. That is why they fail to score.' It was England at their most cagey, but also their most sensible. Why expend precious energy? There might be three more games to come. 'Just get through it' was the maxim.

Second place meant a quarter-final against West Germany, who had an additional day's rest before the game. That he should be confronted by them again held no fears for Alf. Indeed, European opposition was a bonus, for at least they should be equally troubled by the climate. West Germany had arrived in Mexico a fortnight later than England, but they held the crucial advantage of having played all their games in Leon, 722 feet higher than Guadalajara. This was another test. Once more, English preparations were a shambles, disappointing in one as professional as Ramsey. England had booked no rooms in Leon and found themselves in the motel used by the West Germans' wives and girlfriends – hardly ideal. As Ken Jones says, 'We're presently attacking the Germans as arrogant for booking the hotel they want for the World Cup Final in 1998. That's not arrogant, it's preparation. Off the field, England's wasn't good enough in '70.' With only three days between the Czech and West German games, a problem compounded by the travelling, it was as well Ramsey had rested his senior players, though perhaps Bobby Charlton could have been spared too, for as Moore wrote prior to Mexico, 'Bobby is so willing, so eager, that he tends to take more out of himself than he need. He cannot help it . . . a habitual groove. Can he do this in thin air? If only he were lazier it might be better for him.' If he were lazier, would he have been in the side?

Ramsey had his team clear in his mind, his first XI, the side that played Romania. The night before the party travelled to Leon, Banks did not sleep and spent much of the night vomiting, his room-mates Bobby Charlton and Newton suffering a milder version of the illness, supporting Peter Osgood's theory that, 'Somebody got at him – we all did everything together a far as food and drink was concerned. We all ate the same things, we were all on salt tablets and various other pills to protect your stomach, which is why it was so hard to understand.' What with the problems in Bogotá, the noise the night before the Brazil game, and now this, 1970 became a field day for conspiracy theorists (if only Oliver Stone were a football fan). By morning, Banks was a little better and able to get on the coach for the five-hour trek, but within an hour felt unwell and had to miss training the next day. On the day of the game, he was named in the side, attended the team meeting, but was ill again and had to miss out. His deputy was Peter Bonetti. There were no real worries there, for as Peter Osgood confirms, 'Peter was the best professional I ever played with, bar none. He trained right, ate right, drank right, he was a good family man, never went out late, a model pro. He was second in the world behind Banks, no doubt in my mind.' Even so, it was an unwanted disruption, the loss of a potent symbol of 1966. And West Germany were better than then. Their qualifying form had been impressive – where England had struggled to two goals in three games, Gerd Muller had managed seven and the team ten. They'd looked a threat in attack, wingers Libuda and Loehr wreaking havoc, Helmut Schoen using his substitutes with flair, introducing Jürgen Grabowski in the second period, a lightning presence on the flanks against tiring defenders. Consolation for England could be drawn from the fact that Germany's had been a weaker group – Peru, Bulgaria and Morocco – and that both Bulgaria and Morocco had taken the lead. Yet even that proved how resilient the Germans were, coming back in such heat. And in Muller, they had an irresistible, single-minded goalscorer working in tandem with Uwe Seeler.

There was a sharp contrast between the teams. West Germany moved the ball about, England ran and ran – Geoff Hurst, for instance, was told to stay with and challenge the sweeper Karl-Heinz Schnellinger, drawing away his own marker, Moore writing, 'Geoff [soaked up] tremendous physical punishment without complaining and skilfully spearheaded our attack . . . one of Geoff's finest international performances.' That was true, but it was exhausting. Where Hurst was running, Muller was lurking, sharper if a chance came his way. Yet that supreme athleticism seemed to be winning out in the early exchanges. After half an hour of dominance, England forged ahead, Mullery scoring a superb goal that had swept from the left-back position out to the right wing, involving both full-backs and Mullery, instigator and finisher. The game was becoming a rerun of 1966, Beckenbauer ineffective, preoccupied with Charlton, Seeler getting no joy from Mullery, Moore snuffing out Muller. All was going to plan and five minutes into the second period Peters made it 2–0. It was a superb goal too, silencing those who suggested England could not play football. Moore won the ball in his own half, passed to Ball, then on to Hurst, who carried the ball forward before feeding Newton with a beautiful pass as he burst down the right. His cross was as good as any winger could have delivered and on the far post, Peters ghosted in to score. They thought it was all over. It wasn't.

Eight minutes later, Schoen introduced Grabowski, who had been so impressive in the group stage. But why fret? England were in charge, Alan Ball racing around the Germans shouting, '*Auf Wiedersehen.*' The whole team seemed infected by such arrogance and, rather than going on to increase the advantage, they began to fall back, to play out time – 'They're pissing about too early,' as Bobby Charlton memorably declared. With twenty-two minutes left, Beckenbauer was pushed out to the right edge of the box by Mullery, found space where Cooper might have been had he had the energy to get back, and struck a hopeful shot because there was nothing else on. Keeping low, it somehow beat Bonetti and nestled in the far corner. Did the ball move differently in the air, was Bonetti surprised by the pace of such a soft-looking shot as Banks had been against the Czechs? Banks had got away with the misjudgement. Bonetti wasn't so lucky. At 2–1, the game was alive. Then came one of the most controversial decisions of Ramsey's career. As Beckenbauer struck his shot, Bell was warming up, ready to replace Charlton: 'There were no instructions, just fill Bobby's spot, play my normal game. It's easy on TV, you think it's going well, but the climate takes a lot out of you. The theme was just a fresh pair of legs – to play 90 minutes of international football in that heat takes a lot out of you and Bobby always did so much running anyway.' The goal didn't change Ramsey's mind and Bell came on. Within a minute, he'd had a rasping shot saved by Maier and crossed for Hurst to head an inch wide of the goal. Had either gone in, Ramsey would have been hailed a tactical genius. With ten minutes remaining, Peters was removed, Norman Hunter coming on, a signal of English intent – what we have, we hold. (Had Hunter done what he did for Leeds and deposited Beckenbauer into the stand, England would have won.) Seconds later a mishit clearance from Labone found Schnellinger, who lofted the ball into the middle with a first-time cross. Seeler whirled away from Mullery on the right edge of the six-yard box, stretched and managed to get his head to the ball, merely looking to knock it back into play. It ballooned up, floated gently across the box, above the stranded keeper and into the net. Unlike four years earlier, it was England who were exhausted, not the Germans, and they almost snatched victory in normal time. Just as there was only one winner in extra-time in '66, so it was in '70 – England's creativity had gone with Charlton and Peters. Could England hold on? With eleven minutes left, a Grabowski centre was headed back across the face of goal by Loehr, outjumping a shattered Newton. Muller, squat, powerful, a bull of a man, found himself alone between Labone and Moore, leapt into the air and lashed a volley past the helpless Bonetti. Rich irony, indeed – England had been beaten by an indolent forward who had done nothing all afternoon but put this chance in the back of the net, the speciality of another little man called Greaves. England fought back like Champions, but they were Champions no more.

The inquest has lasted twenty-seven years, will probably last twenty-seven more. Was the substitution of Charlton vital? Would Banks have prevented the goals? At 2–0 the game was won, but the entire team was guilty of fatal arrogance. They fell further back into defence, offering the initiative to the Germans, who had nothing to lose anyway, ignoring the fact that they had come from behind twice in the competition already. That was a collective error, though Ramsey takes ultimate responsibility for not urging his players forward. Schoen's introduction of Grabowski, predictable as it was, turned the game. Someone should have stopped him, but Cooper was simply too tired, as Peter Thompson explains: 'You couldn't play as an attacking full-back. It was too much. They were totally exhausted doing one job, never mind two. I played in loads of practice games and I found it so difficult doing my own job. When Grabowski came on, Terry could hardly walk. I'd have loved to have gone on and played against him then! It was red hot and the players were tired – I was soaked to the skin watching from the stand. At half-time I went to the dressing room and they were utterly exhausted, another five minutes and they'd have been asleep. So when Grabowski came on, he was fresh and he tore England to bits.' It was inevitable Grabowski would arrive on the scene, so shouldn't a fresh opponent have come on?

Beckenbauer's goal was unfortunate for Bonetti. He'd have expected to save it. But he wasn't selected until an hour or two before kick-off. Would it not have been better to accept the day before that Banks couldn't play and allow Bonetti proper time to prepare? Given Banks had been ailing for two full days, it was wishful thinking to believe he might recover and be at his best. Instead, Bonetti was dropped in at the deep end at the last minute, never having experienced the behaviour of the ball in match conditions. Paradoxically, England's excellent defence didn't help either, since before the goal Bonetti was scarcely in the match. Maybe he should have played against the Czechs, though you would have found no one voicing that opinion at the time. The blame for the German defeat, though, should not be laid at Bonetti's door.

The substitution of Bobby Charlton is the greatest talking point. Beckenbauer's view is interesting: 'Whereas England had a slice of luck in 1966, I think we did in 1970. After an hour, with England leading 2–0, we were completely dead. We had not had a single chance . . . after I had scored what I thought was a rather soft goal, to make it 2–1, Alf Ramsey decided to substitute Bobby Charlton, who we felt was the heart of the game.' If you follow the maxim that you should always do what your opponent doesn't want you to do, the substitution was an error, yet if Bell's cross had been knocked in, and England had won 3–1, it would have been a masterstroke. Results are used as proof of the correctness of decisions, but are they? Alf's problem was he'd always preached they were and, as Peter Osgood says, 'It's the other side of the Greaves thing in '66. In 1966 his decision worked for him. In 1970, it didn't.' But it could easily have been different.

Charlton was taken off to save him for the anticipated semi-final, but wasn't that over-protective? This was the man Beckenbauer said had the lungs of a horse. He was two years younger than Seeler, who coped admirably. But at 32, and a ceaseless worker, perhaps the heat told on him as Osgood recalls: 'What people don't realize is when Bobby played against Brazil, we played at noon and he lost ten pounds in weight, and Bobby was getting on a bit then. If we'd beaten Germany, the semi-final was three days later, and Alf was desperate to rest Bobby's legs because he was the jewel. He knew the likes of Alan Ball could get through anything, but he had to be careful with Bobby, because he was that bit older, he tried to nurse him a bit but it came unstuck because it released Beckenbauer. For 70 minutes, Bobby had a fantastic game, probably one of his best for England.' Perhaps he shouldn't have played against Czechoslovakia? Yet did it really change the course of the game? West Germany had got a goal back; *that* changed things. And though it's a cliché, 2–0 *is* an awkward lead, not as impregnable as it looks. If the opposition score, they see a way back, while you're mortified, paralysed with the fear of losing a seemingly unassailable position. If you've extra-time to contend with, you're really on the downward slope. And 2–0 forces the opposition into all-out attack, so they're more dangerous. Had Charlton stayed on, Beckenbauer would have ignored him anyway in the hunt for a goal. You need to make it 3–0 before you can feel secure.

Much is made of the psychology of the substitution, giving the Germans hope, but take another look. Bell was warming up as Beckenbauer scored. Had he sat down, England would have looked look rattled. By bringing him on, Ramsey sent out a signal of unconcern. Many back Ramsey's judgement on the matter, Tom Finney saying, 'Having heard his explanation, that Bob was at the age when he was getting tired in the heat, he felt it better to take him off and have him that much fresher for the semi-final, that's a reasonable decision. Unfortunately it backfired.' Bobby Charlton's view was, 'Alf thought [it was right to take me off] and as his judgement has been right in the past, I did not argue. But he might have made a mistake.' Jimmy Armfield reflects, '"If" is a massive word in football – if Banks had been fit, if he hadn't made the substitutions, who knows what might have happened? The result stands and you have to take that, but it's only a result from that one game. I don't think I'd criticize him for taking Bobby off, yet, in saying that, if I'd been manager I might not have done it. But that's part of the make-up of the man, part of the same make-up that won us the World Cup in the first place. He did what he felt was right at the time – perhaps he was thinking things that others weren't. He was looking ahead. But you can't be number one for ever, you can only be at a peak for so long, that's part of life. In football it's more brutal, perhaps – you win one competition and before you've chance to enjoy that, you're on to the next, from World Cup to the European Championships.' And, of course, Alf might have left Charlton on, England might still have lost 3–2, and the debate would centre around why he didn't take him off. Hindsight is the greatest manager.

Substitutions, though, were never Alf's forte – where Schoen was a master of them, Ramsey was not – for it needs the instincts of a gambler. Alf was a man who valued consistency. He was so wedded to his system that it militated against tactical changes. And perhaps that's where errors were made; the system. The two best teams in Mexico were Brazil and West Germany, both of whom used width and looked to score goals. Libuda, Loehr and Grabowski were good wingers, but not great. They were specialists with one main job to do, where Ramsey's all-purpose wing-backs had to do too much. And if conditions were too strenuous, should Charlton have been in the squad, for all his genius? If a man cannot stand up to the ninety minutes, should he be there at all? Because, finally, it was fitness that cost England the game, the increase in altitude playing a part. Charlton came off because he was tiring, Cooper and Newton were exhausted, Mullery and Moore caught out by fatigue for the second and third goals. All had two jobs to do. As Peter Thompson says, 'We stuck to the system and other teams caught up. They could counter us *and* play their own game.' Finally, though, for all that mistakes were made, it was no disgrace to lose to the likes of Seeler,

Beckenbauer, Muller, Wolfgang Overath, Berti Vogts and Sepp Maier. They were a fine side with lots of potential – they were the coming power.

After the match 'Alf didn't say much' according to Peter Osgood. 'He just let us go and have a drink and then said, "We'll be going home now." That was it. What else is there to say? I don't think he could believe it.' Francis Lee adds, 'Everybody was completely shattered and then devastated by the result. Once you've blown it in a competition like that, there's no point having rows about it, because if you haven't done it nobody needs to tell you. We all knew that we dropped it.' Ken Jones feels, 'The loss in Leon crippled Alf. I went looking for him afterwards – the players were by the pool, I wandered around and found Alf by his chalet, two hours after the game. He was sitting there in his tracksuit, he looked up at me, and I said, "Alf, I'm sorry." He asked, "Do you want some champagne? Pour it yourself." Then he said, "Of all the people that had to go sick, it had to be him." That really was the story. But he also knew he'd made a mistake in bringing Bobby off and he apologized to him on the plane home. He told me that Alf had sat down next to him and said he was wrong. He said, "He thanked me for all I'd done for England and I knew then it was my last match."' Later on, in response to questioning, Alf was unrepentant: 'I have never seen England give away such easy goals ... there was no way we could lose to the Germans. I respected them, but it ended there. We couldn't lose and yet we lost. The whole thing was unreal, a freak of nature ... when we went into extra-time there was nothing I could say to the players. They had done so well that I simply had to ask them to keep at it. If I could do this all over again I wouldn't alter anything ... I would like to stay here and see out the rest of the competition. But my place is with my players and so I shall fly home with them.'

They flew back and into the headlines, understandably refusing to give a press conference. Asked if he was glad to be back, Alf replied, 'If you ask a stupid question you'll get a stupid answer ... leave me alone. I have had a very long journey and I'm tired. No autopsies.' When he did speak to the press, he told them, 'We have nothing to learn from Brazil,' a statement which caused uproar. But as Ken Jones argues, he was right: 'Alf was misrepresented because he was a clumsy communicator. What he meant was there was no point trying to play like them, we couldn't do it. They had done what he knew they'd do, there was nothing you could learn from that. He was vilified as a result.' In time, 1970 would be seen as a blip, the Brazilian team among the last great entertainers – has any team since matched the genius of Gerson, Pelé, Tostao, Jairzinho, Rivelino, Carlos Alberto, Everaldo? And they didn't come together by accident – Brazil were in a training camp for months, establishing a rapport. If Ramsey had been given that luxury, he might have produced a side with greater flair. In the time available, he could only introduce organization. He might have pointed out that the very pressmen attacking him for being defensive were the ones responsible – when each game is treated as life and death in their pages, as though the national football team are going off to war, how else can they play? The press and the public are obsessed with results above all else, however much they might pretend otherwise. There is no sense of perspective. But the world goes on. England's defeat meant the end of Terry Collier's marriage in *The Likely Lads*. It allegedly cost Labour the General Election, setting in motion the chain of events that would take Thatcher to the premiership – now *that's* a tragedy.

Brazil blinded everyone to the facts. World football was a game of chess, of organization, not of individuals – unless you had five fully fledged geniuses in your team. England *were* the only team that really troubled Brazil and, with a little luck, might have made the Final again. But since 1966 the game had moved on and others had passed them. West Germany were in the vanguard, playing a game that depended less on perpetual motion and more on moving the ball, a game for all continents. It was time to catch up.

15 1–1

Whenever Ramsey had taken on a new managerial task in the past, he'd done so from a position of strength. At Ipswich, he took over a club that had done nothing and expected to do little. Any improvement was welcome. With England, he was taking over a side that had underachieved, so morale was low and, by removing the selection committee, he won the thanks of the nation. Post-1966, he was the guiding genius that had won the Cup and though he was expected to do it again, he had the country's respect. Now he had to rebuild, but the tide was against him. England had failed in Mexico and Ramsey was the scapegoat because of the Charlton substitution. Not only had he lost the game, he'd removed the nation's favourite and probably ended his career. As Graham Taylor was to find out when he did the same to Gary Lineker, the nation is slow to forgive the slaying of its heroes. Ramsey had now lost much of his respect. The man who believed solely in results had failed – this was a harsh appraisal, for England's performance was scarcely a failure, but that was the mood. Having won the World Cup once, it was now ours by divine right.

Ramsey was now a manager on probation. Just as victory in 1966 was a last glorious fling, the final days of English greatness, defeat in 1970 reaffirmed our lost status. It was a profound blow. The post-war years had seen the loss of Empire, Suez, a diminishing of global authority, a European Community that did not want our participation. The pound in your pocket *had* been affected, and if you were English, so what? No big deal any more. The props were creaking, the currency about to go along with Imperial measurements, the Establishment crumbling – the satirical mood that had begun with *Beyond The Fringe* making it obvious old England had no role, an anachronistic society with no direction for the future. Even The Beatles split. Defeat in Mexico was a profound blow to the psychology of the country. Tony Benn summed up the mood: 'In 1900 it was obvious what being British meant . . . But today? British policy is discussed at the UN, you watch your football game from

Mexico, over an American satellite, you are defended by NATO, you work for Ford, whose export practices have to conform to GATT and whose home market is studied by the IMF, permissive legislation has almost eroded censorship, you are metricating, decimalising . . . Technology appears to be changing everything and producing a sense of loss of cultural identity. This I am sure is the explanation of much of the new nationalism of our time.' That was exacerbated by the fact that now we'd lost to the West Germans for the first time ever in anything that mattered. That was symbolic of our lost stature, especially as the West Germans had enjoyed an economic miracle, were instrumental in shaping the new Europe that we were begging to join – their Europe where our future lay, their Europe that Little Englanders despised. Few would forgive Ramsey for losing at all, but especially to them.

What was the effect on Ramsey himself, how traumatic were those last fifty minutes? This was the man who cocooned himself in self-belief, who convinced himself of his unerring ability to get things right – after all, he'd barely had a setback in his managerial career and few in his playing days, and those he'd dismissed as accidents. His substitutions cost a game that was won, lost England a probable World Cup Final, a triumph in itself even had they lost to Brazil. He'd privately conceded it was his fault by apologizing to Bobby Charlton on the way home. Such a seismic error undermined him with the public, and with himself. It must have been shocking to find just how angry the press and public were with England's incomprehensible failure, a few calling for him to quit. Thereafter, Ramsey would retreat further, hiding in a shell of caution, taking fewer and fewer risks, looking ever more to results for justification, for sanctuary. The vindication of 1966 had evaporated; it had to be replaced. But Alf was forced to do so in less propitious circumstances, with an ageing side. Suddenly, he too looked even more a part of the past, an old man in a young man's game. In 1966 Alf had been scholarly, his tactics capturing the crown. Now he looked reactionary, wedded to old ways and bemused by advances. Substitutions changed the game more radically than most believe, allowing free-thinking managers to ring the changes, to take risks, to pose different questions. A student of the game should be ideally placed to exploit that, but Ramsey wasn't instinctive, nor was he a gambler – leaving Greaves out in '66 wasn't a gamble, it was a logical, calculated decision. And because he thought things through, he wasn't flexible in play. He picked an eleven and they should be able to do the job.

The game was in danger of passing him by. He needed to regroup, quickly.

He was given a helpful draw in qualifying for the Nations Cup – Malta, Greece and Switzerland, none of whom should trouble England. Ramsey had a wonderful opportunity to tear up the England side and start again. But one so devoted to his players could not take it. Looking at the twenty-two who returned from Mexico, who would still be around in Munich in 1974? If they wouldn't, was it time to ease them out? As Peter Osgood says, 'I think after 1970 he should have kept the likes of Mooro in his squad, but not necessarily played them, just used their experience on the new lads. He should have started to rebuild right away, because if we qualified for 1974 it was obvious that Bobby would be too old, and Mullery, Hurst, Lee weren't going to be around. If he'd done that, with the talent we had, the flair players and the likes of Channon, Keegan, McFarland and Todd, we would have qualified in 1974, but he left it too late to bring them in. Mooro played until 1973, which was too long.' England played a friendly with East Germany in November 1970. The side was interesting: Shilton, Hughes, Cooper, Mullery, Sadler, Moore, Lee, Ball, Hurst, Clarke, Peters. Of them, Cooper, Mullery, Moore, Lee, Hurst and Peters would be in their thirties come the next World Cup, hardly geriatrics, but borderline cases given the punishment each received in the Football League – between the two World Cups, each could expect to clock up anything up to 250 appearances for club and country. All were model professionals – Ramsey wouldn't have picked them otherwise – but even they couldn't hold back time. For the time being though, they represented England's best and Ramsey wanted to win games, not look ahead. They beat East Germany 3–1, a confidence booster prior to the start of qualification.

The first game was with Malta, in Valetta, in February, England's second game in seven months. It proved a precursor of the troubles that would assail Alf over the next few years, several players pulling out of the squad with injury, though, as Peter Osgood points out, there was no conspiracy: 'You'd turn up on Sunday night for an international, do a bit of light training on the Monday (that's if you weren't flying away from home), light training Tuesday, play on Wednesday, fly home Thursday, play again for your club on Saturday. We never thought twice about it.' Nevertheless, Ramsey was forced to play an inexperienced side – Roy McFarland, Martin Chivers, Joe Royle and Colin Harvey made debuts, Reaney got his third cap, Moore – suspended by West Ham after a late drinking incident in the company of Greaves and Brian Dear – Lee and Hurst were out, though Banks returned. Roy McFarland recalls the pressure of that first game: 'It was my debut and not only that, I was replacing the great Bobby Moore – I was a bit disappointed Alf didn't make me captain! I played alongside Norman Hunter. It was an important game, and we got through it narrowly. Alf was very thorough, he'd told us all about the opposition. I think he felt that if you were picked, his job was to tell you what the other side might do, but it was up to you to sort yourself out. You already had his confidence, and because he didn't make silly changes you felt you'd earned the right to be there. I remember hearing the anthems and feeling very proud to be representing my country, and Alf instilled a lot of that, made it apparent that you were playing for England and that that was important. He was single-minded, no ifs and buts, straight down the middle, he knew what he wanted and took responsibility for it. When I first came in, I noticed immediately that there was a helluva lot of respect for him as a man and as a manager. People ask me about the coaching with England. Did I learn anything? Did we try new things? But the answer's no, not really. That was very striking. When we'd done our training, Alf would often walk round the individuals and have a little word with you on your own. He came up to me one day and said, "Roy, if you're going to improve your game, I suggest you practise standing jumps. From a run, you're very strong in the air, but from standing, you're not the best and you need to get stronger." And I did practise that. But I remember it vividly because it was unusual, Alf wasn't one to tell you how to play.'

The difficulty of introducing new faces was apparent when England squeaked through 1–0. Had they lost, the clamour for Ramsey's head would have grown shrill; yet he was doing what many wanted, giving the new generation a chance. Things weren't helped by conditions, a factor omitted from most reports. Roy McFarland remembers: 'It had to be the worst football pitch anyone ever made a debut on – most schoolboys make their debut on better pitches than that! It was hard, sandy clay that had been watered and rolled – Banksie had to make a save and when he got up his shorts were ripped and his leg grazed. Maybe worrying about the pitch meant that you didn't worry about the opposition. We had a quiet game at the back, then in the last few minutes Joe Cini got away from me and Banks had to make a great save, which opened my eyes as to how good

Gordon was. He hadn't been involved for eighty minutes, then makes a great save. For a defender, you counted yourself fortunate to play in front of him, and Shilton. They were special.'

That comparative failure upset Ramsey, and for Greece's visit to Wembley in April the old guard returned. Naturally the performance was much better, a 3-0 win, but it was a retrograde step. England had been poor in Malta, but the young talent deserved a second chance – Harvey was never capped again and Royle had to wait almost two years for his second cap. Under fire, Ramsey preferred to surround himself with the players who had brought success rather than uncovering those who'd bring it. To criticize a man for loyalty is harsh (particularly if he is as capable of looking after a friend as Ramsey was with Wilf McGuinness – when he was ousted as manager at Manchester United, Ramsey called him to say, 'Don't mind the bastards, come and have dinner with me,' offering him a job managing an FA XI to keep his hand in) but in competitive sport there's little room for sentiment, and there were many young footballers apparently worthy of a chance. The press screamed for the introduction of Worthington, Marsh, Bowles, Osgood and Hudson, but Ramsey wouldn't relent, though as Ken Jones says, not without reason: 'At one time he thought Alan Hudson was perhaps the most gifted young England footballer he'd ever seen, and he'd picked him provisionally for 1970. He had a bad injury, missed the Cup Final, missed Mexico, and was never the same. Before, he was attacking the defences, running at people, strong, quick, but afterwards he got into a way of playing where he went back into his own half and was knocking other players in.'

One selection personified Ramsey's perverse delight in annoying his critics. Arsenal's Peter Storey was not the most elegant footballer ever to pull on the England shirt and, for some, his elevation was evidence that Ramsey was stuck in a rut. Storey was a replacement for Stiles or Mullery, but he hadn't the same quality. Indeed, there was a dearth of quality in the English game, Ramsey did not have the world-class players that he'd built around in 1966, but then, for the systems man, that shouldn't have been an issue. But while systems might be OK at club level, at international level you need real ability and a special character. Few Englishmen had that. Had Ramsey devised a new system, he might have papered over the cracks but, instead, England atrophied. They'd meet blanket defence and have no reply, minnow nations causing discomfort. There was no spark. In the past England had been solid and had relied on Bobby

Charlton or Geoff Hurst to get a goal out of nothing. They were superb players, that was their forte. But Charlton was finished, Hurst ageing. Where were their replacements? Alf couldn't find them, though his critics suggested that he wasn't looking.

The players had a different view to those on the sidelines. McFarland argues, 'We weren't negative, I never felt that as a player, but I think he had problems getting the balance. Alf always had an anchorman, be it Nobby, Storey, Mullery, he liked that type of player, which made England look more defensive, but you could say that they were freeing the likes of Ball and Peters to be creative. I felt that there was always the likelihood of goals from midfield – Alan was the instigator of so much, Martin was always liable to get a goal. But we didn't always score the goals – we made the chances but they wouldn't always go in. If in the 1970s England had had a Greaves or a Shearer or a Lineker, Alf probably wouldn't have got that criticism. After Franny Lee, nothing was solid for him up front. Franny had that temperament, that class at international level, that arrogance you need to score goals.'

By October 1971, Ramsey could point to three qualifiers, three wins, but few were impressed. If confidence was to be rebuilt, performances also counted. England's were poor. In Basle, where England had won 8–1 in 1963, they struggled to a 3–2 win against lively Swiss opposition, Moore indicating how difficult it would be for Ramsey to leave him out with a stylish performance when the Swiss threatened to swamp them early on. The Swiss came to Wembley the following month to play an England side ravaged by withdrawals and took the lead before Mike Summerbee equalized. It left England needing only to avoid a 4–0 defeat in Athens to qualify for the quarter-finals. A 2–0 win was sealed by Hurst and Chivers. For the manager, it was a job well done, one point lost in six games, and he let down his guard. Roy McFarland remembers, 'After the match in the afternoon, there was a banquet. We had the reception, the meal, the speeches and typical of most footballers, the players drifted off to the bar on the side of the hall. All of a sudden, there was an announcement, and this gorgeous woman got up in the middle of the hall. She was a belly-dancer, so, of course, all the lads started coming back from the bar for a closer look! We'd never seen anything like this before, but she finished, and lads went back to the bar. Myself, Peter Shilton and David Nish walked back to the bus and went and sat down – we were the first three. Then Alf got on, sat down in his usual seat and he could hear us rabbiting away at the back. He just turned his head and said, "Lads! What about the belly-dancer! What a magnificent pair she had, didn't she!" We just cracked up and were laughing about it all night, it was a lovely moment. But it was important, because suddenly he was human – you look at people like Shanks or Cloughie or Alf, and you think of them as Gods; but when you live with them, you see the humour in them in moments like that, which is so important.'

Whether Ramsey was in such good humour when England drew West Germany is doubtful. The first leg was at Wembley at the end of April 1972, four months after England's previous game. The Germans hadn't been impressive since Mexico, had been booed from the field when held to a goalless draw by Poland in their final qualifier. Schoen was denied the services of several regulars following a bribery scandal in the Bundesliga, so there was cause for some hope. But England suffered their own traumas. With Moore and McFarland forming a solid defensive pairing, it was a bitter blow when Clough removed McFarland from the squad, as problematical in its way as Banks' illness in Leon. Ken Jones suggested, 'Alf never forgave Cloughie for that.' Ramsey made the wrong choice of replacement, Norman Hunter. He and Moore had no understanding and played a similar game, mopping up behind a tackling centre-half. Moore was pushed into that job, but was ill at ease. But as Colin Bell points out, 'The English game is hard, you're always going to find players taking knocks, but that's no excuse, there were good enough players about.'

In the event, Wembley hadn't seen anything like it since 1953. As Bell says, 'They were a crack side and they murdered us, they couldn't do a thing wrong. West Germany are hard to beat at the best of times, but that day they were all on song. You can only hold your hands up and say they were better than us.' The game was marshalled from start to finish by Beckenbauer – no Charlton to mark this time – and his accomplice, Gunter Netzer. Netzer was a shock for the Englishmen, Moore commenting that Ramsey had told his men nothing about him. Whether Ramsey had been unfortunate on scouting missions or had simply dismissed him as a strolling playboy is uncertain, but it was an appalling gaffe. Netzer ran the show with an incomparable performance, launching wave after wave of attacks. Uli Hoeness had given the Germans a lead but Lee managed an equalizer to make it square at the break. England failed to regroup and Netzer and Muller added further goals before they declared. It was a lesson in the modern game, as Bell accepts: 'International football is a game of patience, keep ball, not end-to-end stuff; everything would be measured. Our players weren't used to it, it was hard to grasp how the Europeans played.'

The critics were predictably vociferous, Danny Blanchflower sensing this was the beginning of the end: 'There has been a lack of adventure in the England team for years . . . you must get better to hold the same position. To get better you must change a little because you cannot get better and stay the same . . . Sir Alf's team has not gone forward. It has gone back. It would seem too late for him to change now. And change would be out of character.' Equally, Ramsey could argue that he'd picked the press' kind of team and had been crucified for it. In leaving out Storey, or an equivalent player, and playing three strikers, England's aggression allowed Netzer to win the game. Had Storey played, Netzer might not even have finished it. Even that would have been regressive, as the *Sunday Express*' Alan Hoby argued: 'Have the methods of the only man to win the World Cup for England become as dead as the dinosaur? . . . does not Ramsey's ponderous system based on prodigious work-rate, no wingers and endless, top-speed running also burn-up players? . . . a crushing load is placed on England's full-backs . . . "I learned nothing from Mexico," said Ramsey, incredibly . . . well, West Germany certainly did! They learned to cultivate an elegant, almost Latin brand of "touch" football.' This was true, so far as it went. But Tom Finney is right to say, 'He didn't have players as good as the Germans were at that time. Look at the great Hungarian side of the '50s, once they disappeared, they've never done anything since. Management's a thankless job, because as soon as you lose a game or two, you lose a player or two who are past their peak, you just can't replace them at that time, and everyone's out for the manager's blood. Alf was an outstanding manager, with an excellent team who were lucky enough to come together at the same time. That happens in football, you get clusters of players of special qualities coming through together.' The paucity of talent was underlined by Hoby, who offered an alternative selection for the second leg – Banks, Madeley, Hughes, McFarland, Moore, Marsh, Hudson, Hunter, Clarke, Chivers, MacDonald. It had its merits in giving youth its chance, but to win a game against a side including Beckenbauer, Netzer, Muller, Breitner, Maier, Schwarzenbeck and Heynckes? Ken Jones recalls talking to Helmut Schoen before the second leg in Berlin: 'Schoen said, "Do you think he'll give in to the press? I wish he would, because we'll win by six."'

As it was, he reverted to type, putting out a side that looked to stop the opposition, then to pinch a goal if possible. If England could score first, anything might happen. McFarland returned, Hunter moved into midfield in place of Peters, Storey came back, England went 4–4–2. In the first few minutes it almost paid off as England missed a great chance to score. Thereafter, a 0–0 was always on the cards, the Germans, marshalled by Beckenbauer, content to sit on their lead, England keen to stay solid at the back, Moore admitting, 'Above everything we couldn't allow any further goals to be scored against us and lose again.' The selection of Storey and Hunter was a declaration of intent, almost of war, Netzer saying afterwards, 'The fouls my immediate opponent, Storey, made on me had hardly anything to do with football.' Roy McFarland concedes, 'We were very physical in Berlin, no doubt about that at all. The stinging criticism was felt in the camp and we knew how good they were. In Berlin, they kept possession superbly well and we did have to chase the ball a lot. We had to be solid and we were. As a defender, I look back at the game with some pride, even though we didn't play a lot of good football or create many chances, but we were playing a world-class XI and we dealt with it. We had to fight, to get some pride back. In getting a 0–0, we did a bit of that.' Having endured one of the most humiliating experiences in English football, losing 6–3 to Hungary, Ramsey did not want to see the return match repeated – in 1954 England had lost 7–1 in Budapest. It was still all about national pride.

His predicament was underlined at the end of the game. Responding to a question about the lack of ideas, he snapped, 'Where am I to find the forwards?' If he had no faith in them, he had to shore up his defence. If they couldn't score, they must not concede. The press began to scent blood. Knowing that to argue for the inclusion of Marsh and company was popular, Hoby looked for a brave new world. Prior to the Berlin game, he wrote: 'What I dread most is that England will not only lose but that, once again, we shall bore the pants off everyone. If that happens, then Ramsey will really have to watch out. If it is the same old English stodge then there will be only one decisively cruel verdict from that vast jury of watchers. Step down, Alf.' After the game, he was no happier: 'I felt embarrassed and ashamed by the Englishmen's violent, ugly methods . . . this was a sad, bad day for Alf – and England . . . if you cram your team with six midfield players and imbue them with a "they shall not pass" attitude of mind . . . if you go into battle with a 4–4–2 line-up, then a "result" like this is heavily on the cards . . . I do not want to say any more.' Blanchflower was equally depressed: 'What was the point of it? . . . making it difficult for the other team to attack means that you make it difficult for yourself as well. England needed a gamble . . . if they had done that they might have won. They might also have got beaten. Even so they would have learned something by the experience.' But the scribes could afford defeat. Ramsey couldn't. While they harped on about England's deficiencies, Ramsey saw how good the Germans were, knew that all-out attack in Berlin would be suicidal. He would not expose his country to a further thrashing. Nevertheless, as Walter Winter-bottom explains, 'Once the press get against you, you're nowhere. Alf didn't suffer fools, and if any of the press upset him, he'd a strong, hard-hitting response to anyone who attacked him or tried to undermine him. So he made enemies and they were waiting for him.'

It was the end of Geoff Hurst's time with England. Now thirty, he was part of a fading West Ham side that were perennial strugglers at the foot of the First Division. Like Peters before him, after fourteen years at the same club he was becoming stale, as the pressure of having to come up with the goals to preserve the Hammers' First Division place took its toll. Ironically, a transfer to Stoke in August 1972 gave him a new lease of life, but by then it was too late as far as England were concerned. He was substituted in the Wembley game and dropped from the squad for Berlin. He was called up as a replacement but picked up an injury of his own and missed out. He was left with forty-nine caps: 'I just didn't receive a letter for the next game, that was how you knew you were out. There was no call, rightly or wrongly, that's how it happened. There are plenty of players who've said that's not the way it should happen to a senior international, and I think that's a fair comment. It's never been a problem for me, though.' But for the coming generation it was a problem. Where Hurst's age group were used to harsher disciplines and a lack of sentiment about their football – they had grown up in the days of the player as servant, after all – younger people expected to be treated differently. Nowadays if a player is left out without a word, he runs to the press to complain. As Hurst says, it doesn't matter who is right or wrong, it was a sign of the times. For all that he defended their interests, Ramsey wasn't used to mollycoddling players.

He wasn't as intransigent as some suggested, though some

273

changes were half-hearted. For the first game, Rodney Marsh was on the bench, but did think that he 'was in the team on sufferance. When I came on against West Germany at Wembley, the whole crowd of 100,000 was chanting my name and in the end he had to put me on. Possibly he did bow to the outside pressure towards the end. I think there was about fifteen minutes to go and he threw me on as a desperation measure. Then I played in the second leg in Berlin from the start, but he took me off, so he jerked me around a bit.' At last, press and public were having their impact. For the Home Internationals, Alf allowed Marsh, Tony Currie and Malcolm MacDonald games, with mixed results. In Cardiff England won 3–0, a game that had Gordon Banks complaining there was 'too much emphasis being placed on the physical side of the game' (Storey and Terry Yorath kicked lumps out of one another), then lost 1–0 to Northern Ireland at Wembley, finally wining 1–0 at Hampden when the old favourites were restored. As Marsh says, 'There were many games, even though we were winning them, when he'd pull me off, so I never really got to play the way I could. The closest I came to playing like Rodney Marsh at club level was against Wales at Ninian Park. I had a really good game, I did all the things I did at City, and we won 3–0. I scored, and it could have been 13–0! After the game, Alf didn't speak to me, didn't even say well done. He was a very cold man, on the outside anyway.' That coldness to Marsh suggests that he was never part of the inner circle.

Footballers were changing, as was society. Ramsey was forever in monochrome, a man of the war years. Marsh and Currie were technicolour people, products of the 1970s. Ramsey was quiet, hard-working, serious about his craft, where Marsh was raucous, funny, apparently flippant, liable to stop playing and have a chat to the crowd before taking a corner or a throw-in. These mavericks were serious about their football, but that didn't mean you couldn't play with a smile, couldn't enjoy your talents and entertain the punters. They wore long hair and loud suits, where Ramsey was immaculate, utterly conservative. They had money and were willing to flaunt it; Ramsey had little interest in it. They enjoyed being outrageous; Ramsey preferred humility. In every sense they were diametrically opposed. Rodney Marsh admits that they didn't really see eye to eye: 'I don't think he liked my attitude to football, which was playing off the cuff; I always played that way. When you've got a player like that, you've either got to discard him or build a team round him – you can't harness a player like that to a system, you have to give them their head, and Alf wasn't like that. Under Alf, preparation was completely thorough, everything was laid out and documented. I remember vividly he had a clipboard and notes that he used at team talks, so it was all very professionally organized, meticulous to the last detail. Training was never laboured, which it can be at club level. Alf kept it short and to the point. He wasn't open to suggestions, he was very strict, the team kept to a certain system, a rigid 4–4–2, the two forwards, of which I was one, were told exactly what to do, and you didn't deviate from that.' Ramsey wasn't oblivious to Marsh's talents, but he did have a blind spot where his sense of humour was concerned: 'I made a sarcastic comment to Alf in a team talk. Before the Wales game at Wembley in January 1973, he was talking to players individually, and he said to me, "You don't work hard enough when you play for England. If you don't work harder in this game, then I'm going to pull you off at half-time." So I said, "Christ, we only get a cup of tea and an orange at Manchester City!" I think it went over his head, but that was my last game for England! It had been the same against West Germany at Wembley. He said, "Rodney, you'll be taking the penalty kicks this evening. Is that all right with you?" "Fine, Alf. But I'm substitute."'

Ramsey didn't understand men like Marsh. As George Robb says, 'He'd be happier dealing with people with whom he could talk, people who wouldn't make a smart remark back to him.' In the past, he'd had Wilson, Cohen, Hurst, Stiles, and the Charltons, men who had grown up during and just after the war, men like him in many ways, who valued discipline, understood the pre-war values and shared many of them. These were the men who had submitted to the Army-style disciplines of Lilleshall, something he could never recreate with the players of the 1970s. Jimmy Armfield suggests that, 'In '66 we were post-war lads, we'd grown up with austerity, rationing. As players, most of us had seen the bad times, when there was no freedom of contract, the maximum wage. We weren't going to miss out on the benefits after that, so perhaps we were a serious squad.' Where men like Bobby Charlton had enough flair for any team, Ramsey did not retreat from that because he knew that while Charlton might do something off the cuff, work some magic, he'd also do eighty-five minutes of running and fulfil a function. Marsh wouldn't. Like Osgood, he was a product of the rock'n'roll generation, a man with different aspirations and a different way of looking at the world. They weren't going to be told their place. Osgood had missed training when dropped in Mexico and that worried Ramsey. Might they all do that? There was a generation gap and, for all that every player in England respected Ramsey, it was a gulf that could not be bridged. *Monty Python* became as good a way of expressing that gap as any: you either got it or you didn't. They did. Ramsey didn't.

Whether these players were good enough for the world stage is a moot point. We never found out because Ramsey preferred men he could trust, preferred a system to footballing anarchy. By definition, he had to use players of lesser gifts and got poorer results. In 1966 all our world-class players, bar Greaves, played, because he believed in them. By 1972, our *potential* world-class players couldn't get a game, because he didn't – in fairness, some, like Bowles and Hudson, wore their non-conformity like a badge of pride, determined to be awkward. Francis Lee makes the point that Ramsey would not stand for people undermining his authority: 'He had the attitude: "If you want to play for your country, I'm the man who makes it happen. You go wrong on me and it will never happen."' Lee also notes, 'If you get four or five caps for your country, you've had a chance, and it's up to you to take it.' The England manager doesn't have the luxury of road-testing players because there aren't the same number of games available to him; each match is a pressure occasion. If Ramsey were to persist with a player through ten or fifteen games, he'd be in the side for nearly two years through to the finals of a tournament, and if the player's not good enough, you've got a problem. As the 1966 squad proved, football's not just about ability, it's about character, and Alf was a shrewd judge of that. If Bowles and Worthington didn't get a chance, it was because he felt they were flawed off the field as much as on it, though Geoff Hurst makes an important point: 'The flair players in the seventies couldn't compare with those in the sixties – if you look at Moore and Charlton against whoever, they weren't of the same quality. With the greatest respect, there's flair and then there's genius. And perhaps Alf didn't think they were the right sort of characters for him and his side of secure, solid, tougher players. The flair players in the seventies weren't in the same class, and so he couldn't trust them with a free role in the way he could Bobby Charlton. Had there been a Bobby Charlton in the seventies, he'd have been in the team. You can't pick flair for its own sake; they have to be top internationals.' Neeskens or Ardiles had flair, but they also had a calculating football brain, they knew what to do, when to do it, how to do it; whereas Bowles or Worthington were entertainers, would try things at inappropriate moments, blow hot and cold. If a genuine genius like Greaves couldn't find a place in the team, Ramsey certainly couldn't accommodate Frank Worthington, who wasn't in that class.

Roy McFarland makes an equally persuasive case in Ramsey's defence: 'There was a lot of talk about Hudson, Currie, MacDonald getting games, but Alf was concerned with the blend not with individuals. Alf felt he couldn't trust some to do what he wanted every time. It wasn't just flair players that were treated that way either – Tommy Smith had a game or two, was in the squad a few times, then got left out because Alf didn't think he was international class, however good a job he did for Liverpool. Same happened to Larry Lloyd. Alf made assessments on all of us, and with some players he felt he couldn't hang his hat on them. There is a step up, a difference between good club players and internationals. His assessment wasn't often wrong, and while some might think that Hudson and so on could have been given their head, Alf felt not. Alf was maybe too loyal – maybe Bobby or Geoff played one or two games too many – but it's always hard to know when it's right to end with great players. And I don't think Alf had the confidence in some that were looking to replace them. He introduced a few and if they came up to his standards, they stayed in; if they didn't, he'd quickly move them out. There was always a rotation, but there was a solid base of Banks, Moore, Ball, Hurst, Peters, to revolve around.' As Alf's old Southampton colleague Joe Mallett confirms, 'He liked the kind of player that was going to do his job as opposed to others who might dribble past six defenders or might lose it in their own penalty area. Alf liked reliability.' But reliability without invention leads to stale, stereotyped football. Because Alf hadn't yet found another Charlton, England were predictable, though in mitigation, Marsh points out that, 'Many people have said that people like myself or Alan Hudson should have been given a long run in the team, but then that wouldn't have been Alf Ramsey, it wouldn't have been his team.' And if you wanted an exciting side, Ramsey was never the man to provide it – that was as likely in 1972 as Richard Nixon telling the truth. Ramsey was the results man, so determined that England should not be beaten that he perhaps lost sight of the wider picture. As Mick Channon recalls, 'If you look at the Home Internationals, they were very hard games, another league at the end of the season. Nobody wanted to get beat and I think it was good for football. Instead of all the meaningless friendlies they try to arrange now with countries where the result doesn't matter, you got three games at the end of the year when the manager could have a look at a couple of players – playing Scotland at Hampden or Wales at Wembley is a bloody sight harder than playing Lithuania in a friendly that nobody cares about. In Alf's day the best team always played against the Jocks because he fucking hated them! They're open about that towards England, and Alf was the same towards them. To this day, because Alf instilled it in us, I never want to lose to Scotland!'

There were no summer matches for England in 1972 and the cricket season must have dragged for Ramsey. The draw had been made for World Cup qualification and it set England in a three-team group alongside Wales and Poland. Most observers saw this as an easy passage, but it was anything but. Three-team groups are fraught with danger – one slip and there's no time to recover. Contrast that with England's qualification for France '98: defeat at home to Italy seemed to be the end of the world, but in a five-team group there were enough matches left to claw that deficit back. As to the opposition, Wales were dismissed, but that was a juvenile attitude. As Colin Bell says, 'You prefer not to play the British teams because you're expected to win, on a hiding to nothing, and they know how you play. They step up a gear too.' The Welsh were compact, with good pros like Mike England and Terry Hennessey at the back, Leighton James and John Toshack always likely to pinch a goal, so they could cause trouble. Poland were an unknown quantity, and travelling to Eastern Europe was always tough. And in their Nations Cup qualifiers they had held West Germany to a 0–0 draw, goalkeeper Jan Tomaszewski keeping Muller and company at bay.

The theme of poor preparation continued. There was just one friendly prior to the first game against Wales, and that was at home to Yugoslavia. As Roy McFarland suggests: 'West Germany had put the question marks against England because they beat us comfortably at Wembley. They were simply better than us. We were in transition, Hurst, Lee and Moore were coming to the end, Terry Cooper dropped out, and so at times like that you're vulnerable. Alf looked for evolution rather than revolution and that was what won him the loyalty. You felt part of the set-up: you knew you were doing well because he kept picking you, it wasn't a case of being in and out of the squad, experiments going on all the time. It was a good contrast with working for Brian Clough, who was open, abrasive and would speak his mind, where Alf was clinical and methodical, but when he had to be strong he was.'

England needed a good performance against Yugoslavia to re-establish their authority. By the time Ramsey had picked through what was left, he handed debuts to Mick Mills, Frank Lampard, Jeff Blockley and Mick Channon, Joe Royle returning for his second cap in two years. This was hardly ideal preparation for the World Cup, even though Channon had been around the squad for some time: 'I always thought the great thing about Alf was that by the time you got in the team, he'd used the Under-23s to have a look at you. Alf knew what you could do and never asked you to do something you couldn't. He wasn't interested in any weaknesses you might have, all he wanted was your strengths, for you to do what you were best at. The way he put his team together would counter everything else, would give you the balance. His team talks would be: "The German number 6, he's got a very good left foot." He could have been talking about Beckenbauer! But they didn't matter, he didn't frighten you with them. I always thought that when he spoke, he believed we were the best, and as long as we played like that, we'd be OK. His football was common sense, he took the best of what the players had. I played like I did for Southampton – obviously you make your own adjustments because the style and pace of international football's a bit different, but he just wanted you to play. He didn't need to give you instructions or tactics.' That's a sharp contrast to Rodney Marsh's memories and further suggests Ramsey was coerced into playing him.

England struggled through to a 1–1 draw with Yugoslavia. It was obvious that change had to come, perhaps that it was too late. England had managed six goals in six games. Then, on 22 October 1972, came another bitter blow. Gordon Banks was involved in the car crash that cost him his career. The rock of England's rearguard was gone and, though Peter Shilton and Ray Clemence were sound deputies, to lose Banks' experience was a hammer blow. The first qualifier against Wales in Cardiff was less than a month away and Ramsey spent the intervening period sifting through his defence. Ray Clemence was selected to make his debut in a game where Ramsey again picked three forwards, Chivers, Marsh and Kevin Keegan, the latter also making his debut. It was an attacking policy, but it failed to have the desired effect, England limping home with a goal from Bell. Ramsey's balance wasn't there and he was on the run, Keegan writing, 'I do not think Alf rated me as a player . . .

pressure from outside influenced his decision to call me into the squad and select me for the team ... [usually he] picked players who he believed were capable of doing a job for him. How else could a player like Peter Storey have won so many caps? No doubt Sir Alf would disagree but other people wanted me to play and he had reached a situation where he had to try something new.' It was something that could never have happened two years earlier, but now Alf was desperate. The fabled self-confidence of yore had been smashed.

With hindsight, it's easy to say that Ramsey had left it too long to change personnel, but had he begun to make reckless changes, the fabric of his teams would have been irredeemably altered. And almost every manager you can name has held on to his players too long, because they're not simply names on a teamsheet but friends, colleagues, men who have shared great times. But change has to come. Alex Ferguson's greatest achievement at Manchester United is not found in the titles he's won, they're a by-product. It's that he's built two successful sides with no lull – even Busby endured fallow periods at Old Trafford. He was at his best when he sold Ince, Kanchelskis and Hughes to refresh his team with youth and vigour and, most important, the hunger of Butt, Beckham and Scholes. Ramsey chose not to introduce new faces, though at international level, it's far harder to do so. Where Ferguson could endure a thrashing at Villa Park straight after the loss of that trio, would Ramsey have survived a similar beating? He still had Moore, Ball, Peters as the bulwark, still fine players, perhaps the best in their positions, but did they still have the hunger, the drive to go that extra yard to create or destroy? But who was pressing for their places? That was the dichotomy – I need to change, I can't change.

The rematch with Wales took place in January. There were no team changes but Wales got a 1–1 draw in a sour game that emphasized England's relish, almost fetish, for physical battle. Ramsey then confirmed his distaste for Keegan by dropping him and recalling Channon, relying on the height of Chivers to solve England's problems. Allan Clarke returned to a settled side, which took England through the Home Internationals with a 100 per cent record prior to a gruelling summer tour that included the qualifier in Poland. Wales had beaten the Poles 2–0 in Cardiff, so a draw in Katowice would put England in the driving seat, though as Roy McFarland says, 'After a long season, it may not be a great idea to play key qualifiers. I think that with a summer tour, you want to be playing friendlies, not World Cup games. If we'd played Poland in September, maybe it would have been better. Our top division is notorious. Make no mistake, it is a long, hard season and you do need your rest.' England played in Prague, drawing 1–1, but all eyes were on Katowice. Having used three forwards on a regular basis, Ramsey's caution got the better of him and he fell back on 4–4–2, dropping Channon and using Storey as an anchor. Channon recalls, 'It wasn't until the morning of the Poland game that he named the team, and I was gutted because I'd played all the games leading up to it. He pulled me aside later and said, "I'm only doing it for tactical reasons. I want to pull another defender in and not give anything away." I had so much respect for him, there was no problem. He never admitted it to me but I did hear later that he reckoned it was a mistake.'

Alf prepared his players for what they'd face. Roy McFarland remembers: 'Alf knew who the good players were, he knew Deyna, picked him out before the game. They had pace up front and I felt they would be a threat at Wembley on the counter, but I wasn't so concerned about playing in Poland. I thought they feared us. To lose there was a disappointment because I thought we were better than them, we just didn't take our chances, and I think we proved that again at Wembley when we had the possession but didn't get the goals. In Katowice, I felt comfortable, didn't think they could hurt us, but when we went one down in the first half it meant we had to over-commit to get back into it and they caught us with a sucker punch, when the ball went under Bobby's foot and Lubanski went on to score. Then Ballie got sent off out of frustration.' Ball's dismissal was evidence that the wheels were falling off. As passionate and obsessive about the game as his manager, he'd kept his temper under control for eight years in England colours, but finally frustration boiled over. England had a useful side, but they couldn't create chances and the few they did, they could not finish.

The 2–0 defeat was as shattering as the defeat in Leon and, in truth, Ramsey was more culpable, for his caution put England in trouble. Furthermore he hadn't tried to rectify matters with substitutions, allowing the same eleven to play through. To his credit, though, he made no attempt to shift the blame. McFarland recalls: 'Bobby Moore and Alan Ball had the corner room in the hotel. After the game, we got a couple of crates of beer and they invited us all to their room – Katowice was a mining town, there was nothing to do, so we were stuck in the hotel. There were no high jinks or anything, we were all deflated, sitting round talking about the game. For me, as a comparative youngster, it was enlightening to listen to Ball, Moore and Peters talking about football. There was a knock on the door. Alf came in. We started to get up, but he told us to sit down. He had a beer, sat down and said, "It was my fault. For the first goal, I should have got somebody into the hole." (The first goal came from a free-kick on the left, the ball was knocked into the near post, Gadocha beat Bobby Moore on the run and headed it in. Colin Bell should have been in the hole, but Colin was drawn out – I think he committed the foul and stayed out to make a two-man wall.) Alf felt he should have someone else to cover it. Colin was in the room too, he said it was his fault, that he felt he was doing the right thing trying to stop them taking a quick free-kick, and Bobby and myself were saying that we should have organized quicker, so we weren't looking for excuses. Alf drank his beer and we argued with him to a man. He finished his drink, got up, said, "Thank you very much for the beer, boys," then as he got to the door, his last words were, "It was still my fault." And that was all we saw of him that night! Situations like that show what feeling he had for the players, it was good man management, that's why the players loved Alf.'

There was no such romance with the FA. Sir Harold Thompson had travelled and felt he might endear himself to the players by addressing them by their surnames. On one occasion he entered the breakfast room smoking a huge cigar, wafting the smoke towards the players. He was not amused when Ramsey ordered him to put it out. While the rest of the country mourned England's defeat, there were elements in the FA who revelled in their manager's discomfiture. Ken Jones makes the point that, 'He stripped the FA of all power, which was the most important thing that happened to English football. If that hadn't happened, they wouldn't have won in 1966, for sure. They weren't important any more and he'd proved they'd been holding England back. From the moment he got the job there were people gunning for him, notably Harold Thompson. He never liked Alf and was plotting to overthrow him from the start – when England won in '66 it must have been a disappointment to him. Alf had contempt for them and didn't mind showing it – we were in Troon for a Scotland game and Alf was talking to the press, he'd given us the team and at the end he said, "I suppose I'd better go off and give it to *those* people," meaning the FA party.' Bobby

Moore underlined the rift in *England! England!*: 'We usually go to a banquet or official reception after a match in England. The coach is often timed to leave Hendon Hall hotel at eight o'clock. On two occasions FA officials who accompany the playing party were not ready to leave at eight. On Sir Alf's instructions the coach went without them . . . but it is a different matter if a player is not present at the right time. That is important and Harold Shepherdson will organise an immediate search.'

The summer tour lurched into Moscow, where England won 2–1, and on to Italy and a 2–0 defeat. Ramsey knew that his future was on the line. Ken Jones recalls, 'Cloughie said, "How is it the England manager can't pick a team from 2000 players?" And that incensed Alf. I brought it up with him, and he said, "Have you got a copy of *Rothmans*? Go through it and when you've had a look, tell me how many you think I'm picking from." So I went through it, eliminated the bottom three divisions for a start, then all the Scots, Welsh, Irish, and those who had been in the side and had been dropped or were too old, then those who obviously weren't up to it, and I was left with thirty-six. So I rang him back, and he said, "That's three more than I've got!" It was fashionable to have a dig at him.'

England had a friendly with Austria in September, as Wales met Poland in Katowice. Finally, it seemed Ramsey was alive to the dangers. Storey was jettisoned and in his place came the cultured Currie in a three-man midfield alongside the equally graceful Peters and Bell. Up front were Chivers, Clarke and Channon. The biggest change was the omission of Moore, in dispute with West Ham. Moore said later that Ramsey expected him to be back in the World Cup, proof of how difficult it was for Ramsey to say goodbye to a man with whom he had done so much – by June 1974, Moore was a Second Division footballer. Mick Channon saw how difficult it was for Alf to part with his captain: 'Bobby was the symbol of everything Alf had achieved. Bobby was very much like Alf, he did things in a quiet way, he took Alf on to the pitch, if you like, in that he was very competitive, he was desperate to win, but he never showed it. He did it with style, with dignity. You'd almost say the two of them didn't care, but if you knew 'em, they cared, they had that mean streak! None of us like to face the fact that it's time to move on or you're too old, but in football it happens to you very early in life, when you're in your early thirties. Being so close to Bobby, it was hard for Alf to say, "OK, your time's up."'

Against the Austrians, England put on a polished performance, Currie prompting cleverly, Channon and Clarke each scoring twice in a 7–0 win. Had Ramsey found the formula at the death? Things certainly looked more promising when Poland beat Wales 3–0. England knew what they had to do to qualify: beat Poland at Wembley. It was England's most important game in years, arguably as big as the World Cup Final itself in its implications. Sensibly, Ramsey asked that he be able to pull his squad together as much as a week in advance of the game. The Football League refused, decreeing that all players should play for their clubs on the Saturday. For Mick Channon, that wasn't a problem: 'We'd meet up on the Sunday and so you didn't get a lot of time but if you've got to coach the best players in the country you're in trouble anyway! You need a bit of time for your set pieces and your general organization, but if you've got to coach players in how to play the game they shouldn't be internationals. Although there was only a couple of days before the international, people didn't seem to get injured as much then. It was pretty physical, with the likes of Tommy Smith, Ron Harris, Norman Hunter, Jack Charlton and the tackle from behind, so it was no picnic! I played 600 or 700 games over 20 odd years and if I'd waited until I was properly fit before I played, I might have managed 100, and I certainly wouldn't have played 46 times for England! If you had a niggle, a dead leg, a strain, it didn't stop you from playing, the only thing that mattered was getting out on a Saturday afternoon and a Wednesday night. If you want to be fit, you're fit.' Channon's thesis was borne out when Ramsey was able to select an unchanged side, but it was almost very different. As Geoff Hurst recalls, 'I understand from the grapevine that he was looking to bring me back into the team, but he felt that he didn't want to bring me back only to leave me out again, he didn't feel the disappointment would be good for me personally.' Ken Jones confirms, 'He watched Hurst play at Arsenal and he was brilliant, doing all the things that had been so effective, but he felt if it went wrong, not only would he get stick, so would Geoff, so he decided not to.' It was a final affirmation of his depth of feeling for his players, something which Roy McFarland backs up: 'Alf wasn't aloof, he was a warm man, this frostiness or arrogance only came over him around the press or officials. With the players he was very warm, joined in a bit of fun on the training ground. He wanted loyalty and gave it back – I can never remember him slaughtering a player in the press, unless they'd failed to turn up or something like that, and I remember him being aggressive about other managers not allowing players to play for England, but he never said anything about the players who turned out. The press would try to goad him into saying that, say, Bobby Moore was over the hill, but Alf would just come back with, "They are good players, worthy of playing for England."' Francis Lee is one of few who disagrees with that assessment: 'He *was* aloof and unapproachable. He wasn't easy to get along with because you couldn't sit down and have a long conversation with him, because he was curt, and just always made it clear that you were there to play for England by his grace. He was obviously in charge, and liked it that way. Coming into the Poland game, I'd been out of the reckoning for about a year, but I'd played against Gornik for Manchester City home and away and in the Cup-Winners Cup Final, I knew most of their players. I was thinking of ringing him up and saying, "Alf, I know you haven't picked me, but I know these players really well and I think you should," but I never did. I thought, "No I won't, because he'll just say, 'Frahncis, bugger off!'!"'

England dominated the first half, were scarcely out of Poland's half, but Tomaszewski, the keeper described as a clown by Brian Clough, pulled off save after save. The second-half was a carbon copy, until suddenly the Poles broke free with Lato on the left. Hunter went across to tackle, but rather than clattering everything into touch he tried to retain possession to launch another attack. He missed his tackle, leaving McFarland exposed as the only covering defender. Lato squared the ball to Domarski on the edge of the box and his shot squirmed under Shilton, much as Beckenbauer's had under Bonetti. Now England needed two to salvage their World Cup place. Poland were under siege, but England's route to goal was always blocked. They played the ball about nicely, but couldn't turn possession into clear chances. The Polish full-backs had been identified as a weakness, yet seldom did England trouble them, for they played without width. Moore, on the bench beside Ramsey, wrote, 'He sat there an almost agonised figure, occasionally rocking slightly with the tension. He was still bland yet he was boiling inside. The man we all cared for so much was in trouble, and was ever-so-slightly showing it.' Fifteen minutes from time, Moore urged him to make a substitution, to use Kevin Hector, Derby's prolific goalscorer, to probe down the left – Ramsey's response was to push Hunter forward. Eventually, with minutes left, England won a penalty, which Clarke coolly converted. With two minutes to go, Hector came on. In those 120 seconds, he made a couple of clear chances for himself, one of which brushed the post. Moore argued that, 'Predictably Alf got criticism, especially over the substitution. But it wouldn't have been too late if Hector had scored, and he so nearly did.' But that was taking loyalty to extremes. Had Hector had fifteen or twenty minutes, on that form he might have had a hat-trick. Eventually, the final whistle blew. As Barry Davies said in commentary, it was 'the end of an era'. Brian Glanville's epitaph for that era was stark: 'With a more adventurous and flexible manager than Sir Alf Ramsey, England might have prevailed . . . England pressed for most of the evening but hadn't the wit to make clear chances. The game was drawn 1–1, England were out; and so, after his one splendid success and eight years of anti-climax, was Ramsey.'

The players were shattered, disbelieving. Roy McFarland says, 'I've watched that game a few times since, and every time I think, "We've got to score here! There's got to be a goal now!"' As Mick Channon recalls, 'All the inquests were saying we should have been more patient, but how could we be more patient? We had complete control of the game, had the ball for ninety minutes, were camped in their half, raining shots in on the goal. What difference would it have made if you were patient? That was just one of those games where, whatever you do, the bloody ball won't go in! You had to be pleased with the performance because we played well, it was just Norman and Shilts making mistakes that cost us the game, but that happens. That's not just football, it's life! Alf didn't dwell on things, he was disappointed, obviously, because the best team didn't go through, but there's no point shouting and screaming once it's over. He knew we were as upset as he was. That game wasn't a failure – OK, it meant we didn't qualify for the World Cup, but that's the way things go sometimes. What more could England have done?' On that night, nothing at all, but the roots of failure went deeper. Qualification was lost when Wales got a draw against an insipid England at Wembley. It was lost in Katowice when a safety-first outfit wasn't safe enough. It was lost in friendlies when old hands were left in too long. It was lost because England hadn't the players and hadn't the system. As Peter Osgood points out, 'Alf was wedded to his tactics. He could have changed at the last minute against Poland, say, and picked four or five flair players, so the variety would have been there, there would have been different angles and kinds of attack. At home, we could have taken people on a lot more and beaten them comfortably, but Alf wasn't that flexible. He felt that Nobby, Roger Hunt, Mullery, were dependable. He had players who could potentially do a better job, but he was frightened to make that decision, thinking they might let him down.'

England had failed to qualify for the World Cup for the first time. In eight years they'd gone from being World Champions to being nobodies. Had Hector's last-gasp effort gone in, England would have gone to West Germany and quite possibly done well – Poland came third, after all. But it hadn't. Peter Osgood believes, 'Alf should have gone after the Poland game, because it was obvious it was the end for him, he'd done his stint. He should have resigned as a proud man, saying, "I've restored English football, won you the World Cup, it's time for somebody with a fresh outlook to take it on now." It would have been nice if he'd gone upstairs, maybe, and let Bobby Moore take over alongside him, the way Beckenbauer took over in West Germany. It does work keeping the disciplines and it would have been ideal. But it's not the way we do things over here.' But Ramsey was no quitter. He'd have to be pushed. That would have happened in days had it not been for one thing. Two days before the Poland game, Brian Clough resigned as manager of Derby County. If Ramsey had been sacked then, the people's choice would have been ready and waiting – and that was a far bigger nightmare than having Ramsey in the job. As Roy McFarland remembers, 'That was the worst week of my career. Cloughie resigned and we missed out on the World Cup, which I was desperate to play in. Driving home from Wembley back to Derby was one of the most miserable nights I've had in football. But the FA said from day one that Brian Clough would never, ever get the job. He was too outspoken. Brian would be the last bloke in the world they'd want! Alf was never a yes-man, but the thing with him was it was "Alf's Team". Nobody could interfere with that and so long as that was the case, Alf wouldn't trouble the FA. Brian would have turned the place upside down!'

So Ramsey had a few more games in charge, the FA council making that clear on 5 November, when the minutes of their meeting stated: 'On behalf of the members of the Committee, Mr Wragg expressed sincere regrets to Sir Alfred Ramsey that the England Team had been eliminated from the World Cup but he wished to place on record that Sir Alfred Ramsey had the unanimous support and confidence of the Senior Committee.' Would there still be time to redeem himself? Nine days later, England entertained Italy and there was a recall for Peter Osgood and Bobby Moore, Ken Jones arguing that, 'The idea he was inflexible was nonsense – he told me he was going to change, experiment with man-to-man marking, and playing Bobby as a proper sweeper for the first time. It was alien to the players and they lost 1–0, but that's where he was moving. He knew the time had come to amend the system.' But time was running out, the vultures gathering. On 26 November, the next council meeting was forced to record that, 'Sir Harold Thompson stated that this Minute did not represent the feeling of all members of the Council and whilst he agreed that the Senior Committee were perfectly within their rights in recording the view expressed in the Minute, he felt it should not preclude a wider discussion by the Council or some other select group at a later date.' Thompson was moving in for the kill, as Ray Wilson explains: 'Alf made some enemies, not intentionally, but because he knew how he wanted to run things. The people who'd run the international side previous to that, the selectors, were pushed out of the way. I don't think they could wait to have a go at him. It was very embarrassing the way they did it. I remember Martin Peters telling me that one guy rushed past him after one game when they had a bad result and said something like, "We've got the bastard now. He's down." That was sad. I think they were against him for a long time, and that tends to rub off on everybody. Then we had the Poland game. Sometimes everything just turns against you after a while. If ever a side deserved to win a game, England did, it was just an incredible night – Kevin Hector had about ninety seconds and he nearly had a hat-trick! But that's the sort of thing that happens when you're coming to the end. And then they really had him.' Roy McFarland confirms that, 'Sir Harold Thompson wanted him out, that was the feeling we had, the whispers we heard. Even though football was changing, I felt it was a grave mistake, because Alf's knowledge, his dogmatic approach, would still have succeeded.'

In February, an FA sub-committee was set up 'to consider our future policy in respect of the promotion of international football' under the leadership of Sir Harold Thompson – Bert Millichip, Brian Mears, Dr Andrew Stephen and League President Len Shipman were the other members. Ramsey could see where that was heading, and made a pre-emptive strike, presenting a three-point plan to improve English performances, asking for three days' preparation for friendlies, a week for competition games, and one international a month in the season, raising the slogan 'Club or Country?'. That these were reasonable demands was underlined when, of the squad selected for a Football League game against the

Scottish League, seven players withdrew, drawing the arch observation that, 'We were told they are injured, but I suggest they will be fit to play this weekend.' His determination to change the pattern was clear, for Stan Bowles, Martin Dobson, Colin Todd, Trevor Brooking and Dennis Tueart all played, a huge leap for Ramsey, tantamount to an admission that his recent policy had been flawed. He then took England to Lisbon in April, but was forced to make nine squad changes, as managers remained unwilling to release players now England were out of the World Cup. Ramsey's view was, 'There is only one thing to do – punish the clubs concerned. If a player does not report for an international match or a training session, he should not be permitted to play for his club on the following Saturday.' Sticking to his new, bold policy, Ramsey did not scuttle back to the old boys, but bravely named six debutants – Phil Parkes, Mike Pejic, Dobson, Dave Watson, Brooking and Bowles. England played some measured football in a 0–0 draw and, as Brian Glanville noted, 'It was pleasing to see that the Portuguese critics gave great credit to our players' individual technique, as well as their formidable physique. Times may indeed be changing.' He later pointed out that Bowles 'had shown himself no more than a brilliant club player, who cannot take the great leap forward into international football,' suggesting Ramsey's judgement had been sound. Even so, Bowles, Worthington, Keith Weller, MacDonald and all the other Portuguese debutants were in Ramsey's squad for the summer internationals that would cover the Home series, a game with Argentina and a foray into Eastern Europe. There were no assassins. It was as if Ramsey had needed the enormous shock of failure to jolt him back to reality. From 1970, some decisions seemed mechanical, made by rote, oblivious to events around him. Had Leon traumatized him that badly? Or, more likely, was his simple faith in English qualities so great that he could not envisage failure? Now, at last, he seemed to be drawing lessons from the West German beating. That team in Lisbon was elegant if nothing else, players of grace and quality, technically adept. A year too late, Ramsey was forging a new future for England, one that might embrace total football. It's a radical thought, given Ramsey's reputation for tactical rigidity, yet it had a resonance in his philosophy first put forward in *Talking Football*, that every player on the team should be looking to score and create goals.

Would he have turned the tide? We'll never know. On 19 April, a day after he'd announced his summer squad, Thompson's sub-committee made its report. Ramsey was at Lancaster Gate to hear its findings, which included 'a unanimous recommendation that Sir Alf Ramsey should be replaced as England team manager'. Ramsey termed it 'the most devastating half hour of my life . . . I stood in a room almost full of staring committee men. It was just like I was on trial. I thought I was going to be hanged . . . typically I was never given a reason for the sack.' The FA agreed not to announce the decision until Ramsey was away on holiday to spare him the ordeal of dealing with the press. He was reportedly given a golden – he called it a tissue – handshake of £8000 and a meagre pension. The FA placed on record their appreciation of his 'unbending loyalty and dedication and the high level of integrity he has brought to world football'. And that was it. In the end, Thompson was a greater, more implacable foe than even the West Germans. Len Shipman pointed out that the committee was far from unanimous, adding, 'I am very upset. It is very disturbing. But what can you do when your hand is forced?' Amazingly, the two-month inquiry had failed to uncover a replacement, and Joe Mercer was given caretaker control of the squad Ramsey had selected for the summer – Thompson had only been interested in sacking Ramsey, not replacing him.

Had the time come for a change? If he'd left office the day after the Poland game, there'd have been no debate. A manager who talks only of results lives or dies by them. And there was plenty of evidence against him. Ray Wilson's view is, 'I can't deny you can be in a job too long. I do believe that. Most people, if they're good at things, only have one way, one system of doing it. That tires, people catch up, somebody comes up with something else. Probably Alf did go on too long, perhaps he knows that.' Glanville wrote that '[Alf's] attitudes had become so rigid and subjective that they had slight contact with the realities.' Rodney Marsh suggests, 'He did try to change things towards the end with people like myself and Tony Currie, but it was a little bit too late. Alf had gone past his sell-by date. I don't mean that with any disrespect, it's just the rest of the world had caught up from 1966. I've always thought that a manager can be in a job too long. Any manager that lasts with a team for ten years has swum the Channel with diver's boots on.' Undeniably, a manager can only say the same things to the same players for so long before it ceases to be effective. You must change one or other.

Ramsey *was* a sophisticated manager. The 4–1–3–2 formation with which he won the World Cup was clever, offering the option to go 5–3–2 with wing-backs and three central defenders, or a more offensive 4–4–2, even 4–3–3, at will, as the game dictated. Although his strategy was flawed in 1970, asking the full-backs to do too much, he put out an England side of much greater quality than the build-up had suggested possible. That indicates that an England manager could only succeed once he'd qualified for a World Cup, when, at last, he'd be given the players for a month, to do with as he wished. He was looking to introduce a sweeper system in his last two games, making a last-gasp statement, because he felt it was impossible to do that amid the rough and tumble of the season. Few, if any, English clubs employed that system, one which needed work to bring to fruition. With players arriving on Sunday for a game two days later, how could he school his defence? Even now, how many English clubs promise to operate with a sweeper system then abandon it quickly? Both Hoddle and Gullit were supposed to play that role for Chelsea but rarely did. Few other clubs have had the nerve to even try. Had England beaten Poland, there's every chance they'd have played a sweeper in West Germany, revolutionizing English football in the process, but Alf ran out of time. Had he had the nerve to try it against Greece and Malta and risked defeat back in 1971, it might have paid dividends, but he lacked the courage in the wake of the volley of abuse he'd received post-Leon.

A club manager can change tactics after a period, even match to match. An England manager doesn't have time. By definition, his tactics must be less sophisticated because he cannot work them through with the players – look at Graham Taylor's failure in 1993 against Norway when he used Pallister at left-back. There wasn't time to work on the policy and it failed. On the other hand, when England were in their camp for Italia '90 they worked on their own version of the sweeper system – more of a third centre-back – which carried them to the semi-finals. Ramsey won his first battle in wresting selection from the FA but he could not win the war with the Football League, as he complained in his final piece for *FA News*, written days before his dismissal, attacking 'the cheating clubs and managers who [keep] their players away from internationals . . . it is ludicrous that any international team manager should not have available a team of full strength. I find it difficult to believe that any other national activity – sport, art, political – at home or abroad would tolerate this state of affairs! . . . I do not consider full international matches to be the time to experiment with several comparative newcomers.' Since the advent of the Premiership, that problem has eased, the FA giving Glenn Hoddle free weekends before virtually every international fixture, insisting that injured players report to the England medical team to assess whether they can or can't play. If Ramsey had had that luxury, and the increased time with players, it's interesting to speculate on his final years at the helm. Would he have embraced the sweeper earlier? Perhaps, but it's as convincing an argument to say he would have persisted with his pet 4–4–2 at the expense of any experimentation and that it was only failure that drove him to look for something new – he did, after all, persist with Ipswich's 'Leadbetter' formation the year after they won the title even as it faltered.

England's failure was not merely a blow to national pride, it had financial implications. The FA lost money by not reaching the World Cup finals and, with status reduced, couldn't command the lucrative guarantees for friendlies that had boosted their coffers. Who wanted to play England now? And other chickens came home to roost. If Alf's hostility to the FA had left hostages to fortune, so did his tempestuous dealings with the media. As the 1970s wore on, the media became increasingly important, and Ramsey was hopeless with it, Jeff Powell writing in the *Daily Mail* that, 'Ramsey waged twelve years of closed warfare with old reactionaries within the FA under the handicap of an assumed personality which fitted him like a rain-sodden overcoat two sizes too small . . . his tactics were as much imprisoned in a straitjacket as his personality.' His 1950s demeanour was out of synch with the glam 1970s. He was the public face of the FA, so if the public were unhappy with him, it reflected on Lancaster Gate. As a gesture, the FA had tried again to supply him with a PR man post-Poland, but he rejected it. It wasn't just that he personally didn't want to talk with the press, he felt that the England manager shouldn't have to. He might have been correct – certainly good media relations haven't helped any of his successors – but it was an impossible way to continue. The media monster demanded food and the England manager was obliged to provide it. And, ultimately, did anyone genuinely believe that a 58-year-old could lead England to another finals in South America with all the problems that posed? Worse yet, the 1978 World Cup would be held in Argentina – how could Ramsey go there after the controversy of 1966? The hatred of Mexico would be nothing compared to the reaction of a nation on a religious crusade. Despite his attempts to ring the changes, 1974 was perhaps the right time for him to make his exit.

That does not excuse the botched nature of his dismissal. To wait five months after the Polish game was cruel. As Mick Channon says, 'We thought he'd weathered the storm. It never entered my head that he'd get the sack until it happened. He'd been so successful, changed the face of football with the system he put together and the players he used. It was an exciting time because it was the start of a new England side.' George Cohen feels that, 'To sack him was absurd, quite ludicrous, it would never have been done on the Continent. We lost all continuity.' Ken Jones adds, 'It was such a waste when he went – he'd come in in '63 knowing nothing about it, learned so much, and then they lost all that experience and intelligence.' But what was the alternative? Geoff Hurst thinks, 'It was wrong to remove him as England manager. In the light of what he'd achieved, he did not deserve that. He had done things his own way, he wasn't very communicative with the press, didn't go out of his way to create relationships with them because he didn't think it was important. The changing of the times perhaps caught him out there. But he could have gone on longer with a younger deputy to liaise between him and the younger players, because he was still very shrewd.' It's an interesting idea, but could Ramsey have worked with an assistant? He was a dictator, insisting that the job be done to his exacting standards. What would a deputy's function be? How would tactical disputes be settled? Do these consultancy relationships ever work – look at Manchester United post-Busby or Dalglish at Blackburn Rovers. If a new manager and a new direction were needed, better a clean break. However, Ramsey's subsequent treatment by the FA has been shameful, though as Ken Jones says, 'Once he'd gone, the guys who did him in were still there, so he wasn't going to get invited to anything.' There was no honorary position within the hierarchy, few opportunities to attend England matches as the guest of honour, scarcely any recognition at all for all his work. But then a man who'd grown up in the era of player serfdom would hardly expect anything else. As he said when he left, 'The trouble is, the amateurs are back in charge.'

16   Keep Right on to the End of the Road

In the immediate aftermath of Ramsey's sacking, there was a flurry of activity. His few friends in the press leapt to his defence while his enemies feigned horror. There was no shortage of offers of work. Ajax and Athletic Bilbao made lucrative offers, but were rebuffed. It's hard to imagine one as English to the core as Ramsey working abroad, and he said as much: 'I want to continue to work with English footballers. I know I still have a lot to give.' Aston Villa offered him the manager's job, but with Villa in the Second Division, it seemed a retrograde step. After all, if you've been England boss, you should be worthy of a job in the top flight. But the offers dried up, the call from one of the big clubs never came, in spite of the fact that Leeds, Liverpool, Tottenham, Chelsea, Manchester City and West Ham all made changes in management over the next year. It was clear that many in the board rooms felt that Ramsey would wrest control from them, or that he was yesterday's man, that his media profile was simply not what they wanted at a time when his appointment would put him under intense scrutiny.

But as Jimmy Leadbetter says, 'He loved being in football, he was a football man.' Late in 1975, he was approached to join the board of Birmingham City, taking up that appointment in January 1976. Ramsey declared, 'After all these years I will be learning something new about another aspect of the business. Directorship is a part of football which I have never experienced . . . I think that before I am in a position to pass any opinion I will have to get to know much more about the club, always remembering that there is a chairman [Keith Coombs] and a manager [Willie Bell] to make statements about issues of vital importance . . . after a twenty-month break I feel fresh and anxious to be taking an active part . . . I am now fully prepared to devote as much time, energy and application to the game as Birmingham require.' Ramsey continued to live in Ipswich and Coombs announced that, 'Sir Alf will not have executive powers and he will not interfere with the playing side of the club.' As the local press noted, 'It seems Birmingham City have taken on Sir Alf to do nothing except be there.'

Certainly it was an uncharacteristic role for him, merely a face in the background. Birmingham wanted him for prestige value, because there was little for him to do there, though maybe they regarded him as an insurance policy in case the team struggled. What did Ramsey get from it? The involvement with football again. To leave it after almost thirty years in its employ was a dreadful wrench for one obsessed with the game in all its facets. He seemed glad to be back in any capacity. And, good as his word, he kept a low profile, making very few statements to the press, but always on hand on matchdays if any member of staff needed to seek his advice. He even went on pre-season tour with the team, defender Tony Want recalling, 'It was all behind closed doors, training and everything. Kenny Burns went out one night and by the time he got back he was in an "unfit state", while the rest of us were sitting down to eat. Kenny's head appeared round the door, on his knees, and Alf said, "Would somebody mind going and picking Kenny up and putting him to bed."' (It may be coincidental, but by July 1977 Burns was on his way.) Fighting their seemingly perennial battle with relegation, the Blues survived by just three points in 1975–76, but the next year, they consolidated and survived by four.

When the 1977–78 season opened badly, the writing was on the wall for Bell. After five straight defeats and just one goal he was shown the exit and left the Blues looking for a new manager. There were no obvious candidates, so Coombs offered Sir Alf the manager's chair, which he accepted in a caretaker capacity, though Coombs did not rule out the possibility of a longer-term arrangement: 'Sir Alf's situation really depends on what he means by temporary. He may feel like staying longer than he anticipates at the moment.' Within a week, Jack Charlton had turned down an offer to manage the club and it seemed Ramsey would be in charge for some time. The players were amazed at developments, Tony Want remembering that Ramsey seemed as surprised as they were: 'He came into the dressing room and told us that he hadn't come to Birmingham to be manager, but that because of circumstances he was willing to help out. He said it was up to the experienced lads to get us out of trouble. He let them dictate their feelings, he wanted to hear from them, get them talking and get things moving. If he saw younger players, like Kevin Dillon, he'd bring them through – we had a rush of them, because we had a good youth scheme at the time. We were pleased to have him, to see him take the time to do the job, and it was a privilege to say you played under the man who won the World Cup.' Kevin Dillon, then just 17, recalls, 'He had something about him, an aura. He got us all together in a meeting, and the first thing he said was, "Don't call me gaffer or manager, just call me sir," and that broke the ice, really. He was very quietly spoken but when he said something, you listened.'

He got off to a great start, winning 2–1 at Middlesbrough then beating Newcastle at St Andrews, though as Tony Want says, 'With all due respect, when you change the manager at that level, something always happens. People start playing for places, there's usually a little run, every game becomes a Cup-tie. You always play for your own pride anyway, but when there's a new manager coming in, it just adds that bit extra, it's a kick up the backside!' They went on to take nine points from the first twelve – the only defeat was at the Hawthorns – before they were thumped at Ipswich. Ramsey had certainly made the team solid, looking for a straightforward 4–4–2 with no frills, Jimmy Calderwood, Gary Pendrey, Want and Pat Howard keeping things tight in front of goalkeeper Jim Montgomery, Malcolm Page, Tony Towers, Terry Hibbitt and Gary Emmanuel foraging in the middle. Up front there was the rangy Keith Bertschin and Birmingham's undoubted superstar, Trevor Francis. Year in, year out, it was Francis' goals that kept Birmingham afloat and each year he was the subject of transfer rumours, yet it was his striking partners Latchford, Hatton and Burns who were off-loaded. Now Francis was becoming bigger than the club, his performance in the 5–2 defeat at Ipswich described as world-class by the local *Sports Argus*. But he still worked tremendously hard for the team that had given him his break, and Ramsey appreciated that. Francis would again be central to Birmingham's season.

As Tony Want explains, 'Sir Alf didn't get involved in training, he wasn't a tracksuit manager then, he just supervised training and picked the team. He talked to the players and had immense respect from everybody. He was pretty fair, giving everybody a chance. Age didn't come into it, you weren't too old or too young for him, it was just whether you could do a job for him.' It was Ramsey who gave Kevin Dillon a chance: 'I don't think he wanted to be involved day to day, he was just doing the chairman a favour, but he did the thing properly. He came out every day, he used to commute from Ipswich, which was a long way to come. I was just 17 when I first played, and afterwards he spoke very well of me, saying that at that age I was better than Martin Peters, which was a nice thing to say. I wasn't fazed by the fact that he'd won the World Cup, I was too young for it to matter. It didn't really click in until years later. He gave me my debut. I was still an apprentice and it was my weekend off, so I was going home to Sunderland. He came up to me and said, "Excuse me, Kevin, I don't think you'll be going home tomorrow. I need you for tomorrow's game." That was all he said; he didn't say I was playing, or anything. That was the way he went about it, very calm. There were no instructions, just play. I was playing really well and he took me off with ten minutes to go. He got a bit of stick from the crowd for it, but he was straight with me, he said, "I've taken you off for a reason. I want you to play next week and I wanted to give you a rest." He got your trust by being straight as a die – apart from the contract he tried to offer me. I think he still lived in the 1950s 'cause the wages weren't that good! He got my parents down to go through it all and he was very professional in everything he did. He left a lasting impression that way. I think he thought £10 was a lot of money. I held out though, and he laughed about it later. He thought it was a good contract!'

Dillon made rapid progress at Birmingham and was soon a regular. England recognition followed swiftly: 'I got selected to play for England Youth. I was away for four days for a game against France at Crystal Palace and I didn't play, and I was one of the only lads who was a regular in the First Division. Sir Alf went absolutely mad, he said he wouldn't let me go and play for England again if they were going to mess me about like that, which I thought was great, because I felt like that as well, that there was a bit of favouritism because lads who were only in their club reserve or youth teams were in ahead of me. Sir Alf was fuming, he phoned the FA and asked them what they were doing messing one of his players about!' So which side of the club versus country debate was Alf on now? But it did show that, even in this low-key role, Ramsey would fight tigerishly for the rights of his players.

In early November, he resigned from the board and was appointed Football Consultant. Mike Smith, the Welsh manager, had been offered the manager's job but, upon these developments, the offer was withdrawn by mutual consent, Ramsey taking control of the general running of the club. The Blues endured another sticky patch through December but they came out of it brightly enough with some wonderful results, as Kevin Dillon remembers: 'At Liverpool we were 3–0 up and won 3–2, but that was one of the biggest results ever for the Blues. It was like the Alamo!' They also won at Old Trafford, yet dropped points to West Ham, Chelsea and Middlesbrough. The team needed strengthening and the money just wasn't there. On 20 February, Alf attended a board meeting at which he recommended that Trevor Francis and Joe Gallagher be sold. The board accepted, then three days later reneged. Again, controversy centred around a star player. Francis was Birmingham's greatest asset, as was proven twelve months later when he went to Nottingham Forest as the first £1,000,000 man. If money were required, his transfer would provide it. He had outgrown the club, their inconsistency stifling his international ambitions, his own personality cult overshadowing the team. Reports would not be about what Birmingham had done, but what Francis had done, deflecting from the team ethos Ramsey tried to instil. From the directors' viewpoint, Ramsey's logic was sound, but they knew the flak they'd take if the move went wrong and the Blues were relegated. The sale of other big names down the years made it apparent that Birmingham had no ambition, but the likes of Latchford were nothing compared with Trev, who was worshipped by the supporters. The loss of Francis would cause outrage among the faithful. It was a step too far for the board, something they'd rather put off for as long as possible. Twelve days later, Birmingham lost 4–0 at Coventry and Alf said: 'I joined this club as a director two years ago last January and that is the worst performance I have seen. They were disgraceful and I must take part of the blame.' It was a convenient moment to take his leave of the club, though he had decided to do so the moment the board went back on their word.

As Kevin Dillon says, 'He turned it round very quickly, we stayed up pretty easily. But the club needed something more permanent. He'd steadied the ship and then, as quickly as he came, he'd gone. Maybe at the Blues the problem was we had a lot of older players with strong personalities that were difficult for others to deal with, but when Sir Alf came in they were playing for somebody who'd dealt with the best in the world. They were just like schoolboys, really, listening to what he said and getting on with it. There were no rumblings or arguments, he just had the respect of everybody.' And he had fun there, according to Tony Want: 'He wasn't under any pressure because he didn't need the job, and he just enjoyed himself for a while, a little taste for the game again.' But as he left St Andrews, Alf knew he was leaving the game for good. He tried a very brief spell as technical adviser to the Greek side Panathinaikos in 1980, but European football was not for him. And in England, there was nowhere left for him to go. It was sad that such a glorious career should end with a 4–0 defeat at Highfield Road, but he could reflect that his first senior game, for the Army at the Dell, had ended in a 10–3 battering. At least there'd been some improvement in the intervening years.

17 '. . . It's the Only Thing'

Some of football's greatest men have monuments to them: Sir Matt Busby has Old Trafford and Sir Matt Busby Way; Sir Tom Finney is commemorated in the stand that bears his name at his beloved Deepdale; Herbert Chapman graces Arsenal's marble hall; a statue of Billy Wright welcomes visitors to Molineux; and, belatedly, a similar statue of Bill Shankly stands at the Kop, near the Shankly Gates. Yet England's greatest triumph and its architect have no such honours. It's as if 1966 never happened. And if we do remember it, it's in pictures of Geoff Hurst and Bobby Moore, not Alf Ramsey. References to Ramsey, certainly post-1970, have mostly been derogatory ones, attacking him for ruining the beautiful game with his obsession with work-rate, effort and sweat. But these are sweeping generalizations made from beyond the touchlines. As the testimonies in this book have shown, within the game, Ramsey is a figure who commands nothing but respect. That's how it should be. Winning the World Cup takes some doing.

He's taken the blame for many of football's ills down the years, but is that fair? The most common criticism is that he destroyed wing play in England, and there's a grain of truth in that, but no more. When he came to the England post, he had one task and one alone, to win in 1966. The wingers that he had available to him weren't the kind of players that could do that – if he'd had Finney and Matthews in their prime, does anyone believe he wouldn't have formulated a different strategy to make use of them? Look at the players, devise a system. The post-'66 years did see a dramatic decrease in goals scored and in attacking football across Europe, statistics generally put down to a change towards Ramsey's system. Managers did put a premium on not conceding, where in the past they'd concentrated on scoring goals, but to blame Ramsey for that is absurd. It merely proved that there were a lot of very poor coaches in English football, men who were happy to copy blindly with no thought for the resources they had. The system that beat West Germany required a certain kind of footballer, adaptable, intelligent, fit, inventive and imaginative. There are few of them in the world game, never mind the English First Division. How many clubs had a Bobby Charlton, a Ball, a Peters? To copy that was as daft as Doncaster looking to emulate the total football of the Dutch.

Ramsey's England did leave a far more positive legacy to the game than is admitted. There are arguments as to who got there first, but the football with which Liverpool dominated Europe was not dissimilar to that which won the World Cup. They had a superb goalkeeper in Ray Clemence, full-backs like Phil Neal and Alan Kennedy who could augment the attack, crunching tacklers like Phil Thompson or Tommy Smith, and cultured defenders like Alan Hansen, who could bring the ball forward. They had fearsome ball-winners in Jimmy Case or Graeme Souness, clever, creative midfielders like Ray Kennedy and Terry McDermott, who could weigh in with vital goals. And up front there were hard runners like Kevin Keegan or David Johnson, great finishers like Ian Rush, and the genius of Kenny Dalglish. Liverpool built from the back, they were patient, they'd probe the other side for gaps, for weaknesses, they'd spray the ball around with clinical precision, keeping hold of it until an opportunity arose, and would then strike quickly and decisively. They'd go away and play keep-ball, quietening hostile crowds, drawing the sting from the opposition. Liverpool were able to take the England blueprint on further – they had the benefit of club familiarity and the chance to draft in other nationalities – but they were built on similar foundations.

That's where Ramsey was so bright. Where other coaches suggested English football was outdated, needed radical change, revolution was essential, he'd have none of it. He understood each nation has its own peculiarities, its own way of doing things, its good, its bad. The English League is frantic, frenetic, too congested and does, at times, eulogize mediocrity. But it breeds passion, strength, determination and a will to win that outstrips most other countries, countries far more technically gifted than we are. Rather than looking to mask our weaknesses, Alf wanted to build on our strengths. So we had guts aplenty, power and stamina in every department, creating a playing environment in which our great players could operate most effectively, restoring belief in English qualities. Ramsey's use of Bobby Charlton was superb, the way in which he found roles for Ball and Peters remarkably perceptive, the introduction of Hurst inspirational. He'd have pleased his critics if Connelly and Thompson had played together, but would they have fed Charlton as reliably as Stiles, would they have run that extra yard to fetch the ball for Hurst as Ball did in extra-time? We can all select a World XI in the comfort of a pub, and we might decide that the absolute best front two would be Shearer and Ronaldo, but we don't have to put them out on the pitch together. Would they be compatible or would they just get in each other's way? Ramsey's real legacy was to underline the importance of team building, lessons picked up by the likes of Shankly, Paisley, Ferguson and Clough, while others thought it was all about formations. If a few more managers had built cohesive teams rather than strapping players into straitjackets, football might have been brighter. And if you want to argue that Ramsey's pet 4–4–2 is unavoidably dull, what formation has Manchester United's success been built on? If you're an intelligent manager, as Ferguson is, you make of formations what you will, depending on who you have available.

Your verdict on Ramsey depends on your version of football's acid test. Must football teams win games, or should they entertain the public? To combine the two is the ideal, but it's not always possible. England bored against Argentina in 1966, they were dull against Czechoslovakia in 1970, but for an hour in Mexico were thrilling against West Germany. Which result would you take? The truth about Ramsey is that he was, in his way, a prophet, not so much in the football his teams played, but in the spirit in which they played it. Twenty or thirty years ago, people despised him for his pragmatism, mocked him when he said that his job was to win football matches at a time when football was still a sport. But he'd be right at home now, when it's become a business, when managers have to worry about share prices as much as the League table. How far are we from the FA plc? Ramsey would be the perfect manager today. His teams weren't about art. They were about life, about having to work hard for anything you got, struggling, succeeding, not indulging the whims of those whose livelihoods did not depend on football. I would rather watch one of Ossie Ardiles' teams than one of Ramsey's, but if my team needed saving from relegation, I know who I'd call for first.

That brings us back to the original question. What do we really, really want from the England side? Nobody has answered that question better than Sir Alf Ramsey. As Jimmy Armfield says, 'Whatever his successes or failures, above all he was a good football man, and he was good for football in that he gave the English game something to pin the future on. I know we were at home, but Alf proved we could win the World Cup. It gave us the belief that we could beat the rest of the world, and that was a great achievement.' That achievement has sustained England through some pretty dark footballing days and it provides the answer. Ramsey is not the root of all footballing evil. It's the majority who want to win, win and win again. However much they might complain about a grinding 1–0 win over Belgium, they'd rather see that than a brilliant 5–4 defeat against Romania. Because winning isn't everything. It's the only thing.

Career Record

AS ENGLAND INTERNATIONAL

1/12/48	Switzerland	Highbury	6–0	FR
30/11/49	Italy	W. Hart Lane	2–0	FR
15/4/50	Scotland	Glasgow	1–0	WC/HI
14/5/50	Portugal	Lisbon	5–3	FR
18/5/50	Belgium	Brussels	4–1	FR
15/6/50	Chile	Rio	2–0	WC
29/6/50	USA	Belo Horizonte	0–1	WC
2/7/50	Spain	Rio	0–1	WC
7/10/50	Northern Ireland	Belfast	4–1	HI
15/11/50	Wales	Roker Park	4–2	HI
22/11/50	Yugoslavia	Highbury	2–2	FR
14/4/51	Scotland	Wembley	2–3	HI
9/5/51	Argentina	Wembley	2–1	FR
19/5/51	Portugal	Goodison Park	5–2	FR
3/10/51	France	Highbury	2–2	FR
20/10/51	Wales	Cardiff	1–1	HI
14/11/51	Northern Ireland	Villa Park	2–0	HI
28/11/51	Austria	Wembley	2–2	FR
5/4/52	Scotland	Glasgow	2–1	HI
18/5/52	Italy	Florence	1–1	FR
25/5/52	Austria	Vienna	3–2	FR
28/5/52	Switzerland	Zurich	3–0	FR
4/10/52	Northern Ireland	Belfast	2–2	HI
12/11/52	Wales	Wembley	5–2	HI
26/11/52	Belgium	Wembley	5–0	FR
18/4/53	Scotland	Wembley	2–2	HI
17/5/53	Argentina (abandoned after 23 minutes)	Buenos Aires	0–0	FR
24/5/53	Chile	Santiago	2–1	FR
31/5/53	Uruguay	Montevideo	1–2	FR
8/6/53	USA	New York	6–3	FR
21/10/53	Rest of Europe	Wembley	4–4	FR
25/11/53	Hungary	Wembley	3–6	FR

AS ENGLAND MANAGER

27/2/63	France	Paris	2–5	EC
6/4/63	Scotland	Wembley	1–2	HI
8/5/63	Brazil	Wembley	1–1	FR
20/5/63	Czechoslovakia	Bratislava	4–2	FR
2/6/63	East Germany	Leipzig	2–1	FR
5/6/63	Switzerland	Basle	8–1	FR
12/10/63	Wales	Cardiff	4–0	HI
23/10/63	Rest of the World	Wembley	2–1	FR
20/11/63	Northern Ireland	Wembley	8–3	HI
11/4/64	Scotland	Glasgow	0–1	HI
6/5/64	Uruguay	Wembley	2–1	FR
17/5/64	Portugal	Lisbon	4–3	FR
24/5/64	Republic of Ireland	Dublin	3–1	FR
27/5/64	USA	New York	10–0	FR
30/5/64	Brazil	Rio	1–5	LWC
4/6/64	Portugal	São Paolo	1–1	LWC
6/6/64	Argentina	Rio	0–1	LWC
3/10/64	Northern Ireland	Belfast	4–3	HI
21/10/64	Belgium	Wembley	2–2	FR
18/11/64	Wales	Wembley	2–1	HI
9/12/64	Netherlands	Amsterdam	1–1	FR
10/4/65	Scotland	Wembley	2–2	HI
5/5/65	Hungary	Wembley	1–0	FR
9/5/65	Yugoslavia	Belgrade	1–1	FR
12/5/65	West Germany	Nuremburg	1–0	FR
16/5/65	Sweden	Gothenburg	2–1	FR
2/10/65	Wales	Cardiff	0–0	HI
20/10/65	Austria	Wembley	2–3	FR
10/11/65	Northern Ireland	Wembley	2–1	HI
8/12/65	Spain	Madrid	2–0	FR
5/1/66	Poland	Liverpool	1–1	FR
23/2/66	West Germany	Wembley	1–0	FR
2/4/66	Scotland	Glasgow	4–3	HI
4/5/66	Yugoslavia	Wembley	2–0	FR
26/6/66	Finland	Helsinki	3–0	FR
29/6/66	Norway	Oslo	6–1	FR
3/7/66	Denmark	Copenhagen	2–0	FR
5/7/66	Poland	Chorzow	1–0	FR
11/7/66	Uruguay	Wembley	0–0	WC
16/7/66	Mexico	Wembley	2–0	WC

20/7/66	France	Wembley	2–0	WC
23/7/66	Argentina	Wembley	1–0	WC
26/7/66	Portugal	Wembley	2–1	WC
30/7/66	West Germany	Wembley	4–2	WC
22/10/66	Northern Ireland	Belfast	2–0	HI/EC
2/11/66	Czechoslovakia	Wembley	0–0	FR
16/11/66	Wales	Wembley	5–1	HI/EC
15/4/67	Scotland	Wembley	2–3	HI/EC
24/5/67	Spain	Wembley	2–0	FR
27/5/67	Austria	Vienna	1–0	FR
21/10/67	Wales	Cardiff	3–0	HI/EC
22/11/67	Northern Ireland	Wembley	2–0	HI/EC
6/12/67	USSR	Wembley	2–2	FR
24/2/68	Scotland	Glasgow	1–1	HI/EC
3/4/68	Spain	Wembley	1–0	EC
8/5/68	Spain	Madrid	2–1	EC
22/5/68	Sweden	Wembley	3–1	FR
1/6/68	West Germany	Hanover	0–1	FR
5/6/68	Yugoslavia	Florence	0–1	EC
8/6/68	USSR	Rome	2–0	EC
6/11/68	Romania	Bucharest	0–0	FR
11/12/68	Bulgaria	Wembley	1–1	FR
15/1/69	Romania	Wembley	1–1	FR
12/3/69	France	Wembley	5–0	FR
3/5/69	Northern Ireland	Belfast	3–1	HI
7/5/69	Wales	Wembley	2–1	HI
10/5/69	Scotland	Wembley	4–1	HI
1/6/69	Mexico	Mexico City	0–0	FR
8/6/69	Uruguay	Montevideo	2–1	FR
12/6/69	Brazil	Rio	1–2	FR
5/11/69	Netherlands	Amsterdam	1–0	FR
10/12/69	Portugal	Wembley	1–0	FR
14/1/70	Netherlands	Wembley	0–0	FR
25/2/70	Belgium	Brussels	3–1	FR
18/4/70	Wales	Cardiff	1–1	HI
21/4/70	Northern Ireland	Wembley	3–1	HI
25/4/70	Scotland	Glasgow	0–0	HI
20/5/70	Colombia	Bogotá	4–0	FR
24/5/70	Ecuador	Quito	2–0	FR
2/6/70	Romania	Guadalajara	1–0	WC
7/6/70	Brazil	Guadalajara	0–1	WC
11/6/70	Czechoslovakia	Guadalajara	1–0	WC
14/6/70	West Germany	Leon	2–3	WC
25/11/70	East Germany	Wembley	3–1	FR

3/2/71	Malta	Valletta	1–0	EC
21/4/71	Greece	Wembley	3–0	EC
12/5/71	Malta	Wembley	5–0	EC
15/5/71	Northern Ireland	Belfast	1–0	HI
19/5/71	Wales	Wembley	0–0	HI
22/5/71	Scotland	Wembley	3–1	HI
13/10/71	Switzerland	Basle	3–2	EC
10/11/71	Switzerland	Wembley	1–1	EC
1/12/71	Greece	Athens	2–0	EC
29/4/72	West Germany	Wembley	1–3	EC
13/5/72	West Germany	Berlin	0–0	EC
20/5/72	Wales	Cardiff	3–0	HI
23/5/72	Northern Ireland	Wembley	0–1	HI
27/5/72	Scotland	Glasgow	1–0	HI
11/10/72	Yugoslavia	Wembley	1–1	FR
15/11/72	Wales	Cardiff	1–0	WC
24/1/73	Wales	Wembley	1–1	WC
14/2/73	Scotland	Glasgow	5–0	FR
12/5/73	Northern Ireland	Liverpool	2–1	HI
15/5/73	Wales	Wembley	3–0	HI
19/5/73	Scotland	Wembley	1–0	HI
27/5/73	Czechoslovakia	Prague	1–1	FR
6/6/73	Poland	Chorzow	0–2	WC
10/6/73	USSR	Moscow	2–1	FR
13/6/73	Italy	Turin	0–2	FR
26/9/73	Austria	Wembley	7–0	FR
17/10/73	Poland	Wembley	1–1	WC
14/11/73	Italy	Wembley	0–1	FR
3/4/74	Portugal	Lisbon	0–0	FR

KEY:
FR – Friendly
HI – Home Internationals
WC – World Cup
LWC – Little World Cup
EC – European Nations Cup

Bibliography

Ball, Alan, *Ball Of Fire* (Pelham, 1967)

Banks, Gordon with Norman Giller, *Banks Of England* (Arthur Baker, 1980)

Bowler, Dave, *Danny Blanchflower – A Biography of a Visionary* (Gollancz, 1997)

Butler, Bryon & Ron Greenwood, *Soccer Choice* (Pelham, 1979)

Chalk, Gary & Duncan Holley, *Saints – A Complete Record Of Southampton FC 1885–1987* (Breedon Books, 1987)

Clough, Brian with John Sadler, *Clough The Autobiography* (Partridge Press, 1994)

Dunphy, Eamon, *A Strange Kind Of Glory* (Heinemann, 1991)

Evans, Brian, *Bygone Dagenham And Rainham* (Phillimore, 1992)

Finn, Ralph, *World Cup 1970* (Robert Hale, 1970)

Finn, Ralph, *The Official History Of Tottenham Hotspur FC 1882–1972* (Robert Hale, 1972)

Gibson, John, *Wor Jackie: The Jackie Milburn Story* (Sportsprint, 1990)

Glanville, Brian, *The Story Of The World Cup* (Faber, 1997)

Goodwin, Bob, *The Spurs Alphabet* (ACL & Polar, 1992)

Goodwin, Bob, *An Illustrated History Of Tottenham Hotspur* (Breedon Books, 1997)

Greaves, Jimmy with Norman Giller, *Don't Shoot The Manager* (Boxtree, 1987)

Hill, Dave, *England's Glory* (Pan, 1996)

Home, Dr Robert, *A Township Complete In Itself* (University of East London, 1997)

Hughes, Emlyn with James Mossop, *Crazy Horse* (Arthur Baker, 1980)

Hugman, Barry J., *Football League Players Records 1946–1992* (Tony Williams, 1992)

Hutchinson, Roger, *. . . It Is Now!* (Mainstream, 1995)

Keegan, Kevin with John Roberts, *Kevin Keegan* (Arthur Baker, 1977)

Law, Denis with Ron Gubba, *An Autobiography* (Queen Anne, 1979)

Liversedge, Stan, *This England Job* (Soccer Book Publishing)

Marquis, Max, *Anatomy Of A Football Manager* (Arthur Baker, 1970)

Mayes, Harold, *The Football Association World Cup Report 1966* (Heinemann, 1967)

McIlvanney, Hugh, *McIlvanney On Football* (Mainstream, 1994)

McIlvanney, Hugh, *World Cup '66* (Eyre & Spottiswoode, 1966)

McIlvanney, Hugh & Arthur Hopcraft, *World Cup '70* (Eyre & Spottiswoode, 1970)

Miller, David, *The Boys Of '66* (Pavilion, 1996)

Moore, Bobby, *England! England!* (Stanley Paul, 1970)

Moore, Bobby with Kevin Moseley, *Moore On Mexico* (Stanley Paul, 1970)

Moyse, Tony, *Suffolk Punch – Ipswich Town FC 1936–96* (Extra Cover, 1996)

Pelé & Robert L. Fish, *My Life And The Beautiful Game* (New English Library, 1977)

Powell, Jeff, *Bobby Moore: The Life & Times Of A Sporting Hero* (Robson, 1993)

Ramsey, Alf, *Talking Football* (Stanley Paul, 1952)

Robinson, John, *The European Championships 1958–1996* (Soccer Book Publishing, 1996)

Rogan, Johnny, *The Football Managers* (Queen Anne, 1989)

Rubinstein, Antonia (ed.), *Just Like The Country* (Age Exchange, 1991)

Shepherdson, Harold, *The Magic Sponge* (Pelham, 1968)

Smailes, Gordon, *The Breedon Book Of Football League Records* (Breedon Books, 1992)

Soar, Phil, *And The Spurs Go Marching On . . .* (Hamlyn, 1982)

Stiles, Nobby, *Soccer My Battlefield* (Stanley Paul, 1968)

Taylor, Rogan & Andrew Taylor, *Kicking And Screaming* (Robson, 1995)

Thomson, David, *4–2* (Bloomsbury, 1996)

Wolstenholme, Kenneth, *They Think It's All Over . . .* (Robson Books, 1996)

Wright, Billy, *The World's My Football Pitch* (Arrow, 1956)

Rothmans Football Yearbooks

Index